SpringerWienNewYork

T0180936

CISM COURSES AND LECTURES

The series presents lecture notes, monographs, edited works and proceedings in the field of Mechanics, Engineering, Computer Science and Applied Mathematics.
Purpose of the series is to make known in the international scientific and technical community results obtained in some of the activities organized by CISM, the International Centre for Mechanical Sciences.

INTERNATIONAL CENTRE FOR MECHANICAL SCIENCES

COURSES AND LECTURES - No. 504

PREFERENCES AND SIMILARITIES

EDITED BY

GIACOMO DELLA RICCIA
UNIVERSITY OF UDINE

DIDIER DUBOIS
UNIVERSITY OF TOULOUSE

RUDOLF KRUSE
UNIVERSITY OF MAGDEBURG

HANS-JOACHIM LENZ
FREIE UNIVERSITÄT BERLIN

SpringerWienNewYork

This volume contains 29 illustrations

ISBN 978-3-211-99941-7
e-ISBN 978-3-211-85432-7

PREFACE

This volume entitled "Preferences and Similarities" and read at the 8th International Workshop of the International School for the Synthesis of Expert Knowledge (ISSEK), Udine, Italy, October, 5th–7th, 2006, contains thirteen papers. All papers were thoroughly reviewed by the scientific program committee after they were presented, and were carefully prepared for publication. As its preceding ones, this workshop was hosted by the Centre International des Sciences Mécaniques (CISM), and was held in the picturesque Palazzo del Torso, Udine.

The workshop was jointly organised by Professors G. Della Riccia, University of Udine, D. Dubois, CNRS and University of Toulouse, R. Kruse, University of Magdeburg, and H.-J. Lenz, Freie Universität Berlin. As the workshop was an invitational one, the four organisers invited international research workers with a significant contribution to the field of interest. This volume focuses on preference and similarity, issues that have gained much attention in various scientific communities over the last couple of years. It is worthwhile mentioning, that the scope of similarity and preference is still broadening due to the exploration of new fields of application. This is caused by the strong impact of vagueness, imprecision, uncertainty and dominance on human and agent information, communication, planning, decision, action, and control as well as by the technical progress of the information technology itself. The subject is equally of interest to computer scientists, statisticians, operations researchers, experts in AI, cognitive psychologists and economists. Areas of applications may include robotics, database and information retrieval, agent and decision theory, data analysis or data mining. This fact is furthermore evident from the strongly increasing influence of communication and co-operation in electronic markets using the Internet. Information is expected to be available in time, at every site, personalized, and disseminated to privileged users irrespective of their hardware devices,

cf. SOA, and Web Services. Planning agents and guides are yet other representatives of this development. If data or information from several sources is integrated into a single database and embedded into a context, the figures can be interpreted and utilised as knowledge for planning, decision-making or control. In all these cases preferences on decision alternatives, and distances or similarities between pairs of objects measured by corresponding variables are of main interest.

Chapter 1: Similarity, Dominance, Fuzzy Logic and Efficiency. De Baets, Bernard: Similarity of Fuzzy Sets and Dominance of Random Variables: A Quest for Transitivity. The author puts the focus on the occurrence of various types of transitivity in two relational frameworks for expressing similarities and preferences in a quantitative way. The first framework is that of fuzzy relations where transitivity is defined by means of a general conjunction operation. He discusses two approaches to the measurement of similarity of fuzzy sets: a logical approach based on bi-residual operators and a cardinal approach based on fuzzy set cardinalities. The second framework is that of reciprocal relations; the corresponding notion of transitivity is cycle-transitivity, a symmetric form of transitivity. It plays a crucial role in the description of different types of transitivity arising in the comparison of random variables in terms of winning probabilities. Ruspini, Enrique: A Logic-Based View of Similarities and Preferences. After recalling basic concepts of the interpretation of fuzzy logic in terms of metrics in a finite set of states, he considers the nature of the information required to generate the underlying metrics. He concludes that similarity measures are typically derived from preference relations. The relation between similarity measures and utility functions is used to extend his similarity-based approach to marginal and conditional preferences. Some examples motivate basic requirements for a comprehensive logic-based approach to a calculus of similarity and preferences. Such a formalism allows considering the relative desirability of attaining potential system states from the perspective of different preference criteria. Bonnefon, Jean-François, Dubois, Didier and Fargier, Hélène: An overview of bipolar qualitative decision rules. People often evaluate decisions by listing their positive and negative features. The problem is then to compare such sets. Assuming bipolarity of evaluations and qualitative ratings, they present and axiomatically characterise some decision rules based on the idea of focusing on the most salient features, that are capable of handling positive and negative affects. The simplest are extensions of the maximin and maximax criteria to the bipolar case but they suffer from a lack of discrimination power. In order to overcome this weakness of the decision rules, refinements are proposed, capturing both the Pareto-efficiency principle and the order-of-magnitude reasoning principle of neglecting less important criteria. The most decisive rule uses a lexicographic ranking of the pros and cons. This turns out to be a special kind of the Cumulative Prospect Theory, and subsumes the "Take the best" heuristic.

Chapter 2: Uncertainty, Vagueness, Incompleteness, Truthlikeliness and Proximity. Godo, Luis and Rodríguez, Ricardo O.: Logical approaches to similarity-based reasoning: An overview. The paper surveys different approaches to formalize similarity-based reasoning mainly from the view point of a graded notion of truthlikeliness. The difference between the traditional concepts of uncertainty and vagueness and truthlikeliness is explained. Fuzzy similarity relations are used to model truthlikeliness with a graded notion. They follow up an approach, that may be named semantically oriented, which considers a similarity relation on set of possible worlds rather than on propositions. This approach has its roots in work on approximate truth by Ruspini. Finally, the authors analyse non-monotonic similarity-based reasoning. The idea is to consider various kinds of similarity-based orderings in order to define non-monotonic consequence relations and operators for revision. Golińska-Pilarek and Orlowska, Ewa: Logics of similarity and their dual Tableaux. A Survey. The authors survey qualitative similarity models for information systems based on databases from the standpoint of rough sets. Their formal approach is relevant for information systems with incomplete data and uncertainty of knowledge. Their concept of similarity relations includes a qualitative degree of similarity as well as the relevant context. In an axiomatic way they present modal logics characterized by the classes of relational systems based on a subset of those similarity relations. A relational inference system for those logics is based on dual tableaux. Relational proof theory enables the authors to establish a proof system for non-classical logics—represented as a deduction rule set—in a modular way. Lenz, Hans-J.: Proximities in Statistics: Similarity and Distance. The author surveys similarity and distance measures used in statistics for clustering, classification, or multi-dimensional scaling etc. Such pairwise relations are fulfilling conditions like symmetry and reflexivity. Special attention is paid to the type of scales of a variable (attribute), i.e. nominal (often binary), ordinal, metric (interval and ratio), and mixed types of scales. The paper considers the algebraic structure of proximities as suggested by Hartigan (1967) and Cormack (1971), information-theoretic measures as introduced by Jardine and Sibson (1971), and a probabilistic measure as proposed by Skarabis (1970) in more detail. This W-distance not only measures as usual the proximity between pairs of observations in a given finite dimensional data space but allows to establish a preorder on pairs of observations based upon the corresponding probability distribution. This makes it possible to discriminate even between two pairs of objects that have the same distance value but strongly differ with respect to the likelihood of the observations.

Chapter 3: Similarity, Independence, Probability and Game Theory. Klawonn, Frank and Kruse, Rudolf: Similarity Relations and Independence Concepts. The paper focuses on similarity relations, their connection to fuzzy systems, and the inherent independence assumption that are implicitly taken in models using possibility theory, belief functions etc. Motivated by the sound definition of independence in statistics some approaches to distance-based similarity relations are proposed and analysed. The results give evidence of strong differences between the independence concept used in probability theory and useful for similarity relations. Sudkamp, Tom: Imprecision and Structure in Modelling Subjective Similarity. This paper generalises feature-based similarity to gain flexibility in modelling subjective similarity judgements. The presence-absence taxonomic feature approach is extended to attributes that take partial membership or fuzzy sets as values. The minimum specificity principle is applied to obtain possibilistic bounds on the combination of similarity values. Priority and bipolarity are added to model inter-object relationships and constraints in similarity judgements. Shafer, Glenn: Defensive Forecasting. The theory of defensive forecasting uses game theory for the notation of probability thus replacing measure theory by game theory. This approach allows to prove a classical theorem of probability theory such as the law of large numbers by a betting strategy that multiplies the capital at risk by a large factor if the theorem's prediction fails. Defensive forecast-

ing first identifies a strategy that succeeds if the probabilistic forecasts are inaccurate and then makes forecasts that will defeat this strategy. Both betting strategy and forecasts are based on the similarity of the current and previous situation.

Chapter 4: Argument-based Decision Making, Qualitative Preferences Reasoning, and Label Rankings. Amgoud, Leila and Prade, Henri: Comparing decisions on the basis of a bipolar typology of arguments. The authors consider argument-based decision-making. They pick up their former proposal of a typology with eight types of arguments instead of just one, i.e. pro or con. They emphasize the bipolar nature of selecting alternatives, i.e. by explicit considering prioritised goals and rejections that are certainly or possibly to be avoided. Decisions can be attacked or supported by arguments, and have a status. The logic properties of this argumentative framework are presented. Domshlak, Carmel: A Snapshot on Reasoning with Qualitative preference Statements in AI. The paper is devoted to the interpretation and formal reasoning about sets of qualitative preference statements—generally not complete—in the context of ordinal preferences of a decision maker. The author sketches a general scheme for reasoning about user preferences that unifies the treatment of this cognitive paradigm in an analogous way as done in the field of artificial intelligence. As up to now no requirements are specified for such systems in any specific context, the author votes for more interaction between academics and practioneers. Hüllermeier, Eyke and Fürnkranz, Johannes: Learning Preference Models from Data: On the Problem of Label Rankings and its Variants. In label ranking, the problem is to learn a ranking function that maps from an instance space to rankings over a finite set of labels. A ranking function thus defined can be considered as a generalization of a conventional classification function. To solve the label ranking problems the authors propose an approach based on the idea of ranking by pairwise comparison (RPC). Having a learning sample at hand, first of all, a binary preference relation is induced by applying a generalisation of pairwise classification. Then a ranking is derived, by transforming the preference relation. This procedure can be adapted to different loss functions simply by selecting different ranking procedures. Therefore it gives much flexibility. A related ranking procedure called "ranking through iterated choice" is experimentally investigated. Rossi, Francesca: Constraints and

Preferences: Modelling Frameworks and Multi-Agent Settings. The author aims for a unifying formalism to model preferences and constraints and manage them efficiently. The preferences she considers are of various kinds: qualitative/quantitative, marginal/conditional, negative/positive. The constraints may be soft or hard. She reviews existing formalisms for representing both entities, especially soft constraints and CP nets. Voting theory comes in when multi agent preference aggregation is considered. Several semantics for preference aggregation are proposed, and notions such as incompleteness and non-manipulability. Arrow's famous theorem on "Fairness" shows theoretical limitations for any formalism.

The editors of this volume are very thankful to all our authors for re-submitting their papers, and Mrs. Angelika Wnuk, Freie Universität Berlin, for her diligent work as a workshop convenor. We would like to thank the following institutions for substantial help on various levels:

- *The International School for the Synthesis of Expert Knowledge (ISSEK) again for promoting the workshop.*
- *The University of Udine for administrative support.*
- *The Centre International des Sciences Mécaniques (CISM) for hosting a group of enthusiastic people with a common interest in preferences, similarities and cappuccino.*

On behalf of all participants we express our deep gratitude to FONDAZIONE CASSA di RISPARMIO di UDINE e PORDENONE for their financial support of our participants.

Giacomo Della Riccia (University of Udine)
Didier Dubois (University of Toulouse)
Rudolf Kruse (University of Magdeburg)
Hans-Joachim Lenz (Freie Universität Berlin)

5th April, 2008

CONTENTS

Chapter 4: Argument-based Decision Making, Qualitative Preferences Reasoning, and Label Rankings

Similarity of Fuzzy Sets and Dominance of Random Variables: a Quest for Transitivity

Bernard De Baets

Department of Applied Mathematics, Biometrics and Process Control,
Ghent University, Coupure links 653, B-9000 Gent, Belgium

Abstract We present several relational frameworks for expressing similarities and preferences in a quantitative way. The main focus is on the occurrence of various types of transitivity in these frameworks. The first framework is that of fuzzy relations; the corresponding notion of transitivity is C-transitivity, with C a conjunctor. We discuss two approaches to the measurement of similarity of fuzzy sets: a logical approach based on biresidual operators and a cardinal approach based on fuzzy set cardinalities. The second framework is that of reciprocal relations; the corresponding notion of transitivity is cycle-transitivity. It plays a crucial role in the description of different types of transitivity arising in the comparison of random variables in terms of winning probabilities.

1 Introduction

Comparing objects in order to group together similar ones or distinguish better from worse is inherent to human activities in general and scientific disciplines in particular. In this overview paper, we present some relational frameworks that allow to express the results of such a comparison in a numerical way, typically by means of numbers in the unit interval. A first framework is that of fuzzy relations and we discuss how it can be used to develop cardinality-based, i.e. based on the counting of features, similarity measurement techniques. A second framework is that of reciprocal relations and we discuss how it can be used to develop methods for comparing random variables. Rationality considerations demand the presence of some kind of transitivity. We therefore review in detail the available notions of transitivity and point out where they occur.

This chapter is organised as follows. In Section 2, we present the two relational frameworks mentioned, the corresponding notions of transitivity and the connections between them. In Section 3, we explore the framework of fuzzy relations and its capacity for expressing the similarity of fuzzy sets. Section 4 is dedicated to the framework of reciprocal relations and its potential for the development of methods for the comparison of random variables. We wrap up in Section 5 with a short conclusion.

2 Relational frameworks and their transitivity

2.1 Fuzzy relations

Transitivity is an essential property of relations. A (binary) *relation R* on a universe X (the *universe of discourse* or the *set of alternatives*) is called *transitive* if for any $(a, b, c) \in X^3$ it holds that $(a, b) \in R \wedge (b, c) \in R$ implies $(a, c) \in R$. Identifying R with its characteristic mapping, *i.e.* defining $R(a, b) = 1$ if $(a, b) \in R$, and $R(a, b) = 0$ if $(a, b) \notin R$, transitivity can be stated equivalently as $R(a, b) = 1 \wedge R(b, c) = 1$ implies $R(a, c) = 1$. Other equivalent formulations may be devised, such as

$$(R(a, b) \geq \alpha \wedge R(b, c) \geq \alpha) \Rightarrow R(a, c) \geq \alpha, \tag{1}$$

for any $\alpha \in]0, 1]$. Transitivity can also be expressed in the following functional form

$$\min(R(a, b), R(b, c)) \leq R(a, c). \tag{2}$$

Note that on $\{0, 1\}^2$ the minimum operation is nothing else but the Boolean conjunction.

A *fuzzy relation R* on X is an $X^2 \to [0, 1]$ mapping that expresses the degree of relationship between elements of X: $R(a, b) = 0$ means a and b are not related at all, $R(a, b) = 1$ expresses full relationship, while $R(a, b) \in]0, 1[$ indicates a partial degree of relationship only. In fuzzy set theory, formulation (2) has led to the popular notion of T-transitivity, where a t-norm is used to generalize Boolean conjunction. A binary operation $T : [0, 1]^2 \to [0, 1]$ is called a *t-norm* if it is increasing in each variable, has neutral element 1 and is commutative and associative. The three main continuous t-norms are the minimum operator $T_\mathbf{M}$, the algebraic product $T_\mathbf{P}$ and the Łukasiewicz t-norm $T_\mathbf{L}$ (defined by $T_\mathbf{L}(x, y) = \max(x + y - 1, 0)$). For an excellent monograph on t-norms and t-conorms, we refer to Klement et al. (2000).

However, we prefer to work with a more general class of operations called *conjunctors*. A *conjunctor* is a binary operation $C : [0, 1]^2 \to [0, 1]$ that is increasing in each variable and coincides on $\{0, 1\}^2$ with the Boolean conjunction.

Definition 2.1. Let C be a conjunctor. A fuzzy relation R on X is called *C-transitive* if for any $(a, b, c) \in X^3$ it holds that

$$C(R(a, b), R(b, c)) \leq R(a, c). \tag{3}$$

Interesting classes of conjunctors are the classes of semi-copulas, quasi-copulas, copulas and t-norms. *Semi-copulas* are nothing else but conjunctors with neutral element 1 (Durante and Sempi (2005)). Where t-norms have the additional properties of commutativity and associativity, quasi-copulas have the 1-Lipschitz property (Genest et al. (1999); Nelsen (1998)). A *quasi-copula* is a semi-copula that is *1-Lipschitz*: for any $(x, y, u, v) \in [0, 1]^4$ it holds that $|C(x, u) - C(y, v)| \leq |x - y| + |u - v|$. If instead of 1-Lipschitz continuity, C satisfies the *moderate growth property* (also called 2-monotonicity): for any $(x, y, u, v) \in [0, 1]^4$ such that $x \leq y$ and $u \leq v$ it holds that $C(x, v) + C(y, u) \leq C(x, u) + C(y, v)$, then C is called a *copula*.

Any copula is a quasi-copula, and therefore has the 1-Lipschitz property; the converse is not true. It is well known that a copula is a t-norm if and only if it is associative; conversely, a t-norm is a copula if and only if it is 1-Lipschitz. The t-norms $T_\mathbf{M}$, $T_\mathbf{P}$ and $T_\mathbf{L}$ are copulas as well. For any quasi-copula C it holds that $T_\mathbf{L} \leq C \leq T_\mathbf{M}$. For an excellent monograph on copulas, we refer to Nelsen (1998).

2.2   Reciprocal relations

Another interesting class of $X^2 \to [0, 1]$ mappings is the class of *reciprocal relations* Q (also called *ipsodual relations* or *probabilistic relations*) satisfying $Q(a, b) + Q(b, a) = 1$, for any $a, b \in X$. For such relations, it holds in particular that $Q(a, a) = 1/2$. Reciprocity is linked with completeness: let R be a complete ($\{0, 1\}$-valued) relation on X, which means that $\max(R(a, b), R(b, a)) = 1$ for any $a, b \in X$, then R has an equivalent $\{0, 1/2, 1\}$-valued reciprocal representation Q given by $Q(a, b) = 1/2(1 + R(a, b) - R(b, a))$.

Stochastic transitivity   Transitivity properties for reciprocal relations rather have the logical flavor of expression (1). There exist various kinds of stochastic transitivity for reciprocal relations (David (1963); Monjardet (1988)). For instance, a reciprocal relation Q on X is called *weakly stochastic transitive* if for any $(a, b, c) \in X^3$ it holds that $Q(a, b) \geq 1/2 \land Q(b, c) \geq 1/2$ implies $Q(a, c) \geq 1/2$, which corresponds to the choice of $\alpha = 1/2$ in (1). In De Baets et al. (2006a), the following generalization of stochastic transitivity was proposed.

Definition 2.2. Let g be an increasing $[1/2, 1]^2 \to [0, 1]$ mapping such that $g(1/2, 1/2) \leq 1/2$. A reciprocal relation Q on X is called g-stochastic transitive if for any $(a, b, c) \in X^3$ it holds that

$$(Q(a,b) \geq 1/2 \; \wedge \; Q(b,c) \geq 1/2) \;\Rightarrow\; Q(a,c) \geq g(Q(a,b), Q(b,c)).$$

Note that the condition $g(1/2, 1/2) \leq 1/2$ ensures that the reciprocal representation Q of any transitive complete relation R is always g-stochastic transitive. In other words, g-stochastic transitivity generalizes transitivity of complete relations. This definition includes the standard types of stochastic transitivity (Monjardet (1988)):

    (i) *strong* stochastic transitivity when $g = \max$;

    (ii) *moderate* stochastic transitivity when $g = \min$;

    (iii) *weak* stochastic transitivity when $g = 1/2$.

    In De Baets et al. (2006a), also a special type of stochastic transitivity has been introduced.

Definition 2.3. Let g be an increasing $[1/2, 1]^2 \to [0, 1]$ mapping such that $g(1/2, 1/2) = 1/2$ and $g(1/2, 1) = g(1, 1/2) = 1$. A reciprocal relation Q on X is called g-isostochastic transitive if for any $(a, b, c) \in X^3$ it holds that

$$(Q(a,b) \geq 1/2 \; \wedge \; Q(b,c) \geq 1/2) \;\Rightarrow\; Q(a,c) = g(Q(a,b), Q(b,c)).$$

The conditions imposed upon g again ensure that g-isostochastic transitivity generalizes transitivity of complete relations. Note that for a given mapping g, the property of g-isostochastic transitivity is much more restrictive than the property of g-stochastic transitivity.

FG-**transitivity**   The framework of *FG*-transitivity, developed by Switalski (2001, 2003), formally generalizes g-stochastic transitivity in the sense that $Q(a, c)$ is bounded both from below and above by $[1/2, 1]^2 \to [0, 1]$ mappings.

Definition 2.4. Let F and G be two $[1/2, 1]^2 \to [0, 1]$ mappings such that $F(1/2, 1/2) \leq 1/2 \leq G(1/2, 1/2)$, and $G(1/2, 1) = G(1, 1/2) = G(1, 1) = 1$ and $F \leq G$. A reciprocal relation Q on X is called *FG*-transitive if for any $(a, b, c) \in X^3$ it holds that

$$(Q(a,b) \geq 1/2 \wedge Q(b,c) \geq 1/2)$$

$$\Downarrow$$

$$F(Q(a,b), Q(b,c)) \leq Q(a,c) \leq G(Q(a,b), Q(b,c)).$$

Cycle-transitivity For a reciprocal relation Q, we define for all $(a, b, c) \in X^3$ the following quantities, see De Baets et al. (2006a):

$$\alpha_{abc} = \min(Q(a, b), Q(b, c), Q(c, a)),$$

$$\beta_{abc} = \text{median}(Q(a, b), Q(b, c), Q(c, a)),$$

$$\gamma_{abc} = \max(Q(a, b), Q(b, c), Q(c, a)).$$

Let us also denote $\Delta = \{(x, y, z) \in [0, 1]^3 \mid x \leq y \leq z\}$. A function $U : \Delta \to \mathbb{R}$ is called an upper bound function if it satisfies:

(i) $U(0, 0, 1) \geq 0$ and $U(0, 1, 1) \geq 1$;

(ii) for any $(\alpha, \beta, \gamma) \in \Delta$:

$$U(\alpha, \beta, \gamma) + U(1 - \gamma, 1 - \beta, 1 - \alpha) \geq 1. \tag{4}$$

The function $L : \Delta \to \mathbb{R}$ defined by $L(\alpha, \beta, \gamma) = 1 - U(1 - \gamma, 1 - \beta, 1 - \alpha)$ is called the *dual lower bound function* of a given upper bound function U. Inequality (4) then simply expresses that $L \leq U$. Condition (i) again guarantees that cycle-transitivity generalizes transitivity of complete relations.

Definition 2.5. A reciprocal relation Q on X is called cycle-transitive w.r.t. an upper bound function U if for any $(a, b, c) \in X^3$ it holds that

$$L(\alpha_{abc}, \beta_{abc}, \gamma_{abc}) \leq \alpha_{abc} + \beta_{abc} + \gamma_{abc} - 1 \leq U(\alpha_{abc}, \beta_{abc}, \gamma_{abc}), \tag{5}$$

where L is the dual lower bound function of U.

Due to the built-in duality, it holds that if (5) is true for some (a, b, c), then this is also the case for any permutation of (a, b, c). In practice, it is therefore sufficient to check (5) for a single permutation of any $(a, b, c) \in X^3$. Alternatively, due to the same duality, it is also sufficient to verify the right-hand inequality (or equivalently, the left-hand inequality) for two permutations of any $(a, b, c) \in X^3$ (not being cyclic permutations of one another), e.g. (a, b, c) and (c, b, a). Hence, (5) can be replaced by

$$\alpha_{abc} + \beta_{abc} + \gamma_{abc} - 1 \leq U(\alpha_{abc}, \beta_{abc}, \gamma_{abc}).$$

Note that a value of $U(\alpha, \beta, \gamma)$ equal to 2 is used to express that for the given values there is no restriction at all (as $\alpha + \beta + \gamma - 1$ is always bounded by 2).

Two upper bound functions U_1 and U_2 are called *equivalent* if for any $(\alpha, \beta, \gamma) \in \Delta$ it holds that $\alpha + \beta + \gamma - 1 \leq U_1(\alpha, \beta, \gamma)$ is equivalent to $\alpha + \beta + \gamma - 1 \leq U_2(\alpha, \beta, \gamma)$.

If it happens that in (4) the equality holds for all $(\alpha, \beta, \gamma) \in \Delta$, then the upper bound function U is said to be *self-dual*, since in that case it coincides with its dual lower bound function L. Consequently, also (5) and (2.2) can only hold with equality. Furthermore, it then holds that $U(0,0,1) = 0$ and $U(0,1,1) = 1$.

Although C-transitivity is not intended to be applied to reciprocal relations, it can be cast quite nicely into the cycle-transitivity framework of De Baets et al. (2006a).

Proposition 2.6. *Let C be a commutative conjunctor such that $C \leq T_{\mathbf{M}}$. A reciprocal relation Q on X is C-transitive if and only if it is cycle-transitive w.r.t. the upper bound function U_f defined by*

$$U_C(\alpha, \beta, \gamma) = \min(\alpha + \beta - C(\alpha, \beta), \beta + \gamma - C(\beta, \gamma), \gamma + \alpha - C(\gamma, \alpha)).$$

Moreover, if C is 1-Lipschitz, then U_C is given by

$$U_C(\alpha, \beta, \gamma) = \alpha + \beta - C(\alpha, \beta).$$

Consider the three basic t-norms (copulas) $T_{\mathbf{M}}$, $T_{\mathbf{P}}$ and $T_{\mathbf{L}}$:

(i) For $C = T_{\mathbf{M}}$, we immediately obtain as upper bound function the median (the simplest self-dual upper bound function):

$$U_{T_{\mathbf{M}}}(\alpha, \beta, \gamma) = \beta.$$

(ii) For $C = T_{\mathbf{P}}$, we find

$$U_{T_{\mathbf{P}}}(\alpha, \beta, \gamma) = \alpha + \beta - \alpha\beta.$$

(iii) For $C = T_{\mathbf{L}}$, we obtain

$$U_{T_{\mathbf{L}}}(\alpha, \beta, \gamma) = \begin{cases} \alpha + \beta & , \text{ if } \alpha + \beta < 1, \\ 1 & , \text{ if } \alpha + \beta \geq 1. \end{cases}$$

An equivalent upper bound function is given by $U'_{T_{\mathbf{L}}}(\alpha, \beta, \gamma) = 1$.

Cycle-transitivity also incorporates stochastic transitivity, although the latter fits more naturally in the FG-transitivity framework; in particular, isostochastic transitivity corresponds to cycle-transitivity w.r.t. particular self-dual upper bound functions (De Baets et al. (2006a)). We have shown that cycle-transitivity and FG-transitivity frameworks cannot easily be translated into one another, which underlines that these are two essentially different frameworks (De Baets and De Meyer (2005b)).

One particular form of stochastic transitivity deserves our attention. A probabilistic relation Q on X is called *partially stochastic transitive* (Fishburn (1973)) if for any $(a, b, c) \in X^3$ it holds that

$$(Q(a, b) > 1/2 \land Q(b, c) > 1/2) \Rightarrow Q(a, c) \geq \min(Q(a, b), Q(b, c)).$$

Clearly, it is a slight weakening of moderate stochastic transitivity. Interestingly, also this type of transitivity can be expressed elegantly in the cycle-transitivity framework (De Meyer et al. (2007)) by means of a simple upper bound function.

Proposition 2.7. *Cycle-transitivity w.r.t. the upper bound function U_{ps} defined by*

$$U_{ps}(\alpha, \beta, \gamma) = \gamma$$

is equivalent to partial stochastic transitivity.

3   Similarity of fuzzy sets

3.1   Basic notions

Recall that an *equivalence relation E* on X is a reflexive, symmetric and transitive relation on X and that there exists a one-to-one correspondence between equivalence relations on X and partitions of X. In fuzzy set theory, the counterpart of an equivalence relation is a *T-equivalence*: given a t-norm T, a T-equivalence E on X is a fuzzy relation on X that is reflexive ($E(x, x) = 1$), symmetric ($E(x, y) = E(y, x)$) and T-transitive. A T-equivalence is called a *T-equality* if $E(x, y)$ implies $x = y$.

For the prototypical t-norms, it is interesting to note that (see e.g. De Baets and Mesiar (1997, 2002)):

(i) A fuzzy relation E on X is a $T_{\mathbf{L}}$-equivalence if and only if $d = 1 - E$ is a pseudo-metric on X.

(ii) A fuzzy relation E on X is a $T_{\mathbf{P}}$-equivalence if and only if $d = -\log E$ is a pseudo-metric on X.

(iii) A fuzzy relation E on X is a $T_{\mathbf{M}}$-equivalence if and only if $d = 1 - E$ is a pseudo-ultra-metric on X. Another interesting characterization is that a fuzzy relation E on X is a $T_{\mathbf{M}}$-equivalence if and only if for any $\alpha \in [0, 1]$ its α-cut $E_\alpha = \{(x, y) \in X^2 \mid E(x, y) \geq \alpha\}$ is an equivalence relation on X. The equivalence classes of E_α become smaller for increasing α leading to the concept of a partition tree (see e.g. De Meyer et al. (2004)).

3.2 A logical approach

To any left-continuous t-norm T, there corresponds a residual implicator $I_T : [0,1]^2 \to [0,1]$ defined by

$$I_T(x,y) = \sup\{z \in [0,1] \mid T(x,z) \leq y\},$$

which can be considered as a generalization of Boolean implication. Note that $I_T(x,y) = 1$ if and only if $x \leq y$. In case $y < x$, one gets for the prototypical t-norms: $I_\mathbf{M}(x,y) = y$, $I_\mathbf{P}(x,y) = y/x$ and $I_\mathbf{L}(x,y) = \min(1 - x+y, 1)$. An essential property of the residual implicator of a left-continuous t-norm is related to the classical syllogism:

$$T(I_T(x,y), I_T(y,z)) \leq I_T(x,z)),$$

for any $(x,y,z) \in [0,1]^3$. The residual implicator is the main constituent of the biresidual operator $\mathcal{E}_T : [0,1]^2 \to [0,1]$ defined by

$$\mathcal{E}_T(x,y) = \min(I_T(x,y), I_T(y,x)) = I_T(\max(x,y), \min(x,y)),$$

which can be considered as a generalization of Boolean equivalence. Note that $\mathcal{E}_T(x,y) = 1$ if and only if $x = y$. In case $x \neq y$, one gets for the prototypical t-norms: $\mathcal{E}_\mathbf{M}(x,y) = \min(x,y)$, $\mathcal{E}_\mathbf{P}(x,y) = \min(x,y)/\max(x,y)$ and $\mathcal{E}_\mathbf{L}(x,y) = 1 - |x-y|$.

Of particular importance in this discussion is the fact that $\mathcal{E}_T$ is a T-equality on $[0,1]$. The biresidual operator obviously serves as a means for measuring equality of membership degrees. Any T-equality E on $[0,1]$ can be extended in a natural way to $\mathcal{F}(X)$, the class of fuzzy sets in X:

$$E'(A,B) = \inf_{x \in X} E(A(x), B(x)).$$

It then holds that E' is a T-equality on $\mathcal{F}(X)$ if and only if E is a T-equality on $[0,1]$. Starting from $\mathcal{E}_T$ we obtain the T-equality E^T. A second way of defining a T-equality on $\mathcal{F}(X)$ is by defining

$$E_T(A,B) = T(\inf_{x \in X} I_T(A(x), B(x)), \inf_{x \in X} I_T(B(x), A(x))).$$

The underlying idea is that in order to measure equality of two (fuzzy) sets A and B, one should both measure inclusion of A in B, and of B in A. Note that in general $E_T \subseteq E^T$, while $E_\mathbf{M} = E^\mathbf{M}$. These T-equivalences can be used as a starting point for building metrics on $\mathcal{F}(X)$. The above ways of measuring equality of fuzzy sets are very strict in the sense that the "worst" element decides upon the value.

Without going into detail, it is worth mentioning that there exist an appropriate notion of fuzzy partition, called T-partition (De Baets and Mesiar (1998)), so that there exists a one-to-one correspondence between T-equalities on X and T-partitions of X (De Baets and Mesiar (2002)).

3.3   A cardinal approach

Classical cardinality-based similarity measures   A common recipe for comparing objects is to select an appropriate set of features and to construct for each object a binary vector encoding the presence (1) or absence (0) of each of these features. Such a binary vector can be formally identified with the corresponding set of present features. The degree of similarity of two objects is then often expressed in terms of the cardinalities of the latter sets. We focus our attention on a family of $[0,1]$-valued similarity measures that are rational expressions in the cardinalities of the sets involved, see De Baets et al. (2001):

$$S(A,B) = \frac{x\,\alpha_{A,B} + t\,\omega_{A,B} + y\,\delta_{A,B} + z\,\nu_{A,B}}{x'\,\alpha_{A,B} + t'\,\omega_{A,B} + y'\,\delta_{A,B} + z'\,\nu_{A,B}},$$

with $A, B \in \mathcal{P}(X)$ (the powerset of a finite universe X),

$$\alpha_{A,B} = \min(|A \setminus B|, |B \setminus A|),$$
$$\omega_{A,B} = \max(|A \setminus B|, |B \setminus A|),$$
$$\delta_{A,B} = |A \cap B|,$$
$$\nu_{A,B} = |(A \cup B)^c|,$$

and $x, t, y, z, x', t', y', z' \in \{0,1\}$. Note that these similarity measures are symmetric, $i.e.$ $S(A,B) = S(B,A)$ for any $A, B \in \mathcal{P}(X)$.

Reflexive similarity measures, $i.e.$ $S(A,A) = 1$ for any $A \in \mathcal{P}(X)$, are characterized by $y = y'$ and $z = z'$. We restrict our attention to the (still large) subfamily obtained by putting also $t = x$ and $t' = x'$ (De Baets and De Meyer (2005a); De Baets et al. (to appear)), $i.e.$

$$S(A,B) = \frac{x\,\triangle_{A,B} + y\,\delta_{A,B} + z\,\nu_{A,B}}{x'\,\triangle_{A,B} + y\,\delta_{A,B} + z\,\nu_{A,B}}, \tag{6}$$

with $\triangle_{A,B} = |A \triangle B| = |A \setminus B| + |B \setminus A|$. On the other hand, we allow more freedom by letting the parameters x, y, z and x' take positive real values. Note that these parameters can always be scaled to the unit interval by dividing both numerator and denominator of (6) by the greatest among the parameters. In order to guarantee that $S(A,B) \in [0,1]$, we need to impose the restriction $0 \le x \le x'$. Since the case $x = x'$ leads to trivial measures taking value 1 only, we consider from here on $0 \le x < x'$. The similarity measures gathered in Table 1 all belong to family (6); the corresponding parameter values are indicated in the table.

The $T_{\mathbf{L}}$- or $T_{\mathbf{P}}$-transitive members of family (6) are characterized in the following proposition (De Baets et al. (to appear)).

Measure	expression	x	x'	y	z	T
Jaccard (1908)	$\frac{|A\cap B|}{|A\cup B|}$	0	1	0	1	$T_{\mathbf{L}}$
Simple Matching (Sokal and Michener, 1958)	$1-\frac{|A\triangle B|}{n}$	0	1	1	1	$T_{\mathbf{L}}$
Dice (1945)	$\frac{2|A\cap B|}{|A\triangle B|+2|A\cap B|}$	0	1	2	0	–
Rogers and Tanimoto (1960)	$\frac{n-|A\triangle B|}{n+|A\triangle B|}$	0	2	1	1	$T_{\mathbf{L}}$
Sneath and Sokal (1973)	$\frac{|A\cap B|}{|A\cap B|+2|A\triangle B|}$	0	2	1	0	$T_{\mathbf{L}}$
Sneath and Sokal (1973)	$1-\frac{|A\triangle B|}{2n-|A\triangle B|}$	0	1	2	2	–

Table 1. Some well-known cardinality-based similarity measures.

Proposition 3.1.
  (i) The $T_{\mathbf{L}}$-transitive members of family (6) are characterized by the necessary and sufficient condition $x' \geq \max(y, z)$.
  (ii) The $T_{\mathbf{P}}$-transitive members of family (6) are characterized by the necessary and sufficient condition $x\,x' \geq \max(y^2, z^2)$.

Fuzzy cardinality-based similarity measures Often, the presence or absence of a feature is not clear-cut and is rather a matter of degree. Hence, if instead of binary vectors we have to compare vectors with components in the real unit interval $[0,1]$ (the higher the number, the more the feature is present), the need arises to generalize the aforementioned similarity measures. In fact, in the same way as binary vectors can be identified with ordinary subsets of a finite universe X, vectors with components in $[0,1]$ can be identified with fuzzy sets in X.

In order to generalize cardinality-based similarity measure to fuzzy sets, we clearly need fuzzification rules that define the cardinality of a fuzzy set and translate the classical set-theoretic operations to fuzzy sets. As to the first, we stick to the following simple way of defining the cardinality of a fuzzy set, also known as the sigma-count of A (Zadeh (1965)): $|A| = \sum_{x\in X} A(x)$. As to the second, we define the intersection of two fuzzy sets A and B in X in a pointwise manner by $A\cap B(x) = C(A(x), B(x))$, for any $x \in X$, where C is a commutative conjunctor. In De Baets et al. (to appear), we have argued that commutative quasi-copulas are the most appropriate conjunctors for our purpose. Commutative quasi-copulas not only allow to introduce set-theoretic operations on fuzzy sets, such as $A \setminus B(x) = A(x) - C(A(x), B(x))$ and $A \triangle B(x) = A(x) + B(x) - 2C(A(x), B(x))$, they also preserve classical identities on cardinalities, such as $|A \setminus B| = |A| - |A \cap B|$

and $|A \triangle B| = |A \setminus B| + |B \setminus A| = |A| + |B| - 2|A \cap B|$. These identities allow to rewrite and fuzzify family (6) as

$$S(A, B) = \frac{x(a + b - 2u) + yu + z(n - a - b + u)}{x'(a + b - 2u) + yu + z(n - a - b + u)}, \qquad (7)$$

with $a = |A|$, $b = |B|$ and $u = |A \cap B|$.

Bell-inequalities and preservation of transitivity Studying the transitivity of (fuzzy) cardinality-based similarity measures inevitably leads to the verification of inequalities on (fuzzy) cardinalities. We have established several powerful meta-theorems that provide an efficient and intelligent way of verifying whether a classical inequality on cardinalities carries over to fuzzy cardinalities (De Baets et al. (2006b)). These meta-theorems state that certain classical inequalities are preserved under fuzzification when modelling fuzzy set intersection by means of a commutative conjunctor that fulfills a number of Bell-type inequalities.

In Janssens et al. (2004a), we introduced the classical Bell inequalities in the context of fuzzy probability calculus and proved that the following Bell-type inequalities for commutative conjunctors are necessary and sufficient conditions for the corresponding Bell-type inequalities for fuzzy probabilities to hold. The Bell-type inequalities for a commutative conjunctor C read as follows:

$$B_1 : T_{\mathbf{L}}(p, q) \leq C(p, q) \leq T_{\mathbf{M}}(p, q)$$
$$B_2 : 0 \leq p - C(p, q) - C(p, r) + C(q, r)$$
$$B_3 : p + q + r - C(p, q) - C(p, r) - C(q, r) \leq 1$$

for any $p, q, r \in [0, 1]$. Inequality B_2 is fulfilled for any commutative quasi-copula, while inequality B_3 only holds for certain t-norms Janssens et al. (2004b), including the members of the Frank t-norm family $T_\lambda^{\mathbf{F}}$ with $\lambda \leq 9 + 4\sqrt{5}$ (Pykacz and D'Hooghe (2001)). Also note that inequality B_1 follows from inequality B_2.

Theorem 3.2. *(De Baets et al. (2006b)) Consider a commutative conjunctor I that satisfies Bell inequalities B_2 and B_3. If for any ordinary subsets A, B and C of an arbitrary finite universe X it holds that*

$$\mathcal{H}(|A|, |B|, |C|, |A \cap B|, |A \cap C|, |B \cap C|, |X|) \geq 0,$$

where $\mathcal{H}$ denotes a continuous function which is homogeneous in its arguments, then it also holds for any fuzzy sets in an arbitrary finite universe Y.

If the function $\mathcal{H}$ does not depend explicitly upon $|X|$, then Bell inequality B_3 can be omitted. This meta-theorem allows us to identify conditions on the parameters of the members of family (7) leading to $T_{\mathbf{L}}$-transitive or $T_{\mathbf{P}}$-transitive fuzzy similarity measures. As our fuzzification is based on a commutative quasi-copula C, condition B_2 holds by default. The following proposition then is an immediate application (De Baets et al. (2006b)).

Proposition 3.3.
   (i) Consider a commutative quasi-copula C that satisfies B_3. The $T_{\mathbf{L}}$-transitive members of family (7) are characterized by $x' \geq \max(y, z)$.
   (ii) The $T_{\mathbf{L}}$-transitive members of family (7) with $z = 0$ are characterized by $x' \geq y$.
   (iii) Consider a commutative quasi-copula C that satisfies B_3. The $T_{\mathbf{P}}$-transitive members of family (7) are characterized by $x\,x' \geq \max(y^2, z^2)$.
   (iv) The $T_{\mathbf{P}}$-transitive members of family (7) with $z = 0$ are characterized by $xx' \geq y^2$.

However, as our meta-theorem is very general, it does not necessarily always provide the strongest results. For instance, tedious and lengthy direct proofs allow to eliminate condition B_3 from the previous theorem, leading to the following general result (De Baets et al. (2006b)).

Proposition 3.4. *Consider a commutative quasi-copula C.*
   (i) The $T_{\mathbf{L}}$-transitive members of family (7) are characterized by the necessary and sufficient condition $x' \geq \max(y, z)$.
   (ii) The $T_{\mathbf{P}}$-transitive members of family (7) are characterized by the necessary and sufficient condition $x\,x' \geq \max(y^2, z^2)$.

4   Comparison of random variables

4.1   Dice-transitivity

Consider three dice A, B and C which, instead of the usual numbers, carry the following integers on their faces:

$$A = \{1, 3, 4, 15, 16, 17\}, \quad B = \{2, 10, 11, 12, 13, 14\}, \quad C = \{5, 6, 7, 8, 9, 18\}.$$

Denoting by $\mathcal{P}(X, Y)$ the probability that dice X wins from dice Y, we have $\mathcal{P}(A, B) = 20/36$, $\mathcal{P}(B, C) = 25/36$ and $\mathcal{P}(C, A) = 21/36$. It is natural to say that dice X is strictly preferred to dice Y if $\mathcal{P}(X, Y) > 1/2$, which reflects that dice X wins from dice Y in the long run (or that X statistically wins from Y, denoted $X >_s Y$). Note that $\mathcal{P}(Y, X) = 1 - \mathcal{P}(X, Y)$ which implies that the relation $>_s$ is asymmetric. In the above example, it holds that $A >_s B$, $B >_s C$ and $C >_s A$: the relation $>_s$ is not transitive and forms a cycle. In other words, if we interpret the probabilities $\mathcal{P}(X, Y)$ as constituents of a reciprocal relation on the set of alternatives $\{A, B, C\}$, then this reciprocal relation is even not weakly stochastic transitive.

This example can be generalized as follows: we allow the dice to possess any number of faces (whether or not this can be materialized) and allow identical numbers on the faces of a single or multiple dice. In other words, a generalized dice can be identified with a multiset of integers. Given a collection of m such generalized dice, we can still build a reciprocal relation Q containing the *winning probabilities* for each pair of dice (De Schuymer et al. (2003)). For any two such dice A and B, we define

$$Q(A, B) = \mathcal{P}\{A \text{ wins from } B\} + \frac{1}{2}\mathcal{P}\{A \text{ and } B \text{ end in a tie}\}.$$

The dice or integer multisets may be identified with independent discrete random variables that are uniformly distributed on these multisets (i.e. the probability of an integer is proportional to its number of occurences); the reciprocal relation Q may be regarded as a quantitative description of the pairwise comparison of these random variables.

In the characterization of the transitivity of this reciprocal relation, a type of cycle-transitivity, which can neither be seen as a type of C-transitivity, nor as a type of FG-transitivity, has proven to play a predominant role. For obvious reasons, this new type of transitivity has been called dice-transitivity.

Definition 4.1. Cycle-transitivity w.r.t. the upper bound function U_D defined by

$$U_D(\alpha, \beta, \gamma) = \beta + \gamma - \beta\gamma,$$

is called *dice-transitivity*.

Dice-transitivity is closely related to $T_{\mathbf{P}}$-transitivity. However, it uses the quantities β and γ instead of the quantities α and β, and is therefore less restrictive. Dice-transitivity can be situated between $T_{\mathbf{L}}$-transitivity and $T_{\mathbf{P}}$-transitivity, and also between $T_{\mathbf{L}}$-transitivity and moderate stochastic transitivity.

Proposition 4.2. *(De Schuymer et al. (2003)) The reciprocal relation generated by a collection of generalized dice is dice-transitive.*

4.2   A method for comparing random variables

Many methods can be established for the comparison of the components (random variables, r.v.) of a random vector $(X_1, \ldots, X_n)$, as there exist many ways to extract useful information from the joint cumulative distribution function (c.d.f.) $F_{X_1, \ldots, X_n}$ that characterizes the random vector. A

first simplification consists in comparing the r.v. two by two. It means that
a method for comparing r.v. should only use the information contained in
the bivariate c.d.f. F_{X_i,X_j}. Therefore, one can very well ignore the existence
of a multivariate c.d.f. and just describe mutual dependencies between the
r.v. by means of the bivariate c.d.f. Of course one should be aware that
not all choices of bivariate c.d.f. are compatible with a multivariate c.d.f.
The problem of characterizing those ensembles of bivariate c.d.f. that can
be identified with the marginal bivariate c.d.f. of a single multivariate c.d.f.,
is known as the *compatibility problem* (Nelsen (1998)).

A second simplifying step often made is to bypass the information contained in the bivariate c.d.f. to devise a comparison method that entirely
relies on the one-dimensional marginal c.d.f. In this case there is even not
a compatibility problem, as for any set of univariate c.d.f. F_{X_i}, the product $F_{X_1} F_{X_2} \cdots F_{X_n}$ is a valid joint c.d.f., namely the one expressing the
independence of the r.v. There are many ways to compare one-dimensional
c.d.f., and by far the simplest one is the method that builds a partial order on the set of r.v. using the principle of first order stochastic dominance
(Levy (1998)). It states that a r.v. X is weakly preferred to a r.v. Y if for
all $u \in \mathbb{R}$ it holds that $F_X(u) \leq F_Y(u)$. At the extreme end of the chain of
simplifications, are the methods that compare r.v. by means of a characteristic or a function of some characteristics derived from the one-dimensional
marginal c.d.f. The simplest example is the weak order induced by the
expected values of the r.v.

Proceeding along the line of thought of the previous section, a random
vector $(X_1, X_2, \ldots, X_m)$ generates a reciprocal relation by means of the
following recipe.

Definition 4.3. Given a random vector $(X_1, X_2, \ldots, X_m)$, the binary relation Q defined by

$$Q(X_i, X_j) = \mathcal{P}\{X_i > X_j\} + \frac{1}{2}\mathcal{P}\{X_i = X_j\}$$

is a reciprocal relation.

For two discrete r.v. X_i and X_j, $Q(X_i, X_j)$ can be computed as

$$Q(X_i, X_j) = \sum_{k>l} p_{X_i,X_j}(k,l) + \frac{1}{2}\sum_k p_{X_i,X_j}(k,k),$$

with p_{X_i,X_j} the joint probability mass function (p.m.f.) of (X_i, X_j). For
two continuous r.v. X_i and X_j, $Q(X_i, X_j)$ can be computed as:

$$Q(X_i, X_j) = \int_{-\infty}^{+\infty} dx \int_{-\infty}^{x} f_{X_i,X_j}(x,y)\, dy,$$

with f_{X_i,X_j} the joint probability density function (p.d.f.) of (X_i, X_j).

For this pairwise comparison, one needs the two-dimensional marginal distributions. Sklar's theorem (Sklar (1959); Nelsen (1998)) tells us that if a joint cumulative distribution function F_{X_i,X_j} has marginals F_{X_i} and F_{X_j}, then there exists a copula C_{ij} such that for all x, y:

$$F_{X_i,X_j}(x,y) = C_{ij}(F_{X_i}(x), F_{X_j}(y)).$$

If X_i and X_j are continuous, then C_{ij} is unique; otherwise, C_{ij} is uniquely determined on $\mathrm{Ran}(F_{X_i}) \times \mathrm{Ran}(F_{X_j})$.

As the above comparison method takes into account the bivariate marginal c.d.f. it takes into account the dependence of the components of the random vector. The information contained in the reciprocal relation is therefore much richer than if, for instance, we would have based the comparison of X_i and X_j solely on their expected values. Despite the fact that the dependence structure is entirely captured by the multivariate c.d.f., the pairwise comparison is only apt to take into account pairwise dependence, as only bivariate c.d.f. are involved. Indeed, the bivariate c.d.f. do not fully disclose the dependence structure; the r.v. may even be pairwise independent while not mutually independent.

Since the copulas C_{ij} that couple the univariate marginal c.d.f. into the bivariate marginal c.d.f. can be different from another, the analysis of the reciprocal relation and in particular the identification of its transitivity properties appear rather cumbersome. It is nonetheless possible to state in general, without making any assumptions on the bivariate c.d.f., that the probabilistic relation Q generated by an arbitrary random vector always shows some minimal form of transitivity (De Baets and De Meyer (2008)).

Proposition 4.4. *The reciprocal relation Q generated by a random vector is $T_{\mathbf{L}}$-transitive.*

4.3 Artificial coupling of random variables

Our further interest is to study the situation where abstraction is made that the r.v. are components of a random vector, and all bivariate c.d.f. are enforced to depend in the same way upon the univariate c.d.f., in other words, we consider the situation of all copulas being the same, realizing that this might not be possible at all. In fact, this simplification is equivalent to considering instead of a random vector, a collection of r.v. and to artificially compare them, all in the same manner and based upon a same copula. The pairwise comparison then relies upon the knowledge of the one-dimensional marginal c.d.f. solely, as is the case in stochastic dominance methods. Our comparison method, however, is not equivalent to any known kind of stochastic dominance, but should rather be regarded as a graded variant of it (see also De Baets and De Meyer (2007)).

The case $C = T_{\mathbf{P}}$ generalizes Proposition 4.2, and applies in particular to a collection of independent r.v. where all copulas effectively equal $T_{\mathbf{P}}$.

Proposition 4.5. *(De Schuymer et al. (2003, 2005)) The reciprocal relation Q generated by a collection of r.v. pairwisely coupled by $T_{\mathbf{P}}$ is dice-transitive,* i.e. *it is cycle-transitive w.r.t. the upper bound function given by* $U_D(\alpha, \beta, \gamma) = \beta + \gamma - \beta\gamma$.

Next, we discuss the case when using one of the extreme copulas to artificially couple the r.v. In case $C = T_{\mathbf{M}}$, the r.v. are coupled comonotonically. Note that this case is possible in reality.

Proposition 4.6. *(De Schuymer et al. (2007); De Meyer et al. (2007)) The reciprocal relation Q generated by a collection of r.v. pairwisely coupled by $T_{\mathbf{M}}$ is cycle-transitive w.r.t. to the upper bound function U given by* $U(\alpha, \beta, \gamma) = \min(\beta + \gamma, 1)$. *Cycle-transitivity w.r.t. the upper bound function U is equivalent to $T_{\mathbf{L}}$-transitivity.*

In case $C = T_{\mathbf{L}}$, the r.v. are coupled countermonotonically. This assumption can never represent a true dependence structure for more than two r.v., due to the compatibility problem.

Proposition 4.7. *(De Schuymer et al. (2007); De Meyer et al. (2007)) The reciprocal relation Q generated by a collection of r.v. pairwisely coupled by $T_{\mathbf{L}}$ is partially stochastic transitive,* i.e. *it is cycle-transitive w.r.t. to the upper bound function defined by* $U_{ps}(\alpha, \beta, \gamma) = \max(\beta, \gamma) = \gamma$.

The proofs of these propositions were first given for discrete uniformly distributed r.v. (De Schuymer et al. (2003, 2007)). It allowed for an interpretation of the values $Q(X_i, X_j)$ as winning probabilities in a hypothetical dice game, or equivalently, as a method for the pairwise comparison of ordered lists of numbers. Subsequently, we have shown that as far as transitivity is concerned, this situation is generic and therefore characterizes the type of transitivity observed in general (De Meyer et al. (2007); De Schuymer et al. (2005)).

The above results can be seen as particular cases of a more general result (see De Baets and De Meyer (2008)).

Proposition 4.8. *Let C be a commutative copula such that for any $n > 1$ and for any $0 \le x_1 \le \cdots \le x_n \le 1$ and $0 \le y_1 \le \cdots \le y_n \le 1$, it holds that*

$$\sum_i C(x_i, y_i) - \sum_i C(x_{n-2i}, y_{n-2i-1}) - \sum_i C(x_{n-2i-1}, y_{n-2i})$$

$$\le C\left(x_n + \sum_i C(x_{n-2i-2}, y_{n-2i-1}) - \sum_i C(x_{n-2i}, y_{n-2i-1}), \right.$$

$$\left. y_n + \sum_i C(x_{n-2i-1}, y_{n-2i-2}) - \sum_i C(x_{n-2i-1}, y_{n-2i}) \right), \quad (8)$$

where the sums extend over all integer values that lead to meaningful indices of x and y. Then the reciprocal relation Q generated by a collection of random variables pairwisely coupled by C is cycle-transitive w.r.t. to the upper bound function U^C defined by:

$$U^C(\alpha, \beta, \gamma) = \max(\beta + C(1-\beta, \gamma), \gamma + C(\beta, 1-\gamma)).$$

Inequality (8) is called the *twisted staircase condition* and appears to be quite complicated. Although its origin is well understood (see De Baets and De Meyer (2008)), it is not yet clear for which commutative copulas it holds. We strongly conjecture that it holds for all Frank copulas.

4.4 Comparison of special independent random variables

Dice-transitivity is the generic type of transitivity shared by the reciprocal relations generated by a collection of independent r.v. If one considers independent r.v. with densities all belonging to one of the one-parameter families in Table 2, the corresponding reciprocal relation shows the corresponding type of cycle-transitivity listed in Table 4.4 (De Schuymer et al. (2005)).

Note that all upper bound functions in Table 3 are self-dual. More striking is that the two families of power-law distributions (one-parameter subfamilies of the two-parameter Beta and Pareto families) and the family of Gumbel distributions, all yield the same type of transitivity as exponential distributions, namely cycle-transitivity w.r.t. the self-dual upper bound function U_E defined by:

$$U_E(\alpha, \beta, \gamma) = \alpha\beta + \alpha\gamma + \beta\gamma - 2\alpha\beta\gamma.$$

Cycle-transitivity w.r.t. U_E can also be expressed as

$$\alpha_{abc}\beta_{abc}\gamma_{abc} = (1 - \alpha_{abc})(1 - \beta_{abc})(1 - \gamma_{abc}),$$

Table 2. Parametric families of continuous distributions.

Name	Density function $f(x)$		
Exponential	$\lambda e^{-\lambda x}$	$\lambda > 0$	$x \in [0, \infty[$
Beta	$\lambda x^{(\lambda-1)}$	$\lambda > 0$	$x \in [0, 1]$
Pareto	$\lambda x^{-(\lambda+1)}$	$\lambda > 0$	$x \in [1, \infty[$
Gumbel	$\mu e^{-\mu(x-\lambda)} e^{-e^{-\mu(x-\lambda)}}$	$\lambda \in \mathbb{R}, \mu > 0$	$x \in]-\infty, \infty[$
Uniform	$1/a$	$\lambda \in \mathbb{R}, a > 0$	$x \in [\lambda, \lambda + a]$
Laplace	$(e^{-|x-\lambda|/\mu)})/(2\mu)$	$\lambda \in \mathbb{R}, \mu > 0$	$x \in]-\infty, \infty[$
Normal	$(e^{-(x-\lambda)^2/2\sigma^2})/\sqrt{2\pi\sigma^2}$	$\lambda \in \mathbb{R}, \sigma > 0$	$x \in]-\infty, \infty[$

which is equivalent to the notion of multiplicative transitivity of Tanino (1988). A reciprocal relation Q on X is called *multiplicatively transitive* if for any $(a, b, c) \in X^3$ it holds that

$$\frac{Q(a,c)}{Q(c,a)} = \frac{Q(a,b)}{Q(b,a)} \cdot \frac{Q(b,c)}{Q(c,b)}.$$

In the cases of the unimodal uniform, Gumbel, Laplace and normal distributions we have fixed one of the two parameters in order to restrict the family to a one-parameter subfamily, mainly because with two free parameters, the formulae become utmost cumbersome. The one exception is the two-dimensional family of normal distributions. In De Schuymer et al. (2005), we have shown that the corresponding reciprocal relation is in that case moderately stochastic transitive.

5   Conclusion

We have introduced the reader to two relational frameworks and the wide variety of transitivity notions available in them. The presentation was rather dense and more information can be found following the many literature pointers given.

Anticipating on future work, in particular on applications, we can identify two important directions. The first direction concerns the use of fuzzy similarity measures. Moser (2006) has shown recently that the T-equality E^T, with $T = T_\mathbf{P}$ or $T = T_\mathbf{L}$, is positive semi-definite. We are currently tackling the same question for the fuzzy cardinality-based similarity measures. Results of this type allow to bridge the gap between the fuzzy set

Table 3. Cycle-transitivity for the continuous distributions in Table 1.

Name	Upper bound function $U(\alpha, \beta, \gamma)$
Exponential Beta Pareto Gumbel	$\alpha\beta + \alpha\gamma + \beta\gamma - 2\alpha\beta\gamma$
Uniform	$\begin{cases} \beta + \gamma - 1 + \dfrac{1}{2}[\max(\sqrt{2(1-\beta)} + \sqrt{2(1-\gamma)} - 1, 0)]^2 & , \beta \geq 1/2 \\ \alpha + \beta - \dfrac{1}{2}[\max(\sqrt{2\alpha} + \sqrt{2\beta} - 1, 0)]^2 & , \beta < 1/2 \end{cases}$
Laplace	$\begin{cases} \beta + \gamma - 1 + f^{-1}(f(1-\beta) + f(1-\gamma)) & , \beta \geq 1/2 \\ \alpha + \beta - f^{-1}(f(\alpha) + f(\beta)) & , \beta < 1/2 \end{cases}$ with $f^{-1}(x) = \frac{1}{2}\left(1 + \frac{x}{2}\right)e^{-x}$
Normal	$\begin{cases} \beta + \gamma - 1 + \Phi(\Phi^{-1}(1-\beta) + \Phi(1-\gamma)) & , \beta \geq 1/2 \\ \alpha + \beta - \Phi(\Phi^{-1}(\alpha) + \Phi^{-1}(\beta)) & , \beta < 1/2 \end{cases}$ with $\Phi(x) = (\sqrt{2\pi})^{-1} \int_{-\infty}^{x} e^{-t^2/2} dt$

community and the machine learning community, making some fuzzy similarity measures available as potential kernels for the popular kernel-based learning methods, either on their own or in combination with existing kernels (see e.g. Maenhout et al. (2007) for an application of this type).

The second direction concerns the further exploitation of the results on the comparison of random variables. As mentioned, the approach followed here can be seen as a graded variant of the increasingly popular notion of stochastic dominance. Future research will have to clarify how these graded variants can be defuzzified in order to come up with meaningful partial orderings of random variables that are more informative than the classical notions of stochastic dominance. First results into that direction can be found in De Baets and De Meyer (2007); De Loof et al. (2006).

Bibliography

H.A. David. *The Method of Paired Comparisons*, volume 12 of *Griffin's Statistical Monographs & Courses*. Charles Griffin & Co. Ltd., London, 1963.

B. De Baets and H. De Meyer. Transitivity-preserving fuzzification schemes for cardinality-based similarity measures. *European J. Oper. Res.*, 160: 726–740, 2005a.

B. De Baets and H. De Meyer. Transitivity frameworks for reciprocal relations: cycle-transitivity versus FG-transitivity. *Fuzzy Sets and Systems*, 152:249–270, 2005b.

B. De Baets and H. De Meyer. Cycle-transitive comparison of artificially coupled random variables. *Internat. J. Approximate Reasoning*, 47:306–322, 2008.

B. De Baets and H. De Meyer. Toward graded and nongraded variants of stochastic dominance. In I. Batyrshin, J. Kacprzyk, L. Sheremetov, and L. Zadeh, editors, *Perception-based Data Mining and Decision Making in Economics and Finance*, volume 36 of *Studies in Computational Intelligence*, pages 261–274. Springer, 2007.

B. De Baets and R. Mesiar. Pseudo-metrics and T-equivalences. *J. Fuzzy Math.*, 5:471–481, 1997.

B. De Baets and R. Mesiar. T-partitions. *Fuzzy Sets and Systems*, 97: 211–223, 1998.

B. De Baets and R. Mesiar. Metrics and T-equalities. *J. Math. Anal. Appl.*, 267:531–547, 2002.

B. De Baets, H. De Meyer, and H. Naessens. A class of rational cardinality-based similarity measures. *J. Comput. Appl. Math.*, 132:51–69, 2001.

B. De Baets, H. De Meyer, B. De Schuymer, and S. Jenei. Cyclic evaluation of transitivity of reciprocal relations. *Social Choice and Welfare*, 26: 217–238, 2006a.

B. De Baets, S. Janssens, and H. De Meyer. Meta-theorems on inequalities for scalar fuzzy set cardinalities. *Fuzzy Sets and Systems*, 157:1463–1476, 2006b.

B. De Baets, S. Janssens, and H. De Meyer. On the transitivity of a parametric family of cardinality-based similarity measures. *Internat. J. Approximate Reasoning*, to appear. doi: 10.1016/j.ijar.2008.03.006.

K. De Loof, H. De Meyer, and B. De Baets. Graded stochastic dominance as a tool for ranking the elements of a poset. In J. Lawry, E. Miranda, A. Bugarin, S. Li, M.A. Gil, P. Grzegorzewski, and O. Hryniewicz, editors, *Soft Methods for Integrated Uncertainty Modelling*, Advances in Soft Computing, pages 273–280. Springer, 2006.

H. De Meyer, H. Naessens, and B. De Baets. Algorithms for computing the min-transitive closure and associated partition tree of a symmetric fuzzy relation. *European J. Oper. Res.*, 155:226–238, 2004.

H. De Meyer, B. De Baets, and B. De Schuymer. On the transitivity of the comonotonic and countermonotonic comparison of random variables. *J. Multivariate Analysis*, 98:177–193, 2007.

B. De Schuymer, H. De Meyer, B. De Baets, and S. Jenei. On the cycle-transitivity of the dice model. *Theory and Decision*, 54:264–285, 2003.

B. De Schuymer, H. De Meyer, and B. De Baets. Cycle-transitive comparison of independent random variables. *J. Multivariate Analysis*, 96: 352–373, 2005.

B. De Schuymer, H. De Meyer, and B. De Baets. Extreme copulas and the comparison of ordered lists. *Theory and Decision*, 62:195–217, 2007.

L. Dice. Measures of the amount of ecologic associations between species. *Ecology*, 26:297–302, 1945.

F. Durante and C. Sempi. Semicopulæ. *Kybernetika*, 41:315–328, 2005.

P. Fishburn. Binary choice probabilities: On the varieties of stochastic transitivity. *J. Math. Psych.*, 10:327–352, 1973.

C. Genest, J.J. Quesada-Molina, J.A. Rodríguez-Lallena, and C. Sempi. A characterization of quasi-copulas. *Journal of Multivariate Analysis*, 69: 193–205, 1999.

P. Jaccard. Nouvelles recherches sur la distribution florale. *Bulletin de la Sociétée Vaudoise des Sciences Naturelles*, 44:223–270, 1908.

S. Janssens, B. De Baets, and H. De Meyer. Bell-type inequalities for quasi-copulas. *Fuzzy Sets and Systems*, 148:263–278, 2004a.

S. Janssens, B. De Baets, and H. De Meyer. Bell-type inequalities for parametric families of triangular norms. *Kybernetika*, 40:89–106, 2004b.

E. Klement, R. Mesiar, and E. Pap. *Triangular Norms*, volume 8 of *Trends in Logic, Studia Logica Library*. Kluwer Academic Publishers, 2000.

H. Levy. *Stochastic Dominance*. Kluwer Academic Publishers, 1998.

S. Maenhout, B. De Baets, G. Haesaert, and E. Van Bockstaele. Support vector machine regression for the prediction of maize hybrid performance. *Theoretical and Applied Genetics*, 115:1003–1013, 2007.

B. Monjardet. A generalisation of probabilistic consistency: linearity conditions for valued preference relations. In J. Kacprzyk and M. Roubens, editors, *Non-Conventional Preference Relations in Decision Making*, volume 301 of *Lecture Notes in Economics and Mathematical Systems*. Springer, 1988.

B. Moser. On representing and generating kernels by fuzzy equivalence relations. *Journal of Machine Learning Research*, 7:2603–2620, 2006.

R. Nelsen. *An Introduction to Copulas*, volume 139 of *Lecture Notes in Statistics*. Springer-Verlag, 1998.

J. Pykacz and B. D'Hooghe. Bell-type inequalities in fuzzy probability calculus. *Internat. J. of Uncertainty, Fuzziness and Knowledge-Based Systems*, 9:263–275, 2001.

D. Rogers and T. Tanimoto. A computer program for classifying plants. *Science*, 132:1115–1118, 1960.

A. Sklar. Fonctions de répartition à n dimensions et leurs marges. *Publ. Inst. Statist. Univ. Paris*, 8:229–231, 1959.

P. Sneath and R. Sokal. *Numerical Taxonomy*. WH Freeman, San Francisco, 1973.

R. Sokal and C. Michener. A statistical method for evaluating systematic relationships. *Univ. of Kansas Science Bulletin*, 38:1409–1438, 1958.

Z. Switalski. Transitivity of fuzzy preference relations – an empirical study. *Fuzzy Sets and Systems*, 118:503–508, 2001.

Z. Switalski. General transitivity conditions for fuzzy reciprocal preference matrices. *Fuzzy Sets and Systems*, 137:85–100, 2003.

T. Tanino. Fuzzy preference relations in group decision making. In J. Kacprzyk and M. Roubens, editors, *Non-Conventional Preference Relations in Decision Making*, volume 301 of *Lecture Notes in Economics and Mathematical Systems*. Springer, 1988.

L. Zadeh. Fuzzy sets. *Information and Control*, 8:338–353, 1965.

A Logic-based View
of Similarities and Preferences

Enrique H. Ruspini

Artificial Intelligence Center, SRI International, Menlo Park, California, USA

E-mail: ruspini@ai.sri.com

Abstract We start by recalling previous work leading to an interpretation of fuzzy logic in terms of metric structures defined in a set of possible worlds. These possible worlds, or possible states of a system, are characterized by the truth values of classical logical assertions about the state of the world.

We consider next the nature of the information required to generate the underlying metrics, concluding that similarity measures are typically derived from preference relations that induce a generalized order in the space of possible worlds. Recalling the relation between similarity measures and utility functions underlying several fundamental results such as the representation theorem of Valverde, we extend our similarity-based formalism by introduction of corresponding utilitarian notions, such as marginal preference and conditional preference. On the basis of these definitions we derive a formula to infer the value of marginal preference functions.

Finally we briefly present several examples of the application of these ideas to the development of intelligent planners and controllers for robots and teams of robots. These examples motivate basic requirements for a comprehensive logic-based approach to a calculus of similarities and preferences. We note that logic-based preference formalisms permit to explicitly specify context-dependent formulas that tradeoff the relative utilities of attaining potential system states from the perspective of different preference criteria, allow specification of the interaction of individual agents, and control the behavior of groups of interacting agents.

1 Similarities, Preferences, and Logic

The ability to recognize similarities between concepts, objects, and events is the basis of a number of important cognitive processes (Shafir, 2003). Classification of entities along partition schemes that facilitate understanding of the underlying systems is the basis for the generation of conceptual knowledge structures. The correspondence between the extensional concept of set and the intentional notion of logical predicate provides a connection between partitions of a set—that is, a summary description of that set as a collection of classes where pairs of members of each class are thought as being similar or equivalent—and logical structures that states rules and criteria employed to produce the partition.

When equivalence relations are extended to consider gradual notions of similarity the resulting measures are described by a fuzzy similarity relation (Zadeh, 1971b). These similarity relations define a metric structure in a classical set and may be thought of as being the complement of a bounded distance function that assigns maximum similarity (i.e., 1) to identical elements while indicating that two elements that are far away from each other have the minimum possible similarity (i.e., 0).

The notion of similarity has been generally regarded as being metric in character permitting to express proximity or resemblance, from some viewpoint, using a numeric scale, which, in fuzzy-set theory, is the $[0, 1]$ interval of the real line. In this spirit, Ruspini (1969) introduced their use in the context of unsupervised pattern recognition (*fuzzy clustering*). In the context of this type of applications, similarity measures generalize the defining properties of equivalence relations—reflexivity, symmetry, and transitivity—resulting in classification frameworks having desirable formal properties.

In 1991, Ruspini (1991), while examining possible interpretations of the fuzzy-logic notion of possibility (Zadeh, 1978), proposed an explanation of the basic structures of fuzzy logic in terms of notions of similarity. Triangular norms (Klement, 2000), for example, were shown to arise naturally from rational requirements on the notion of generalized transitivity rather than from arguments about possible generalizations of the notion of logical conjunction.

The connections between metric and generalized logical structures presented in that work provided semantic bases for the notion of fuzzy possibility that differed substantially in character and properties from their probabilistic counterparts. Rather than stressing on the tendency, or likelihood, of certain systems to exhibit certain behaviors or properties, similarity-based interpretations of fuzzy-logic structures, focus on the resemblance, or proximity, between possible states of the systems under consideration. This interpretation is similar in character to those generated when examining the notion of truthlikeness (Niiniluoto, 1987; Oddie, 1987), that is, the idea that certain statements about the real world, although possibly false, are more adequate descriptions of the state of affairs than others.

This emphasis on representing uncertainty about the state of the world in terms of its proximity to designated subsets of possible states is very different in nature to statements about the relative frequency of occurrence of a possible state. This interpretation is also close in spirit to methods to measure information complexity based on the notion of radius of uncertainty (Traub et al., 1998).[1]

In this paper we review the basic ideas linking the metric concept of similarity and the fundamental concepts and procedures of fuzzy logic. We turn then our attention to the problem of defining metrics that capture the semantics of a particular problem proceeding to discuss the relation between the concepts of preference and similarity. We extend our similarity-based formalism to the preference relations introducing the notions of extended, conditional, and marginal preference and derive a result permitting to infer marginal preference values from knowledge of conditional preference values and related marginal preference values.

Finally, we present applications of the concepts of similarity and utility to control and planning problems in robotics as a motivation for the development of a comprehensive approach to control based on the definition and synthesis of functions describing the relative desirability of a system being in a possible state (i.e.,possible world) as opposed to being in another. In this discussion, we will consider also issues related to the need to handle and aggregate multiple criteria, the preferences of different decision-making agents, and relations between preferences of individual and teams of decision-making agents.

2   Fuzzy Logic and Similarity

In this section we will discuss interpretations of the fundamental concepts of fuzzy logic in terms of the metric notion of similarity measure. Our presentation follows the outline of the more extensive account of Ruspini and Esteva (1998).

Our studies on the semantics of the basic concepts and structures of fuzzy logic were motivated by the need to develop a sound formal framework that permits to differentiate possibilistic constructs from those of other approaches to the representation of imprecision and uncertainty, notably the calculus of probability. While a number of formulations had been proposed to provide solid conceptual foundations for fuzzy logic these formalisms were typically axiomatic in nature, concentrating on the rationality and consis-

---

[1] Other interpretations of fuzzy and possibilistic logics have been advanced (Dubois et al., 1994) explaining its role in the representation of beliefs, which is the central concern of subjective probability.

tency of the extensions of classical set theory and classical logic proposed by the theory rather than on interpretation of its basic notions in terms of more primitive concepts.

Although often, as remarked by Giles (1988), specific formalisms had been developed with implicit interpretations in mind, the lack of clear characterizations of fundamental concepts, such as the notion of degree of membership, led to doubts about the potential probabilistic nature of those concepts or the to the "inevitability" (Lindley, 1982) of their eventual rejection in favor of probabilistic frameworks.

In addition to requirements to resolve these epistemological quandaries, there was also an important pragmatic reason to provide a better understanding of fuzzy-logic concepts. Computer-based implementations of of possibilistic methods produce fuzzy sets and possibility distributions as results of the solution of practical problems. The validity of these results, and that of the programs that produce them, could not possibly be evaluated unless correctness tests were clearly specified. Such specification is not possible without a practical interpretation of the meaning of those results that permits to assess their validity and to estimate the consequences of potential errors.

2.1   Similarity-based Interpretations

The metric concepts of similarity, resemblance, proximity, and closeness are the bases for a number of important cognitive analogical processes (Shafir, 2003). Quantitative measures of similarity have been also proposed as a possible basis for certain aspects of language understanding (Lewis, 1973). Computational methods such as case-based reasoning (Kolodner, 1993; Carbonell, 1982), cluster analysis (Bezdek, 1998), and rough-set techniques (Pawlak, 1992) are also based on the concept of similarity or on its classical counterpart notion of equivalence relation. Recently, similarity-based methods have acquired a heightened importance because of their role in bioinformatics (Mount, 2004), chemistry (Nikolova and Jaworska, 2003; Glen and Adams, 2006), and semantic information retrieval (Stroulia and Wang, 2005).

In spite of interest in analogical methods both at the conceptual and practical levels, a theory of similarity, providing firm bases for the concept and illuminating its many aspects, has yet to be developed. It is perhaps for this reason that other forms of approximate reasoning such as probabilistic analysis or utility-based reasoning have received more attention as both inductive and deductive tools.

Our similarity-based interpretation of fuzzy logic was both motivated by the need to provide explanation of its concepts in terms of more primitive notions and by our desire to further explore the central role of the notion of generalized equivalence relation (Zadeh, 1971a), which as noted by other authors (Valverde, 1985; Trillas and Valverde, 1985; Ovchinnikov, 1991) played a central role in the inferential processes of fuzzy logic.

The Similarity-based Model   The similarity-based logic **SL** (Ruspini, 1991) extends modal-logic formalisms by considering a nested family of *accessibility relations* that are defined by a similarity, or fuzzy equivalence, relation. This logic **SL** has been extended and generalized in a number of regards (Esteva et al., 1994a, 1997; Dubois et al., 1997; Rodríguez et al., 1996).

We will discuss this model in the context of a *universe of discourse* $\mathcal{U}$ (or *universe*, for short), that is, a nonempty set of *possible worlds*, possible states of a system, or possible solutions of a problem. Each possible world will be assumed to either satisfy or not some declarative statements about that possible world. These propositions correspond, as is customary in propositional logic, to sentences in a language $\mathcal{L}$ formed, employing the usual well-formedness rules, by combination of symbols in an alphabet $\mathcal{A}$ and the logical operators $\neg, \vee, \wedge, \rightarrow$ and $\leftrightarrow$.

Possible worlds in $\mathcal{U}$ are related to the truth value of propositions in $\mathcal{L}$ by a *valuation* function V that assigns a value of either **true** or **false** to every pair (w, p) of possible world w and propositions p. As is customary in classical logic, we will write $w \models p$ to indicate that the valuation V assigns the truth value **true** to a pair (w, p). The notation $[p]$ will be used to represent the subset of possible worlds where p is true. Obviously, $w \models p$ if and only if $w \in [p]$. As is also common in conventional logic, we will say that the subset of possible worlds $[p]$ is an interpretation of p.

We will also consider a nonempty subset $\mathcal{E}$ of the universe $\mathcal{U}$, called the *evidential set*, modelling the set of possible worlds that are consistent with available evidence. In what follows, abusing the language, we will also denote by $\mathcal{E}$ any proposition p having $\mathcal{E}$ as its extension, i.e., such that $[p] = \mathcal{E}$.

If this conventional modal framework is enhanced by introduction of a similarity measure S we may characterize, in an informal fashion, the **SL** interpretation of possibility distributions as measures of the similarity of the evidential set $\mathcal{E}$ (i.e., the set that available evidence indicts as containing the "true" state of the system) to arbitrary possible worlds in $\mathcal{U}$. In other words, any possible world is similar to the degree $S(w, w_{\mathcal{E}})$ to some evidential world $w_{\mathcal{E}}$. The closest evidential world provides a measure of the *possible truth* of w, that is, how much we have to "stretch" the truth to encompass w. Even if w is not in the evidential set, this measure quantifies the extent to which competing explanations are more adequate description of the possible state of affairs. This interpretation is close in spirit to the concept of truthlikeness (Niiniluoto, 1987).

This measure of potential truth of a single possible world w can be readily extended to a measure of necessary truth of a nonempty subset of possible worlds W as the extent to which W has to be "stretched" to encompass the evidential set $\mathcal{E}$, i.e., the smallest metric neighborhood of W that includes $\mathcal{E}$. [2]

Being able, through the introduction of a metric structure, to measure the similarity between subsets of the universe $\mathcal{U}$ allows to readily extend the main inferential procedure of *modus ponens* into its generalized counterpart, providing an interpretation for the *compositional rule of inference*, or *generalized modus ponens* of Zadeh (1979). Under this interpretation, this rule bounds the distance from the evidential set $\mathcal{E}$ to the set $[q]$ (i.e., the conclusion) on the basis of information of the similarity of $\mathcal{E}$ and $[p]$ (the premise), and that of the distance between $[p]$ and $[q]$ (the conditional rule or implication). In other words, the similarity logic **SL** regards the modus ponens as an expression of the inclusion relation between metric neighbourhoods of sets in the space $\mathcal{U}$, generalizing the classical modus ponens, which expresses the transitivity of the classical relation of set inclusion:

If $[p]$ is a subset of $[q]$, and if $[q]$ is a subset of $[r]$, then $[p]$ is a subset of $[r]$.

This metric approach to characterize the truth of statements in terms of similarities between sets of possible worlds is completely different in nature to that emphasized in probabilistic approaches where the truth of a proposition p given the evidence $\mathcal{E}$ is defined in terms of numeric measures of the extent of overlap of the sets $\mathcal{E} \cap [p]$ and $\mathcal{E}$.

Similarity Relations   We recall that a *fuzzy similarity* (Zadeh, 1971a), or generalized equivalence relation, S is a function

$$S : \mathcal{U} \times \mathcal{U} \mapsto [0, 1]\,,$$

mapping each pair of possible worlds (w, w') to a numerical *degree of similarity* between 0 (corresponding to maximum dissimilarity) to 1 (corresponding

---

[2]In a typical fuzzy-logic application sets W of practical concern are defined as the sets $[X = x]$) where a system variable X takes the value x.

to maximum similarity) satisfying the constraints

$$
\begin{aligned}
S(w, w') &= 1, && \text{if and only if } w = w', \\
S(w, w') &= S(w', w), && \text{for all } w, w' \text{ in } \mathcal{U}, \\
S(w, w') &\geq S(w, w'') \circledast S(w'', w') && \text{for all } w, w', w'' \text{ in } \mathcal{U}
\end{aligned}
$$

where $\circledast$ is one of a family of operators, called *triangular norms* (or *T-norms*, for short), which are important in several fields (Schweizer and Sklar, 1983; Trillas and Valverde, 1985). It is important to remark that, in multivalued logics such as fuzzy logic, T-norms are the result of logical considerations as generalizations for the truth table for the logical conjunction operator $\wedge$. In our original formulation (Ruspini, 1991), however, T-norms arise from the imposition of reasonable axiomatic requirements intended to provide the relation S with the semantics commonly associated with concepts such as proximity or resemblance.

From a modal-logic (Hughes and Cresswell, 1996) viewpoint, the similarity relation S permits definition of a generalized accessibility relation. In conventional modal systems, accessibility relations are binary relations defined between pairs of possible worlds that make possible to formalize the notions of *possibility* and *necessity*. In **SL** the similarity relation S defines an extended, gradual, relation of accessibility leading to numeric notions of possibility and necessity. The following notions of graded modality extend the unary operators $\mathbf{N}$ and Π of modal logic to the infinite family of unary operators $\mathbf{N}_\alpha$ and Π_α, where α is a real number in $[0, 1]$:

$$
\begin{aligned}
w \models \Pi_\alpha p, &\quad \text{if and only if there exists } w' \text{ such that } w' \models p \text{ and } S(w, w') \geq \alpha, \\
w \models \mathbf{N}_\alpha p, &\quad \text{if and only if for all } w' \text{ such that } S(w, w') \geq \alpha, \text{ it is } w' \models p.
\end{aligned}
$$

If $w \models \Pi_\alpha p$, it is said that the possibility of p is greater or equal than α. Similarly, if $w \models \mathbf{N}_\alpha p$, it is said that the necessity of p is greater or equal than α.

Possibility Distributions The isomorphism between propositions and subsets of possible worlds that model the proposition, i.e., the set $[p] = \{w \colon w \models p\}$, permits to regard the relation of set inclusion in $\mathcal{U}$ as the counterpart of the notion of logical implication in $\mathcal{L}$. The similarity relation S allows generalization of this notion by application of the approach commonly employed in metric spaces, namely the Hausdorff distance (Dieudonné, 1960), to extend a metric between points to a metric between sets

Definition: The *degree of implication* of p by q is the value

$$\mathbf{I}(p \mid q) = \inf_{w' \models q} \ \sup_{w \models p} \ S(w, w').$$

The degree of implication $\mathbf{I}(p \mid q)$ is a measure of the size of the minimal neighbourhood of $[q]$ that intersect $[p]$ in the sense that if $\beta \leq \mathbf{I}(p \mid q)$, then

$$q \Rightarrow \Pi_\beta(p).$$

In addition, $\mathbf{I}(p \mid q)$ is the largest real value β for which the above statement may be made. The similarity between two propositions p and q may now be defined as the "Hausdorff similarity" [3] between the subsets of possible worlds $[p]$ and $[q]$

$$\hat{S}(p, q) = \min\big(\mathbf{I}(p \mid q), \mathbf{I}(q \mid p)\big).$$

If the similarity measure S is , then the extended similarity relation $\hat{S}$ is also ⊛-transitive.

A notion dual to the degree of implication, called the *degree of consistence* gauges the extent of the neighborhood of $[q]$ that simply intersects $[p]$:

Definition: The *degree of consistence* of p and q is the value

$$\mathbf{C}(p \mid q) = \sup_{w' \models q} \ \sup_{w \models p} \ S(w, w').$$

We are now in a position to introduce the notions of generalized possibility and necessity distributions in terms of the degree of implication and degree of consistency functions:

Definition: If $\mathcal{E}$ is a nonempty subset of $\mathcal{U}$, then a function $\mathbf{N}_\mathcal{E}(\cdot)$, defined over propositions in the language $\mathcal{L}$, is called an *necessity distribution* for $\mathcal{E}$ if

$$\mathbf{N}_\mathcal{E}(p) \leq \mathbf{I}(p \mid \mathcal{E}),$$

and

Definition: If $\mathcal{E}$ is a nonempty subset of $\mathcal{U}$, then a function $\Pi_\mathcal{E}(\cdot)$, defined over propositions in the language $\mathcal{L}$, is called an *possibility distribution* for $\mathcal{E}$ if

$$\Pi_\mathcal{E}(p) \geq \mathbf{C}(p \mid \mathcal{E}).$$

---

[3]It is important to recall that similarity measures are a form of complement of metric distances.

If $\mathcal{E}$ is thought as the set of possible worlds compatible with the evidence or, informally, the set of possible states of the system under consideration, then the necessity distribution $\Pi_{\mathcal{E}}(p)$ is the lower bound of the similarity between *any* evidential world and a possible world where p is true. Correspondingly, possibility distributions are upper bounds on the similarities of possible worlds in $\mathcal{E}$ and in $[p]$.

To derive the notions of conditional necessity and independence, we will need to recall the definition of the concept of the *residuation*, or *pseudoinverse*, function associated with a triangular norm $\circledast$ (Valverde, 1985):

Definition: If $\circledast$ is a triangular norm, its *pseudoinverse* $\oslash$ is the function defined over pairs of numbers in the unit interval of the real line by the expression

$$a \oslash b = \sup\{\, c : \; b \circledast c \leq a \,\}.$$

The pseudoinverse function permits to define conditional possibility and necessity distributions. with respect to an evidential set $\mathcal{E}$, as as measures of the proximity of worlds on the evidential set $\mathcal{E}$ to (some or all) worlds satisfying a proposition p *relative* to their proximity to (some or all) the worlds that satisfy another (conditioning) proposition q:[4]

Definition: Let $\mathcal{E}$ be a nonempty subset of $\mathcal{U}$. A function $\mathbf{N}_{\mathcal{E}}(\cdot|\cdot)$ mapping pairs of propositions in the language $\mathcal{L}$ into $[0,1]$ is called a *conditional necessity distribution* for $\mathcal{E}$ if

$$\mathbf{N}_{\mathcal{E}}(p|q) \leq \inf_{w \models \mathcal{E}} \left[\, \mathbf{I}(p\,|\,w) \oslash \mathbf{I}(q\,|\,w) \,\right],$$

for any propositions p and q.

Definition: Let $\mathcal{E}$ be a nonempty subset of $\mathcal{U}$. A function $\mathbf{N}_{\mathcal{E}}(\cdot|\cdot)$ mapping pairs of propositions in the language $\mathcal{L}$ into $[0,1]$ is called a *conditional possibility distribution* for $\mathcal{E}$ if

$$\Pi_{\mathcal{E}}(p|q) \geq \sup_{w \models \mathcal{E}} \left[\, \mathbf{I}(p\,|\,w) \oslash \mathbf{I}(q\,|\,w) \,\right],$$

for any propositions p and q.

Generalized Modus Ponens The following results generalize (Esteva et al., 1994b,a) original theorems of Ruspini (1991) that interpret the fundamental operation of fuzzy logic in terms of the similarity-based logic **SL**.

---

[4] In a way reminiscent of the definition of conditional probability in probability theory, we are now comparing the similarity between $\mathcal{E}$ and $[p]$ as a "fraction" of the similarity between $\mathcal{E}$ and $[q]$.

Before being able to state them we need to characterize the well-known notion of partition in the context of possible-worlds models:

Definition (Partition of $\mathcal{L}$): If $\mathbf{P} = \{p_i \text{ in } \mathcal{L}, i \text{ in } I\}$ is a collection of propositions such that their extensions, as subsets of possible worlds, satisfy $\cup_I[p_i] = \mathcal{U}$, then $\mathbf{P}$ is called a *partition* of $\mathcal{L}$. We will also say occasionally that $\mathbf{P}$ is a partition of $\mathcal{U}$.

Theorem: *(Generalized Modus Ponens for Necessity Distributions)*: Let $\{p_i, i \text{ in } I\}$ be a family of propositions and let $\mathcal{E}$ and $\mathcal{F}$ be nonempty subsets of $\mathcal{U}$. Then, it is

$$\sup_I \left[\mathbf{N}_\mathcal{F}(q|p_i) \circledast \mathbf{N}_\mathcal{E}(p_i) \right] \leq \mathbf{N}_{\mathcal{E} \cap \mathcal{F}}(q).$$

Theorem: *(Generalized Modus Ponens for Possibility Distributions)*: Let $\{p_i, i \text{ in } I\}$ be a partition of $\mathcal{U}$ and let $\mathcal{E}$ and $\mathcal{F}$ be nonempty subsets of $\mathcal{U}$. Then, it is

$$\sup_I \left[\Pi_\mathcal{F}(q|p_i) \circledast \Pi_\mathcal{E}(p_i) \right] \geq \Pi_{\mathcal{E} \cap \mathcal{F}}(q).$$

These results validate the inferential scheme:

If w is in $\mathcal{E}$, then w is necessarily (respectively, possibly) similar to p,
If w is in $\mathcal{F}$, then
    if w is necessarily (respectively, possibly) similar to p,
    then it is necessarily (respectively, possibly) similar to q,

---

If w is in $\mathcal{E} \cap \mathcal{F}$, then w is necessarily (respectively, possibly) similar to q.

It is important to note that the above formulation involves two evidential sources $\mathcal{E}$ and $\mathcal{F}$. The evidential set $\mathcal{E}$ represents the background evidence while the evidential set $\mathcal{F}$ models the major syllogistic premises, that is. the rules in a knowledge-based system. The inferential process estimates the possible necessity and possibility of the conclusion if both sources of evidence are true.

Formal Characterization of the Similarity Logic SL We now state, in a formal fashion, the similarity based model in terms of the extended language $\mathcal{L}_{\mathbf{SL}}$ defined from the propositional language $\mathcal{L}$ as follows:

$$\mathcal{L}_{\mathbf{SL}} = \left\{ (p, [\alpha, \beta]) : p \in \mathcal{L}, \ 0 \leq \alpha, \beta \leq 1 \right\}.$$

In a formula $(p, [\alpha, \beta])$ in $\mathbf{SL}$, the value α indicates a lower bound of the degree of implication of p while the value β indicates a lower bound of its degree of consistence. The formula $(p, [\alpha, \beta])$ states therefore that, given the evidence $\mathcal{E}$, p is true at least to the degree α and that it is compatible with $\mathcal{E}$ at most to the degree β.

A **SL** model is a pair $(S, \mathcal{E})$ where S is a $\circledast$-similarity relation in the set $\mathcal{U}$ of possible worlds and where $\mathcal{E}$ is a nonempty subset of $\mathcal{U}$. The satisfaction relation is defined as follows:

$$(S, \mathcal{E}) \models_{\mathbf{SL}} (p, [\alpha, \beta]) \iff \alpha \leq \mathbf{I}(p \mid \mathcal{E}) \text{ and } \mathbf{C}(p \mid \mathcal{E}) \leq \beta.$$

The possibilistic logic **PL** was introduced by Dubois and Prade (1988) as a formalization of seminal ideas of Zadeh. This formalism is noteworthy for its ability to represent uncertainty and vagueness, its handling of partial inconsistence, its deductive methods, and its relations to nonmonotonic logic. Although **SL** and **PL** are not logically equivalent since, for example, the possibilistic logic **PL** models conditional statements by means of material implication while **SL** employs conditional measures, there are several significant relations between both formalisms, which have been studied by Esteva et al. (1994a). This work deals also with relations of the possibility and similarity logics to the fuzzy-truth valued logic **FTL** (Godó et al., 1991).

3 Utility and Logic

The similarity-based interpretation of fuzzy logic embodied in the logic **SL** provides both an explanation of the basic structures of fuzzy logic while clarifying the role of analogic reasoning—commonly regarded as an unsound form of reasoning—as a sound approach to derive knowledge of the state of affairs in some situations by extension of propositions known to be true in similar situations.

A significant remaining issue, however, is the nature and source of similarity measures. In this regard, it is important to note first a fundamental difference between probability distributions—the bases of probabilistic reasoning—and the metric notion of similarity. Probabilities (at least in their objectivist interpretation) are formal charaterizations of the notion of *frequency*, that is, they measure the tendency of certain systems to exhibit certain behaviors. As such they can be estimated from experimental data as it is usually done with system variables and descriptive parameters.

Similarity relations, on the other hand, are arbitrary metrics introduced to measure resemblance from some perspective. Their definitions, although arbitrary, reflect needs to manage analytical complexity in the same way that classical partitions, which similarities generalize, are introduced to improve system understanding. Similarity measures do not, therefore, reflect properties of the real world but must, nonetheless, have a clear analytical purpose and, most importantly, assertions made on their bases (e.g., "the pressure is small") must be true according to a clear interpretation, such as that given before, of the notion of validity of generalized propositions.

The significant conceptual difference between the notions of probability and similarity should be easily understood by noting that the latter is dependent on a wide variety of criteria to judge proximity while the former is a formalization of the concept of statistical frequency. As noted, for example, by Tversky (1977), if countries are compared in terms of their similarity, then Jamaica might be considered to be close to Cuba on the basis of geographic proximity while Cuba was, when Tversky wrote his paper, close to Russia in terms of their political systems.[5] Similarities are structures introduced for convenience to permit analogical reasoning and to extend, by a form of logical extrapolation, existing knowledge. Probabilities, on the other hand, are an expression of the likelihood that, under certain specified circumstances, a system will behave in certain ways.

In general, however, direct synthesis of useful similarity relations is not usually straightforward. In the few situations where similarity relations may be specified, rules mapping one measure of similarity into another are not easily derived. Utility and preference measures, however, appear naturally in the context of system analysis and system optimization problems and formal relations, presented below, between preference and similarity relations facilitate definition of the latter.

3.1   Preference-based Interpretations

The interpretation of fuzzy sets as elastic constraints—i.e., constraints that may be satisfied to some degree— is one of the earliest explanations of the concept. Bellman and Zadeh (1970) proposed in 1970 the interpretation of fuzzy constraints as measures to quantitatively rank alternative solutions of a decision problem from the point of view of their desirability. Zadeh later extended this view in the formulation of possibility theory (Zadeh, 1978), which is based on a set of *translation rules* that permit the derivation of global measures of adequacy by logical aggregation of goal-specific preferences. Giles (1988) examined utility-based interpretations of fuzzy sets in the context of a decision-oriented framework where grades of membership where defined as the payoff, to a rational agent. associated with the truth

---

[5]Tversky actually introduced this example to cast doubt on the requirement that similarities be transitive. In our view, we will simply say that we are actually dealing with several similarity functions. emphasizing, in one case geographical considerations and, in the other, political criteria.

of a proposition.

From an epistemological viewpoint, preference relations are the most important source, in our view, of the problem-specific criteria that permit to employ analogical methods based on possibility distributions while showing them to be sound procedures rather than useful, but logically suspect, schemes. When confronting the need to determine if a statement known to be applicable in one situation (or possible world) is also an appropriate assertion (perhaps in a modified fashion) about the state of affairs in another situation, we must determine what are the consequences of making such an assertion, that is the potential utility (or cost) of assuming that such is the case.

In our interpretation of the notion of similarity relation stems directly from consideration of one of the major components of decision analysis: the utility associated with the outcome of taking an action under certain circumstances. In our discussion in Section 4 of the application of these ideas to various problems in autonomous control we introduce the term *desirability* to denote structures that gauge the relative utility, from some viewpoint, of following a number of alternative courses of action. From such a perspective two alternative actions, or decisions, are similar if the consequences of applying either action have similar utility values from every applicable perspective. When the utility values associated with two possible courses of action (e.g., as when choosing how to control the motion of an autonomous robot) are equal or nearly the same, then there is little reason to prefer one over the other and the actions should be considered similar. If on the other hand, the payoffs associated are very different, then the outcomes (and the associated actions) are different and little may be inferred from what is true in one case to what is true in the other.

In the following sections we sketch the basic formal elements of an approach to the definition, representation, and manipulation of utilitarian notions. This formalism is both intended to provide a formal utilitarian basis for analogical reasoning while establishing the required notions to permit a calculus of utilities and preferences that might serve as the formal counterpart of existing notions in probability theory.

Preference Relations   Our discussion will start with the introduction of a very simple notion of preference relation that follows the original ideas of Zadeh (1971a) to generalize the conventional notion of order relation to fuzzy set theory, Fodor and Roubens (1994) provide a more extensive discussion of fuzzy relations,—obeying additional properties—that model various notions of preference .

In the context of this paper, a fuzzy, or valued, preference relation is a

$\circledast$-transitive preorder in $\mathcal{U}$, i.e., a function $\pi \colon \mathcal{U} \times \mathcal{U} \mapsto [0,1]$ such that

$$
\begin{aligned}
\pi(w,w) &= 1\,, & &\text{for all } w \text{ in } \mathcal{U}\,, \\
\pi(w,w') &\geq \pi(w,w'') \circledast \pi(w'',w')\,, & &\text{for all } w,w',w'' \text{ in } \mathcal{U}\,.
\end{aligned}
$$

The value $\pi(w,w')$ is a measure of the degree to which w is preferable to w' or, informally, the degree of truth of the statement: "The state of affairs represented by w is, at least, as preferable (or desirable) as that represented by w'."

We turn our attention next to the relations between preference and similarity relations.

Similarity and Preference   The following results relate the important notions of preference and similarity and provide the semantic basis to regard similarities as measures of proximity along criteria deemed to have utility by a rational decision-making agent.

If π is a preference relation, then the relation S, defined by the equation

$$
S(w,w') = \min\big(\pi(w,w'),\pi(w',w)\big)\,,
$$

is a $\circledast$-similarity relation. Informally, this equation may be interpreted as stating that two possible worlds are similar from the limited perspective of a single preference relation π if either of them is not significantly better than the other as far as π is concerned.

Now, if U is a fuzzy set in $\mathcal{U}$, then the function π defined by the equation

$$
\pi(w,w') = U(w) \oslash U(w')\,,
$$

is a $\circledast$-transitive preference relation in $\mathcal{U}$ (Valverde, 1985). If the fuzzy set U is thought of as a utility function, i.e., a ranking of possible worlds in terms of their desirability, then $\pi(w,w')$ expresses the degree to which w is preferable to w' from the perspective of π. If $U(w) \geq U(w')$, then w is, at least, equally preferable to w' (i.e., $\pi(w,w') = 1)$). If, on the other hand, $U(w) < U(w')$, then w' is preferable and $\big(U(w) \oslash U(w')\big)$ measures the strength of that preference.

Typically, several preference measures (or notions of problem-specific utility) might need to be considered in the context of a problem. Given a family $\{U_i \colon i \text{ in } I\}$, of fuzzy sets, the preference functions $\{U_i(w) \oslash U_i(w') \colon i \text{ in } I\}$ may be combined in a number of ways to derive an aggregate preference relation. A simple approach to produce such an aggregate, yielding a $\circledast$-transitive preference relation U, is expressed by the formula

$$
\pi(w,w') = \inf_{I} \{\, (U_i(w) \oslash U_i(w')) \,\}\,.
$$

This formula requires that two possible worlds be similar from every applicable viewpoint if they are to be considered similar from a joint perspective. Other possible formulations trade off preference requirements to construct suitable preference-combination formulas.

The following theorem (Valverde, 1985) assures that any $\circledast$-transitive relation may be written as the infimum of a utility-specific preference relations:

Theorem: *(Valverde's Representation Theorem for Preference Relations):* Let π be a $\circledast$-preference relation in $\mathcal{U}$. Then there exists a family $\{U_i : i$ in $I\}$ of fuzzy sets in $\mathcal{U}$ such that

$$\pi(w, w') = \inf_I \{U_i(w) \oslash U_i(w')\}.$$

The previously mentioned relation between preference and similarity relations leads to a counterpart of this theorem for similarity relations

Theorem: *(Valverde's Representation Theorem for Similarity Relations):* Let S be a $\circledast$-similarity relation in $\mathcal{U}$. Then there exists a family $\{U_i : i$ in $I\}$, of fuzzy sets in $\mathcal{U}$ such that

$$\pi(w, w') = \inf_I \{\, |U_i(w) \oslash U_i(w')| \,\},$$

where

$$|U_i(w) \oslash U_i(w')| = \min \big(U_i(w) \oslash U_i(w'),\ U_i(w') \oslash U_i(w) \big).$$

The concepts of preference and similarity relations, as we will discuss below, play a fundamental role in problems in control, planning, and decision making where the basic object is to reason about actions that lead to preferred outcomes and where knowledge of actions that are desirable in certain situations provides insights on possible actions in similar situations. In pattern recognition, pattern matching, and object description problems, preference relations permit to rank alternative interpretations of complex data patterns in terms of their compliance with known prototypes or paradigms.

Marginal and Conditional Preferences We propose now generalizations of the notion of preference relation, as a fuzzy relation between pairs of possible worlds, to preference relations defined between pairs of propositions in $\mathcal{L}$, or, by equivalence, between pairs of subsets of $\mathcal{U}$. Our motivation in this regard is similar to that guiding our exploration of similarity relations, that is, to provide a semantic basis for fuzzy logic (in this case as a calculus of preferences).

As was also the case with similarity relations, we recur to notion of Hausdorff distance to yield the required generalization.

Definition (Extended Preference Relation): Let π be a $\circledast$-preference relation in $\mathcal{U}$. The function

$$\widehat{\pi}\colon \mathcal{L}\times\mathcal{L}\colon (p,q)\mapsto \inf_{w\models p}\ \sup_{w'\models q}\ \pi(w,w')\,.$$

is is called the *extended preference relation* of π, or, simply, the extension of π.

The value $\widehat{\pi}(p,q)$ measures the degree to which p is preferable to q in the sense that every p-world is, at least, preferable to every q-world to the degree $\widehat{\pi}(p,q)$ (as, for every p-world w, the value $\sup_{w'\models q}\ \pi(w,w')$ measures the degree to which some q-world w' is as preferable as w.

The following result is a straightforward consequence of the definition of extended preference relation:

Theorem (Transitivity of $\widehat{\pi}$): Let π be a $\circledast$-preference relation in $\mathcal{U}$. Then its extension $\widehat{\pi}$ is also $\circledast$-preference relation in $\mathcal{L}$, i.e.,

$$\widehat{\pi}(p,p) \;=\; 1\,, \qquad\qquad \text{for all } p \text{ in } \mathcal{L}\,,$$
$$\widehat{\pi}(p,q) \;\geq\; \widehat{\pi}(p,r)\circledast\widehat{\pi}(r,q)\,, \quad \text{for all } p,q,r \text{ in } \mathcal{L}\,.$$

As was the case with similarity relations, the importance of this result lies on its role as the basis for a logical calculus of preferences having desirable properties that extend the inferential mechanisms of classical logic. We sketch, in the remainder of this Section, some significant concepts and results.

We first introduce the notion of marginal preference intended to provide the formal basis to define extended preference relations over a coarsening of the universe $\mathcal{U}$. The coarsening is modeled via a partition of the language $\mathcal{L}$:

Definition (Marginal Preference): If $\mathbf{P} = \{p_i \text{ in } \mathcal{L}, i \text{ in } I\}$ is a partition of $\mathcal{L}$, then the *marginal preference* of π with respect to $\mathbf{P}$ is the function

$$\widehat{\pi}^{\mathbf{P}}\colon\ \mathbf{P}\times\mathbf{P}\colon (p_i,p_j)\mapsto \widehat{\pi}(p_i,p_j)\,.$$

In practice, the partition $\mathbf{P}$ is usually a disjoint partition, i.e., if p and q are two elements of the partition that are not logically equivalent, then their extensions do not intersect, i.e., $[p]\cap[q]=\emptyset$.

The notion of conditional preference is amenable to various types of interpretations. The most natural is based on the interpretation of a condition as evidence that the true state of affairs is a possible world lying in a subset $\mathcal{E}$ (the evidential set) of the universe $\mathcal{U}$. [6] In this interpretation, the evidence $\mathcal{E}$ has effectively eliminated from consideration all possible worlds outside $\mathcal{E}$. effectively making the evidential set the new frame of reference. When estimating the extent to which p-worlds are preferable to q-worlds, it makes sense, in this view, to consider only those worlds that are consistent with the evidence. This view readily leads to the following definition:

Definition (Strict Preference): Let r be a proposition in $\mathcal{L}$ and let π be a ⊛-preference relation in $\mathcal{U}$. The *strict conditional preference* of π with respect to $\mathcal{E}$ is the preference relation in $\mathcal{L}$ defined by

$$\widehat{\pi}(\cdot,\cdot)_{\mathcal{E}}: (p,q) \mapsto \widehat{\pi}(p \wedge \mathcal{E}, q \wedge \mathcal{E}).$$

Another approach to the definition of conditional preference—similar in spirit to that employed in the definition of similarity relations—still considers all possible worlds in $\mathcal{U}$ since even worlds that are not strictly compatible with the evidence may be suitable approximations of the true state of affairs. Under this interpretation, conditional preferences are a measure of the extent to which p-worlds are preferred to $\mathcal{E}$-worlds as compared to the extent that q-worlds are preferred to $\mathcal{E}$-worlds. This viewpoint suggests the following definition:

Definition (Relative Preference): Let $\mathcal{E}$ be a proposition in $\mathcal{L}$ and let π be a ⊛-preference relation in $\mathcal{U}$. The *relative conditional preference* of π with respect to $\mathcal{E}$ is the preference relation in $\mathcal{L}$ defined by

$$\widehat{\pi}(\cdot,\cdot\,|\,\mathcal{E}): (p,q) \mapsto \widehat{\pi}(p,\mathcal{E}) \oslash \widehat{\pi}(q,\mathcal{E}).$$

As was the case with similarity relations, this definition leads to an inferential procedure to estimate values of $\widehat{\pi}(p,q)$ (the conclusion) from values of $\widehat{\pi}(q,\mathcal{E})$ (the premise) and the relative conditional preference $\widehat{\pi}(p,q|\,\mathcal{E})$ (the inferential rule):

Theorem (Generalized Modus Ponens for Preference Relations): Let p,q be propositions in $\mathcal{L}$ and let $\widehat{\pi}$ and $\widehat{\pi}(\cdot,\cdot\,|\,\mathcal{E})$ be the extension and conditional preferences of the ⊛-preference relation π. The following relation then holds:

$$\widehat{\pi}(p,\mathcal{E}) \geq \widehat{\pi}(p,q|\,\mathcal{E}) \circledast \widehat{\pi}(q,\mathcal{E}).$$

---

[6]We recall that, for simplicity, we loosely refer to $\mathcal{E}$ as a subset of possible worlds or, equivalenty, to any proposition in $\mathcal{L}$ having that subset as its extension.

4 Similarity and Preference in Decision and Control

The theoretical developments outlined above have been motivated by the need to treat a number of important problems in System control and in computer science. In this Section we briefly discuss the major considerations leading to the development of formal structures for the principled treatment of problems involving notions of similarity and preference.

Issues to be examined include questions arising from the need to plan and control the behavior of autonomous robots and of teams of autonomous robots. These problems exemplify various decision and control applications where performance objectives and goals change in time as a consequence of changes in the operational environment and where goals have different degrees of importance for each of several interacting decision agents. The formal notions discussed in this paper have also guided the development of methods for the qualitative description of complex objects (Zwir and Ruspini, 1999a,b; Zwir et al., 2002) and for the approximate matching of patterns in large databases (Wolverton et al., 2003).

4.1 Autonomous Robot Control

The ability to express preference by means of a logical framework permits to express not only overall system goals ("Keep CO_2 emissions in the low range") but also conditional statements ("If the speed is medium, open the throttle slowly") describing actions that are important in in certain contexts. Typically, these actions are derived by analysis of context-dependent objectives (Saffiotti et al., 1995).

A number of important decision and control problems—exemplified by the control of autonomous robots—are characterized both by the complexity of the system being controlled and that of its operational environment. In these problems, it is usually necessary to consider a number of context-specific objectives, mainly related to needs to *react* to changing circumstances (e.g., "near an obstacle, avoid obstacle") in the operational environment, in addition to the *purposive* goals underlying the control problem (e.g., "go to point P and enter the office"). In these cases it is necessary to employ effective methods for the dynamic management of multiple objectives. Intelligent behavior-based controllers (Arkin, 1998) based on treatment of multiple notions of preference have been successfully developed and implemented (Konolige et al., 1997) to control commercial autonomous robots on the basis of some of the formal concepts and structures discussed in this paper.

These control mechanisms essentially produce aggregated measures of adequacy by combination of simpler constraints in a way that generalizes the combination mechanisms of multi-attribute utility theory (Keeney and Raiffa, 1976) while permitting to interpret the aggregates employing possibilistic translation rules. These rules map logical expressions describing notions of desirable behavior into numeric formulas measuring the extent to which a control action is preferable to another.

The basic concept employed to construct the behavior-based controllers is the notion of desirability, that is, a function $D(x, u)$, taking values in $[0, 1]$, of the state x of the system and its operational environment and of the potential control actions u that may be taken when in that state. In practice, several such measures, $\{D_i(x, u)\}$ need to be considered at any time during the control process. Each such function is usually associated with a behavior, that is a sequence of actions intended to attain some specific objective. Decomposition of the overall control into a number of interacting behaviors permits the synthesis of complex behavior controllers as an aggregation of simpler, objective-specific, controllers (Mataric, 1997). Application of the ideas discussed in this paper leads to aggregation formulas such as

$$D(x, u) = \bigwedge_I \left(\mathrm{Ctxt}_i(x) \to D_i(x, u) \right),$$

where $\{\mathrm{Ctxt}(i): \ i \in I\}$ is a collection of logical predicates, each measuring the extent to which an elastic contextual condition (e.g., "near obstacle") is being met, and where the logical operators $\wedge$ and $\to$ are modelled by a T-norm and its pseudoinverse, respectively.

The expression above permits to attach context-dependent weights to each of the interacting behaviors. In other words, the possibly conflicting requirements leading to the desirability functions D_i are traded off according to criteria depending on the current operational context. When near an obstacle, for example, the context function $\mathrm{Ctxt}_i(x)$ associated with that condition takes a value close to 1 and the value of the conjunct $(\mathrm{Ctxt}_i(x) \to D_i(x, u))$ is very close to that of $D_i(x, u)$. When away from an obstacle, on the other hand, the value of the context function $\mathrm{Ctxt}_i(x)$ is close to zero while that of $(\mathrm{Ctxt}_i(x) \to D_i(x, u))$ is close to 1. The corresponding conjunct, therefore, does not influence the value of the result, effectively meaning that, whenever the contextual condition is not being met, then the corresponding constraint is ignored.

The aggregation mechanisms suggested by this utility-oriented interpretation of the degree of satisfaction of elastic constraints may be applied in a hierarchical fashion to construct ever more complex utility functions, employing combination techniques that are identical in spirit to those of multi-attribute utility theory. The control of teams of autonomous robots is the source of numerous problems where such aggregation techniques may be employed. The perspicuous nature of the logic-based preference and aggregation functions permits the explicit specification of mechanisms to be applied in a wide variety of situations.

Saffiotti et al. (2000) first applied this approach to the control of teams of autonomous robots introducing schemes that differentiate the objectives and behavior of individual team members from that of the group as a whole. Group behaviors such as "maintain wedge formation" where blended with individual behaviors such as "avoid obstacle" by means of expressions that specified the relative importance of each constraint in various operational contexts. In another application, involving search and pursuit of moving objects by a team of autonomous robots, complex "handoff" behaviors emerged from application of simple rules to the behaviors regulating individual team members.

In another application, Ruspini (1998) considered the control of teams of teams of autonomous flying vehicles. In this case, the control problem was again decomposed in a hierarchy of simpler problems. At the lowermost level of this hierarchy controllers were synthesized by blending of behaviors regulating individual team members. The next level in the hierarchy was intended to regulate the behavior of team members with respect to each other. Controllers at this level performed tasks such as formation maintenance or resulted in actions such transfer of responsibilities (handoff) between team members. In many cases, these behaviors were formulated in terms of *control points* and *control structures*, that is, regions in space-time employed to define the nature of the result being sought (e.g., the spatial area of operations of the team). These parameters were then controlled by the next regulatory level, which was concerned with actions such as the movement of the whole team. This hierarchical arrangement was then repeated to regulate teams of teams so as to produce, for example, team-rendezvous actions.

5   Conclusion

Cognitive processes based on notions of similarity and preference are extremely important in human reasoning. The formal approaches to the characterization of analogical and utilitarian concepts discussed in this paper provide a foundation for the development of a theory of similarity and preference that may be regarded as a counterpart of probability theory. Furthermore, the relations between similarity and preference concepts described in this paper lay the basis for the consideration of complex control and decision problems such as the control of autonomous robots and of teams of autonomous robots. Finally, the results discussed in this paper facilitate the interpretation of fuzzy and possibilistic logic concepts and the understanding of their role as tools for the solution of complex system-analysis problems.

Bibliography

Ronald C. Arkin. *Behavior-based robotics*. MIT Press, 1998.

Richard E. Bellman and Lotfi A. Zadeh. Decision-making in a fuzzy environment. *Management Science*, 17:141–164, 1970.

James C. Bezdek. Fuzzy clustering. In E. H. Ruspini, P. P. Bonissone, and W. Pedrycz, editors, *Handbook of Fuzzy Computation*, chapter F6.2. Institute of Physics Press, 1998.

Jaime G. Carbonell. Learning by analogy: formulating and generalizing plans from past. In Ryszard S. Michalski, Jaime G. Carbonell, and Tom M. Mitchell, editors, *Machine learning: an AI approach*. Tioga Press, Palo Alto, California, 1982.

Jean Dieudonné. *Foundations of Modern Analysis*. Academic Press, New York, 1960.

Didier Dubois and Henri Prade. An introduction to possibilistic and fuzzy logics. In Didier Dubois, Henri Prade, and P. Smets, editors, *Non-Standard Logics for Automated Reasoning*. Academic Press, 1988.

Didier Dubois, Jerome Lang, and Henri Prade. Possibilistic logic. In Dov M. Gabbay, Christopher J. Hogger, and John A. Robinson, editors, *Handbook of Logic in AI and Logic Programming*, volume 3. Oxford University Press, 1994.

Didier Dubois, Francesc Esteva, Pere García, Lluís Godó, and Henri Prade. A logical approach to interpolation based on similarity relations. *International Journal of Approximate Reasoning*, 17:1–36, 1997.

Francesc Esteva, Pere García, and Lluis Godó. Relating and extending approaches to possibilistic reasoning. *International Journal of Approximate Reasoning*, 10:311–344, 1994a.

Francesc Esteva, Pere García, Lluís Godó, Llorenç Valverde, and Enrique H. Ruspini. On similarity logic and the generalized modus ponens. In *Proceedings of the 1994 IEEE International Conference on Fuzzy Systems*, pages 1423–1427, Orlando, Florida, 1994b. IEEEE Press.

Francesc Esteva, Pere García, Lluís Godó, and Ricardo Rodríguez. A modal account of similarity-based reasoning. *International Journal of Approximate Reasoning*, 16:235–260, 1997.

János Fodor and Marc Roubens. *Fuzzy Preference Modelling and Multicriteria Decision Support*. Kluwer Academic Publishers, 1994.

Robin Giles. The concept of grade of membership. *Fuzzy Sets and Systems*, 25(3):297–323, 1988.

Robert C. Glen and Samuel E. Adams. Similarity metrics and descriptor spaces. *QSAR Comb. Sci.*, 25(12):1133–1142, 2006.

Lluís Godó, Francesc Esteva, Pere García, and J. Aguist-Cullel. A formal semantic approach to fuzzy logic. In *Proceedings of the 21st International Symposium on Multiple-Valued Logic*, pages 72–79. IEEE Computer Society Press, 1991.

George E. Hughes and Maxwell J. Cresswell. *A New Introduction to Modal Logic*. Routledge, 1996.

Ralph W. Keeney and Howard Raiffa. *Decisions with multiple objectives: preferences and value tradeoffs*. Wiley, 1976.

Erich Peter Klement. *Triangular Norms*. Kluwer, Dordrecht, 2000.

Janet Kolodner. *Case-Based Reasoning*. Morgan-Kauffman Publishers, San Mateo, California, 1993.

Kurt Konolige, Karen L. Myers, Enrique H. Ruspini, and Alessandro Saffiotti. The Saphira architecture: A design for autonomy. *Journal of experimental & theoretical artificial intelligence: JETAI*, 9(1):215–235, 1997.

David K. Lewis. *Counterfactuals*. Harvard University Press, Cambridge, Massachusetts, 1973.

Dennis V. Lindley. Scoring rules and the inevitability of probability. *Int. Stat. Rev.*, 50:1–26, 1982.

Maja J. Mataric. Behavior-based control: Examples from navigation, learning, and group behavior. *Journal of Experimental and Theoretical Artificial Intelligence*, 9(2–3), 1997.

David W. Mount. *Bioinformatics: Sequence and Genome Analysis*. Cold Spring Harbor Laboratory Press, Cold Sping Harbor, NY, 2nd ed. edition, 2004.

Ilkka Niiniluoto. *Truthlikeness*. Reidel, Dordrecht, 1987.

Nina Nikolova and Joanna Jaworska. Approaches to measure chemical similarity—a review. *QSAR Comb. Sci.*, 22(9–10):1006–1026, 2003.

Graham Oddie. *Likeness to Truth*. Western Ontario Series on Philosophy of Science. Reidel, Dordrecht, 1987.

Sergei V. Ovchinnikov. Similarity relations, fuzzy partitions, and fuzzy orderings. *Fuzzy Sets and Systems*, 40:107–126, 1991.

Zdzisław Pawlak. Rough sets—basic concepts. ICS Research Report 13/92, Institute of Computer Science, Warsaw, 1992.

Ricardo Rodríguez, Pere García, and Lluís Godó. Using fuzzy similarity relations to revise and update a knowledge base. *Mathware & Soft Computing*, III:357–370, 1996.

Enrique H. Ruspini. A new approach to clustering. *Information and Control*, 15(1):22–32, 1969.

Enrique H. Ruspini. Applications of intelligent multiobjective decision making. In Okyay Kaynak, Lotfi A. Zadeh, Burhan Turksen, and Imre J. Rudas, editors, *Computational Intelligence: Soft Computing and Fuzzy Neurointegration with Applications*, NATO ASI Series. Series F, Computer and System Sciences. Springer-Verlag, 1998.

Enrique H. Ruspini. On the semantics of fuzzy logic. *Int. J. of Approximate Reasoning*, 5:45–88, 1991.

Enrique H. Ruspini and Francesc Esteva. Interpretations of fuzzy sets. In Enrique H. Ruspini, Piero P. Bonissone, and Witold Pedrycz, editors, *The Handbook of Fuzzy Computation*. Institute of Physics, 1998.

Alessandro Saffiotti, Kurt Konolige, and Enrique H. Ruspini. A multivalued-logic approach to integrating planning and control. *Artificial Intelligence*, 76(1-2):481–526, 1995.

Alessandro Saffiotti, Nina B. Zumel, and Enrique H. Ruspini. Multirobot team coordination using desirabilities. In *Proceedings of IAS-6: Sixth Intl. Conf. on Intelligent Autonomous Systems*, Venice, Italy, 2000.

Berthold Schweizer and Abe Sklar. Associative functions and abstract semigroups. *Publ. Math. Debrecen*, 10:69–81, 1983.

Eldar Shafir, editor. *Preference, Belief, Similarity: Selected Writings of Amos Tversky*. The MIT Press, 2003.

Eleni Stroulia and Yiqiao Wang. Structural and semantic matching for assessing web-service similarity. *International Journal of Cooperative Information Systems*, 14(4):407–437, 2005.

Joseph F. Traub, Grzegoz W. Wasilkowski, and Henryk Woźniakowski. *Information-based Complexity*. Academic Press, 1998.

Enric Trillas and Llorenç Valverde. On mode and implication in approximate reasoning. In Madam M. Gupta, Abe Kandel, Willis Bandler, and Jerzy B. Kiszka, editors, *Approximate Reasoning in Expert Systems*, pages 157–166. North Holland, Amsterdam, 1985.

Amos Tversky. Features of similarity. *Psychological Review*, 84:327–352, 1977.

Llorenç Valverde. On the structure of f-indistinguishability operators. *Fuzzy Sets and Systems*, 17:313–328, 1985.

Michael Wolverton, Pauline Berry, Ian Harrison, John Lowrance, David Morley, Andrés Rodriguez, Enrique Ruspini, and Jerome Thomere. LAW: A workbench for approximate pattern matching in relational data. In *Proceedings of the Fifteenth Innovative Applications of Artificial Intelligence Conference (IAAI-03)*, 2003.

Lotfi A. Zadeh. Similarity relations and fuzzy orderings. *Information Sciences*, 3:177–200, 1971a.

Lotfi A. Zadeh. Similarity relations and fuzzy orderings. *Information Sciences*, 3:177–200, 1971b.

Lotfi. A. Zadeh. A theory of approximate reasoning. In J. Hayes, D. Mitchie, and L. Mikulich, editors, *Machine Intelligence*, pages 149–194. Wiley, 1979.

Lotfi A. Zadeh. Fuzzy sets as the basis for a theory of possibility. *Fuzzy Sets and Systems*, 1:3–28, 1978.

Igor S. Zwir and Enrique H. Ruspini. Automated qualitative description of measurements. In *Proc. 16th IEEE Instrumentation and Measurement Technology Conf.*, 1999a.

Igor S. Zwir and Enrique H. Ruspini. Qualitative object description: Initial reports of the exploration of the frontier. In *Proc. Joint EUROFUSE-SIC'99 Intl. Conf.*, 1999b.

Igor S. Zwir, Rocío Romero Zaliz, and Enrique H. Ruspini. Automated biological sequence description by genetic multiobjective generalized clustering. *Annals of the New York Academy of Sciences*, 980, December 2002.

An overview of bipolar qualitative decision rules

Jean-François Bonnefon[†] Didier Dubois[‡] and Hélène Fargier[‡]

[†] CLLE, CNRS and Université de Toulouse, France
[‡] IRIT, CNRS and Université de Toulouse, France

Abstract Making a good decision is often a matter of listing and comparing positive and negative arguments, as studies in cognitive psychology have shown. In such cases, the evaluation scale should be considered bipolar, that is, negative and positive values are explicitly distinguished. Generally, positive and negative features are evaluated separately, as done in Cumulative Prospect Theory. However, contrary to the latter framework that presupposes genuine numerical assessments, decisions are often made on the basis of an ordinal ranking of the pros and the cons, and focusing on the most salient features, i.e., the decision process is qualitative. In this paper, we report on a project aiming at characterizing several decision rules, based on possibilistic order of magnitude reasoning, and tailored for the joint handling of positive and negative affects, and at testing their empirical validity. The simplest rules can be viewed as extensions of the maximin and maximax criteria to the bipolar case and, like them, suffer from a lack of discrimination power. More decisive rules that refine them are also proposed. They account for both the principle of Pareto-efficiency and the notion of order of magnitude reasoning. The most decisive one uses a lexicographic ranking of the pros and cons. It comes down to a special case of Cumulative Prospect Theory, and subsumes the "Take the best" heuristic.

1 Introduction

It is known from many experiments in cognitive psychology that humans often evaluate alternatives or objects for the purpose of decision-making by considering positive and negative aspects separately. Psychologists have shown (Osgood et al., 1957; Cacioppo and Berntson, 1994; Slovic et al., 2002) that the simultaneous presence of positive and negative arguments prevents decisions from being simple to make, except when all the arguments have different order of magnitude. Under this bipolar view, comparing two decisions comes down to comparing pairs of sets of arguments or features, namely, the set of pros and cons pertaining to one decision versus the set of pros and cons pertaining to the other. Such kind of information involving negative and positive features is called *bipolar*. Dubois and Prade (2006) provide a general discussion on the bipolar representation of information. Classical utility theory does not exploit bipolarity. Utility functions are defined up to an increasing affine transformation (they rely on an interval scale), and the separation between positive and negative evaluations has no special meaning.

Cumulative Prospect Theory (CPT, for short) proposed by Tversky and Kahneman (1992) is an attempt to explicitly account for positive and negative evaluations in the numerical setting. It computes the so-called net predisposition for a decision, viewed as the difference between two numbers, the first one measuring the importance of the group of positive features, the second one the importance of the group of negative features. Such group importance evaluations are modelled by non-additive set functions called capacities. More general numerical models, namely bi-capacities(Grabisch and Labreuche, 2002) and bipolar capacities (Greco et al., 2002) encompass situations where positive and negative criteria are not independent from each other.

However, Gigerenzer et al. (1999) have argued that human decisions are often made on the basis of an ordinal ranking of the strength of criteria rather than on numerical evaluations, hence the qualitative nature of the decision process. People choose according to the most salient arguments in favor of a decision or against the others. They seldom resort to explicit numerical computations of figures of merit. This idea is also exploited in Artificial Intelligence in qualitative decision theory (Doyle and Thomason, 1999). Qualitative criteria like Wald's rule (Wald, 1950) and variants or extensions thereof have been axiomatized along the line of decision theory; see (Dubois and Fargier, 2003) for a survey. So-called conditional preference networks (CP-nets) have been introduced by Boutilier et al. (2004) for an easier representation of preference relations on multidimensional sets of alternatives, using local preference statements interpreted ceteris paribus.

The above qualitative models use preference relations that express statements like "decision a is better than decision b for an agent." However, people also have some idea of what is good and what is bad for them, a notion that simple preference relations cannot express. Using these poorly expressive models, the best available choice may fail to be really suitable for the decision-maker. In other circumstances, even the worst ranked option remains somewhat acceptable. To discriminate between these two situations, one absolute landmark or reference point expressing neutrality or indifference, and explicitly separating the positive and the negative judgments, must appear in the model.

Other qualitative formalisms exist in which such a neutral reference point exists, e.g., fuzzy constraint satisfaction problems (Dubois et al., 1996) and possibilistic logic (Benferhat et al., 2001). They indeed presuppose that the different criteria evaluate decisions in terms of merits by means of some kind of utility functions mapping on any ordinal *negative* scale whose bottom value expresses an unacceptable degree of violation of some constraint, and the top expresses indifference. Decisions are then ranked according to the merit of their worst evaluation, following a pessimistic attitude. But this kind of approach is devoted to the handling of negative arguments. When no constraint is violated, it is not possible to express a positive evaluation that would be better than neutral.

The case of ordinal ranking procedures using bipolar (both positive and negative) information has recently retained the attention of a few scholars. The kind of bipolarity accounted for in (Benferhat et al., 2006) differentiates between prioritized constraints on the one hand and goals or desires on the other hand. Constraints expressed as logical formulas have a prominent role and first select the most tolerated decisions; positive preferences (goals and desire) then act to discriminate among this set of tolerated decisions. Hence a positive evaluation, even if high, can never outperform a negative evaluation even if very weak. In this approach, negative features prevail over positive ones. The latter matter only when no constraint is violated. In the approach proposed here, positive and negative arguments play symmetric roles.

In this chapter, we consider a bipolar and qualitative setting (Dubois and Fargier, 2005), and survey a family of decision rules based on the comparison of positive and negative arguments, and the properties they satisfy. The basic ordinal and bipolar decision rules have been recently axiomatized (Dubois and Fargier, 2006; Bonnefon et al., 2008a). We also briefly report on their empirical validity (Bonnefon and Fargier, 2006; Bonnefon et al., 2008b). Unsurprizingly, these rules are strongly related to possibility theory (Lewis, 1973; Dubois, 1986; Dubois and Prade, 1988), and rely on a bipolar extension of possibility measures tailored to the comparison of sets with elements having positive or negative polarity.

The paper is structured as follows. Section 2 presents a simple framework for qualitative bipolar decision rules and properties that capture the principles of *qualitative* bipolar decision-making. Specific qualitiative bipolar decision rules are then reviewed that range from the most basic (but less decisive) ones in Section 3 to the most decisive ones in Section 4. Section 5 discusses related works and Section 6 comments on the empirical validation study.

2   Qualitative bipolar choice and ranking: basic framework and properties

In this section we first give a simplified framework for bipolar decision rules together with an example. Then we provide a general setting for bipolar preference relations for comparing sets of arguments. Finally we recall assumptions that are characteristic of a qualitative approach to bipolar decision-making (Dubois and Fargier, 2006).

2.1   A simple framework for qualitative bipolar evaluation

A formal elementary framework for bipolar multicriteria decision analysis requires

- a finite set D of potential decisions $a, b, c, \ldots$;
- a set X of criteria, viewed as mappings x with domain D ranging on a bipolar scale V;
- and a totally ordered scale L expressing the relative importance of criteria or groups of criteria.

For simplicity, we use the simplest example of a bipolar scale $V = \{-, 0, +\}$, whose elements reflect negativity, neutrality and positivity respectively: each argument x is either a complete pro or a complete opponent (or is totally indifferent) w.r.t. each decision $a \in D$, in the spirit of cooperative bigames (Bilbao et al., 2000). This is clearly a simpler approach than usual MCDM frameworks where each $x \in X$ is a full-fledged criterion rated on a bipolar utility scale like $V = [-1, +1]$ containing a neutral value 0 (Labreuche and Grabisch, 2006). Amgoud et al. (2005) also compare decisions in terms of positive or negative arguments. They use a complex scheme for evaluating the strength or arguments, whereby an argument possesses both a level of importance and a degree of certainty, and the approach involves criteria whose satisfaction is a matter of degree. We only assume gradual importance of arguments here.

Due to their all-or-nothing nature, criteria can be viewed as simple arguments in favor or against a decision. Let $A = \{x, x(a) \neq 0\}$ be the set of relevant (non-indifferent) arguments for decision a, $A^- = \{x, x(a) = -\}$ be the set of arguments against decision a and $A^+ = \{x, x(a) = +\}$ in favor of a. It comes down to enumerating the pros and the cons of a. So, comparing decisions a and b comes down to comparing the pairs of disjoint sets (A^-, A^+) and (B^-, B^+).

For the sake of simplicity, we suppose in the following that X is made of two subsets: X^+ is the set of positive arguments (taking their value in the set $\{0,+\}$) , X^- is the set of negative arguments (taking their value in the set $\{-,0\}$). The difference between this simplified model with respect to the previous one is that, in the latter, when comparing decisions a and b, one may have $A^- \cap B^+ \neq \emptyset$ and $A^+ \cap B^- \neq \emptyset$, while these sets are disjoint in the simplified model. This is done without loss of generality and will not affect the validity of our results in the ordinal setting. Indeed, any x that may give a valuation in the full domain $\{-,0,+\}$ can be duplicated, leading to an attribute x_+ in X^+ and an attribute x_- in X^-. This transformation moreover enlarges the framework so as to allow an attribute to be positive and negative simultaneously (e.g., "eating chocolate" can have both a positive and a negative aspect).

Even if in our setting, arguments or criteria are Boolean, they can be more or less important. Levels of importance of individual criteria are expressed by a function $\pi : X \mapsto L$. The scale L is unipolar positive. It has top 1_L (full importance) and bottom 0_L (no importance). Within a qualitative approach, L is typically finite. $\pi(x) = 0_L$ means that the decision maker is indifferent to argument x ; 1_L is the highest level of attraction or repulsion (according to whether it applies to a positive or negative argument). Assignment π is supposed to be non trivial, i.e., at least one x has a positive level of importance. One hypothesis made here is that the importance of a group of criteria only depends on the importance of the individual ones. It drastically reduces the type of interaction allowed between criteria, but it facilitates computations when evaluating decisions.

In a nutshell, each criterion (viewed as an argument) $x \in X$ is Boolean (presence vs. absence) but has

- a *polarity*: the presence of x is either good or bad (its absence is always neutral).
- an *importance* $\pi(x) \in L$.

Since we are looking for *qualitative* decision rules, the approach relies on two modelling assumptions:

- *The use of finite qualitative importance scales*: the qualitativeness of L means that there is a big step between one level of merit and the next lower one. Arguments are ranked in terms of the *order of magnitude* of their figures of importance by means of the mapping π.
- *Focalization* : the order of magnitude of the importance of a group A of arguments with a prescribed polarity is the one of the most important argument, in the group. This assumption perfectly suits the intuition of a qualitative scale as it means that several weaker arguments are always negligible compared with a single stronger one.

Example 2.1. Luc has to choose a holiday destination and considers two options for which he has listed the pros and cons. Option 1 is in a very attractive region (a strong pro); but it is very expensive, and the plane company has a terrible reputation (two strong cons). Option 2 is in a non-democratic country, and Luc considers it a strong con. On the other hand, Option 2 includes a tennis court, a disco, and a swimming pool. These are three pros, but not very decisive: they do matter, but not as much as the other arguments.

Note that Luc can only provide a rough evaluation of how strong a pro or a con is. He can only say that the attractiveness of the region, the price, the reputation of the company, and the fact of being in a non-democratic country are four arguments of comparable importance; and that swimming pool, tennis and disco are three positive arguments of comparable, but lesser importance. Formally, let:

$$X^+ = \{tennis^+, swimming^+, disco^+\} \text{ be the subset of pros ;}$$
$$X^- = \{price^{--}, company^{--}, non-demo^{--}\} \text{ be the subset of cons.}$$

By convention in the above lists, doubling the sign symbol appearing in superscript indicates higher importance.
Available decisions are described by :

$$\text{Option 1 : } A^+ = \{region^{++}\}; A^- = \{company^{--}, price^{--}\}.$$
$$\text{Option 2 : } B^+ = \{tennis^+, swimming^+, disco^+\}; B^- = \{non-demo^{--}\}.$$

2.2 Monotonic bipolar set relations

In our setting, each decision rule defines a preference relation comparing the subsets A and B of relevant arguments for each pair of decisions $a, b \in D$, respectively. Let $\succeq$ be a preference relation on 2^X, $A \succeq B$ meaning that decision (with relevant arguments forming set) A is at least as good as decision (with relevant arguments forming set) B. Relations used here are not necessarily complete nor transitive:

Definition 2.2. Any relation $\succeq$ includes:
- a symmetric part : $A \sim B \Leftrightarrow A \succeq B$ and $B \succeq A$;
- an asymmetric part: $A \succ B \Leftrightarrow A \succeq B$ and $not(B \succeq A)$;
- an incomparability relation : $A \bowtie B \Leftrightarrow not(A \succeq B)$ and $not(B \succeq A)$.

$\succeq$ is said to be *quasi-transitive* when $\succ$ is transitive. The transitivity of $\succeq$ obviously implies its quasi-transitivity, be it complete or not. The converse implication generally does not hold. When the relation is complete,

$\approx$ is empty. $\succeq$ is said to be a *weak order* iff it is complete (and thus reflexive) and transitive. Any (weak) preference relation, is supposed to be at least reflexive and quasi transitive, which are *sine qua non* conditions for rationality.

In the following, we also use the notion of refinement of a relation :

Definition 2.3. $\succeq'$ refines $\succeq$ iff $\forall A, B : A \succ B \Rightarrow A \succ' B$

The refined relation $\succeq'$ thus follows the strict preference of $\succeq$ when any, but can make a difference between decisions when $\succeq$ cannot : it may happen that $A \succ' B$ when $A \sim B$ or $A \approx B$.

The basic notion of bipolar reasoning over sets of arguments is the separation of X in good and bad arguments. The neutral landmark is naturally represented by the empty set. A positive argument $x \in X^+$ is then such that $\{x\} \succ \emptyset$, a negative argument $x \in X^-$ such that $\emptyset \succ \{x\}$. The relation $\succeq$ must thus satisfy the postulate of :

Clarity of Arguments (CA) : $\forall x \in X, \{x\} \succeq \emptyset$ or $\emptyset \succeq \{x\}$,

stating that any argument is either positive or negative in the wide sense, i.e., better than nothing or worse than nothing. One can then partition X in positive, negative and null arguments. In particular, $X^0 = \{x, \emptyset \sim \{x\}\}$ is the set of unimportant arguments, that should obviously not affect the preference. This is the meaning of the next axiom:

Statu Quo Consistency (SQC) :
   If $\{x\} \sim \emptyset$ then $\forall A, B \subseteq X, A \succeq B \;\Leftrightarrow\; A \cup \{x\} \succeq B \;\Leftrightarrow\; A \succeq B \cup \{x\}$

The SQC axiom allows to forget about X_0 without loss of generality. So, we shall suppose that $X_0 = \emptyset$ in the following.

Let us consider the property of monotony of $\succeq$ in the sense of inclusion ($A \subseteq B$ implies $B \succeq A$), which expresses that the larger a group of criteria, the more important it is. This property obviously does not apply to the bipolar framework. Indeed, if B is a set of negative arguments, it generally holds that $A \succ A \cup B$. We rather need axioms of monotony *specific to* positive and negative arguments – basically, the one of bipolar capacities (Greco et al., 2002), expressed in a comparative way.

Positive monotony : $\forall C, C' \subseteq X^+, \forall A, B : A \succeq B \Rightarrow C \cup A \succeq B \setminus C'$
Negative monotony : $\forall C, C' \subseteq X^-, \forall A, B : A \succeq B \Rightarrow C \setminus A \succeq B \cup C'$

Clearly, as a consequence, the restriction of $\succeq$ to sets of positive arguments $A \subseteq X^+$ is monotonic in the sense of inclusion and the restriction of $\succeq$ to sets of negative arguments $A \subseteq X^-$ is likewise antimonotonic.

Now, another assumption is that only the positive side and the negative side of A and B are to be taken into account when comparing them: if A is at least as good as B on both the positive and the negative sides, then A is at least as good as B. This is expressed by the axiom of weak unanimity.

Weak Unanimity : $\forall A, B, A^+ \succeq B^+$ and $A^- \succeq B^- \Rightarrow A \succeq B$

All the relations presented later will satisfy weak unanimity. The axiom of weak unanimity can in some cases be reinforced into a more demanding axiom, strong unanimity. It claims that only indifference on both sides results in indifference.

Strong Unanimity: For any $A, B \subseteq X$:

$$A^+ \succeq B^+ \quad \text{and} \quad A^- \succeq B^- \;\Rightarrow\; A \succeq B;$$
$$A^+ \succeq B^+ \quad \text{and} \quad A^- \succ B^- \;\Rightarrow\; A \succ B;$$
$$A^+ \succ B^+ \quad \text{and} \quad A^- \succeq B^- \;\Rightarrow\; A \succ B.$$

Finally, we add an axiom of non-triviality:

Non-Triviality: $X^+ \succ X^-$.

All in all, we get the following bipolar generalization of comparative capacities:

Definition 2.4. A relation on a power set 2^X is a *monotonic bipolar set relation* iff it is reflexive, quasi-transitive and satisfies the properties CA, SQC, Non-Triviality, Weak Unanimity, Positive and Negative Monotony.

Clearly, monotonic bipolar set relations satisfy a *property of bivariate monotony*: using the above conventions for positive and negative arguments in subsets A and B, if $A^- \subseteq B^-, B^+ \subseteq A^+$, then the corresponding decision a should be obviously preferred to b in the wide sense.

2.3 Extracting the importance or arguments

Definition 2.4 is actually very general and encompasses numerous models, be they qualitative or not (e.g., cumulative prospect theory in its full generality). In the present work, we are interested in relations that are entirely determined by the strength and the polarity of the individual arguments X. This basic information is captured by the restriction of $\succeq$ to $\mathbb{X}$

$= X \cup \{\emptyset\}$ (we add $\emptyset$ so as to keep track of the polarity of the arguments). Let us denote it $\succeq_X$. Formally, it is defined by:

$$x \succeq_X y \iff \{x\} \succeq \{y\}; \quad x \succeq_X \emptyset \iff \{x\} \succeq \emptyset; \quad \emptyset \succeq_X x \iff \emptyset \succeq \{x\}.$$

In the sequel, $\succeq_X$ is called the *ground relation* of $\succeq$.

In agreement with the existence of a totally ordered scale for weighting arguments, the ground relation $\succeq_X$ is supposed to be a weak order. Then a minimal condition of coherence with $\succeq_X$ is that if an argument is replaced by a better one (resp., a worse one), the preference cannot be reversed. This can be viewed as a condition of monotony with respect to $\succeq_X$:

"Ground Monotony": $\forall A, B, x, x'$ such that $A \cap \{x, x'\} = \emptyset$ and $x' \succeq_X x$:

$$
\begin{aligned}
A \cup \{x\} \succ B &\Rightarrow A \cup \{x'\} \succ B; & A \cup \{x\} \sim B &\Rightarrow A \cup \{x'\} \succeq B \\
B \succ A \cup \{x'\} &\Rightarrow B \succ A \cup \{x\}; & B \sim A \cup \{x'\} &\Rightarrow B \succeq A \cup \{x\}
\end{aligned}
$$

This very natural axiom is richer that it seems. For instance, it implies a property of substitutability of equally strong positive (resp., negative) arguments, This kind of property is often called "anonymity" in social choice and decision theory.

A property close to anonymity should also be required when a positive argument blocks a negative argument of the same strength: this blocking effect should not depend on the arguments themselves, but on their position in the scale only. Hence the axioms of positive and negative cancellation:

Positive Cancellation (C⁺): $\forall x, z \in X^+, y \in X^-$, $\{x, y\} \sim \emptyset$ and $\{z, y\} \sim \emptyset \Rightarrow x \sim_X z$.

Negative Cancellation (C⁻) : $\forall x, z \in X^-, y \in X^+$, $\{x, y\} \sim \emptyset$ and $\{z, y\} \sim \emptyset \Rightarrow x \sim_X z$.

It makes sense to summarize the above requirement into a single axiom we call *Simple Grounding* as follows:

Simple Grounding: $\succeq$ is said to be simply grounded if and only if its ground relation is a weak order, $\succeq$ is ground-monotonic, and satisfies positive and negative cancellation.

Given a simply grounded monotonic bipolar relation, it is possible to reconstruct the importance scale L and the importance mapping π. Let us define an importance relation $\geq$ on $\mathbb{X}$, based on $\succeq$, as follows: $\geq = \succeq_{\mathbb{X}}$ on X^+ and on X^-. Moreover, $x > \emptyset, \forall x \in X$. The tricky point is to compare arguments of different polarities as to their importance. Then, for $x \in X^+, y \in X^-$: define $x \geq y \iff not(\emptyset \succ \{x, y\})$. Relation $\geq$ is complete by definition. It is routine to prove its transitivity, by examining the various possible cases. For instance, suppose that $x \geq y$ and $y \geq z$:

- $x \in X^+$, $y \in X^-$ and $z \in X^-$. Then by definition, $x \geq y$ means $\{x, y\} \succeq \emptyset$ and $y \geq z$ means $\{z\} \succeq \{y\}$. By Ground Monotony we can replace y by z without reversing the preference: $\{x, z\} \succeq \emptyset$, i.e., $x \geq z$.
- $y \in X^+$ $x \in X^-$ and $z \in X^-$. Suppose that $\{x, y\} \preceq \emptyset$ ($x \geq y$), $\{z, y\} \succeq \emptyset$ ($y \geq z$) and $\{x\} \succ \{z\}$ ($z > x$ for negative arguments). If $\{z, y\} \succ \emptyset$, then $\mathbb{X} - monotony$ implies $\{x, y\} \succ \emptyset$ (thus a contradiction). If $\emptyset \succ \{x, y\}$ then Ground Monotony implies $\emptyset \succ \{z, y\}$ (second contradiction). Last case, if $\{x, y\} \sim \emptyset$ and $\{z, y\} \sim \emptyset$, then property C^+ implies $\{x\} \sim \{z\}$ (last contradiction). So, $z > x$ does not hold and thus, by completeness of $\geq$, $x \geq z$.
- $y \in X^-$ $x \in X^+$ and $z \in X^+$. The proof of $x \geq z$ is similar to the one in the previous item, using property C^- instead of C^+.

So, $\geq$ is a weak order. It can be encoded by a possibility distribution reflecting the importance of arguments $\pi : \mathbb{X} \mapsto L$, a totally ordered scale. The bottom level 0_L is the level of $\emptyset$.

2.4 Qualitative monotonic bipolar set relations

As we are interested in qualitative preference rules, we now focus on properties that account for the principle of focalization.

The basic principle in qualitative reasoning is *Negligibility*. It presupposes that each level of importance should be interpreted as an order of magnitude much higher than the next lower level. It is expressed by the following property:

$$A \succ B \text{ and } A \succ C \Rightarrow A \succ B \cup C$$

This kind of property, at the basis of possibility theory (Dubois, 1986), was extensively used in Artificial Intelligence by, for instance, Lehmann (1996); Halpern (1997); Dubois and Fargier (2004).

The coarsest variant of qualitative reasoning generally comes along with a notion of indifference preservation, that does away with the idea of counting:

$$A \sim B \text{ and } A \sim C \Rightarrow A \sim B \cup C$$

$$B \succeq C \Rightarrow B \sim B \cup C.$$

These properties are justified when all arguments have positive polarity. Technically, they enforce a possibility measure for measuring the importance of a set of positive arguments (Dubois, 1986):

$$OM(A) = \max_{x \in A} \pi(x).$$

In fact, we only use comparative possibility relations (Lewis, 1973), interpreted in term of order of magnitude of importance, hence the notation OM, here. It means that there is no synergy between criteria, which are in some sense considered as redundant with respect to one another.

But they are not sufficient when negative arguments are involved as well. We need for instance to express that if there is a set of very bad arguments B, so bad that $A \succ B$ and $C \succ B$, then whatever the negative arguments in A and C, B is still worse than $A \cup C$: $\forall A, B, C : A \succ B$ and $C \succ B \Rightarrow A \cup C \succ B$. This property is meaningful for negative sets of arguments and trivial on X^+; hence it can be introduced soundly in the framework. Other cases can be checked, that compare sets with both negative and positive elements. All these properties can be expressed by the following axiom of *global negligibility*:

$GNEG : \forall A, B, C, D : A \succ B$ and $C \succ D \Rightarrow A \cup C \succ B \cup D.$

This property is valid in a unipolar setting – in this case, it is a consequence of simple Negligibility and Positive Monotony. This is no longer true in the bipolar setting.

A property of generalized preservation of weak preference must also be stated:

$GCLO : \forall A, B, C, D : A \succeq B$ and $C \succeq D \Rightarrow A \cup C \succeq B \cup D.$

Hence the following bipolar generalization of possibility relations:

Definition 2.5. A relation on a power set 2^X is a *qualitative monotonic bipolar set relation* iff it is a qualitative monotonic bipolar set relation that satisfies GNEG and GCLO.

3 Examples of qualitative bipolar decision rules

This section examines two basic qualitative decision rules for balancing pros and cons and some of their refinements (Dubois and Fargier, 2006). They decide on the basis of the most salient features of the available options, and thus belong to the family of "focus heuristics" (Bonnefon et al., 2008b). The corresponding ordering is either complete or transitive, and is usually weakly discriminant.

3.1 A Bipolar Qualitative Pareto Dominance Rule

The order of magnitude of a bipolar set A is no longer a unique value in L like in the unipolar case, but a pair $(OM(A^+), OM(A^-))$. It is then tempting to propose the following reflexive and transitive Pareto rule, which does not assume commensurateness between the respective importances of positive and negative arguments:

Definition 3.1. The qualitative bipolar Pareto dominance relation reads:
$A \succeq^P B \iff OM(A^+) \geq OM(B^+)$ and $OM(A^-) \leq OM(B^-)$

$\succeq^P$ collapses to Wald's pessimistic ordering if $X = X^-$, and to its optimistic max-based counterpart if $X = X^+$.

On Luc's example, there is a strong argument for Option 1, but only weak arguments for Option 2 : $OM(A^+) > OM(B^+)$. In parallel, there are strong arguments both against A and against B: $OM(A^-) = OM(B^-)$. Luc will choose Option 1.

Now, consider a weak order $\succeq_{\mathbb{X}}$ on $\mathbb{X}$, encoding the polarity and the relative order of magnitude of the arguments. Applying the principles of qualitative bipolar reasoning described by the previous axioms can lead to several different rules. But $\succeq^P$ is the unique relation induced by $\succeq_{\mathbb{X}}$ by applying the principles of (i) bipolar qualitative decision making and (ii) weak and strong unanimity *only*. Indeed, any other preference relation in the family refines it. This unsurprising result can be formalized as follows (Dubois and Fargier, 2006): Let $\mathcal{F}(\succeq_{\mathbb{X}})$ be the set of monotonic bipolar set relations grounded on $\succeq_{\mathbb{X}}$.

Theorem 3.2. *For any weak order $\succeq_{\mathbb{X}}$ on $\mathbb{X}$, $\succeq^P$ is the least refined* transitive *monotonic bipolar set relation in $\mathcal{F}(\succeq_{\mathbb{X}})$ that satisfies axioms GNEG and GCLO and the principle of strong unanimity.*

Theorem 3.2 shows that the Bipolar Qualitative Pareto Dominance rule is the least committed qualitative bipolar monotonic relation that follows from strong unanimity.

When the preference patterns between positive and negative arguments are conflicting, the rule concludes to an incomparability. This information should not be confused with indifference. In case of incomparability, the decision maker is perplex and no alternative looks better than the other:

any choice goes along with a reason to regret it. In case of indifference, both alternatives are equally satisfactory, and either choice can be made without any regret.

Notice that $\succeq^P$ concludes to incomparability in some cases when a preference would sound more natural. When A has both pros and cons, it is incomparable with the empty set even if the importance of the cons in A is negligible in front of the importance of its pros. Another drawback of this rule can observed when the two decisions have the same evaluation on one of the two dimensions. Namely, if $OM(A^-) = OM(B^-) > OM(A^+) > 0 = OM(B^+)$, then $A >^P B$, and this despite the fact $OM(A^+)$ may be very weak. In other terms, this rule does not completely obey the principle of focalization on the most important arguments, especially when A^- and B^- do not contain the same number of arguments. In Luc 's example, Option 1 is preferred despite its two major drawbacks.

To overcome this kind of problematic behavior, the next section relaxes the unanimity postulate, requiring *weak unanimity* only and assuming completeness.

3.2 The Bipolar Possibility Relation

The problem with the above decision rule is that it does not account for the fact that the two evaluations *share a common importance scale*. The next decision rule for comparing A and B focuses on arguments of maximal strength in $A \cup B$, i.e., those at level $\max_{y \in A \cup B} \pi(y) = OM(A \cup B)$. The principle at work in this rule is simple: any argument against A (resp. against B) is an argument pro B (resp., pro A) and conversely. The most supported decision is preferred.

Definition 3.3 (Bipolar Possibility Relation).
$A \succeq^{B\Pi} B \iff OM(A^+ \cup B^-) \geq OM(B^+ \cup A^-)$.

This rule decides that A is at least as good as B as son as there are maximally important arguments in favor of A or attacking B; $A \succ^{B\Pi} B$ if and only if at the highest level of importance, there is no argument against A and none for B. Obviously, $\succeq^{B\Pi}$ collapses to Wald's pessimistic ordering if $X = X^-$ and to its optimistic counterpart when $X = X^+$.

In Luc's example 2.1, Option 1 = $\{region^{++}, company^{--}, price^{--}\}$ and Option 2 = $\{non - demo^{--}, tennis^+, swimming^+, disco^+\}$ are considered as very bad and thus indifferent since one trusts a bad airplane company and the other takes place in a non-democratic country.

In some sense, this definition is the most straightforward generalization of possibility measures to the bipolar case. The bipolar possibility relation clearly satisfies GNEG and GCLO. It does not define a weak order:

Proposition 3.4. $\succeq^{B\Pi}$ *is complete and quasi-transitive, that is, its strict part* $\succ^{B\Pi}$ *is transitive.*

But the associated indifference relation is generally not transitive : neither $A \sim^{B\Pi} B$ and $B \sim^{B\Pi} C$ imply $A \sim^{B\Pi} C$ nor $A \succ^{B\Pi} B$ and $B \sim^{B\Pi} C$ imply $A \succ^{B\Pi} C$. For simplicity, let us denote $a^+ = OM(A^+), a^- = OM(A^-), b^+ = OM(B^+), b^- = OM(B^-), c^+ = OM(C^+), c^- = OM(C^-)$

- Assume $\max(a^+, b^-) > \max(a^-, b^+)$ and $\max(b^+, c^-) = \max(b^-, c^+)$. Consider the case when $a^+ = c^+ = c^- = 1_L$. We have $1_L > \max(a^-, b^+)$, hence $\max(a^+, c^-) = \max(a^-, c^+) = 1$.
- Assume $\max(a^+, b^-) = \max(a^-, b^+)$ and $\max(b^+, c^-) = \max(b^-, c^+)$. Assume $b^+ = b^- = 1_L$. Then the two equalities hold regardless of the values a^+, a^-, c^+, c^-. So the values $\max(a^+, c^-)$ and $\max(a^-, c^+)$ can be anything.

$\succeq^{B\Pi}$ is thus very different from, and less dubious than $\succeq^P$. But, it is obviously a very rough rule that may be not decisive enough. This weakness of $\succeq^{B\Pi}$ lies in the usual drowning effect of possibility theory: the presence of at least one argument of maximal importance (e.g., the high price) on each side cancels all arguments of less importance. The drowning effect is also at work in $\succeq^P$, clearly. Despite this weakness, this rule has the merit of capturing the essence of qualitative bipolar decision-making, as shown by the following representation result Dubois and Fargier (2006):

Theorem 3.5. *The following propositions are equivalent:*
  - $\succeq$ is a simply grounded complete *monotonic bipolar set relation on* 2^X, *that satisfies GNEG and GCLO.*
  - There exists a mapping $\pi : X \mapsto [0_L, 1_L]$ *such that* $\succeq \equiv \succeq^{B\Pi}$.

We pointed out already that, when $\succeq$ is complete and simply grounded, a ranking $\geq$ can be built that rank-orders the arguments with respect to their strength, and coincides with $\succeq_X$ within X^+ and within X^-. It can thus be encoded by a mapping $\pi : X \mapsto [0_L, 1_L]$ such that $\pi(x) = 0_L \iff x \in X^0$. Notice that this construction is valid for any simple grounded complete bipolar relation, and not only for qualitative ones. The sequel of the proof then uses the axioms of GNEG and GCLO to show that $\succeq \equiv \succeq^{B\Pi}$.

3.3   Leximax refinement of $\succeq^{B\Pi}$

$\succeq^{B\Pi}$ suffers from a drowning effect, as usual in standard possibility theory. For instance, when B is strictly included in A, which contains positive arguments only, then A is not strictly preferred to B, when arguments in

$A \setminus B$ are of equal or lesser importance. A tempting way of refining $\succeq^{B\Pi}$ is to notice that the bipolar possibility relation basically relies on a comparison of indices of the form $\max(a^+, b^-)$ and $\max(b^+, a^-)$. Then using a purely mathematical intuition, a natural way of breaking ties is to compare the pairs (a^+, b^-) and (b^+, a^-) using the leximax ranking rather than the max one.

The leximax ranking procedure suits the comparison of vectors of any length. When restricted to the comparison of pairs of values, it can be written as follows: $(u_1, u_2) \geq_{lmax} (v_1, v_2)$ iff either $\max(u_1, u_2) > \max(v_1, v_2)$ or $\max(u_1, u_2) = \max(v_1, v_2)$ and $\min(u_1, u_2) \geq \min(v_1, v2)$. Hence the definition:

Definition 3.6. $A \succeq_{B\Pi L} B \iff$
either $(A \succ^{B\Pi} B)$ or $(A \sim^{B\Pi} B$ and $\min(a^+, b^-) > \min(b^+, a^-))$.

$\succeq_{B\Pi L}$ is complete and transitive, as is the leximax ranking of vectors of any length. It refines $\succeq^{B\Pi}$, as any leximax ranking refines the max ranking. More surprisingly, it can be shown that it also refines $\succeq^P$. This is worth noticing: as pointed out in Section 3 that $\succeq^P$ sometimes leads to a counterintuitive strict preference. As a refinement of $\succeq^P$, $\succeq^{B\Pi L}$ follows its misleading behavior and suffers of some of its important drawbacks. Its is thus not an attractive refinement of $\succeq^{B\Pi}$.

3.4   The implicative bipolar decision rule

The implicative decision rule proposed by Dubois and Fargier (2005) follows the same focalization principle as $\succeq^{B\Pi}$: when comparing A and B, it focuses on arguments of maximal strength in $A \cup B$. It adds to this principle a separation, reminiscent of $\succeq^P$, between arguments in favor of A and B and against them : A is at least as good as B iff, at the highest importance level, the existence of arguments in favor of B is counterbalanced by the existence of arguments in favor of A and the existence of arguments against A is cancelled by the existence of arguments against B. This heuristic is called *the straw and beam* by Bonnefon et al. (2008b) so as to reflect the argumentative flavor of this decision rule. Formally, the implicative bipolar rule can be described as follows:

Definition 3.7. $A \succeq^{Im} B$ if and only if

$$OM(B^+) = OM(A \cup B) \implies OM(A^+) = OM(A \cup B)$$
$$OM(A^-) = OM(A \cup B) \implies OM(B^-) = OM(A \cup B)$$

It is easy to check that $\succeq^{Im}$ is a bipolar monotonic relation. Like $\succeq^{B\Pi}$, when there are positive arguments only, relation $\succeq^{Im}$ collapses to the maximum rule. It also obeys the principle of weak unanimity. Moreover, $\succeq^{Im}$ is transitive.

On Luc's dilemma, where the bipolar possibility rule concludes to an indifference, the implicative rule will rather select Option 1, because there are important arguments against both decisions while only Option 1 is supported by an important pro (there is no important pro supporting Option 2).

Let us make the cases when $A \succeq^{Im} B$ more explicit. Once again, denote $a^+ = OM(A^+), a^- = OM(A^-), b^+ = OM(b^+), b^- = OM(B^-)$.

Proposition 3.8.

- $A \sim^{Im} B \iff$ *either* $a^+ = b^+ = a^- = b^-$ *or* $a^+ = b^+ > \max(a^-, b^-)$ *or yet* $a^- = b^- > \max(a^+, b^+)$.
- $A \simeq^{Im} B \iff$ *either* $a^+ = a^- > \max(b^-, b^+)$ *or* $b^+ = b^- > \max(a^-, a^+)$.
- $A \succ^{Im} B \iff$ *either* $\max(a^+, b^-) > \max(a^-, b^+)$ *or* $a^+ = a^- = b^- > b^+$ *or yet* $b^+ = b^- = a^+ > a^-$.

Since $\max(a^+, b^-) > \max(a^-, b^+)$, i.e., $A \succ^{B\Pi} B$, is one of the conditions of $A \succ^{Im} B$ in the above proposition, it obviously follows that:

Proposition 3.9. $\succeq^{Im}$ *is a refinement of* $\succeq^{B\Pi}$

Moreover, incomparability $A \simeq^{Im} B$ arises in two cases only, when $a^+ = a^- > \max(b^-, b^+)$ or in the symmetric case $b^+ = b^- > \max(a^-, a^+)$, i.e., when one of the two sets, e.g., A, displays an *internal contradiction* at the highest level, while the arguments in the other set are too weak to matter: in this case, A is as good as bad. In particular, $a^+ = a^- > 0_L$ if and only if $A \simeq^{Im} \emptyset$. For instance, a dangerous travel in an exceptional, and mysterious part of a far tropical forest displays such an internal conflict, and I do not know whether I prefer staying at home or not. Such a conflict appears also in Luc's first option (which is very attractive but high priced). On the other hand, considering a non conflicting (and non-empty) A, either $OM(A^+) > OM(A^-)$ and then $A \succ^{Im} \emptyset$ (well, the travel is reasonably dangerous, so I travel), or $OM(A^-) > OM(A^+)$ and then $\emptyset \succ^{Im} A$ (there is a war near the border and I prefer staying home); in these two latter cases, the $\succeq^P$ rule would have concluded to an incomparability. The range of incompleteness of $\succeq^{Im}$ is thus very different from the one of $\succeq^P$, which does not account for any notion of internal conflict.

Relation is $\succeq^{Im}$ interesting from a theoretic descriptive point of view, both because of its way of handling the conflict, and because it refines $\succeq^{B\Pi}$. But it still may happen that A and B differ only on their negative part (e.g., $A^+ = B^+ > A^- > B^-$) and $A \sim^{Im} B$. A dangerous travel in a quite uninteresting part of the forest is not worse than if it were in an interesting one. One may be tempted to notice that, on this very example, the Pareto rule would have made a difference in favor of the intuitively best decision. Since $\succeq^{Im}$ is compatible with the Pareto rule ($A \succeq^P B \implies A \succeq^{Im} B$), it is possible to mix the two rules, breaking ties in $\sim^{Im}$ (but keeping its interesting range of incompleteness).

On the other hand, even if more decisive than $\succeq^{B\Pi}$ and $\succeq^{Im}$, this refined rule does not satisfy preferential independence: like the previous ones, it collapses with Wald's criterion (resp., the max rule) on the negative (resp., positive) sub-scale X^- (resp., X^+), and can thus suffer of the drowning effect. So, let us now focus on set of refinements that do satisfy Preferential Independence, and are thus Pareto-efficient both positively and negatively.

4 Efficient qualitative bipolar decision rules

Any decision rule in accordance with GNEG has to follow the strict preference prescribed by $\succ^{B\Pi}$. On the other hand, $\succeq^{B\Pi}$ and its refinements so far suffer from a drowning effect, as usual in standard possibility theory. For instance, when B is strictly included in A, which contains positive arguments only, then A is not strictly preferred to B, when arguments in $A \setminus B$ are of equal or lesser importance. This is because GCLO forbids the counting of equally important arguments and concludes to indifference. GNEG does not discriminate in cases when additional arguments in $A \setminus B$ are of strictly lesser importance. In such cases, we would like to apply the so-called principle of efficiency to make the decision.

4.1 The efficiency principle

Like the monotony principle, the efficiency axiom is well known on positive sets. Its proper extension to the bipolar framework, that should be at work here, has one positive and one negative side:

Positive Efficiency : $B \subseteq A$ and $A \setminus B \succ \emptyset \Rightarrow A \succ B$;
Negative Efficiency : $B \subseteq A$ and $A \setminus B \prec \emptyset \Rightarrow A \prec B$.

$\succeq^{B\Pi}$ and $\succeq^P$ also fail the classical condition of preferential independence, also called the principle of additivity. This condition simply says that arguments present in both A and B should not influence the decision:

Preferential Independence: $\forall A, B, C, (A \cup B) \cap C = \emptyset : A \succeq B \iff A \cup C \succeq B \cup C$.

This axiom is well-known in uncertain reasoning, as one of the fundamental axioms of comparative probabilities; see (Fishburn, 1986) for a survey. Notice that it implies the above conditions of efficiency (provided that completeness holds).

Except in very special cases where all arguments are of different levels of importance ($\succeq_X$ is a linear order), these axioms are incompatible with a qualitative approach when completeness or transitivity are enforced. It is already true in the pure positive case, i.e., when X^- is empty (Fargier and Sabbadin, 2005). But this impossibility result is not damning: to overcome the lack of decisiveness of the previous rules, we now propose comparison principles that refine them, that is, relations $\succeq$ compatible with $\succeq^{B\Pi}$ but more decisive, i.e., such that $A \succ^{B\Pi} B \Rightarrow A \succ B$. We shall give up $\succeq^P$ because of its important drawbacks.

The bipolar "Discrimax" rule (Dubois and Fargier, 2005) just adds the principle of preferential independence to the ones proposed by $\succeq^{B\Pi}$, simply cancelling the elements that appear in both sets before applying the rule:

Definition 4.1 (Bipolar Discrimax). $A \succeq^D B \iff A \setminus B \succeq^{B\Pi} B \setminus A$

$\succeq^D$ is complete and quasi-transitive (its symmetric part is not necessarily transitive). Unsurprizingly, if $X = X^+$, it does not collapse with the *max* rule, but with the discrimax procedure (Dubois and Fargier, 2004).

Consider the choice between two expensive holiday resorts, one for which an expensive visa is requested but that is close to the sea (which is rather pleasant), another one inland, where no visa is needed. Then, options are $A = \{price^{---}, visa^{--}, sea^+\}$ and $B = \{price^{---}\}$, and the Discrimax rule chooses B since once putting away the bad price present in each option, A possesses a relatively strong con, the visa, while B has no cons nor pro. On Luc's example, the two options are indifferent, like for $\succeq^{B\Pi}$ (since the two options do not share any argument).

4.2 Lexicographic refinements of $\succeq^{B\Pi}$

$\succeq^D$ simply cancels any argument appearing in both A and B. One could moreover accept the cancellation of any positive (resp., negative) argument in A by another positive (resp., negative) argument in B of the same strength. Among the two basic axioms of qualitative modeling, it comes down to giving up GCLO, while retaining GNEG. Choosing can then be based on counting arguments of the same strength, but we do not allow an important argument to be superseded by several less important ones, however large is their number. This yields the following two rules based on a levelwise comparison by cardinality. The arguments in A and B are scanned top down, until a level is reached such that the numbers of positive and negative arguments pertaining to the two alternatives are different; then, the set with the least number of negative arguments and the greatest number of positive ones is preferred. There are two such decision rules respectively called "Bivariate Levelwise Tallying" and (univariate) "Levelwise Tallying" by Bonnefon et al. (2008b), according to whether positive and negative arguments are treated separately or not (Dubois and Fargier, 2005).

For any importance level $\lambda \in L$, let $A_\lambda = \{x \in A, \pi(x) = \lambda\}$ be the λ-section of A, the set of arguments of strength λ in A. Let $A_\lambda^+ = A_\lambda \cap X^+$ (resp., $A_\lambda^- = A_\lambda \cap X^-$) be its positive (resp., negative) λ-section. Let $\delta(A, B)$ be the maximal level of importance where either the positive or the negative λ-sections of A and B differ, namely:

$$\delta(A, B) = \max\{\lambda : |A_\lambda^+| \neq |B_\lambda^+| \text{ or } |A_\lambda^-| \neq |B_\pm^+|\}.$$

$\delta(A, B)$ is called the *decisive level* pertaining to (A, B).

Definition 4.2 (Bivariate Levelwise Tallying).
$$A \succeq^{BL} B \iff |A_{\delta(A,B)}^+| \geq |B_{\delta(A,B)}^+| \text{ and } |A_{\delta(A,B)}^-| \leq |B_{\delta(A,B)}^-|$$

It is easy to show that $\succeq^{BL}$ is reflexive, transitive, but not complete. Indeed, $\succeq^{BL}$ concludes to an incomparability if and only if there is a conflict between the positive view and the negative view at the decisive level. From a descriptive point of view, this range of incomparability is a good point in favor of $\succeq^{BL}$. On Luc's example for instance, the difficulty of the dilemma is clearly pointed point by this decision rule: at the highest level, Option 1 involves 3 strong arguments ($price^{--}$, $company^{--}$ and $attractive-region^{++}$) while Option 2 only involves one ($non - demo^{--}$). $\delta(A, B)$ is the highest importance level and Option 1 has more strong negative arguments than Option 2, while Option 2 has one strong positive argument while Option 1 has none. An incomparability results, revealing the difficulty of the choice. On the other example, $\succeq^{BL}$ is well behaved: $\{price^{---}\}$ is preferred to $\{price^{---}, visa^{--}, sea^+\}$ (the price argument on both side is put away and at $\delta(A, B)$ level, only $visa^{--}$ remains as quite a strong con).

Now, if one can assume a compensation between positive and negative arguments at the same level, one on each side canceling each other, the following refinement of $\succeq^{BL}$ can be obtained:

Definition 4.3 (Levelwise Tallying).
$$A \succeq^L B \iff \exists \lambda \in L \backslash 0_L \text{ s. t. } \begin{cases} (\forall \gamma > \lambda, & |A_\gamma^+| - |A_\gamma^-| = |B_\gamma^+| - |B_\gamma^-|) \\ \text{and} & |A_\lambda^+| - |A_\lambda^-| > |B_\lambda^+| - |B_\lambda^-| \end{cases}$$

Interestingly, $\succeq^L$ is a special case of the decision rule originally proposed two centuries ago by Benjamin Franklin (1887). On Luc's dilemna, the strong pro of Option 1 is now cancelled by one of its strong cons - they are discarded. A strong con on each side remains. Because of a tie at this level, the procedure then examines the second priority level: there are 3 weak pros for Option 2 (no cons) and no pro nor con w.r.t. Option 1 : Option 2 is elected. On the other example, $\succeq^L$ also breaks the ties in $\succeq^{B\Pi}$ just as $\succeq^{BL}$ and $\succeq^D$ do : Luc will prefer the destination that does not require a visa.

The two rules proposed in this section obviously stem from monotonic bipolar relations. Each of them refines $\succeq^{B\Pi}$ and satisfies Preferential Independence. Some of these relations refine each other and the most decisive is ($\succ^L$). The latter is moreover complete and transitive.

Proposition 4.4. $A \succ^{B\Pi} B \Rightarrow A \succ^D B \Rightarrow A \succ^{BL} B \Rightarrow A \succ^L B$

Notice that the restriction of both $\succeq^{BL}$ and $\succeq^L$ on X^+ amounts to the leximax preference relation (Deschamps and Gevers, 1978). We can the use classical encoding of the leximax (unipolar) procedure by comparing sums of suitably chosen weights (Moulin, 1988). For instance, ranking and denoting $\lambda_1 = 0_L < \lambda_2 < \cdots < \lambda_l = 1_L$ the l elements of L, we can use the capacity

$$\sigma^+(A) = \sum_{\lambda_i \in L} |A^+_{\lambda_i}| \cdot |X|^i.$$

We can similarly use a second big-stepped sum to represent the importance of sets of negative arguments :

$$\sigma^-(A) = \sum_{\lambda_i \in L} |A^-_{\lambda_i}| \cdot |X|^i$$

It is then easy to show that :

Proposition 4.5. *There exist two capacities σ^+ and σ^- such that:*
$A \succeq^L B \Leftrightarrow \sigma^+(A^+) - \sigma^-(A^-) \geq \sigma^+(B^+) - \sigma^-(B^-)$

$A \succeq^{BL} B \Leftrightarrow$ *and* $\begin{cases} \sigma^+(A^+) & \geq & \sigma^-(B^+) \\ \sigma^+(B^-) & \geq & \sigma^-(A^-) \end{cases}$

This proposition clearly shows that the $\succeq^L$ ranking of decisions is a particular case of the CPT decision rule (using big-stepped probabilities). In summary, $\succeq^L$ complies with the spirit of qualitative bipolar reasoning while being efficient. In the meantime, it has the advantages of numerical measures (transitivity and representability by a pair of functions).

Finally, this relation is the only one that both refines $\succeq^{B\Pi}$, is a weak order and satisfies the principle of preferential independence without introducing any bias on the importance order elementary arguments, that is, preserving the ground relation $\succeq_X$. We could recently prove the following result:

Theorem 4.6. *Let $\succeq$ be a monotonic bipolar set relation and π be a possibility distribution over the elements of X. The following propositions are equivalent:*

    1 $\succeq$ is complete, transitive, satisfies preferential independence and is an unbiased refinement of $\succeq^{B\Pi}$

    2 $\succeq \equiv \succeq^L$

This concludes our argumentation in favor of $\succeq^L$: it is the only bipolar decision rule in agreement with qualitative reasoning while being decisive and practically meaningful.

5 Related works

Qualitative choice heuristics were extensively studied and advocated by Gigerenzer and his colleagues. In the "Take the best" approach (Gigerenzer and Goldstein, 1996), each criterion x is supposed to have a positive side (it generates a positive argument x^+) and a negative side (it generates a negative argument x^-): fulfilling the criterion is a pro, missing it is a con, all the worse as the criterion is important. The criteria are then supposed to be of very different importance, so that they can be ranked lexicographically: there does not exist x, y such that $\pi(x) = \pi(y)$. So, we can rank criteria from the stronger to the weaker when comparing alternatives. Scanning the criteria top down, as soon as we find a criterion that is in favor of decision a and in disfavor of decision b, a is preferred to b (hence the name "Take the best"). Applied to such linearly ranked criteria, the Discrimax Bipolar and Levelwise Tallying rules coincide with "Take the best". But these rules are able to account for more decision situations than the latter heuristic — e.g., when several criteria share the same (and highest) degree of importance. In this sense, they are a natural extension of the "Take the best" qualitative rule advocated by psychologists.

Cumulative Prospect Theory of Tversky and Kahneman (1992) is another attempt to account for positive and negative arguments. Contrary to the "Take the best" approach, it uses quantitative evaluations of decisions. CPT assumes that reasons supporting a decision and reasons against it can be measured by means of two capacities σ^+ and σ^-, σ^+ reflecting the importance of the group of positive arguments, σ^- the importance of the group of negative arguments. The higher σ^+, the more convincing the set of positive arguments and conversely the higher σ^-, the more deterring is the set of negative arguments. This approach moreover admits that it is possible to map these evaluations to a so-called "net predisposition" score expressed on a single scale:

$$\forall A \subseteq X, NP(A) = \sigma^+(A^+) - \sigma^-(A^-)$$

where $A^+ = A \cap X^+, A^- = A \cap X^-$. Alternatives are then ranked according to this net predisposition: $A \succeq^{CPT} B \iff \sigma^+(A^+) - \sigma^-(A^-) \geq \sigma^+(B^+) - \sigma^-(B^-)$. Proposition 4.5 (Section 4) actually shows that that $\succeq^L$ is a particular case of this preference relation (using big-stepped capacities).

Interestingly, the bipolar possibility relation can be directly related to net predisposition comparison. More precisely, it can be viewed as its qualitative counterpart ; indeed, let us first notice that $A \succeq^{CPT} B \iff \sigma^+(A^+) + \sigma^-(B^-) \geq \sigma^+(B^+) + \sigma^-(A^-)$. Then the bipolar possibility decision rule comes down to changing + into max in this comparison. In other words, our framework bridges the gap between Take The Best and CPT, the two main antagonistic approaches to bipolar decision-making.

6   A Glimpse at Experimental Results

The *descriptive* power of the above bipolar decision rules , i.e., their ability to represent the behavior of human decision makers was tested, based on a dataset of more than $2,000$ decisions made by about 60 individuals (see Bonnefon and Fargier (2006)). Results confirm $\succ^{B\Pi}$ as a good basis for ordinal bipolar decision making. They point at $\succeq^L$, as the emergent decision rule for decision-makers that satisfies preferential independence. Moreover, $\succeq^{BL}$ seems to be the best model for that subset of decision-makers for whom conflicts leads to incomparability. Details about the experimental setting can be found in the recent paper by Bonnefon et al. (2008b).

As a general index of descriptive validity, we computed the accuracy of each heuristic—that is, the average number of answers it correctly predicts, across participants. Figure 1 displays the accuracy of most heuristics presented here, in percentage form. $I2$ is the discrimax procedure applied to $\succeq^{Im}$, Tal is the reduction of Levelwise Tallying to simple comparison of cardinalities of arguments regardless of their relative importance.

Figure 1 clearly shows the superiority of the family of heuristics based on counting arguments over the pure Focalization and Discrimax rules. Furthermore, it suggests that Levelwise Tallying ($\succeq^{C3}$) has by far the greatest

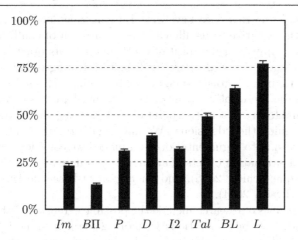

Figure 1. Average percentage of answers correctly predicted by each heuristic.

descriptive validity, with an overall accuracy of 77%. Indeed, Levelwise Tallying always provided the most accurate predictions of *all* participants' choices, at the individual level. The second best heuristic was always Bivariate Levelwise Tallying $\succeq^{C2}$. On average, Levelwise Tallying predicted a reliably larger number of answers than did Bivariate Levelwise Tallying. Similar results were observed when comparing Bivariate Levelwise Tallying to all other procedures.

More interestingly, it is *not* the case that some participants leaned towards one heuristic while some leaned towards another. The responses of *each of the 62 participants* were always closer to the predictions of Levelwise Tallying than to the predictions of the other heuristics. The reader is referred to the paper of Bonnefon et al. (2008b) for more details on the experiment and a detailed analysis of its results.

7 Conclusion

The qualitative bipolar decision rules proposed here are an extension of possibility theory to the handling of sets containing two-sorted elements considered as positive or negative. The Levelwise Tallying rule is the corresponding lexicographic refinement. It generalizes the "Takes the best heuristic" to a proper handling of ties, and is a special case of what could be called bipolar probability, as proposed in Cumulative Prospect Theory.

On the contrary, the Bivariate Levelwise Tallying rule does not merge the positive and the negative, thus allowing the expression of conflicts. These decision rules comply with the spirit of CTP as well at its practical computational advantages. They are Pareto-efficient and in agreement with but more decisive than pure order-of-magnitude reasoning. This study was carried out from the prescriptive point of view, laying bare basic "rationality properties", and from a descriptive point of view, testing whether people use these rules to guide their decisions. We have couched our results in a terminology borrowing to argumentation, and indeed we consider they can be relevant for the evaluation of sets of arguments in inference processes (Cayrol and Lagasquie-Schiex, 2005), and for argument-based decision-making (Amgoud and Prade, 2004).

Some future lines of research include the possible extension of the bipolar possibility and probability relations to more general set-functions, so as to understand whether transitivity can be retained beyond the additive case. Broadening the setting, from Boolean arguments to criteria whose satisfaction is a matter of degree, is also in order.

Bibliography

L. Amgoud and H. Prade. Using arguments for making decisions: A possibilistic logic approach. In M. Chickering and J. Halpern, editors, *Proceedings of the 20th Conference of Uncertainty in Artificial Intelligence (UAI'04)*, pages 10–17, Menlo Park, CA, 2004. AUAI Press.

L. Amgoud, J. F. Bonnefon, and H. Prade. An argumentation-based approach for multiple criteria decision. In L. Godo, editor, *Proceedings of ECSQARU 2005 – LNAI 3571*, pages 269–280, Berlin, 2005. Springer Verlag.

S. Benferhat, D. Dubois, and H. Prade. Towards a possibilistic logic handling of preferences. *Applied Intelligence*, 14(3):303–317, 2001.

S. Benferhat, D. Dubois, S. Kaci, and H. Prade. Bipolar possibility theory in preference modeling: Representation, fusion and optimal solutions. *International Journal on Information Fusion*, 7:135–150, 2006.

J.M. Bilbao, J.R. Fernandez, A. Jiménez Losada, and E. Lebrón. Bicooperative games. In J.M. Bilbao, editor, *Cooperative games on combinatorial structures*, pages 23–26. Kluwer Academic Publishers, Dordrecht, 2000.

J. F. Bonnefon and H. Fargier. Comparing sets of positive and negative arguments: Empirical assessment of seven qualitative rules. In G. Brewka, S. Coradeschi, A. Perini, and P. Traverso, editors, *Proceedings of the 17th European Conference on Artificial Intelligence (ECAI2006)*, pages 16–20, Zurich, 2006. IOS Press.

J.-F Bonnefon, D. Dubois, H. Fargier, and H. Prade. On the qualitative comparison of decisions having positive and negative features. *J. Artificial Intelligence Research, to appear*, 2008a.

J.F. Bonnefon, D. Dubois, H. Fargier, and S. Leblois. Qualitative heuristics for balancing the pros and cons. *Theory and Decision, to appear*, 2008b.

C. Boutilier, R. I. Brafman, C. Domshlak, H. H. Hoos, and D. Poole. CP-nets: A tool for representing and reasoning with conditional ceteris paribus preference statements. *J. Artif. Intell. Res. (JAIR)*, 21:135–191, 2004.

J. T. Cacioppo and G. G. Berntson. Relationship between attitudes and evaluative space: A critical review, with emphasis on the separability of positive and negative substrates. *Psychological Bulletin*, 115:401–423, 1994.

C. Cayrol and M.-C. Lagasquie-Schiex. On the acceptability of arguments in bipolar argumentation frameworks. In *Symbolic and Quantitative Approaches to Reasoning with Uncertainty, Proc. 8th European Conference (ECSQARU 2005)*, volume 3571 of *Lecture Notes in Computer Science*, pages 378–389. Springer, 2005.

R. Deschamps and L. Gevers. Leximin and utilitarian rules : a joint characterization. *Journal of Economic Theory*, 17:143–163, 1978.

J. Doyle and R. Thomason. Background to qualitative decision theory. *The AI Magazine*, 20(2):55–68, 1999.

D. Dubois. Belief structures, possibility theory and decomposable confidence measures on finite sets. *Computers and Artificial Intelligence*, 5(5):403–416, 1986.

D. Dubois and H. Fargier. Qualitative decision rules under uncertainty. In G. Della Riccia, D. Dubois, R. Kruse, and H.-J. Lenz, editors, *Planning Based on Decision Theory*, volume 472 of *CISM*, pages 3–26. Springer Wien, 2003.

D. Dubois and H. Fargier. An axiomatic framework for order of magnitude confidence relations. In M. Chickering and J. Halpern, editors, *Proceedings of the 20th Conference of Uncertainty in Artificial Intelligence (UAI'04)*, pages 138–145, Menlo Park, CA, 2004. AUAI Press.

D. Dubois and H. Fargier. On the qualitative comparison of sets of positive and negative affects. In L. Godo, editor, *Proceedings of ECSQARU 2005 – LNAI 3571*, pages 305–316, Berlin, 2005. Springer Verlag.

D. Dubois and H. Fargier. Qualitative decision making with bipolar information. In P. Doherty, J. Mylopoulos, and C. Welty, editors, *Proceedings of the 10th International Conference on Principles of Knowledge Representation and Reasoning*, pages 175–186, Menlo Park, CA, 2006. AAAI Press.

D. Dubois and H. Prade. Bipolar representations in reasoning, knowledge extraction and decision processes. In *Rough Sets and Current Trends in Computing, 5th International Conference, RSCTC 2006, Kobe, Japan*, volume 4259 of *Lecture Notes in Computer Science*, pages 15–26. Springer, 2006.

D. Dubois and H. Prade. *Possibility Theory: An Approach to Computerized Processing of Uncertainty*. Plenum Press, New York, 1988.

D. Dubois, H. Fargier, and H. Prade. Possibility theory in constraint satisfaction problems: Handling priority, preference and uncertainty. *Applied Intelligence*, 6(4):287–309, 1996.

Hélène Fargier and Régis Sabbadin. Qualitative decision under uncertainty: back to expected utility. *Artificial Intelligence*, 164:245–280, 2005.

P Fishburn. The axioms of subjective probabilities. *Statistical Science*, 1 (3):335–345, 1986.

B. Franklin. *Complete works*, chapter Letter to J. B. Priestley, 1772, page 522. Putnam, New York, 1887.

G. Gigerenzer and D.G. Goldstein. Reasoning the fast and frugal way: Models of bounded rationality. *Psychological Review*, 103:650–669, 1996.

G. Gigerenzer, P. M. Todd, and the ABC group. *Simple heuristics that make us smart*. Oxford University Press, 1999.

M. Grabisch and Ch. Labreuche. Bi-capacities for decision making on bipolar scales. In *EUROFUSE'02 Workshop on Information Systems*, pages 185–190, 2002.

S. Greco, B. Matarazzo, and R. Slowinski. Bipolar Sugeno and Choquet integrals. In *EUROFUSE'02 Workshop on Information Systems*, 2002.

J. Y. Halpern. Defining relative likelihood in partially-ordered structures. *JAIR*, 7:1–24, 1997.

Ch. Labreuche and M. Grabisch. Generalized Choquet-like aggregation functions for handling bipolar scales. *EJOR*, 172(3):931–955, 2006.

D. J. Lehmann. Generalized qualitative probability: Savage revisited. In *UAI*, pages 381–388, 1996.

D. L. Lewis. Counterfactuals and comparative possibility. *Journal of Philosophical Logic*, 2:418–446, 1973.

H. Moulin. *Axioms of Cooperative Decision Making*. Wiley, New-York, 1988.

C. E. Osgood, G.J. Suci, and P. H. Tannenbaum. *The Measurement of Meaning*. University of Illinois Press, Chicago, 1957.

P. Slovic, M. Finucane, E. Peters, and D.G. MacGregor. Rational actors or rational fools? implications of the affect heuristic for behavioral economics. *The Journal of Socio-Economics*, 31:329–342, 2002.

A. Tversky and D. Kahneman. Advances in prospect theory: Cumulative representation of uncertainty. *Journal of Risk and Uncertainty*, 5:297–323, 1992.

A. Wald. *Statistical Decision Functions*. Wiley, 1950.

Logical approaches to fuzzy similarity-based reasoning: an overview

Lluís Godo [*] and Ricardo O. Rodríguez [†]

[*] AI Research Institute, IIIA
Spanish National Research Council, CSIC
08193 Bellaterra, Spain
godo@iiia.csic.es

[†] Computer Science Department, FCEyN
University of Buenos Aires, UBA
1428 Buenos Aires, Argentina
ricardo@dc.uba.ar

Abstract The aim of this paper is to survey a class of logical formalizations of similarity-based reasoning models where similarity is understood as a graded notion of truthlikeness. We basically identify two different kinds of logical approaches that have been used to formalize fuzzy similarity reasoning: syntactically-oriented approaches based on a notion of approximate proof, and semantically-oriented approaches based on several notions of approximate entailments. In particular, for these approximate entailments we provide four different formalisations in terms of suitable systems of modal and conditional logics, including for each class a system of graded operators with classical semantics, as well as a system with many-valued operators. Finally, we also explore some nonmonotonic issues of similarity-based reasoning.

1 Introduction: vagueness, uncertainty and truthlikeness

For many years, classical logic has given a formal basis to the study of human reasoning. However, during the last decades, it has become apparent that human practical reasoning demands more than what traditional deductive logic can offer. For instance, classically, the truth of a statement q with respect to a state of knowledge K is determined whenever every model of K is also model of q. But nothing can be said about its truth value if only *most* of the models of K are also models of q or when models of q are *very "close"* to models of our state of knowledge. Moreover, a statement can only be either true or false, but some human expressions, such as "John is bald", often fail to be semantically determined with bivalued precision since they express gradual properties.

Minsky (Min85) and McDermott (McD87) suggested that classical logic is inappropriate for modeling human reasoning because of the modeling "perfect" nature of the former. They remarked that while classical logical reasoning is both *sound* (all conclusions reached are valid or true) and *complete* (all true facts can be deduced), human reasoning does not possess either one of these qualities. On the contrary, the modeling of human reasoning usually requires "imperfect" knowledge to be taken into account in the form of uncertainty, vagueness, truthlikeness, incompleteness and partial contradictions. These limitations of classical logic in accounting for human reasoning motivated the study of alternative (or perhaps better, complementary) formalisations which already became one of the major research areas in the field of Artificial Intelligence in the recent past.

A variety of *approximate reasoning* models have appeared as possible alternatives and have generated an extensive literature in both Philosophy and Artificial Intelligence. Models of approximate reasoning aim at being more flexible than classical logic and basically work on three "imperfections" information can be pervaded with: vagueness, uncertainty and truthlikeness. Informally, and roughly speaking, we can say that approximate reasoning deals with propositions and "labels" associated to them, which are usually interpreted as degrees of truth, belief or proximity to the truth. Each one of these units of measurement is respectively associated with the notions of vagueness, uncertainty and truthlikeness. Unfortunately, this simplified view does not make clear that each one of these "imperfections" responds to a different semantics. In what follows, we shall try to give an "orthogonal" description of these three "imperfections" which we hope will make clear the distinction among them and then we shall indicate how they may be combined.

The three axes correspond to: crisp vs. many-valued interpretations, complete vs. incomplete information, and error-free vs. mistaken information.

Interpretation Problem

Whenever we have (or fix) a representation language to describe our information about the world, we should provide a form of interpreting the sentences in such a language, i.e. to establish a correspondence between meaning and truth (or as Carnap says (Car37), between theoretical concepts and observations). There is no consensus about what is the best (or most appropriate) theory to define the truth: there are e.g. pragmatic, coherence, correspondence, redundancy or semantic theories. In our opinion, Tarski's correspondence theory is the most adequate form to establish this relationship. He considers that the truth of sentences, statements, judgments, propositions, beliefs or ideas, consists of their "correspondence" with reality, world, or facts. The fundamental difficulty for this theory is to specify what it means to say that a statement "corresponds" to reality. In Tarski's view (Tar56), the truth value of a sentence is determined by an interpretation function e from language $\mathbf{L}$ to models Ω. One familiar objection to Tarski's correspondence theory is that his definition applies only (or at best) to formal languages, but not to natural languages. It is well-known that most of the statements in natural language do not have a precise characterisation of their meanings, i.e. they are not semantically determined (in last sense) because they contain (among other things) different kinds of *vague expressions*, including predicates as 'big', 'short', 'large', etc., modifiers as 'very', 'more or less', 'rather', etc., and quantifiers as 'most', 'some', 'many', 'few', etc.

In brief, some expressions which refer to gradual properties are inherently or semantically vague. In such cases, there are no suitable characterizations of their meaning in terms of true-false interpretations. Hence, if we want to represent knowledge of the type "the mountain is high" we need to increase the interpretation power and hence we have to give up classical logic principles such as the excluded middle principle ($p \vee \neg p$ is always true) or the non-contradiction principle ($p \wedge \neg p$ is always false). In response to this necessity Lotfi Zadeh introduced in 1965 (Zad65) *fuzzy set theory*. His fundamental idea consists in understanding lattice-valued maps as generalised characteristic functions of some new kind of objects, the so-called *fuzzy sets*, of a given universe.

In the context of fuzzy set theory, fuzzy logic (FL) was born as a logical system that aims at the formalisation of the reasoning with vague propositions. The term fuzzy logic has been used through the literature with two different meanings (Zad94):

- *In the narrow sense* fuzzy logic, FL_n, is an extension of many-valued logic, where the notion of "degree of membership" of an element x in an universe X with respect to a fuzzy set A over X is regarded as the degree of truth of the statement "$A(x)$" (usually read as "x is A). However, as it is pointed out by Zadeh in (Zad94), the agenda of FL_n is quite different from that of traditional many-valued logical systems, e.g. Lukasiewicz's logic. He states that concepts such as linguistic variables, canonical forms, fuzzy if-then rules, fuzzy quantifiers and such modes of reasoning as interpolative reasoning, syllogistic reasoning, and dispositional reasoning, are not part of traditional many-valued logical systems.

- *In the broad sense* fuzzy logic, FL_b, is almost synonymous with fuzzy set theory which is a general theory to represent and to reason over "classes" with unsharp boundaries. Fuzzy set theory includes: fuzzy arithmetic, fuzzy mathematical programming, fuzzy topology, fuzzy graph theory, and fuzzy data analysis.

In the last years, many works have been devoted to the development of the formal background of fuzzy logic in narrow sense (as witnessed by a number of important monographs that have appeared in the literature, e. g. (Haj98; NPM99; Got01; Ger01), that is, to formal systems of many-valued logics having the real unit interval as set of truth values, and truth functions defined by fuzzy connectives that behave classically on extremal truth values (0 and 1) and satisfy some natural monotonicity conditions. Actually, these connectives originate from the definition and algebraic study of fuzzy set theoretical operations over the real unit interval.

In this paper we consider vagueness as an interpretation problem and it will be formally addressed by means of the use of some kind of many-valued logic. As in classical logic, in many-valued logics sentences of the representation language get a truth-value, possibly an intermediate value between 0 and 1, in every complete description of the world. But, as we discuss next, it may be not always possible to determinate this value because in general we may not have (or/and it is impossible to have) a complete knowledge about the real world.

Incomplete Information Problem

In a classical logic, there is a clear distinction between a definition of truth (such as it was mentioned above) and a criteria for recognizing the truth. In the latter sense, the truth or validity of a conclusion C is often given in terms of a list of arguments Γ, called premises, knowledge base or theory. Thus, if every interpretation that satisfies Γ (i.e. which is a model of Γ) it satisfies C as well, then we can say that in the context of Γ, C is true or is valid conclusion. On the other hand, the falsehood of C is established when no model of Γ satisfies C. Any other situation (when only some (but not all) models of Γ are also models of C) leaves uncertainty about the truth-value of the conclusion C. Moreover, except for the case in which the theory that describes our knowledge about the state of the world is complete it will not be possible in general to determine the truth or falsehood of every possible conclusion. Therefore, even in classical logic, there are three (not two) different epistemic attitudes on propositions with respect to a given theory modelling the world (Gär88; DP01). This indetermination caused by the third state (ignorance or indetermination) will be referred to as the incomplete information problem.

In practice, it is usual that those dealing with the task of decision or prediction making do not have complete information about the current state of affairs. This prevents from unequivocal assessments of future states and limits the ability to precisely predict the consequence of the possible choices. In such a situation, a classical logical approach as basic formalization of this kind of reasoning would condemn us to "inaction". Fortunately, it is often the case that the available information, even if incomplete, is useful and sufficient for many purposes. For example, knowledge about the laws of evolution of a physical system may be useful to derive that, given an ideal gas, if its pressure P and temperature $Temp$ are known then its volume Vol is determined by the expression $Vol = k\frac{Temp}{P}$. Of course, if the gas is not ideal the result provided by this equation will not be accurate. Hence, in a strict sense, it will not be possible to know the exact volume of the gas, at least from that equation. So, this kind of precise laws have limited applicability in real domains, where e. g. statistical mechanics gives an answer to these questions by using probability theory, that aims at capturing the underlying uncertainty. In such a case, a probability distribution over the possible values of the volume would be obtained, which provides a measure (objective or subjective) of confidence on the accuracy in predicting a value of a physical property, in our example the volume. Other popular theories used to formalize and quantify that uncertainty are possibility theory and Dempster-Shafer theory of evidence.

In general, an uncertainty model attaches numbers to logical propositions which do not indicate a degree of truth (as some authors usually point out) but a degree of confidence or belief in the truth-value of these propositions. In this sense, the measure of uncertainty compensates the lack of knowledge at the propositional level with information at a higher level of abstraction. At this point, it is important to differentiate vagueness or imprecision at propositional level (as it was discussed above) from vagueness at the model or interpretation level, as it is the case in possibilistic logic. In the latter case, each (crisp) interpretation is attached a degree that estimates the extent to which it may represent the real state of the world. Such an attachment defines a fuzzy set of interpretations which is in fact a fuzzy set based modeling of our vague knowledge about what the real world is. In this sense, the degrees of possibility and necessity in possibilistic logic may be understood as uncertainty degrees induced by some kind of vague (and hence incomplete) information.

However, although notions of vagueness (at propositional level) and uncertainty are not the same, there are close links between them and in many occasions they need to live together. For example, as mentioned in (DP88), if all we know is that "John is tall" (i.e. a vague knowledge about John's height) then, about the truth of the sentence "John's height is 1.80 m", one can only say that it is more or less possible. More formally, Dubois and Prade in (DP91a) propose to understand each fuzzy assertion of the sort of "X is *Tall*" (where *Tall* is a fuzzy set of an universe of discourse U and X is a variable taking values in U) as a constraint on the unknown possibility of the crisp assertions $X = x$, with $x \in U$, of the form $\Pi(X = x) \leq \mu_{Tall}(x)$. This example makes it clear that vague, incomplete information also produces uncertainty on conclusions.

As it is argued by Resconi, Klir and St. Clair (RKC92), uncertainty is an intensional or metatheoretical notion. For this reason, modal logics provide a unified framework for representing those uncertain theories (RKCH93; Hal03) and are naturally related to various generalisations of the modal system S4.3. The well-known cases are probabilistic (Car50; Hal03), possibilistic (FH91; HK94; LL96) and Dempster-Shafer logics (Rus87; Hal03).

Summarizing, we will associate the term *uncertainty* to a degree of belief regarding the truth of a proposition, usually crisp but not necessarily so. Formally, the uncertainty should correspond to intensional logics which are non-truth functional (DP01).

Mistaken Information Problem

In classical logic, falsity entails any statement. But, in many occasions, we may want to use "false" theories, for instance, Newton's Gravitational Theory. Although this theory is not true we may accept it is a good approximation to truth. Note that we are not referring to self-contradictory theories, but empirically or factually false ones, i.e. theories that correctly explain most of the observations but have counter-examples. As a first approach, we could measure how close is a theory to the truth according to its amount of counter-examples. According to this measure, it is possible to affirm that there are good reasons to conjecture that Einstein's Gravitational Theory, which is also not true, is a better approximation to the truth than Newton's Theory. In a more general sense, we refer to the notion of "proximity to the truth" of a statement (even though it may not be true or provable) as *truthlikeness* (Odd07).

Popper makes an observation which throws light over the distinction between uncertainty and truthlikeness. He points out that by using the Bayesian inference to establish the strength of belief in a hypothesis h from both a previous knowledge K and an observed evidence e, " if the evidence e contradicts the hypothesis h then the probability $P(h \mid e, K)$ of h given e (in the context of K) is zero; yet, h may be highly truthlike, since false theories (even theories known to be false) may be 'close' to the truth". This point stresses the difference between incompleteness and "falsity" of a theory. The first case indicates its failure to express the whole truth and the second one represents the acceptance of an untrue proposition. For instance, a witness in court who does not lie but conceals some "relevant"[1] of facts, tells an incomplete information. On the contrary, a testimony which is partially true, refers to false information.

In a more pragmatic sense, the concept of truthlikeness appears, for example, when we want to give an answer to a query over a database: if we must match exactly the query against the database, we will possibly need too much time or even we can fail. But, if we allow to match the consult "approximately" enough then a lot of time may be saved. In this case, we also may say that the answer to a query is close to the truth or truthlike. Note that the notion of "approximation" to the truth is in correspondence to the one of error in numerical methods.

If we accept this notion, we will be able to say that a statement is *almost true, nearly true* or *approximately true*, indicating thereby that it is false or unprovable but close to being true. For instance, in this sense, the sentence "the height of Mount Everest is 8.800 m" is close to the truth[2]. This concept of "close" to the truth presupposes some metric which allows us to express the degree of approximate truth. Notice that this last concept is different from the two previous: vagueness and uncertainty. The truth-value of our example "the height of Mount Everest is 8.800 m" is certainly false and precisely formulated, therefore it is neither uncertain nor vague.

Summarising, we may say that vagueness, uncertainty and truthlikeness, until few years ago, were not clearly differentiated from each other, possibly because they are usually coded by real numbers from the unit interval $[0, 1]$. In the last years, much effort has been devoted to clarify the conceptual differences between vagueness and uncertainty as it is witnessed in (BDG+99). However, the distinction between these two notions and truthlikeness is not so clear in the literature. For instance, in (DPB99), similarity logic is classified as a non truth-functional logic dealing with vagueness. We consider that it is useful to clarify the distinctive features of each notion, since they are specially important when we aim to represent knowledge and reason with it.

---

[1]Relevance is an important notion which we do not consider here, but that it should be taking account in a thinner analysis of truthlikeness

[2]The height of Mount Everest that appears in dictionaries is 8,835m.

We think that these three notions, vagueness, uncertainty and truthlikeness, constitute the basic axes of approximate reasoning models. Also, we believe that they may be formalized and combined under a homogeneous framework which should be, we understand, an appropriate extension of fuzzy logic in the narrow sense. Several attempts have been made in this direction. For instance,

- Zadeh in (Zad86) combines fuzziness and probability by suggesting a definition of the probability of a fuzzy proposition.

- In (DP93), the authors extensively survey the literature concerning the relationship between fuzzy sets and probability theories; again, besides pointing out the gaps between them, the authors build bridges between both theories, stressing in this sense the importance of possibility theory.

- In Hájek *et al.*'s paper (HGE95), and in some later elaborations (Haj98; GHE03), there is a further contribution to this bridge building. They propose three different theories in Lukasiewicz-Pavelka's logic to cope with probability, necessity and belief functions respectively. The main idea behind this approach is that uncertainty measures of crisp propositions can be understood as truth-values of some suitable fuzzy propositions associated to crisp propositions (it is worth mentioning that although in this work the propositional variables only take Boolean values it is easy to extend it to the many-valued case).

Truthlikeness is probably the least known of the above three notions. The aim of this paper is to survey some logical formalisations of similarity-based reasoning models, where similarity is understood as truthlikeness. To this end, the paper is structured is as follows. In the next section we provide all necessary background about fuzzy similarity relations. In Section 3, we introduce two different logical approaches, one syntactically and another semantically oriented, in order to formalize fuzzy similarity reasoning. In Section 4 we describe the main ideas behind the syntactic model based on the notion of approximate proof, while Section 5 is devoted to the semantical model based on several notions of approximate entailments. In Section 6, we give four different formalisations of these similarity entailments in terms of suitable systems modal and conditional logics, including for each class a system of graded operators with classical semantics and a system with many-valued operators. Finally, Section 7 explores some nonmonotonic issues of similarity-based reasoning, by considering similarity, instead of distance, as a central notion with which to define epistemic orderings and operators of theory revision.

2   Truthlikeness and graded similarity

As it was mentioned above, the dichotomy of the class of propositions into truths and falsehoods should thus be supplemented with a more fine-grained criterion according to their closeness to the truth. The problem of truthlikeness is to give an adequate account of such a concept and to explore its logical properties and its applications to knowledge representation. While a multitude of apparently different solutions to this problem has been proposed, it is now standard to classify them into two main approaches: the *content approach* and the *likeness approach*. The first approach is based on Popper's idea that any theory (or knowledge base) K may be divided in two parts: its truth content K_T, and its falsity content K_F. This partition into true and false propositions is induced by the real world (obviously the epistemological problem is to know which is this world). Following this idea, a knowledge base is closer to the truth than another if it has more truth content (without engendering more falsity content) and less falsity content (without sacrificing truth content). Unfortunately, this account suffers from a fatal flaw, it entails that no false theory is closer to the truth than any other. This was shown independently by Tichý and Miller (Tic74; Mil74). After the failure of Popper's idea, the modern definition of truthlikeness follows the likeness approach, and has emerged based on similarity and was proposed independently by Risto Hilpinen within possible worlds semantics (Hil76) and by Pavel Tichý within propositional logic (Tic74). The basic idea of this *similarity approach* is that the degree of truthlikeness of a sentence φ depends on the similarity between the states of affairs that are compatible with φ and the true state of the world, see e.g. (Nii87, pag. 198). According to Niiniluoto (Nii87), we will consider the *truthlike* value of a sentence as its degree of "proximity to the truth", even though it may not be true or provable. This degree should be given by the "distance" that separates (or dually, by the similarity between) the models of this sentence and the models of the "reality".

Thus, this notion of truthlikeness can be regarded as a special case of the more general concept of similarity and its logical counterparts to some form of similarity-based reasoning, this last concept being often associated with reasoning by analogy which is an important form of non-demonstrative inference. Similarity-based reasoning aims at studying which kinds of logical consequence relations make sense when taking into account that some propositions may be closer to be true than others. A typical kind of inference which is in the scope of similarity-based reasoning responds to the form "if φ is true then ψ is *close* to be true", in the sense that, although ψ may be false (or not provable), knowing that φ is true leads to infer that

ψ is semantically close (or similar) to some other proposition which is indeed true. Notice again that the fact of ψ being close to (or approximately) true has nothing to do with a problem of uncertainty, i. e. with a problem of missing information not allowing us to know whether ψ is true or false (DP95). Essentially, similarity-based reasoning has been investigated from two different perspectives:

• Qualitative or comparative approaches, where the aim is formalizing e. g. expressions like p is closer to q than r. The works independently developed by Nicod (Nic70), Williamson (Wil88), and Konikowska (Kon97), belong to the first tradition. At the semantical level, Lewis in (Lew73) uses sphere systems in order to formalize the counterfactual reasoning. Given a possible world w, a sphere system is a set of sets of worlds centered on w, nested, and closed under union and intersection. It is meant to carry information about the comparative overall similarity of worlds. Any particular sphere around world w is to contain just those worlds that resemble w to at least a certain degree. If one world lies within some sphere around w and another world lies outside that sphere, then the first world is more closely similar to w than the second.

• Quantitative approaches, that are based somehow on a numerical definition of degree of truthlikeness or similarity, following the last tradition of truthlikeness as it is pointed out by Niiniluoto in (Nii87, pag. 203), and by Weston (Wes87). This kind of approach, although not always within a formal logical framework, has blossomed after the introduction by Zadeh (Zad71) of fuzzy similarity relations as graded modelings of similarity relations, originally to be used in techniques of categorization and clustering. From then, similarity-based reasoning has taken an important place in the context of fuzzy reasoning. In this second group, we may mention works such as (Rus91; DP94; Yin94; EGG94; DEG$^+$95; Kla95; BJ96; DEG$^+$97).

In this paper we will be mainly concerned with reviewing the logical formalizations of similarity-based approaches based in one way or another on the notion of fuzzy similarity relations.

A (binary) fuzzy similarity relation S on a given domain D is a mapping $S : D \times D \to [0,1]$ fulfilling some basic properties trying to capture the notion of similarity.

Reflexivity: $S(u,u) = 1$ for all $u \in D$
Separability: $S(u,v) = 1$ iff $u = v$
Symmetry: $S(u,v) = S(v,u)$, for all $u,v \in D$
$\otimes$-Transivity: $S(u,v) \otimes S(v,w) \leq S(u,w)$, for all $u,v,w \in D$

where $\otimes$ is a t-norm. The reflexivity property establishes that the similarity degree of any world with itself has the highest value. Separability is a bit stronger since it forbids to have $S(u,v) = 1$ for $u \neq v$. Symmetry has a clear meaning, and $\otimes$-Transitivity is a relaxed form of transitivity since it establishes $S(u,v) \otimes S(v,w)$ as a lower bound for $R(u,w)$. Note that $S(u,v) = S(v,w) = 1$ implies $S(u,w) = 1$. Reflexive and symmetric fuzzy relations are often called *closeness* relations, while those further satisfying $\otimes$-transitivity are usually called *$\otimes$-similarity relations*. Sometimes, the name similarity relation is also used to denote in fact min-similarity relations. These relations have the remarkable property that their level cuts $S_\alpha = \{(u,v) \in D \mid S(u,v) \geq \alpha\}$, for any $\alpha \in [0,1]$, are indeed equivalence relations.

The question which set of the above properties better models the intuitive notion of similarity has led to some interesting discussions in the literature (see e.g. the series of papers (DeCK03a; Bod03; Boi03; Jan03; Kla03; DeCK03b)) related to the Poincaré paradox and the $\otimes$-transitivity property, but such a matter is not in the scope of this paper.

Even though Zadeh introduced both the notions of fuzzy sets and fuzzy similarity relations, only recently it has been remarked the duality between these two notions, which in turn generates another duality between fuzzy reasoning and similarity-based reasoning. Moreover, as it is pointed out by Klawonn and Castro (KC95), even if similarity is not the intended interpretation of fuzzy sets, one can not avoid the effects of similarity which are inherent in fuzzy sets and in fuzzy reasoning.

Indeed, a fuzzy similarity relation $S : D \times D \to [0,1]$ defines, for each crisp subset $E \subseteq D$, a corresponding fuzzy set *approx_E* of those elements which are *close* to E (in the sense of being close to *some* element of E), just by defining its membership function $\mu_{approx\_E} : D \to [0,1]$ as

$$\mu_{approx\_E}(u) = \sup\{S(u,v) \mid v \in E\}$$

Note that the membership degree $\mu_{approx\_E}(u)$ is taken as the (highest) similarity degree of u to some element of E, in particular $\mu_{approx\_E}(u) = 1$ if $u \in E$ (and conversely in the case S is separating). Therefore, $E \subseteq$ *approx_E*, and hence *approx_E* can be properly considered an upper (fuzzy) approximation of E. Moreover, if E a set of typical elements satisfying some given property P, $\mu_{approx\_E}(u)$ can also be viewed as a *typicality degree* of u with respect to the property P (in accordance with Niiniluoto's proposal (Nii87)).

Conversely, a fuzzy subset A on a domain D, with membership function $\mu_A : D \to [0,1]$, can be thought of as being defined by

(i) a set of prototypes $E_A = \{u \in D \mid \mu_A(u) = 1\}$, i.e. those elements that fully belong to A, and

(ii) a fuzzy similarity S_A such that the membership degree $\mu_A(u)$ for any $u \in A$ is interpreted as the (highest) similarity degree of u to some prototype of A, that is, $\mu_A(u) = \sup\{S_A(u,v) \mid v \in E_A\}$. Indeed, it suffices to define

$$S_A(u,v) = \min(\mu_A(u) \Rightarrow \mu_A(v), \mu_A(v) \Rightarrow \mu_A(u))$$

for $\Rightarrow$ being the residuum of some (left-continuous) t-norm.

Note, however, that the induced similarity S_A is not unique, it depends on the fuzzy set A.

3 Logical approaches to formalize fuzzy similarity-based reasoning

From a logical point of view, two different paths of research are upheld according to take as primitive notion either a similarity relation between worlds (models), which is then used to define approximate semantical entailments, or a similarity relation between formulas, which is then used to define a notion of approximate (syntactical) proof, by allowing a partial matching mechanism in the inference steps. We mention next main works related to each approach:

• Ruspini presents in (Rus91) "a semantic characterisation of the major concepts and constructs of fuzzy logic in terms of notions of similarity, closeness, and proximity between possible states (*worlds*) of a system that is being reasoned about". Following Ruspini's conception, a family of entailments has been proposed and applied to Case-Based and Interpolative Reasoning (DEG$^+$95; DEG$^+$97; DEG$^+$98). In those works, the characterisation of entailments are strictly semantic. Ruspini's perspective is intrinsically modal, although he never produced a full-fledged modal logical framework. However, this gap may be easily overcome by considering a definition of truthlikeness based on similarity measures between worlds and used as accessibility relations in a Kripke's semantics.

• Ming-Sheng Ying presents in (Yin94) "...a propositional calculus in which the truth values of sentences are true or false exactly, but the reasoning may be approximate by allowing the antecedent of a rule to match its premise only approximately". Thus, he wants to give a notion of an approximate proof like one of approximate calculus in, for example, resolution of systems of equations. In (BG98) the authors generalise Ying's proposal and reduce it to a fuzzy logic in the Hilbert style as defined by Pavelka in (Pav79).

Besides these logical-oriented developments, other more fuzzy set based approaches to model patterns of similarity-based reasoning have been developed. For instance, Klawonn *et al.* have developed interpolation methods to obtain fuzzy control functions which are modelled by similarity relations between terms (KK93; Kla94; Kla95; KC95; KGK95; KN96). The notion of *extensionality* appears as fundamental in their investigations. Independently, Boixader and Jacas (BJ98) have proposed models of approximate reasoning through the same concept of extensionality with respect to a natural ⊗-indistinguishability operator. They consider the degree of indistinguishability between fuzzy sets as a formal measure of its degree of similarity. Although of different nature, it is also worth mentioning Hüllermeier's probabilistic framework for similarity-based inference (Hül01) where he provides a formal model (called similarity profile) of the principle that "similar causes bring about similar effects" which underlies most approaches to similarity-based reasoning and based on a probabilistic characterization of the similarity between observed causes.

In the rest of the paper we overview the above two kinds of logical approaches and related issues.

4   Fuzzy similarity and approximate proofs

Following (Yin94), (BGY00) and (Ses02), the idea is to consider inferences that may be approximated by allowing the antecedent clauses of a rule to match its premises only approximately. In particular, the classical SLD Resolution is modified in order to overcome failure situations in the unification process if the entities involved in the matching have a non-zero similarity degree. Such a procedure allows us to compute numeric values belonging to the interval $[0,1]$, named *approximation degrees*, which provide an approximation measure of the obtained solutions. This framework, which we shall call *Similarity Propositional Logic Programming* (SPLP), is the propositional version of that one proposed by Sessa in (Ses02) which is based upon a first order language. In (GS99b) we find the first proposal to introduce similarity in the frame of the declarative paradigm of Logic Programming. Logic programs on function-free languages are considered and approximate and imprecise information are represented by introducing a similarity relation between constant and predicate symbols. Two transformation techniques of logic programs are defined. In the underlying logic, the inference rule (Resolution rule) as well as the usual crisp representation of the considered universe are not modified. It allows to avoid both the introduction of weights on the clauses, and the use of fuzzy sets as elements of the language. The semantic equivalence between the two inference processes associated to the two kinds of transformed programs has been proved by using an abstract interpretation technique. Moreover, the notion of fuzzy least Herbrand model has been introduced. In (Ses01) the generalization of this approach to the case of programs with function symbols is provided by introducing the general notion of *structural translation* of languages. In (Ses02) the operational counterpart of this extension is faced by introducing a modified SLD Resolution procedure which allows us to perform these kinds of extended computations exploiting the original logic program, without any preprocessing steps in order to transform the given program. Some relations, which allow to state the computational equivalence between these different approaches, has been proved. Finally, for completeness sake, we also cite (FGS00) where a first and different (it takes into account substitutions of variable with sets of symbols) generalized unification algorithm based on similarity has been proposed.

Suppose, as it is the case in (Yin94; BG98; BGY00), that the starting point is a similarity relation S (reflexive, symmetric and min-transitive relation) defined on the set *Var* of propositional variables. A first problem is how to extend the similarity S over *Var* to a similarity over a propositional language **L** built from *Var*. In Ying and Gerla's papers the extension is done in two steps:

(1) First S is extended to $\overline{S}$ on **L** by the following recursive definition,

$$\overline{S}(p,q) = \begin{cases} S(p,q), & \text{if } p, q \in Var \\ S(s,s') \wedge S(t,t'), & \text{if } p = s \to t \text{ and } q = s' \to t' \\ 0, & \text{otherwise} \end{cases}$$

Notice that $\overline{S}$ is not compatible with the logical equivalence. Take, for example, $F \to p \equiv p \to p$ for every $p \in Var$ and a simple computation shows that $\overline{S}(F \to p, p \to p) = 0$.

(2) Second they define what is proved to be the minimal similarity relation S_e over $\mathcal{L}$ compatible with logical equivalence and containing $\overline{S}$, as:

$$S_e(p,q) =$$
$$\sup\{\overline{S}(p_1, p_2) \wedge \ldots \wedge \overline{S}(p_{2n-1}, p_{2n}) \mid p_1 = p, \, p_{2n} = q \text{ and } p_{2k} \equiv p_{2k+1}$$
$$\text{for } k = 1, n - 1\}.$$

The main problem arising from this definition is that it is not evident how to practically compute the relation S_e. Moreover the following results can be proved:

(i) There does not exist a functional extension of S compatible with logical equivalence.

(ii) Any similarity relation preserving logical equivalence defines a similarity relation between classes of logical equivalent formulas and thus a similarity relation between subsets of interpretations, i. e. subsets of Ω. Take into account that, in the finite case, there exists an isomorphism between propositions and subsets of interpretations. Moreover any similarity relation over the set of subsets of Ω defines a similarity relation over $\mathbf{L}$ compatible with logical equivalence.

(iii) Relations $\mathcal{S}_e$ obtained from a similarity relation $\mathcal{S}$ over the set Var by Ying-Gerla's method do not cover all similarity relations compatible with logical equivalence. For example, if $\mathcal{S}_e(p,q) = \alpha \neq 0$, then $\mathcal{S}_e(p, p\wedge q) \geq \min(\overline{S}(p,p), \overline{S}(p\wedge p, p\wedge q)) = \alpha$ and this is not necessarily true in a similarity relation compatible with logical equivalence.

Based on $\mathcal{S}_e$, in (BG98) the authors define a consequence operator, $Con_e :$ $F(\mathbf{L}) \times \mathbf{L} \rightarrow [0,1]$, $F(\mathbf{L})$ being the set of fuzzy subsets of $\mathbf{L}$, by

$$Con_e(\Gamma, q) = \bigvee \{\overline{\mathcal{S}}_e(\mathit{Taut} \cup \Gamma, B) \mid B \vdash q\}$$

where Taut denotes the set of classical tautologies and $\overline{\mathcal{S}}_e$ is defined as,

$$\overline{\mathcal{S}}_e(\Gamma, B) = \bigwedge_{q \in B} \bigvee_{p \in \mathcal{L}} \Gamma(p) \wedge \mathcal{S}_e(p, q)$$

for all $\Gamma \in F(\mathbf{L})$, $B \subseteq \mathbf{L}$ and $p, q \in \mathbf{L}$. The relation $\overline{\mathcal{S}}_e$ is not symmetrical, it may be interpreted as the degree in which B can be considered included in Γ. In fact, if Γ is a crisp set of formulas, then $\overline{\mathcal{S}}_e(\Gamma, B) = 1$ whenever $B \subseteq \Gamma$. An easy computation shows that a form of generalized Modus ponens is preserved by this consequence operator, since the inequality

$$Con_e(\{p \rightarrow q, p'\}, q) \geq \overline{\mathcal{S}}_e(p, p')$$

holds for any propositions p, q and p'.

In the rest of this section we briefly describe an application of these ideas in the framework of logic programming developed in (GS99b; Ses02; FGS00). For simplicity we only consider below the propositional version. We start by recalling that a logic program P on $\mathbf{L}$ is a conjunction of definite clauses of $\mathbf{L}$, denoted as $q \leftarrow p_1, \ldots, p_n$, $n \geq 0$, and a goal is a negative clause, denoted with $\leftarrow q_1, \ldots, q_n$, $n \geq 1$, where the symbol "," that separates the propositional variables has to be interpreted as conjunction, where $p_1, \ldots, p_n, q, q_1, \ldots, q_n \in Var$. A SPLP-program is a pair $(P, \mathcal{S})$, where P is a logic program defined on $\mathbf{L}$ and $\mathcal{S}$ is a similarity on Var. Given P, the least Herbrand model of P is given by $M_P = \{p \in Var \mid P \models p\}$, where $\models$ denotes classical logical entailment. M_P is equivalent to the corresponding procedural semantics of P, defined by considering the SLD Resolution. In the classical case, a mismatch between two propositional constant names causes a failure of the unification process. Then, it is rather natural to admit a more flexible unification in which the syntactical identity is substituted by a Similarity $\mathcal{S}$ defined on Var. The modified version of the SLD Resolution, which we shall call *Similarity-based SLD Resolution*, exploits this simple variation in the unification process. The basic idea of this procedure for first order languages has been outlined in (GS99a). The following definitions formalize these ideas in the case of propositional languages.

Definition 4.1. Let $\mathcal{S} : Var \times Var \rightarrow [0,1]$ be a similarity and $p, q \in Var$ be two propositional constants in a propositional language $\mathcal{L}$. We define the *unification-degree of p and q with respect to $\mathcal{S}$* the value $\mathcal{S}(p,q)$. p and q are *λ-unifiable* if $\mathcal{S}(p,q) = \lambda$ with $\lambda > 0$, otherwise we say that they are *not unifiable*.

Definition 4.2. Given a similarity $\mathcal{S} : Var \times Var \rightarrow [0,1]$, a program P and a goal G_0, a *similarity-based SLD derivation of $P \cup \{G_0\}$*, denoted by $G_0 \Rightarrow_{C_1,\alpha_1} G_1 \Rightarrow \cdots \Rightarrow_{C_k,\alpha_k} G_k$, consists of a sequence $G_0, G_1, \ldots, G_k$ of negative clauses, together with a sequence $C_1, C_2, \ldots, C_k$ of clauses from P and a sequence $\alpha_1, \alpha_2, \ldots, \alpha_k$ of values in *[0,1]*, such that for all $i \in \{1, \ldots, k\}$, G_i is a resolvent of G_{i-1} and C_i with unification degree α_i. The approximation degree of the derivation is $\alpha = \inf\{\alpha_1, \ldots, \alpha_k\}$. If G_k is the empty clause $\perp$, for some finite k, the derivation is called a *Similarity-based SLD refutation*, otherwise it is called *failed*.

It is easy to see that when the similarity $\mathcal{S}$ is the identity, the previous definition provides the classical notion of SLD refutation. The values α_i can be considered as constraints that allow the success of the unification processes. Then, it is natural to consider the best unification degree that allows us to satisfy all these constraints. In general, an answer can be obtained with different SLD refutations and different approximation degrees, then the maximum α of these values characterizes the best refutations of the goal. In particular, a refutation with approximation-degree 1 provides an exact solution. Let us stress that α belongs to the set $\lambda_1, \lambda_2, \ldots$ of the possible similarity values in $\mathcal{S}$.

In the sequel, we assume the leftmost selection rule whenever Similarity-based SLD Resolution is considered. However, all the presented results can be analogously stated for any selection rule that does not depend on the propositional constant names and on the history of the derivation (Apt90). Similarity-based SLD Resolution provides a characterization of the fuzzy least Herbrand model $M_{P,\mathcal{S}}$ for $(P, \mathcal{S})$ defined in (GS99b), as stated by the following result.

Proposition 4.3. *Let a similarity S and a logic program P (on a propositional language $\boldsymbol{L}$) be given. For any $q \in Var$, $M_{P,S}(q) = \alpha > 0$ iff α is the maximum value in $(0,1]$ for which there exists a Similarity-based SLD refutation for $P \cup \{\leftarrow q\}$ with approximation degree α.*

Intuitively, the degree of membership $M_{P,S}(q)$ of an atom q is given by the best "tolerance" level $\alpha \in (0,1]$ which allows us to prove q exploiting the Similarity-based SLD Resolution on $P \cup \{\leftarrow q\}$. Moreover, if S is strict and M_P denotes the classical least Herbrand Model of the program P, then $q \in M_P$ iff $M_{P,S}(q) = 1$.

5 Fuzzy similarity and approximate entailments

The starting point in the semantical approaches is to assume that a possible world or state of a system may resemble more to some worlds than to another ones, and this basic fact may help us to evaluate to what extent a partial description (a proposition) may be close or similar to some other.

Under this perspective, an epistemic (in the sense of similarity) state may be modelled by a set of propositions K, modelling the factual information about the world, together with a similarity relation $S : W \times W \to [0,1]$ on the set of possible worlds W for some classical propositional language, modelling how similar or close are worlds among them. Dually, one can think of $\delta = 1 - S$ as a kind of metric on worlds.

Then, using classical reasoning we may know what are the consequences we can infer from K, i.e. those propositions p which logically follow from K, but we can also be interested in those propositions which are approximate consequences of K, in the sense that they are close to some other proposition which is indeed a classical consequence of K.

Since in classical logic we can identify propositions with sets of worlds (in a finitary setting), the above problem reduces to how do we extend the similarity S between worlds to a measure of similarity between sets of worlds. And as well-known, a metric between points does not univocally extend to a meaningful metric between sets of points.

A first consideration is that such a metric has not to be necessarily symmetric, in fact, the logical consequence relation is related to the subsethood relation on sets of worlds ($K \models p$ iff $[K] \subseteq [p]$), not on the equality relation. So, when trying to evaluate to what extent a proposition p is an approximate consequence of K, one is led to measure to what extent the set of K-worlds are close to be included into the set of p-worlds, and not the other way round. In this direction, Ruspini defined the two measures

$$I_S(p \mid q) = \inf_{\omega \models q} \sup_{\omega' \models p} S(\omega, \omega') \qquad and \qquad C_S(p \mid q) = \sup_{\omega \models q} \sup_{\omega' \models p} S(\omega, \omega')$$

which are the lower and upper bounds respectively of the resemblance or proximity degree between p and q. Indeed, I_S is an implication (i.e. inclusion-like) measure, while C_S is a consistency (i.e. intersection-like) measure.

With these measures, he wants to capture inference patterns like so-called generalised modus ponens. The value of $I_S(p \mid q)$ provides the measure of what extent p is close to be true given q for granted and the similarity between worlds represented by S. In particular, when S is separating and the set of worlds is finite then, $I_S(p \mid q) = 1$ iff $q \models p$. Moreover, if S is $\otimes$-transitive, for a t-norm $\otimes$, then I_S is $\otimes$-transitive as well (Rus91), i.e. the inequality

$$I_S(r \mid p) \otimes I_S(p \mid q) \leq I_S(r \mid q)$$

holds for any propositions p, q and r. This property can be seen as a kind of generalized resolution rule

from: $I_S(r \mid p) \geq \alpha$ and $I_S(p \mid q) \geq \beta$
infer: $I_S(r \mid q) \geq \alpha \otimes \beta.$

if one interprets $I_S(\varphi \mid \psi)$ as the truthlike degree of a (non-material) conditional "if ψ then φ". On the other hand, if we keep the conditioning part fixed, I_S fails to cast a generalized pattern of modus ponens of the following kind, given some proposition K:

from: $I_S(p \rightarrow q \mid K) \geq \alpha > 0$ and $I_S(p \mid K) \geq \beta > 0$
infer: $I_S(q \mid K) \geq \alpha \otimes \beta > 0.$

Indeed, one can easily produce a counter-example in which we may have $I_S(p \rightarrow q \mid K) = I_S(p \mid K) \geq \alpha$, with $0 < \alpha < 1$ and α arbitrarily close to 1, but $I_S(q \mid K) = 0$. For instance consider $\mathcal{L}$ generated by only two propositional variables p and q, hence with only four interpretations $\Omega = \{w_1 \ (= p \wedge q), w_2 \ (= p \wedge \neg q), w_3 \ (= \neg p \wedge q), w_4 \ (= \neg p \wedge \neg q)\}$, and let S be such that $S(w_i, w_i) = 1$, $S(w_2, w_4) = S(w_4, w_2) = \alpha$, and $S(w_i, w_j) = 0$ otherwise. If we take $K = \{p \wedge \neg q\}$, then it is easy to check that $I_S(p \rightarrow q \mid K) = \alpha$ and $I_S(p \mid K) = 1$, but $I_S(q \mid K) = 0$.

On the other hand, the value of $C_S(p \mid q)$ provides the measure of what extent p can be considered compatible with the available knowledge q. In particular, in the finite case and with S satisfying separation property, $C_S(p \mid q) = 1$ iff $q \not\models \neg p$. Observe that, when the propositional language is finitely generated and q is equivalent to a maximal consistent set of propositions, both measures coincide because there is a unique world w such that $w \models q$[3]. In addition, it is easy to show that, given a fixed r, the measure $C_S(\cdot \mid r)$ is a possibility measure (DLP94) since the following identities hold true:

1. $C_S(\top \mid r) = 1$
2. $C_S(\bot \mid r) = 0$
3. $C_S(p \vee q \mid r) = \max(C_S(p \mid r), C_S(q \mid r))$.

Therefore, we also have $C_S(p \mid r) = \max\{C_S(p \wedge q \mid r), C_S(p \wedge \neg q \mid r)\}$. In particular, when $C_S(p \wedge q \mid r) > C_S(p \wedge \neg q \mid r)$, it results that $C_S(p \mid r) = C_S(p \wedge q \mid r)$. This can be interpreted as: the $p \wedge q$-worlds are closer (consistent) to the known r-worlds than the $p \wedge \neg q$-worlds are. In this context, the term "closer" is used in the sense of "more similar". We return to this consideration in Subsection 7.1.

Based on the I_S and C_S measures, a first logical system was introduced in (EGG94) where I_S and C_S were used as lower and upper bounds for the truthlikeness degree with which a proposition can be entailed in a given similarity-based epistemic state (K, S). Namely, formulas in this framework are pairs of the form $(p, [\alpha, \beta])$, with $\alpha \leq \beta$ are from the unit interval $[0, 1]$. Then we define

$$(K, S) \models (p, [\alpha, \beta]) \text{ iff } I_S(p \mid K) \geq \alpha \text{ and } C_S(p \mid K) \leq \beta \ .$$

Here we shall go a bit further in this framework along this notion of logical entailment. If we fix the similarity S, the above satisfaction relation can be extended to a consequence relation in the usual way. Let $\Gamma = \{(q_i, [\alpha_i, \beta_i])\}_{i \in I}$ be a set of graded formulas, and say that (K, S) satisfies Γ, written $(K, S) \models \Gamma$, when $(K, S) \models (q_i, [\alpha_i, \beta_i])$ for each $i \in I$. Then we define

$$\Gamma \models_S (p, [\alpha, \beta]) \text{ iff for each } K, (K, S) \models (p, [\alpha, \beta]) \text{ whenever } (K, S) \models \Gamma \ .$$

Analogously to classical logic, this notion of logical consequence can be reduced to involving only worlds. Indeed, if for each proposition p and each world w we define $I(p \mid w) = \sup\{S(w', w) \mid w' \models p\}$, then it can be shown that

$$\Gamma \models_S (p, [\alpha, \beta]) \text{ iff for each } w, w \models_S (p, [\alpha, \beta]) \text{ whenever } w \models_S \Gamma,$$

where $w \models_S (p, [\alpha, \beta])$ iff $\alpha \leq I_S(p \mid w) \leq \beta$, and $w \models_S \Gamma$ iff $w \models_S (q_i, [\alpha_i, \beta_i])$ for each $(q_i, [\alpha_i, \beta_i]) \in \Gamma$.

---

[3] By an abuse of notation, in this case we will also write $I_S(p \mid w)$ or $C_S(p \mid w)$.

Of particular interest are formulas of the kind $(p, [\alpha, 1])$ referring only to lower bounds for I_S, which seem to be more relevant for our purposes. In such a case we can just write (p, α). For this subset of formulas one can define a consequence operator similar to the one defined by Biacino and Gerla for fuzzy sets of formulas. Indeed, a set of graded formulas $\Gamma = \{(q_i, \alpha_i)\}_{i \in I}$ can be seen as a fuzzy set of classical formulas with membership function

$$\Gamma(q) = \begin{cases} \alpha_i, & \text{if } q = q_i \\ 0, & \text{otherwise} \end{cases}.$$

Then one can define a consequence operator $\mathcal{C}_S$ based on S such that, for every fuzzy set of formulas Γ, $\mathcal{C}_S(\Gamma)$ is the fuzzy set of approximate consequences of Γ with the following membership function:

$$\mathcal{C}_S(\Gamma)(p) = \sup\{\alpha \mid \Gamma \models_S (p, \alpha)\},$$

for any proposition p.

Lemma 5.1. $\mathcal{C}_S(\Gamma)(p) = \min\{I_S(p \mid w) \mid w \models_S \Gamma\}$.

In fact, one can show that, for any S, $\mathcal{C}_S$ is a fuzzy consequence operator since it verifies:

(i) $\Gamma \leq \mathcal{C}_S(\Gamma)$
(ii) if $\Gamma \leq \Gamma'$ then $\mathcal{C}_S(\Gamma) \leq \mathcal{C}_S(\Gamma')$
(iii) $\mathcal{C}_S(\mathcal{C}_S(\Gamma)) = \mathcal{C}_S(\Gamma)$

The closure property (iii) is a direct consequence from the above lemma and of the fact that, for any world w, $w \models_S \Gamma$ iff $w \models_S \mathcal{C}(\Gamma)$. When Γ is not a fuzzy but a crisp set of formulas, then it is easy to check that one has

$$\mathcal{C}_S(\Gamma)(p) = I_S(p \mid \wedge\{q \mid q \in \Gamma\}).$$

Another way of looking at the above similarity-based consequence operator is by means of a notion of approximate entailment. Given a $*$-similarity relation S on the set W of classical interpretations of a propositional language, one starts by defining a (graded) approximate satisfaction relation $\models_S^\alpha$, for each $\alpha \in [0, 1]$ by

$$\omega \models_S^\alpha p \quad \text{iff} \quad \text{there exists a model } \omega' \text{ of } p$$
$$\text{which is } \alpha\text{-similar to } \omega, \text{ i.e. } S(\omega, \omega') \geq \alpha$$

If $\omega \models_S^\alpha p$ we say that w is an *approximate model* (at level α) of p. The approximate satisfaction relation can be extended over to an approximate entailment relation in the following way: a proposition p entails a proposition q at degree α, written $p \models^\alpha q$, if each model of p is an approximate model of q at level α, that is,

$p \models_S^\alpha q$ holds iff $w \models_S^\alpha q$ for all model w of p, i.e. iff $I(q \mid p) \geq \alpha$

$p \models_S^\alpha q$ means "p entails q, approximately" and α is a level of strength. The properties of this graded entailment relation are:

(1) **Nestedness:**   if $p \models^\alpha q$ and $\beta \leq \alpha$ then $p \models^\beta q$;
(2) **$\otimes$-Transitivity:**   if $p \models^\alpha r$ and $r \models^\beta q$ then $p \models^{\alpha \otimes \beta} q$;
(3) **Reflexivity:** $p \models^1 p$;
(4) **Right weakening:**   if $p \models^\alpha q$ and $q \models r$ then $p \models^\alpha r$;
(5) **Left strengthening:** if $p \models r$ and $r \models^\alpha q$ then $p \models^\alpha q$;
(6) **Left OR:** $p \vee r \models^\alpha q$ iff $p \models^\alpha q$ and $r \models^\alpha q$;
(7) **Right OR:**   if r has a single model,
                             $r \models^\alpha p \vee q$ iff $r \models^\alpha p$ or $r \models^\alpha q$.

The fourth and fifth properties are consequences of the transitivity property (since $q \models r$ entails $q \models^1 r$) and express a form of monotonicity. The transitivity property is weaker than usual and the graceful degradation of the strength of entailment it expresses, when $\otimes \neq \min$, is rather natural. It must be noticed that $\models^\alpha$ does not satisfy the Right And property, i.e. from $p \models^\alpha q$ and $p \models^\alpha r$ it does not follow in general that $p \models^\alpha q \wedge r$. Hence the set of approximate consequences of p in the sense of $\models^\alpha$ will not be deductively closed. The left OR shows how disjunctive information is handled, while the right OR reflects the decomposability of the approximate satisfaction relation with respect to the $\vee$ connective.

In the case where some (imprecise) knowledge about the world is known and described under the form of some proposition K (i.e. the actual world is in the set of worlds satisfying K), then an approximate entailment relative to K can be straightforwardly defined as

$$p \models_{S,K}^\alpha q \text{ iff } p \wedge K \models_S^\alpha q \text{ iff } I_S(q \mid p \wedge K) \geq \alpha$$

See (DEG$^+$97) for more details and properties of this derived notion of relative entailment.

The above approximate satisfaction relation $w \models_S^\alpha p$ can be also extended over another entailment relation $\models_S$ among propositions as follows: $p \models\!\!\models_S^\alpha q$ holds whenever each approximate model of p at a given level β is also an approximate model of q but at a possibly lower level $\alpha \otimes \beta$. Formally:

$$p \models\!\!\models_S^\alpha q \text{ holds iff for each } w, w \models_S^\beta p \text{ implies } w \models_S^{\alpha \otimes \beta} q$$

Now, $p \models\!\!\models_S^\alpha q$ means "approximately-p entails approximately-q" and α is a level of strength, or in other words, when worlds in the vicinity of p-worlds are also in the vicinity (but possibly a bit farther) of q-worlds. This notion of entailment, called *proximity entailment* in (DEG$^+$97), also admits a characterization in terms of another similarity-based measure

$$J_S(q \mid q) = \inf_w I_S(p \mid w) \Rightarrow I_S(q \mid w)$$

where $\Rightarrow$ is the residuum of the (left-continuous) t-norm $\otimes$ and $I_S(p \mid w) = \sup_{w' \models p} S(w, w')$. Indeed, one can easily check that $p \models^\alpha_S q$ holds iff $J_S(q \mid p) \geq \alpha$. This notion of approximate entailment relation can be easily made relative to a context, described by a set of propositions K we know for sure to hold, sometimes called *background knowledge*, by defining

$$p \models^\alpha_{S,K} q \text{ holds iff for each } w \text{ model of } K, \ w \models^\beta_S p \text{ implies } w \models^{\alpha \otimes \beta}_S q$$

One can analogously characterize this entailment by a generalized measure $J_{S,K}$, namely it holds that $p \models^\alpha_{K_S} q$ iff $J_{K,S}(q \mid p) \geq \alpha$, where $J_{K,S}(q \mid q) = \inf_{w:w \models K} I_S(p \mid w) \Rightarrow I_S(q \mid w)$.

The entailment $\models^\alpha_K$ satisfies similar properties to those satisfied by $\models^\alpha$. Characterizations of both similarity-based graded entailments in terms of these properties are given in (DEG$^+$97). It is also shown there that $\models^\alpha$ and $\models^\alpha$ actually coincide, i.e. when there is no background knowledge K, or equivalently when K is a tautology. However, when K is not a tautology, $\models^\alpha$ is generally stronger than $\models^\alpha_K$.

6   Modal and conditional logic accounts of the similarity-based entailments

In the notions of approximate entailments described in the previous section, the key presence of a similarity relation on the set of interpretations strongly suggests a modal logic setting for similarity-based reasoning. Indeed, modal logic has always received a lot of attention from logicians and after the publication of Kripke's semantics (Kri59a; Kri59b), the notion of possible worlds and of accessibility relation has been inseparably associated with modal logic. For instance, taking classical propositional logic interpretations as possible worlds, each level cut S_α of the (fuzzy) similarity relation S defines an accessibility relation: $(w, w') \in S_\alpha$ if $S(w, w') \geq \alpha$. Therefore it makes sense to consider a modal approach to similarity-based reasoning based on Kripke structures of the form

$$M = (W, S, e),$$

where W is a set of possible worlds, $S : W \times W \rightarrow [0, 1]$ a similarity relation between worlds, and e a classical two-valued truth assignment of propositional variables in each world $e : W \times Var \rightarrow \{0,1\}$. Then, for each $\alpha \in [0,1]$ one can consider the accessibility relation S_α on W, which gives meaning to a pair of dual possibility and necessity modal operators $\Diamond_\alpha$ and $\Box_\alpha$:

$$(M,w) \models \Diamond_\alpha \varphi \text{ if there is } w' \in W \text{ such that } (w,w') \in S_\alpha \text{ and } (M,w') \models \varphi.$$

This defines in fact, a multi-modal logical framework (with as many modalities as level cuts in the similarity relations). Such a multimodal logic setting is systematically developed by Esteva *et al.* (EGGR97) and will be reviewed in Section 6.1.

Note that, if W is the set of classical interpretations of a propositional language $\mathcal{L}$, then the above notion of modal satisfiability for the possibility operators $\Diamond_\alpha$ captures precisely the notion of approximate satisfiability considered in Section 5, in the sense that, for any $p \in \mathcal{L}$, $(M,w) \models \Diamond_\alpha p$ holds iff $w \models_S^\alpha p$ holds. Moreover, the *approximate entailments* $p \models_S^\alpha q$ can also be captured by the formula

$$p \rightarrow \Diamond_\alpha q,$$

in the sense that $p \models_S^\alpha q$ holds iff $M \models p \rightarrow \Diamond_\alpha q$, i.e. iff $p \rightarrow \Diamond_\alpha q$ is valid in $M = (W,S,e)$. As for the *proximity entailments* $\models^\alpha$, recall that $p \models_K^\alpha q$ holds iff for all w model of K and for all β, $w \models^\beta p$ implies $w \models^{\alpha \otimes \beta} q$. Therefore, it cannot be represented in the multi-modal framework unless the similarity relations are forced to have a fixed, predefined set of finitely-many different levels, say $G \subset [0,1]$. In that case, the validity of the formula

$$K \rightarrow (\bigwedge_{\beta \in G} \Diamond_\alpha p \rightarrow \Diamond_{\alpha \otimes \beta} q)$$

in the model (W,S,e) is equivalent to the entailment $p \models_{S,K}^\alpha q$. Obviously, when C is not finite, this representation is not suitable any longer.

Partly due to these difficulties, an alternative approach developed in (Rod02) is to consider a graded conditional logic, where each (approximate and proximity) entailment is directly represented in the object language by a family of binary operators indexed by degrees. Indeed, the idea is to introduce in the language graded binary modalities $>_\alpha$ and $\gg_\alpha$, for each $\alpha \in G$, with the following semantics: given a similarity Kripke model $M = (W,S,e)$, the following satisfiability conditions are defined:

$(M, w) \models \varphi >_\alpha \psi$ iff   for all $w' \in W$, $(W, w') \models \varphi$ implies $(W, w'') \models \psi$ for some w'' s.t. $S(w', w'') \geq \alpha$

$(M, w) \models \varphi \gg_\alpha \psi$ iff   for each β, $(W, w') \models \varphi$ and $S(w, w') \geq \beta$ implies $(W, w'') \models \psi$ for some w'' s.t. $S(w, w'') \geq \alpha \otimes \beta$

Note that the first condition is actually independent from the world w, it is thus a global condition which is indeed equivalent to the validity in M of $\varphi \to \Diamond_\alpha \psi$ in the previous multi-modal framework, and hence to the validity of the approximate entailment $\varphi \models_S^\alpha \psi$ (when φ and ψ are non modal). The second condition is indeed local, and it is easy to check that the condition of $\varphi \gg_\alpha \psi$ being valid in M is indeed captures the proximity entailment $\varphi \models^\alpha \psi$. The technical details of this graded conditional approach will be described in Section 6.2.

In both the graded modal and conditional logical frameworks, the following classes of models will be considered:

$\Sigma_0 \quad = \{M = (W, S, e) \mid S \text{ is a fuzzy relation}\}$,
$\Sigma_1 \quad = \{M = (W, S, e) \mid S \text{ is a serial fuzzy relation}\}$,
$\Sigma_2 \quad = \{M = (W, S, e) \mid S \text{ is a reflexive fuzzy relation}\}$,
$\Sigma_3 \quad = \{M = (W, S, e) \mid S \text{ is a reflexive and symmetric fuzzy relation}\}$,
$\Sigma_4 \quad = \{M = (W, S, e) \mid S \text{ is a reflexive and } \otimes\text{-transitivity fuzzy relation}\}$,
$\Sigma_\otimes \quad = \{M = (W, S, e) \mid S \text{ is a } \otimes\text{-similarity relation}\}$.

where we assume the fuzzy relations to take values on some given countable $C \subset [0,1]$, i.e. $S : W \times W \to C$, and in the class $\Sigma_\otimes$ we are also assuming that the t-norm $\otimes$ is closed on C. Furthermore, the notations Σ_i^* and Σ_{if} will be used to denote the subclasses of Σ_i ($i \in \{1, 2, 3, 4, \otimes\}$) where the fuzzy relation is separating as well, and where the set of worlds is finite, respectively. As it is obvious, we have that $\Sigma_0 \supseteq \Sigma_1 \supseteq \Sigma_2 \supseteq \Sigma_3, \Sigma_4 \supseteq \Sigma_\otimes$ and therefore, their corresponding sets of valid formulas satisfy the inverse inclusion.

Yet another line of modeling, alternative to the two above multi-modal frameworks, has been proposed in the literature. It consists in understanding the grades of the modal and conditional operators as truth-values of some related syntactic many-valued objects. For instance, if p is a proposition, one can consider another (fuzzy) proposition $\Diamond p$, read as "*approximately p*" and, given a similarity Kripke frame (W, S), define the truth-value of $\Diamond p$ in a world w as the value $e(w, \Diamond p) = I_S(p \mid w) \in [0,1]$, i.e. the greatest α for which $(M, w) \models \Diamond_\alpha p$. Then one can use a suitable t-norm based fuzzy logic (Haj98; GH05), like Gödel or Łukasiewicz logics, expanded with truth-constants (EGGN07) as base logic to reason about the modalities. In such a framework, the evaluation $e(w, \overline{\alpha} \to \Diamond p)$ of a formula of the form $\overline{\alpha} \to \Diamond p$, where $\overline{\alpha}$ is a truth-constant representing the value α and $\to$ is interpreted as the residuum of a t-norm, takes value 1 iff $e(w, \Diamond p) \geq \alpha$. Hence, the 1-validity of $\overline{\alpha} \to \Diamond p$ in (W, S) is again equivalent to the validity of $\Diamond_\alpha p$.

Analogously, one may introduce (fuzzy) modalities $>$ and $\gg$ in such a way that the truth values of $p > q$ and $p \gg q$ in a world $w \in W$ be $e(w, p > q) = I_S(q \mid p)$ and $e(w, p \gg q) = J_{S,w}(q \mid q)$. These approaches, fully developed in (Rod02), are recalled in Sections 6.3 and 6.4 respectively.

In what follows we will use the special symbol $\mathcal{M}_S$ to denote the similarity Kripke model (Ω, S, e) where Ω is the set of all boolean interpretations of $\mathbf{L}$, $S : \Omega \times \Omega \to C \subset [0,1]$ is a similarity relation (of some of the above types), and $e : \Omega \times Var \to \{0,1\}$ is the truth-evaluations of variables naturally induced by the elements of Ω, i.e. $e(w, p) = w(p)$ for any $w \in \Omega$ and any propositional variable p.

6.1   Multi-modal logic approach

The use of *graded modalities* is a very well known tool in Philosophy and Computer Science. Several authors, for instance Goble (Glo70), Fine (Fin72), Fattorosi-Barnaba and De Caro (FD85), provide graded modal operators $\Box_n$ (with $n \in N$) interpreted as *"there are more than (or at least) n accessible worlds such that..."*. Graded languages with this interpretation were applied to the areas of epistemic logic (HM92) and of generalised quantifiers (HR91). Here, the conceptual framework and technical features are very different.

A general formalization of the similarity-based graded modal logic, as proposed in (EGGR97), can be summarized as follows:

• Modal Language: The new language $\mathcal{L}$ is built over $\mathbf{L}$ by adding modal operators $\Diamond_\alpha^c$ and $\Diamond_\alpha^o$ for every rational $\alpha \in C$, where $\{0,1\} \subseteq C \subseteq [0,1]$.

• Formulae: They are built from a set V (not necessarily finite) of propositional variables using the classical binary connectives $\wedge$, $\vee$ and $\to$, and the unary operators $\neg$, $\Diamond_\alpha^c$ and $\Diamond_\alpha^o$ for every rational $\alpha \in C$, in the usual way.

• Satisfiability: Let $M = (W, S, e)$, $\omega \in W$ and φ be a formula of $\mathcal{L}$. Then, we define:
$$(M, \omega) \models \Diamond_\alpha^c \varphi \quad \text{if} \quad I_S(\varphi \mid \omega) \geq \alpha,$$
$$(M, \omega) \models \Diamond_\alpha^o \varphi \quad \text{if} \quad I_S(\varphi \mid \omega) > \alpha.$$

The rest of the conditions are the usual ones. Note that this notion of satisfiability needs a definition of implication measure for modal formulas since the definition given above is only valid for non modal formulas. Nevertheless, the implication measure for modal formulas φ is defined as a natural extension in the following way,

$$I_S(\varphi \mid \omega) = \sup\{S(\omega,\omega') \mid (\mathcal{M},\omega') \models \varphi\}.$$

we shall also introduce the corresponding family of dual modal operators $\square_\alpha^c$ and $\square_\alpha^o$ as $\neg\lozenge_\alpha^c\neg$ and $\neg\lozenge_\alpha^o\neg$ respectively, and whose satisfiability conditions are:

$(M,\omega) \models \square_\alpha^c\varphi$ if $I_S(\neg\varphi \mid \omega) < \alpha,$
$(M,\omega) \models \square_\alpha^o\varphi$ if $I_S(\neg\varphi \mid \omega) \le \alpha.$

It is easy to see that whenever W is finite, $\lozenge_\alpha^c$ and $\square_\alpha^c$ have the usual Kripke semantics with respect to the accessibility relation S_α^c defined as

$$\omega S_\alpha^c\omega' \quad \text{iff} \quad S(\omega,\omega') \ge \alpha.$$

In contrast, the *strict* cuts S_α^o of S, i.e. $\omega S_\alpha^o\omega'$ iff $S(\omega,\omega') > \alpha$, always provide the modal operators $\lozenge_\alpha^o$ and $\square_\alpha^o$ with the usual Kripke semantics, even when W is not finite.

• Axioms: For the axiomatic characterization of the different multi-modal systems, let us consider the following schemes, where, as usual, C denotes the range of the fuzzy relations and it is assumed to be of the form $\{0,1\} \subseteq C \subseteq [0,1]$ and closed with respect to the operation $\otimes$:

K^c: $\square_\alpha^c(\varphi \to \psi) \to (\square_\alpha^c\varphi \to \square_\alpha^c\psi), \forall\alpha \in C$
K^o: $\square_\alpha^o(\varphi \to \psi) \to (\square_\alpha^o\varphi \to \square_\alpha^o\psi), \forall\alpha \in C$
D: $\square_1^c\varphi \to \lozenge_1^c\varphi$
T^c: $\square_\alpha^c\varphi \to \varphi, \forall\alpha \in C$
T^o: $\square_\alpha^o\varphi \to \varphi, \text{ for } \alpha < 1$
C^c: $\varphi \to \square_1^c\varphi$
B^c: $\varphi \to \square_\alpha^c\lozenge_\alpha^c\varphi, \text{ for } \alpha > 0$
B^o: $\varphi \to \square_\alpha^o\lozenge_\alpha^o\varphi, \forall\alpha \in C$
4^c: $\square_{\alpha\otimes\beta}^c\varphi \to \square_\beta^c\square_\alpha^c\varphi, \forall\alpha,\beta \in C$
4°: $\square_{\alpha\otimes\beta}^o\varphi \to \square_\beta^o\square_\alpha^o\varphi, \forall\alpha,\beta \in C$
N^c: $\square_\alpha^c\varphi \to \square_\beta^c\varphi, \text{ for } \beta \ge \alpha,$
N^o: $\square_\alpha^o\varphi \to \square_\beta^o\varphi, \text{ for } \beta \ge \alpha$
EX^c: $\lozenge_0^c\varphi,$
EX^o: $\neg\lozenge_1^o\varphi,$
CO: $\square_\alpha^c\varphi \to \square_\alpha^o\varphi, \forall\alpha \in C$
OC: $\square_\alpha^o\varphi \to \square_\beta^c\varphi, \text{ for } \alpha < \beta,$

and the following inference rules

MP: From φ and $\varphi \rightarrow \psi$ infer ψ.

RN^c: From φ infer $\square_\alpha^c \varphi$, for $\alpha > 0$.

RN^o: From φ infer $\square_\alpha^o \varphi$, $\forall \alpha \in C$.

- **Completeness**: The following completeness results, where PL stands for propositional tautologies, have been proved in (EGGR97):

  - The axiom system $\mathbf{MS5(C, \otimes)^{++}} = PL + K^c + K^o + CO + OC + EX^c + EX^o + T^c + B^o + B^c + 4^o + 4^c + C^c$ is complete with respect to the subclass of finite models of $\Sigma_\otimes^*$ when C is a dense and denumerable and $\otimes = \min$.
  - If C is finite, then the axiom system $\mathbf{MS5(C, \otimes)^+}$ consisting of PL, K^c, B^c, 4^c, C^c, N^c, EX^c, plus MP and RN^c is complete with respect to the class of models $\Sigma_\otimes^*$, for any t-norm $\otimes$. In this case we shall see that the open and closed modalities are interdefinable, and the resulting modal system can be simplified.
  - If we remove axiom C^c from the system $\mathbf{MS5(C, \otimes)^{++}}$ we get a complete system with respect to the subclass of models $\Sigma_{\otimes f}$ when C is dense and denumerable and $\otimes = \min$.
  - If C is finite and we remove axiom C^c from the system $\mathbf{MS5(C, \otimes)^+}$ we get a complete system with respect to $\Sigma_\otimes$.
  - If C is finite and we remove axiom 4^c ($+ C^c$ resp.) from the system $\mathbf{MS5(C, \otimes)^+}$ we get a complete system with respect to Σ_2^* (with respect to Σ_2 resp.).

Once the presentation of the logics is done, we are able to formally claim that the basic similarity-based graded consequence relation proposed in (DEG+95) is fully captured inside these multi-modal systems. Namely, given a similarity relation S on the set of interpretations Ω of a propositional language $\mathbf{L}$, if p and q are non-modal formulas, then we have that the *approximate entailment* corresponds to

$$p \models_S^\alpha q \text{ iff } \mathcal{M}_S \models p \rightarrow \lozenge_\alpha^c q.$$

If C is finite, then proximity entailments can be captured as well:

$$p \models_{S,K}^\alpha q \text{ iff } \mathcal{M}_S \models K \rightarrow \bigwedge_{\beta \in C} (\lozenge_\beta^c p \rightarrow \lozenge_{\beta \otimes \alpha}^c q).$$

Finally, we briefly describe three modal systems that can be found in the literature and which are close to the above mentioned ones:

(i) In (LL92; LL95) Liau and Lin define a multi-modal system like the one presented here. One goal of that paper is the relationship of their modal system with *possibilistic logic* and therefore they consider models such that the relation R only satisfies the so-called *serial* property, i.e. for all $\omega \in W$, $\sup_{\omega' \in W} R(\omega, \omega') = 1$. Obviously this property is weaker than reflexivity, but to model truthlikeness does not seem meaningful to consider serial relations which are not reflexive, since in that case the corresponding mapping might be such that the approximation p^* of a proposition p would not contain the set $[p]$ of interpretations of p. In their works, Liau and Lin propose a Quantitative modal logic (QML) with $C = [0,1]$ and prove the following completeness results:

- The axiom system **SK** consisting of PL, K^c, K^o, CO, OC, EX^c, EX^o, together with the MP and RN^o inference rules is complete with respect to the class of models Σ_0.
- The axiom system **SKD** = SK + D is complete with respect to the class of models Σ_1.
- The axiom system **SKT** = SK + T^c is complete with respect to the class of models Σ_2.

(ii) In a very interesting work, Suzuki (Suz97) proposes a more general semantics by considering a partial fuzzy accessibility function instead of a total fuzzy function, as it is the case with our fuzzy similarity relations. He also describes almost all families of modal systems that we considered above. But, he only gives a logic of similarity relations when they are min-transitive. Besides, he only establishes completeness results for the cases that the range of the partial fuzzy function is an arbitrary *finite* subset of $[0,1]$. Moreover, strong completeness is not available in the general case. However, we think this work is important because some other general results which are natural extensions of well-known ones in classical modal logic, are presented in his work, as for instance, the definition of F-filtration, Craig's interpolation theorem, etc.

(iii) Finally, another similar logic is proposed in (CF92). The logic is called lattice-based graded logic and contains modal operators $\Box_\alpha$ which are formed for all α from a finite lattice structure instead of the countable set C considered above where $\{0,1\} \subseteq C \subseteq [0,1]$. They adopt a semantics which involves a family of accessibility relations R_α for each α in the lattice (also called multi-relational model in (FH91)). In the finite case, when R_α's are nested equivalence relations, their semantics is equivalent to the one with min-transitive similarity relations.

6.2 Multi-conditional logic approach

The idea of the graded conditional logic approach is to encode in the language syntactical objects representing both approximate and proximity entailments $p \models^{\alpha} q$ and $p \models^{\alpha} q$. To do so, binary (graded) modal operators are introduced (under some restrictions, e.g. nested modal formulas are not allowed, and the language is finitely generated) and given appropriate semantics in terms of similarity Kripke structures. Following (Rod02), the main notions involved in the graded conditional logical framework to model similarity-based reasoning can be summarized as follows:

- Conditional Language: The propositional language $\mathbf{L}_f$ generated from a finite set *Var* of propositional variables is extended by two families $\{>_{\alpha}\}_{\alpha \in C}$ and $\{\gg_{\alpha}\}_{\alpha \in C}$ of binary operators, where $\{0,1\} \subseteq C \subseteq [0,1]$.

- Conditional Formulae:
    - If p is a propositional formula then it is also a conditional formula.
    - If p and q are propositional formulas in $\mathbf{L}_f$ then for every $\alpha \in C$: $p >_{\alpha} q$ and $p \gg_{\alpha} q$ are conditional formulas.
    - If φ and ϕ are conditional formulas then $\varphi \circ \phi$ is a conditional formula, where $\circ \in \{\wedge, \vee, \rightarrow\}$.
    - If φ is a conditional formula then $\neg\varphi$ is a conditional formula.
Note that in this language, nested modal formulas are not allowed.

- Satisfiability: Given a model $\mathcal{M} = (W, S, \models)$, a world $\omega \in W$ and formulas p and q of $\mathbf{L}_f$, we define:

$$(\mathcal{M}, \omega) \models p >_{\alpha} q \quad \text{if} \quad I_S(q \mid p) \geq \alpha,$$
$$(\mathcal{M}, \omega) \models p \gg_{\alpha} q \quad \text{if} \quad I_{S,\bar{\omega}}(q \mid p) \geq \alpha,$$

where $\bar{\omega}$ is the maximal elementary conjunction[4] corresponding to ω[5]. The rest of the conditions are the usual ones. Note that the notion of satisfiability for $>_{\alpha}$ is independent of any particular world, i.e. it is a global notion. The last conditions of satisfiability make clear that in the object language $p >_{\alpha} q$ and $p \gg_{\alpha} q$ represent lower bounds of $I_S(q \mid p)$ and $I_{S,\bar{\omega}}(q \mid p)$ respectively.

- Axioms: The following schemes will be used to characterise the different classes of models (Σ_i) above mentioned, where p and q are propositional formulas in $\mathbf{L}_f$, and α and β represent any element in the range C of fuzzy relations.

---

[4]A maximal elementary conjunction, m.e.c. for short, is a conjunction where each propositional variable in *Var* appears either in positive or negative form (remember that we are assuming *Var* be finite).

[5]That is, the conjunction $\bar{\omega} = \bigwedge_{p_i \in Var : \omega(p_i) = 1} p_i \wedge \bigwedge_{p_i \in Var : \omega(p_i) = 0} \neg p_i$.

N: $p >_\alpha q \to p >_\beta q$ if $\beta \le \alpha$.

        $p \gg_\alpha q \to p \gg_\beta q$ if $\beta \le \alpha$

CS: $p >_1 q \to (p \to q)$.

        $p \gg_1 q \to (p \to q)$

EX: $p >_0 q$.

        $p \gg_0 q$

B: $r >_\alpha r' \to r' >_\alpha r$, if r and r' are m.e.c.'s

4: $(p >_\alpha q) \wedge (q >_\beta r) \to p >_{\alpha \otimes \beta} r$

        $(p \gg_\alpha q) \wedge (q \gg_\beta r) \to p \gg_{\alpha \otimes \beta} r$

LO: $(p \vee q >_\alpha r) \leftrightarrow (p >_\alpha r) \wedge (q >_\alpha r)$

        $(p \vee q \gg_\alpha r) \leftrightarrow (p \gg_\alpha r) \wedge (q \gg_\alpha r)$

RO: $(r >_\alpha p \vee q) \leftrightarrow (r >_\alpha p) \vee (r >_\alpha q)$, if r is a m.e.c.

        $(s \gg_\alpha p \vee q) \leftrightarrow (s \gg_\alpha p) \vee (s \gg_\alpha q)$

and the following inference rules:

MP: From φ and $\varphi \to \psi$ infer ψ

RK: From $p_1 \wedge \cdots \wedge p_n \to q$ infer $p_1 \wedge \cdots \wedge p_n >_\alpha q$

        From $p_1 \wedge \cdots \wedge p_n \to q$ infer $p_1 \wedge \cdots \wedge p_n \gg_\alpha q$

• Completeness: The following completeness results have been proved (Rod02) for different classes of models Σ in which the set W is fixed to the set of all boolean interpretations of $\mathbf{L}_f$, for any t-norm $\otimes$ and range C. From now on, PL will stand for propositional tautologies. Here, we consider two kinds of logical systems: **CSI** and **CSJ**. In the first, the operators $\gg_\alpha$ do not appear and in the second, the operators $>_\alpha$ are not used. Next we list the available completeness results for the **CSI** logics and for the **CSJ** logics.

- The approximate conditional system $\mathbf{CSI}(\mathbf{C}, \otimes) = PL + N + EX + LO + RO$ and closed under MP and RK is complete with respect to Σ_{2f}. Furthermore, it is possible to prove completeness with respect to the subclasses of models Σ_{3f}, Σ_{4f} and $\Sigma_{\otimes f}$ if we add to $\mathbf{CSI}(\mathbf{C}, \otimes)$ the axioms B, 4 and both B and 4, respectively.

- The system $\mathbf{CSI}(\mathbf{C}, \otimes)^+$, the extension of $\mathbf{CSI}(\mathbf{C}, \otimes)$ with axiom CS, is complete with respect to the subclass of models Σ_{2f}^*. Again, it is possible to extend this result of completeness for the subclasses of models Σ_{3f}^*, Σ_{4f}^* and $\Sigma_{\otimes f}^*$ by adding to $\mathbf{CSI}(\mathbf{C}, \otimes)^+$ the axioms B, 4 and both B and 4, respectively.

- The proximity conditional system $\mathbf{CSJ}(\mathbf{C}, \otimes) = PL + N + EX + LO + RO + 4$ and closed under MP and RK is complete with respect to Σ_{4f}.

- The system $\mathbf{CSJ}(\mathbf{C}, \otimes)^+$, the extension of $\mathbf{CSJ}(\mathbf{C}, \otimes)$ with axiom CS, is complete with respect to the subclass of models Σ^*_{4f}.

Graded approximate and proximity entailments are captured in $\mathbf{CSI}(\mathbf{C}, \otimes)$ and $\mathbf{CSJ}(\mathbf{C}, \otimes)$ as follows:

approximate entailment: $\quad p \models^\alpha_{S,K} q \quad$ iff $\quad \mathcal{M}_S \models K \to p >_\alpha q$

proximity entailment: $\quad p \models^\alpha_{S,K} q \quad$ iff $\quad \mathcal{M}_S \models K \to p \gg_\alpha q$

where $\mathcal{M}_S$ is the similarity Kripke model over the set of all Boolean interpretations of the finitely generated language $\mathbf{L}_f$.

Regarding related work, let us mention that Liau (Lia98) defines what he calls *residuated implication operators* $\overset{\alpha}{\Longrightarrow}$ and $\overset{\alpha^+}{\Longrightarrow}$ corresponding to $\gg_\alpha$ and its strict counterpart, respectively. He shows how to capture the approximate and proximity entailments proposed in (DEG$^+$95) with these implication operators. However, his considerations are purely semantical. Besides, his motivation is very different because he aims at defining a logical system where quantitative and qualitative uncertainty may be combined. According to this author, probabilistic, Dempster-Shafer and possibilistic theories are included in the first kind of uncertainty, and rough sets and nonmonotonic theories belong to the second class. In fact, his residuated implication operators may be seen as graded generalisations of qualitative possibility relations (Dub86). We also mention that Liau and Lin (LL96) define a logic for conditional possibility (LCP) based on Dempster's conditional rule, but LCP is able to model similarity-based entailment only when the similarity relation is min-transitive. Besides, although an axiomatic system for LCP is exhibited in its appendix, completeness results are not established. They mention that their main difficulty in order to obtain a completeness result lies in the infiniteness of the language. This problem is however different from the above conditional logics: the need of considering a finite language was due to properly cope with the Symmetry and Right-Or properties.

6.3 Many-valued modal logic approach

As already mentioned in the introduction of this section, a possibly more elegant way of formalising similarity-based reasoning in a modal framework is to shift from a family of graded classical modalities $\Diamond_\alpha$ (one for each $\alpha \in G$) to a single many-valued modality $\Diamond$. The idea is that, even if p is a two-valued formula, $\Diamond p$, to be read as *approximately p*, is a many-valued formula which takes $I_S(p \mid w) = \sup\{S(w, w') \mid (M, w') \models p\}$ as truth-value in a world w from a model $M = (W, S, e)$, i. e. such that $e(w, \Diamond p) =$

$I_S(p \mid w)$. Therefore one needs to choose a suitable (t-norm based) fuzzy logic as base logic to reason about the modal formulas. If one also wants to reason explicitly with truthlikeness degrees, then the base fuzzy logic has to be expanded with truth constants, for instance by adding a constant $\overline{\alpha}$ for each $\alpha \in C$. These expansions have been studied for instance in (EGGN07) for the case of logics of continuous t-norms (thus including Łukasiewicz, Gödel and Product fuzzy logics).

However, with the above semantics, one would be led to define a language without nested modal operators. If one wants to be as general as possible, one has to generalize the above semantics and allow to deal with modal formulas of the form $\Diamond \varphi$, where φ may be in turn a many-valued formula. Indeed, there have been many attempts in the literature to mix many-valued (or fuzzy) and modal logic semantics, obeying to very different motivations. These logics consider the fuzzification of either the valuation function or the accessibility relation in the Kripke model (or both). A complete analysis of all alternative semantics is provided by Thiele in (Thi93). As it is reported there, there are different ways to face with the problem of how the truth values of a formula p in two worlds ω and ω' can be combined with the "degree of accessibility" of ω' from ω, expressed as the value of a fuzzy relation $R(\omega, \omega')$.

Most of the alternatives have appeared as a direct generalisation of the classical definitions of possibility and necessity. It is easy to see that the classical definitions are equivalent to the following ones:

$$\begin{aligned} e(\omega, \Diamond p) &= \sup_{\omega' \in W} R(\omega, \omega') \wedge e(\omega', p) \\ e(\omega, \Box p) &= \inf_{\omega' \in W} R(\omega, \omega') \Rightarrow e(\omega', p) \end{aligned}$$

where the existential and universal quantifiers are interpreted by supremum and infimum operators, respectively. When we shift from $\{0,1\}$-valued to $[0,1]$-valued evaluations e and accessibility relations R, following the tradition of fuzzy logics the *and* connective $\wedge$ is usually associated to a (left-continuous) t-norm (e. g. Gödel, Łukasiewicz or Product), and the *implication* connective $\Rightarrow$ has is associated to its residuum (although other interpretations exist, see e. g. (Yin88)).

This is the alternative taken by Fitting (see (Fit91; Fit92; Fit95)) in his many-valued modal logic. His many-valued modal logic includes truth constants that are the syntactical counterpart of truth values, but it is confined to the case where the set of truth values is finite and the t-norm is min. As another example of this alternative, although somehow particular, we mention Hájek and Harmancová's work (HH96) (see also (Haj98) for a further elaboration) where they study a modal logic over a Pavelka-like extension of the infinitely valued Łukasiewicz's logic. Their logic is a many-valued counterpart of the well-known classical system **S5** and proved to complete with respect to Kripke models with the universal accessibility relation (i.e. $\forall \omega, \omega' : R(\omega, \omega') = 1$).

But probably the most interesting work for the purposes of modelling similarity-based reasoning is (CR07) where Caicedo and Rodríguez define a very general many-valued modal logic over Gödel fuzzy logic by introducing independently a possibility modal operator $\Diamond$ (with the intended meaning of $\Diamond p$ as *approximately-p*) and a necessity modal operator $\Box$ (since they are are not dual). Moreover, to explicitly deal with similarity degrees in the language they take as base logic the expansion of Gödel logic with rational truth-constants, called RG in (EGN06), but with only a finite set of truth-constants. In the following we summarize the most interesting features of the $\Diamond$-fragment of that related modal systems

- Language: propositional variables, truths constant $\bar{\alpha}$ for each rational $\alpha \in C$ (where $\{0,1\} \subseteq C \subset [0,1]$ is finite) logical connectives of Gödel fuzzy logic $\wedge, \rightarrow$ (other connectives are definable, e.g. $\neg\varphi$ is $\varphi \rightarrow \bar{0}$) and one modality $\Diamond$.

- Formulae: they are built in the usual way from a set *Var* of propositional variables using the binary connectives $\wedge$, $\rightarrow$, truth-constants and the unary operator $\Diamond$

- Satisfiability: models are Gödel similarity Kripke models $M = \langle W, S, e_G \rangle$, in which $W \neq \emptyset$ is a set of possible worlds, S is a similarity relation on $W \times W$ and e represents an evaluation assigning to each atomic formula p_i and each interpretation $w \in W$ a truth value $e(p_i, w) \in [0,1]$ of p_i in w. e is extended to formulas by means of Gödel logic truth functions by defining

$e(\varphi \wedge \psi, w) = \min(e(\varphi, w), e(\psi, w))$,
$e(\varphi \rightarrow \psi, w) = e(\varphi, w) \Rightarrow_G e(\psi, w)$,

where $\Rightarrow_G$ is the well-known Gödel implication function[6], and

$e(\bar{r}, w) = r$, for all $r \in C$,
$e(\Diamond\varphi, w) = \sup_{w' \in W} \min\{S(w, w'), e(\varphi, w')\}$.

- Axioms: we include here below the axioms of Rational Gödel logic and a list of modal axioms

Axioms of Rational Gödel logic (RG):

---

[6] $\Rightarrow_G$ is defined as $x \Rightarrow_G y = 1$ if $x \leq y$ and $x \Rightarrow_G y = y$, otherwise

$$(\varphi \to \psi) \to ((\psi \to \chi) \to (\varphi \to \chi))$$
$$\varphi \to (\psi \to \varphi)$$
$$(\varphi \wedge \psi) \to (\psi \wedge \varphi)$$
$$(\varphi \wedge (\psi \wedge \chi)) \to ((\psi \wedge \varphi) \wedge \chi)$$
$$(\varphi \to (\psi \to \chi)) \equiv ((\varphi \wedge \psi) \to \chi)$$
$$((\varphi \to \psi) \to \chi) \to (((\psi \to \varphi) \to \chi) \to \chi)$$
$$\bar{0} \to \varphi$$
$$\varphi \to (\varphi \wedge \varphi)$$
$$\bar{r} \wedge \bar{s} \equiv \overline{\min\{r,s\}}, \text{ for } r, s \in C$$
$$\bar{r} \to \bar{s} \equiv \overline{r \Rightarrow s}, \text{ for } r, s \in C$$

Modal Axioms:

$D_\Diamond$: $\Diamond(\varphi \vee \psi) \to (\Diamond\varphi \vee \Diamond\psi)$

$Z_\Diamond^+$: $\Diamond\neg\neg\varphi \to \neg\neg\Diamond\varphi$

$T_\Diamond$: $\varphi \to \Diamond\varphi$

$B_\Diamond$: $\varphi \to \neg\Diamond\neg\Diamond\varphi$

$4_\Diamond$: $\Diamond\Diamond\varphi \to \Diamond\varphi$

$R1$: $\Diamond\bar{r} \to \bar{r}$

$R2$: $\Diamond(\bar{r} \to \varphi) \to (\bar{r} \to \Diamond\varphi)$

$R3$: $\Diamond((\varphi \to \bar{r}) \to \bar{r}) \to ((\Diamond\varphi \to \bar{r}) \to \bar{r})$

and the following inference rules:

$RN_\Diamond^+$: From $\varphi \to \psi$ infer $\Diamond\varphi \to \Diamond\psi$

MP: From φ and $\varphi \to \psi$, infer ψ

• Completeness: According to (CR07), the system $FMT_{G,\Diamond}(C, \min) = RG + D_\Diamond + Z_\Diamond^+ + T_\Diamond + R1 + R2 + R3$ is complete with respect to the class of Gödel similarity Kripke models with reflexive similarity relations; the system $FMTB_{G,\Diamond}(C, \min) = FMT_{G,\Diamond}(C, \min) + B_\Diamond$ is complete with respect to the class of Gödel similarity Kripke models with reflexive and symmetric similarity relations, and the system $FMS5_{G,\Diamond}(C, \min) = FMTB_{G,\Diamond}(C, \min) + 4_\Diamond$ is complete with respect to the class of Gödel similarity Kripke models with min-transitive similarity relations. It is worth mentioning that if one adds the axiom

Bool: $\varphi \vee \neg\varphi$, if φ is not modal.

to the above systems, one gets completeness with respect to the corresponding class of models restricted to those where all the propositional (non-modal) formulas are classical (e. g. two-valued), and hence, only the modal formulas can get intermediate truth-values.

As for the question of capturing the approximate and proximity entailments in this many-valued modal framework, it is easy to check that the following statements hold for any Boolean propositions p and q:

approximate entailment: $p \models^\alpha_S q$ iff $\bar{\alpha} \to (p \to \Diamond q)$ is valid in $\mathcal{M}_S$

proximity entailment: $p \models^\alpha_S q$ iff $\bar{\alpha} \to (\Diamond p \to \Diamond q)$ is valid in $\mathcal{M}_S$

where $\mathcal{M}_S = (\Omega, S, e_G)$ is the Gödel similarity Kripke model with Ω being the set of *Boolean* interpretations of the propositional variables *Var*. In other words, $p \models^\alpha_S q$ iff $e(w, \bar{\alpha} \to (p \to \Diamond q)) = 1$ for all $w \in \Omega$, and $p \models^\alpha_S q$ iff $e(w, \bar{\alpha} \to (\Diamond p \to \Diamond q)) = 1$ for all $w \in \Omega$.

It turns out that the main difficulty for defining similar many-valued modal logics over a t-norm-based fuzzy logic different from Gödel logic is the fact that the resulting logics are generally not normal (they do not satisfy axiom K). In particular, this is the case with Łukasiewicz logic with general Kripke semantics (see (GR98) for an attempt), even though in such a case the modal operators $\Diamond$ and $\Box$ are dual ($\Box$ can be defined as $\neg \Diamond \neg$), in contrast to Gödel-based many-valued modal logics . One possibility to avoid this difficulty is to introduce graded modalities $\Box_t$ (where $t \in C$) corresponding to the cuts of the many-valued accessibility relation, i.e. using a semantics of the form

$$e(w, \Box_t \varphi) = \inf\{e(\varphi, w') : R(w, w') \geq t\}$$

to extend the valuation. Then, it is easy to see that all modalities $\Box_t$ are normal. We notice that in some particular cases, axiomatizations for these graded modalities can be found in the literature (see for instance (EGGR97; Suz97; BEGR07)). The case considered in (BEGR07) corresponds to considering the n-valued Łukasiewicz logic $Ł_n$ as base logic and having constants in the language for every element in the standard n-valued Łukasiewicz algebra $AŁ_n = \{0, 1/n, ..., (n-1)/n, n\}$. An interesting fact about this case is that $\Box$ is definable in the new language as

$$\Box \varphi := (\overline{1/n} \to \Box_{1/n} \varphi) \wedge \ldots \wedge (\overline{(n-1)/n} \to \Box_{(n-1)/n} \varphi) \wedge \Box_1 \varphi$$

Finally, let us mention a recent paper by Hansoul and Teheux (HT06) where they axiomatize a modal system over the infinitely-valued Łukasiewicz logic. The proof is based on the construction of a classical canonical model. Surprisingly this proof does not need the presence in the language of constants for every truth value. The trick to avoid the introduction of constants is based on a result of (Ost88) (see (HT06, Definition 5.3)).

6.4 Many-valued conditional logic approach

Combining the approaches of Sections 6.2 and 6.3, the main idea behind a many-valued conditional logic approach is that the truthlikeness degree

with which a (classical) proposition q is an approximate or proximity consequence of another (classical) proposition p is understood as the truth-value
of a (many-valued) conditional formula that has p as its antecedent and
q as its consequent. Therefore one needs to make use of a suitable fuzzy
logic to reason about the conditional formulas. The choice of the particular
fuzzy logic is determined by the class of similarity Kripke models defining
the intended semantics. Namely, if the intended semantics is the class of
$*$-transitive similarity Kripke models, for some (left-continuous) t-norm $*$,
then the fuzzy logic to be chosen will be the t-norm fuzzy logic L_*, extension of MTL or BL, which is complete with respect to the standard
MTL-algebra over $[0,1]_* = ([0,1], *, \Rightarrow, \min, \max, 0, 1)$ defined by t-norm $*$
and its residuum $\Rightarrow$. Such logics have been axiomatized for the whole family
of continuous t-norms (EGM03) as well as for other left-continuous t-norms
(GH05). Moreover if one needs to explicitly deal with degrees then such
logics have to expanded by a countable set of truth-constants (EGGN07).
We will denote by $L_*(\mathcal{C})$ the logic of the t-norm $*$ with truth-constants from
a suitable countable set $C \subset [0,1]$.

In the following we summarize the main characteristics of the many-
valued conditional logic built over the logic $L_*(\mathcal{C})$.

• <u>Language</u>: The language is built from a finite set of propositional variables
Var plus two binary operators $>, \gg$ and a constant $\bar{r}$ for each element r in
the range C. The set of propositional formulas built from Var is denoted
as usual by $\mathbf{L}_f$

• <u>Conditional Formulas</u>: The set of conditional formulas $\mathcal{L}$ is built as follows:

   - Every propositional formula is also a conditional formula.
   - If p and q are propositional formulas in $\mathbf{L}_f$ then $p > q$ and $p \gg q$ are
     (atomic) conditional formulas.
   - Truth-constants $\bar{r}$, with $r \in C$, are conditional formulas.
   - If φ and ϕ are conditional formulas then $\varphi \circ \phi$ is a conditional formula
     where $\circ \in \{\wedge, , \&, \rightarrow\}$ (connectives $\neg$, $\vee$ and $\leftrightarrow$ are definable).

• <u>Satisfiability</u>: A $L_*(\mathcal{C})$-similarity Kripke model is just a usual similarity
Kripke model $M = (W, S, e)$, where now $e(w, \cdot)$ is a $\{0,1\}$-valued interpretation of propositional variables for each $w \in W$, and is extended to atomic
conditional formulas as follows:

$$e(\omega, p > q) \quad = \quad I_S(q \mid p)$$
$$e(\omega, p \gg q) \quad = \quad I_{S,\bar{\omega}}(q \mid p)$$

and to compound conditional formulas as usual ones in t-norm-based
logics, i.e.

$$e(\omega, \varphi \wedge \psi) \quad = \quad \min(e(\omega, \varphi), e(\omega, \psi))$$
$$e(\omega, \varphi \& \psi) \quad = \quad e(\omega, \varphi) * e(\omega, \psi)$$
$$e(\omega, \varphi \to \psi) \quad = \quad e(\omega, \varphi) \Rightarrow e(\omega, \psi)$$

Again, notice that the notion of satisfiability for a conditional formula of the kind $p > q$ is independent of the particular world, i.e. it is global notion, but is not the case with the conditional formulas of the form $p \gg q$. In this case it is also clear that a formula $p > q$ directly represents $I_S(q \mid p)$ whilst $p \gg q$ represents $I_{S,\bar{\omega}}(q \mid p)$.

• Axioms: Besides the axioms of $L_*(\mathcal{C})$, the following axioms will be used to characterise our many-valued conditional logic:

Bool: $\quad p \vee \neg p$, for p propositional (non conditional).

B: $\qquad p > q \to q > p$, if p and q are m.e.c.

4: $\qquad (p > q)\&(q > s) \to p > s$.
$\qquad\quad (p \gg q)\&(q \gg s) \to p \gg s$.

LO: $\qquad (p \vee q) > r \leftrightarrow (p > r) \wedge (q > r)$.
$\qquad\quad (p \vee q) \gg r \leftrightarrow (p \gg r) \wedge (q \gg r)$.

RO: $\qquad (r > p \vee q) \leftrightarrow (r > p) \vee (r > q)$, if r is a m.e.c.
$\qquad\quad (s \gg p \vee q) \leftrightarrow (s \gg p) \vee (s \gg q)$

and the following inference rules:

MP: $\quad$ From φ and $\varphi \to \psi$ infer ψ
RK: $\quad$ From $p \to q$ infer $p > q$
$\qquad\quad$ From $p \to q$ infer $p \gg q$

• Completeness: Again, two kinds of systems are considered: approximate fuzzy conditional systems **FCSI** and proximity fuzzy conditional systems **FCSJ**. In the first case only the operator $>$ is used and in the second case, the operator $\gg$ is the only used. The completeness results may be summarised as follows:

- The system **FCSI**$(\mathbf{C}, \otimes)$, which has as axioms: $L_\otimes(\mathcal{C}) + Bool + LO + RO$ and is closed under MP and RK, is complete with respect to the class of models Σ_{2f}. Moreover, we obtain completeness with respect to the subclasses of models Σ_{3f}, Σ_{4f} and $\Sigma_{\otimes f}$ if we add to **FCSI**$(\mathbf{C}, \otimes)$ the axioms B, 4 and both B and 4, respectively.
- The system **FCSJ**$(\mathbf{C}, \otimes) = L_\otimes(\mathcal{C}) + Bool + LO + RO + 4$ and closed under MP and RK is complete with respect to Σ_{4f}.

Note that these conditional logics do not have the axiom CS as in the multi-conditional framework and hence they cannot be complete for the classes of models Σ_i^* (with $i \in \{1, 2, 3, 4, \otimes\}$). To be so, one would need to introduce in the logics Baaz's projection connective Δ.

If S is $\otimes$-transitive similarity relation on the set Ω of all Boolean interpretations of the propositional language $\mathbf{L}_f$, the corresponding approximate and proximity entailments are captured by the $\mathbf{FCSI}(\mathbf{C}, \otimes)$ and $\mathbf{FCSJ}(\mathbf{C}, \otimes)$ systems in the following sense:

approximate entailment: $p \models^\alpha_S q$ iff $\overline{\alpha} \to (p > q)$ is valid in $\mathcal{M}_S$

proximity entailment: $p \models^\alpha_{S,K} q$ iff $\overline{\alpha} \to (K \to (p \gg q))$ is valid in $\mathcal{M}_S$

where $\mathcal{M}_S = (\Omega, S, e)$ is defined as in the previous section.

7   Other issues in similarity-based reasoning

Traditional entailments are always monotonic: adding new premises never invalidate old conclusions, i.e. the set of conclusions increases monotonically with the set of premises. In this sense, the approximate and proximity entailments are also monotonic, because due to their definitions of satisfiability, for any similarity relation S, the following occurs:

$$p \models^\alpha_S q \quad \text{implies} \quad p \wedge r \models^\alpha_S q$$
$$p \models^\alpha_{S,K} q \quad \text{implies} \quad p \wedge r \models^\alpha_{S,K} q$$

However, in some kinds of reasoning like approximate, case-based or interpolative where the notion of similarity between situations plays a central role, sometimes it is necessary to have nonmonotonic entailments based on similarity like Lehmann's Stereotypical reasoning (Leh98), or a most recent proposal to provide a logical interpretation (in terms of nonmonotonic inferences) of dilation and erosion operators used in mathematical morphology techniques (BL02). Essentially, this kind of reasoning tries to "jump" to conclusions without having complete information about the state of the world, i.e. since the descriptions of complex domains are naturally incomplete it is necessary to resort to assumptions, "defaults" , etc. in order to "fill up" holes of ignorance with assumptions which are taken as valid while there is not any evidence against them. They are nonmonotonic in the sense that the increase of the amount of available information as premises may sometimes lead to the loss of some of previously drawn conclusions. This is in contrast with the situation for purely deductive reasoning.

In this section we describe some forms of nonmonotonic inference based on similarity measures between situations as discussed in (GR02), in particular, those that can be interpreted in terms of consistency and implication measures. Finally, we also consider the relation between similarity reasoning and a very close topic to nonmonotonic reasoning which is belief revision.

7.1 Similarity-based nonmonotonic reasoning

In the recent past, a lot of efforts have been devoted for developing various approaches to combine uncertain and nonmonotonic reasoning. For instance, probabilistic semantics for defaults have been developed by Geffner (Gef88) and Pearl (Pea88) on the basis of Adam's logic of conditionals, and the relation between possibilistic logic and nonmonotonicity was early established by Dubois and Prade (DP91c).

In (GR02), the authors consider the issue of combining both similarity-based and nonmonotonic reasonings. Namely, they study which kinds of nonmonotonic inference relations naturally arise when using implication and consistency measures to rank propositions à la Gärdenfors and Makinson (GM94). These measures generate two different types of nonmonotonic inferences, namely pessimistic and optimistic inferences. The approach based on *consistency* measures is indeed very close to Possibility theory, and we refer to it as optimistic because it takes into account the "closest" or "best" situations. On the contrary, the approach based on *implication* measures is based on two new ideas: a new kind of orderings between sentences called *inclusion orderings* and a new implication-like measure, which is called *counter-implication* measure, where $L_S(p \mid K)$ indicates the degree to how close is $\neg p$ to imply $\neg K$. This approach may be called pessimistic because it considers the worst situation in order to make an assumption. These two notions are combined to obtain a new form to define comparative entailments.

In both cases, the starting point is to use an ordering between formulas to determinate when a proposition p nonmonotonically implies another proposition q meaning that q follows from p together with all the propositions that are expected in the light of p. In order to formalise this notion of expectation, Makinson and Gärdenfors in (GM94) assume that there is an ordering $\leq^E$ of the sentences in a given language $\mathcal{L}$. Thus, given two sentences p and q, $p \leq^E q$ should be interpreted as "q is at least as expected as p" or "p is at least as surprising as q" (we shall write "$p <^E q$" as an abbreviation for "not $q \leq^E p$"). Makinson and Gärdenfors propose three properties which, they argue, must be satisfied by any reasonable ordering. They are:

transitivity: If $p \leq^E q$ and $q \leq^E r$, then $p \leq^E r$.
dominance: If $p \models q$, then $p \leq^E q$.
conjunctiveness: $p \leq^E (p \wedge q)$ or $q \leq^E (p \wedge q)$.

The authors point out that the first postulate on *expectation ordering* is very natural for an ordering relation, the second postulate says that a logically stronger sentence is always less expected and the third constraint concerns the relation between the degrees of expectation of a conjunction $p \wedge q$ and the corresponding degrees of p and q respectively. Note that the three conditions imply reflexivity ($p \leq^E p$) and connectivity (either $p \leq^E q$ or $q \leq^E p$). By way of comparison, it may be mentioned that these axioms are three of the five conditions used in (Gär88) and (GM94) to define the notion of *epistemical entrenchment* for the logic of theory change (see next section).

Now this ordering can be used to determine when p nonmonotonically implies q in the case q follows from p together with all the propositions that are expected in the light of p. The natural idea, according to Makinson and Gärdenfors, is to require that the added sentences must be those which are strictly more expected than $\neg p$. This motivates the following definition of comparative entailment $\mid\!\sim$:

$$p \mid\!\sim q \ \text{ iff } \ p \models q \ \text{ or there exists } r \text{ such that } p \wedge r \models q \text{ and } \neg p <^E r, \quad (1)$$

where $\leq^E$ is an ordering satisfying transitivity, dominance and conjunctiveness.

It has been proved in (GM94) that comparative entailments satisfy the desirable properties of Supraclassicality (SC), Left Logical Equivalence (LLE), And, Consistency Preservation (CP), Cut, Or and Rational Monotony (RM) (see (GM94) for their definitions) and vice-versa. So these properties characterize comparative entailments.

An alternative form to define an ordering $\leq^F$ between sentences is proposed by (FHL94), it is called *possibility ordering* and it is required to satisfy the axioms of transitivity, dominance together with:

disjunctiveness $p \vee q \leq^F p$ or $p \vee q \leq^F q$

In this case, $p \leq^F q$ denotes that q is at least as possible as p.

As pointed out in (FHL94), the dual of a possibility ordering, defined as $p \leq^F q$ iff $\neg q \leq^E \neg p$, is an expectation ordering in the above sense of Gärdenfors and Makinson. So, if the condition $\neg p <^E r$ is changed by $\neg r <^F p$ in (1), we shall obtain an equivalent comparative entailment. Furthermore, in (FHL94) it is shown that the following three clauses are equivalent for a possibility ordering $\leq^F$:

1. there is a proposition r such that $p \wedge r \models q$ and $\neg r <^F p$.
2. $p \wedge \neg q <^F p$.
3. $p \wedge \neg q <^F p \wedge q$.

These conditions allow us to give different (but equivalent) versions of (1) in terms of possibility orderings, e. g. $p \mid\!\sim_F q$ iff either $p \models q$ or $p \wedge \neg q <^F p \wedge q$.

Now, we are in condition to focus on the orderings on propositions that a body of evidence K and a similarity measure S on worlds induce when the corresponding consistency measure $C_S(\cdot \mid K)$ is used to rank propositions. As it was mentioned in Section 5, since the consistency measure $C_S(\cdot \mid K)$ is also a possibility measure, the ordering induced on formulas defined by:

$$p \leq_C q \text{ iff } C_S(p \mid K) \leq C_S(q \mid K),\qquad(2)$$

read as "q is at least as consistent (with K) as p", is is a *qualitative possibility* relation in the sense of Dubois (Dub86), i.e. the qualitative counterpart of a possibility measure. A qualitative possibility relation is a possibility ordering (as defined above) together with this further axiom

non-triviality: $\perp <_C \top$

where $<_C$ is the strict part of the ordering $\leq_C$. According to the previous section, the corresponding comparative entailment $\vdash_C$ is then defined as

$$p \vdash_C q \text{ iff either } p \models q \text{ or } p \wedge \neg q <_C p \wedge q.$$

Although some are stronger than the others, in (FHL94) it is shown that qualitative possibility relations and possibility orderings generate the same family of nonmonotonic entailments [7]. Consequently, a consequence relation $\vdash$ satisfies SC, LLE, And, CP, Cut, Or and RM iff there exists a proposition K and a similarity S on possible worlds such that $p \vdash q$ iff $p \models q$ or $C_S(p \wedge q \mid K) > C_S(p \wedge \neg q \mid K)$. Indeed, although the orderings of sentences defined by consistency measures $\leq_C$ are qualitative possibility orderings, they have a different meaning because $p \leq_C q$ means q is at least as consistent with K as p, where the level of consistency is understood as a degree of closeness to K. This way of interpreting the ordering is different to the ones based on preference or possibility. Next, we consider another way to define nonmonotonic inference relations from a more interesting perspective because the ordering is induced taking into account the most distant worlds instead of the closest ones.

As it is pointed out by Makinson in (Mak94, pag. 46), if we want to abandon monotony then we will also have to abandon contraposition. However, in many occasions, the information we get is in a different way from the one we need it. For instance, we know for sure that if the battery is discharged the car will not start, thus a very common trouble shooting rule is the following: "if a car engine does not start up then it is possible that its battery is discharged". And from this rule of thumb, one can derive,

---

[7]However, the non-triviality property will become relevant when we will analyse the relationship between similarity logic and belief revision

by contraposition, another rule, in this case a predictive rule: "If the car battery is charged up then probably the engine will start up". Note that this last rule (like the first one) is nonmonotonic because it is not intended to assert that the antecedent alone is a sufficient condition of the consequent, but jointly with a set of assumptions commonly accepted in the context of this rule. In order to capture this intuition, we now consider a notion of nonmonotonic consequence $p \mathrel{|\sim} q$ that it is based in the degree of implication of $\neg p$ by $\neg q$.

As we have already mentioned, an implication measure $I_S(\cdot \mid K)$ does not verify any interesting decomposability property and this makes it quite difficult to grasp which properties may satisfy an ordering on propositions defined as

$$p \leq_I q \text{ iff } I_S(p \mid K) \leq I_S(q \mid K)$$

However, in (GR02) they find a way out by contrapositive reasoning. Namely, if $I_S(p \mid K)$ measures to what extent p is implied by K, one can also consider another implication-like index $L_S(p \mid K)$ measuring to what extent $\neg p$ implies $\neg K$ defined by:

$$L_S(p \mid K) = I_S(\neg K \mid \neg p).$$

L_S is called a *counter-implication* measure. It is easy to show that, given a fixed consistent K, the measure $L_S(\cdot \mid K)$ fulfills the following properties:

1. $L_S(\top \mid K) = 1$
2. $L_S(p \wedge q \mid K) = \min(L_S(p \mid K), L_S(q \mid K))$

but fails to satisfy $L_S(\bot \mid K) = 0$. This means that $L_S(\cdot \mid K)$ is very close to a necessity measure[8]. So close, that the ordering induced by it,

$$p \leq_L q \text{ iff } L_S(p \mid K) \leq L_S(q \mid K), \tag{3}$$

is a genuine expectation ordering, that is, it satisfies transitivity, dominance and conjunctiveness. Indeed, the ordering $\leq_L$ will be a qualitative necessity relation (i.e. the dual of a qualitative possibility relation) and the condition $\bot <_L \top$ will hold, if S is separating . Therefore we can also prove that an inference relation $\mathrel{|\sim}$ satisfies SC, LLE, And, Or, RM, CP, Cut, Or and RM iff there exists a proposition K and a similarity S on possible worlds such that $p \mathrel{|\sim} q$ iff either $p \models q$ or $L_S(p \to q \mid K) > L_S(p \to \neg q \mid K)$.

Finally, it is interesting to also express $\mathrel{|\sim}_L$ in terms of the graded approximate entailment $\models^\alpha$ introduced in Section 2. Just by applying the

---

[8]A formal study of a weaker notion of necessity which it is not required to satisfy that the measure of $\bot$ should be 0 is given in (BG92)

definitions, it turns out that the following condition holds:

$$p \mathrel{|\!\sim_L} q \quad \text{iff} \quad \text{either } p \models q \text{ or there exists } \alpha \in [0,1] \text{ such that}$$
$$p \wedge \neg q \models^{\alpha} \neg K \text{ and } p \wedge q \not\models^{\alpha} \neg K.$$

In other words, q nonmonotonically follows from p, in a context of K and S, when $\neg K$ is approximately entailed by $\neg(p \to q)$ to a higher degree than by $\neg(p \to \neg q)$, or roughly speaking, when falsifying $p \to q$ falsifies K *more* than when falsifying $p \to \neg q$.

7.2 Belief revision and similarity logic

Theory change formalisms deal with mechanisms for adding (or retracting) a proposition to (from) an existing knowledge base. The natural question addressed by these formalisms is what should the resulting theory be. In particular, one of the basic problems is whether the new information to be added is inconsistent with the given knowledge base. Concerning this problem, most relevant works take as a departure point the postulates proposed by Alchourrón, Gärdenfors and Makinson (AGM85) for the so-called belief revision operators. More specifically, in (AGM85), the authors proposed eight postulates which, they argued, must be satisfied by any reasonable revision operator $\star$. In what follows, given a knowledge base K and a formula φ, $K \star \varphi$ denotes the result of adding φ to K. The postulates consist of [9]:

- six basic postulates

    Closure: $K \star \varphi = Cn(K \star \varphi)$
    Success: $\varphi \in K \star \varphi$
    Inclusion: $K \star \varphi \subseteq Cn(K \cup \{\varphi\})$
    Vacuity: If $\neg\varphi \notin Cn(K)$, then $Cn(K \cup \{\varphi\}) \subseteq K \star \varphi$
    Consistency: If $\neg\varphi \notin Cn(\emptyset)$ then $\bot \notin Cn(K \star \varphi)$
    Extensionality: If $\varphi \leftrightarrow \psi \in Cn(\emptyset)$, then $K \star \varphi = K \star \psi$

- and two supplementary postulates

    Superexpansion: $K \star (\varphi \wedge \psi) \subseteq Cn((K \star \varphi) \cup \{\psi\})$
    Subexpansion: If $\neg\psi \notin Cn(K \star \varphi)$,
    $\qquad\qquad$ then $Cn((K \star \varphi) \cup \{\psi\}) \subseteq K \star (\varphi \wedge \psi)$

Gärdenfors (Gär90) has suggested that nonmonotic reasoning and belief revision are two sides of a same coin. This is specially true for nonmonotonic logic based on *expectation orderings*. In fact, while the above postulates leave the choice of the revision operator quite open, Gärdenfors proves

---

[9] where Cn is any consequence operator which includes classical propositional logic, is compact and satisfies the deduction theorem.

(Gär88) that any a such operator underlines an ordering $\leq_{EE}$ on the formulas of a knowledge base that guides the revision procedure. He calls this ordering *epistemic entrenchment*, and it is an expectation ordering (i.e. it satisfies the *transitivity, dominance* and *conjunctiveness* properties) which additionally satisfies two further properties:

Minimality: If $\bot \notin Cn(K)$, then $\varphi \notin Cn(K)$ iff $\varphi \leq_{EE} \psi$ for all ψ
Maximality: If $\psi \leq_{EE} \varphi$ for all ψ, then $\varphi \in Cn(\emptyset)$

The connections between epistemic entrenchment orderings and revision operators is witnessed by the following relationships (Gär88; LR91; Rot91):

- given an epistemic entrenchment ordering $\leq$ on a consistent belief set K the operator $\star$ defined by

  (EBR) $\psi \in K \star \varphi$ iff either $(\varphi \to \neg\psi) < (\varphi \to \psi)$ or $\varphi \vdash \bot$.

  is a belief revision that satisfies the eight AGM postulates.
- conversely, if $\star$ is an operation on a consistent belief set K that satisfies the eight AGM postulates, then the relation $\leq$ defined from $\star$ by

  $(C \leq)$ $\varphi \leq \psi$ iff: If $\varphi \in K \star \neg(\varphi \wedge \psi)$ then $\psi \in K \star \neg(\varphi \wedge \psi)$.

  is an epistemic entrenchment ordering.

According to these relationships between orderings and belief revision, and taking account the previous subsection, it is not surprising then that there is also a connection between similarity-based logical formalism and belief revision. Indeed, in (DP92), Dubois and Prade have pointed out that the relation $\leq_{EE}$ has exactly the same properties as a qualitative necessity relation. Hence, the only numerical counterpart of epistemic entrenchment orderings are exactly those induced by necessity measures. Taking this into account, the above two relationships also hold when the ordering is an $\leq_C$- (or $\leq_L$)-ordering, as defined in (2) and in (3) respectively, induced by a separating similarity relation S. As a final remark, let us notice that, actually, the symmetry and transitivity properties of the similarity relations are not needed to generate the orders for defining revision operators. Therefore it is possible to consider models with a fuzzy binary relation, representing some more general notion of similarity or "closeness", for which only the reflexivity and separating (discriminant) properties would be required.

8   Summary and conclusions

In this paper we have surveyed different approaches to formalize similarity-based reasoning, in the sense of logical systems that provide a formal account of the graded notion of truthlikeness. For this, we have first clarified the differences between the notion of truthlikeness and the better known notions of uncertainty and vagueness and we have introduced fuzzy similarity relations as the main tool used to model a graded notion of truthlikeness. In fact, fuzzy similarity relations can be used, either syntactically or semantically, to define notions of approximate proofs or approximate entailments respectively. Although both have been addressed in the paper, we have put more emphasis on the semantical approach where the starting point is to assume there are possible worlds or situations that resemble more than others, and this is reflected by a given fuzzy similarity relation between worlds. Indeed, we have shown how similarity relations on possible worlds can be used to extend the classical notion of logical consequence leading to new notions of graded entailments, basically the so-called approximate and proximity entailments. These ideas go back to Ruspini (Rus91) and are captured by similarity-based Kripke structures. Based on these semantics, we have described in detail four formalisations, based on different modal and conditional logical frameworks, capturing different aspects of these similarity entailments. Finally, we also have addressed the issue of exploring nonmonotonic aspects in similarity-based reasoning. By following ideas of Gärdenfors and Makinson (GM94), where they reduce the notion of nonmonotonic reasoning to the notion of ordering between formulas, we have described some approaches that consider different kinds of similarity-based orderings to define nonmonotonic consequence relations and operators of theory revision.

As concluding remarks we may point out that similarity-based reasoning is a research topic that has many different and interesting facets. In this paper we have addressed only some issues in the task of logical formalisation of different notions of approximate consequence that make sense in this framework. Therefore we have not covered many other reasoning models where the notion of similarity or truthlikeness plays a key role, like case-based reasoning or case-based decision. Finally, regarding open problems, we note a couple of questions. In subsection 6.3, we have described a many-valued modal system, based on Gödel logic semantics, only for a $\Diamond$ operator. This logic is very important because it allows us to formalize other related notions, like interpolative reasoning (DEG$^+$97), similarity-based SLD resolution (BGR05), and fuzzy description logic (Haj05). However, Gödel logic is only one of prominent fuzzy logics. One of the main open problems in this field is the search for axiomatization for similar many-valued modal systems based on other fuzzy logics. The difficulty is essentially due to their lack of normality, i. e. they do not satisfy the K axiom. In Section 7 we have considered two kinds of nonmonotonic inference based on similarity orderings. Another approach would be to follow Schlechta's ideas in (Sch97) where he reduces the notion of nonmonotonic reasoning to the notion of distance. The use of similarity relations instead of distances seems an interesting line for future research.

Acknowledgments

The authors are indebted to José Álvarez for helpful and interesting discussions on different parts of this paper as well as to the anonymous reviewers for their comments and remarks that have helped to improve the final version of this paper. The authors also acknowledge partial support of a bilateral cooperation CSIC-CONICET project, ref. 2005AR0092. Godo also acknowledges the Spanish project MULOG2, TIN2007-68005-C04-01, and Rodríguez acknowledges the Argentinean project PIP-CONICET 2005-2007 5541.

Bibliography

[AGM85] C. Alchourrón, P. Gärdenfors, and D. Makinson. On the logic of theory change: partial meet contraction and revision function. *Journal Symbolic Logic*, 50:510–530, 1985.

[Apt90] R.K. Apt. Logic Programming. In J. van Leeuwen (Ed.), *Handbook of Theoretical Computer Science*, vol. B, Elsevier, Amsterdam, 1990, pp. 492-574.

[BG92] L. Biacino and G. Gerla. Generated necessities and possibilities. *International Journal of Intelligent Systems*, 7:445–454, 1992.

[BG98] L. Biacino and G. Gerla. Logics with approximate premises. *International Journal of Intelligent Systems*, 13:1–10, 1998.

[BGY00] L. Biacino, G. Gerla and M. Ying Approximate Reasoning based on Similarity. *Mathematical Logic Quaterly* 46 (1), 77-86, 2000.

[BGR05] L. Blandi, L. Godo, and R. Rodríguez. A connection between similarity logic programming and Gödel modal logic. In *Proc. of EUSFLAT-LFA 2005*, Barcelona, Sept. 2005, pp. 775-780.

[BL02] I. Bloch and J. Lang. Towards mathematical morpho-logics. Proc. of IPMU'2000. Revised version in *Technologies for Constructing Intelligent Systems*, Vol. 2, 367-380, Springer-Verlag, 2002.

[Bod03] U. Bodenhofer. A note on approximate equality versus the Poincar paradox. *Fuzzy Sets and Systems* 133 (2) 2003, pp.155-160.

[Boi03] D. Boixader. On the relationship between T-transitivity and approximate equality. *Fuzzy Sets and Systems*133 (2) 2003, pp. 161-169.

[BJ96] D. Boixader and J. Jacas. CRI as approximate reasoning tool: an analysis via T-indistinguishability operators. In *Proc. of FUZZ-IEEE'96*, pages 2094–2097, New Orleans, USA, 1996. IEEE Press.

[BJ98] D. Boixader and J. Jacas. Extensionality based approximate reasoning. *International Journal of Approximate Reasoning*, 19:221–230, 1998.

[BEGR07] F. Bou, F. Esteva, L. Godo, and R. Rodríguez. On many-valued modal logics over finite residuated lattices. Manuscript in preparation. Abstract presented in TANCL'07 (Oxford, August 2007) and in IX Congreso Dr. Antonio Monteiro (Bahía Blanca, May 2007).

[BDG+99] B. Bouchon-Meunier, D. Dubois, L. Godo, and H. Prade. Fuzzy sets and possibility theory in approximate and plausible reasoning. In J. Bezdek, D. Dubois, and H. Prade, editors, *Fuzzy Sets in Approximate Reasoning and Information Systems*, The Handbooks of Fuzzy Sets Series, Chapter 1, pages 15–190. Kluwer Academic Publishers, 1999.

[CR07] X. Caicedo and R. Rodríguez. A Gödel similarity-based modal logic. Manuscript. A shortened version was published as "A Gödel modal logic", in: Proc. of Logic, Computability and Randomness 2004. Córdoba, Argentina, 2007.

[Car37] R. Carnap. Treatability and meaning. *Philosophy of Science*, (3 – 4), 1937.

[Car50] R. Carnap. *The Logical Foundations of Probability*. University Chicago Press, Chicago, 1950.

[CF92] P. Chatalic and C. Froidevaux. Lattice-based graded logic: A multimodal approach. In *Proceedings 8th Conference on Uncertainty in Artificial Intelligence*, pages 33–40, Stanford, CA, 1992.

[CDM00] R. Cignoli, I.M.L. D'Ottaviano, and D. Mundici. *Algebraic foundations of many-valued reasoning*, volume 7 of *Trends in Logic—Studia Logica Library*. Kluwer Academic Publishers, Dordrecht, 2000.

[DeCK03a] M. De Cock and E. Kerre. On (un)suitable fuzzy relations to model approximate equality. *Fuzzy Sets and Systems* 133 (2) 2003, pp.137–153.

[DeCK03b] M. De Cock and E. Kerre. Why fuzzy -equivalence relations do not resolve the Poincar paradox, and related issues. *Fuzzy Sets and Systems* 133 (2) 2003, pp. 181-192.

[DD92] D. Driankov and P. Doherty. A nonmonotonic fuzzy logic. In *Fuzzy logic for the management of uncertainty*, Eds. L. Zadeh and J. Kacprzyk, John Wiley & Sons, 1992.

[Dub86] D. Dubois. Belief structures, possibility theory and decomposable confidence measures. *Computers and Artificial Intelligence*, 5:403–416, 1986.

[DEG+98] D. Dubois, F. Esteva, P. Garcia, L. Godo, R. Lopez de Mántaras, and H. Prade. Fuzzy set modelling in case-based reasoning. *International Journal of Intelligent Systems*, pages 345-373, 1998.

[DEG+95] D. Dubois, F. Esteva, P. Garcia, L. Godo, and H. Prade. Similarity-based consequente relations. In Christine Froidevaux and Jürg Kohlas, editors, *Symbolic and Quantitative Approaches to Reasoning and Uncertainty*, volume 946 of *Lecture Note in Artificial Intelligence*, pages 168–174, Fribourg, Switzerland, July 1995. Springer.

[DEG+97] D. Dubois, F. Esteva, P. Garcia, L. Godo, and H. Prade. A logical approach to interpolation based on similarity relations. *International Journal of Approximate Reasoning*, 17:1–36, 1997.

[DLP94] D. Dubois, J. Lang, and H. Prade. Possibilistic logic. In D.M. Gabbay, C.J. Hogger, and J.A. Robinson, editors, *Handbook of Logic in Artificial Intelligence and Logic Programming. Volume 3: Nonmonotonic Reasoning and Uncertain Reasoning*, pages 439–513. Oxford University Press, 1994.

[DP88] D. Dubois and H. Prade. An introduction to possibilistic and fuzzy logics. In P. Smets, A. Mamdani, D. Dubois, and H. Prade, editors, *Non-Standard Logics for Automatic Reasoning*. Academic Press, 1988.

[DP91a] D. Dubois and H. Prade. Fuzzy sets in approximate reasoning, part 1: Inference with possibility distributions. *Fuzzy Sets ans Systems*, 40:143–202, 1991.

[DP91b] D. Dubois and H. Prade. Fuzzy sets in approximate reasoning, part 2: Logical approaches. *Fuzzy Sets and Systems*, 40:203–244, 1991.

[DP91c] D. Dubois and H. Prade. Possibilistic logic, preferencial models, non-monotonicity and related issues. In *Proc. of IJCAI'91*, pages 419–424, 1991.

[DP92] D. Dubois and H. Prade. Belief change and possibility theory. In Peter Gärdenfors, editor, *Belief Revision*, volume 29 of *Cambridge Tracts in Theoretical Computer Science*, pages 142–182. Cambridge University Press, 1992.

[DP93] D. Dubois and H. Prade. Fuzzy sets and probability: Misunderstandings, bridges and gaps. In *Second IEEE International Conference on Fuzzy Systems*, volume II, pages 501–506, San Francisco, California, April 1993.

[DP94] D. Dubois and H. Prade. Similarity-based approximate reasoning. In J.M. Zurada, R.J. MarksII, and C.J. Robinson, editors, *Computacional Intelligence: Imitating Life*, pages 69–80. IEEE Press, New York, 1994.

[DP95] D. Dubois and H. Prade. Comparison of two fuzzy set-based logics: similarity logic and posibilistic logic. In Proc. of *FUZZ-IEEE'95*, pages 1319–1326, Yokohama, Japan, July 1995. IEEE Press.

[DP01] D. Dubois and H. Prade. Possibility theory, probability theory and multiple-valued logics: A clarification. *Annals of Mathematics and Artificial Intelligence* 32, 35-66, 2001.

[DPB99] D. Dubois, H. Prade, and J. Bezdek. Introduction: fuzzy sets in approximate reasoning and intelligent information systems technology. In J. Bezdek, D. Dubois, and H. Prade, editors, *Fuzzy Sets in Approximate Reasoning and Information Systems*, The handbooks of Fuzzy Sets Series, pages 1–13. Kluwer Academic Publishers, 1999.

[EGG94] F. Esteva, P. Garcia, and L. Godo. Relating and extending semantical approaches to possibilistic reasoning. *International Journal of Approximate Reasoning*, 10:313–344, 1994.

[EGGR97] F. Esteva, P. Garcia, L. Godo, and R. Rodriguez. A modal account of similarity-based reasoning. *International Journal of Approximate Reasoning*, 16(3-4):235–261, 1997.

[EGGN07] F. Esteva, J. Gispert, L. Godo, and C. Noguera. Adding truth-constants to continuous t-norm based logics: axiomatization and completeness results. *Fuzzy Sets and Systems* 158: 597–618, 2007.

[EG99] F. Esteva and L. Godo. Putting Łukasiewicz and product logic together. *Mathware and Soft Computing*, Vol. VI, n.2-3, pp. 219-234, 1999.

[EGHN00] F. Esteva, L. Godo, P. Hájek, and M. Navara. Residuated fuzzy logics with an involutive negation. *Archive for Mathematical Logic*, 39: 103-124, 2000.

[EGM03] F. Esteva, L. Godo and F. Montagna. Equational characterization of the subvarieties of BL generated by t-norm algebras. *Studia Logica* 76, 161-200, 2004.

[EGN06] F. Esteva , L. Godo, C. Noguera. On Rational Weak Nilpotent Minimum Logics. *Journal of Multiple-Valued Logic and Soft Computing* Vol. 12, Number 1-2, pp. 9-32, 2006.

[FH91] L. Fariñas del Cerro and A. Herzig. A modal analysis of possibility theory. volume 535 of *Lecture Notes in Computer Sciences*, pages 11–18. Springer Verlag, Berlin, 1991.

[FHL94] L. Fariñas del Cerro, A. Herzig, and J. Lang. From ordering-based nonmonotonic reasoning to conditional logics. *Artificial Intelligence*, 66:375–394, 1994.

[FD85] M. Fattorosi-Barnaba and F. De Caro. Graded modalities. *Studia Logica*, 2:197–221, 1985.

[Fin72] K. Fine. In so many possible worlds. *Notre Dame Journal of Formal Logic*, 13(4):516–520, october 1972.

[Fit91] M. Fitting. Many-valued modal logics. *Fundamenta Informaticae*, 15:235–254, 1991.

[Fit92] M. Fitting. Many-valued modal logics, II. *Fundamenta Informaticae*, 17:55–73, 1992.

[Fit95] M. Fitting. Tableaus for many-valued modal logic. *Studia Logica*, 55(1):63–87, 1995.

[FGS00] F. Formato, G. Gerla, and M.I. Sessa. Similarity-based unification. *Fundamenta Informaticae* 40, 2000, pp. 1-22.

[Gär88] P. Gärdenfors. *Knowledge in Flux: Modeling the Dynamics of Epistemic States*. The MIT Press, Cambridge, 1988.

[Gär90] P. Gärdenfors. Belief revision and non-monotonic logic: two sides of the same coin? In *Proceedings of the 9th European Conference of Artificial Intelligence*, Stockholm, Sweden, August 6-10 1990. Pitman.

[GM91] P. Gärdenfors and D. Makinson. Relations between the logic of theory change and nonmonotonic logic. In A. Furman and M. Morreau, editors, *Lecture Notes in Artificial Intelligence*, volume 465, pages 185–205. Springer Verlag, 1991.

[GM94] P. Gärdenfors and D. Makinson. Nonmonotonic inference based on expectations. *Artificial Intelligence*, 65:197–245, 1994.

[Gef88] H. Geffner. On the logic of defaults. In *Proc. of the 7th. AAAI National Conference on Artificial Intelligence*, 449–454, St. Paul, 1988.

[Ger01] G. Gerla (2001) *Fuzzy Logic: Mathematical Tols for Approximate Reasoning*. Trends in Logic, vol. 11. Kluwer Academic Publishers.

[GS99a] G. Gerla, M.I. Sessa. Similarity Logic and Similarity PROLOG. In *Proc. Joint EUROFUSE-SIC99 International Conference*, 25-28 May 1999, Budapest, Hungary, pp.367-372.

[GS99b] G. Gerla and M.I. Sessa. Similarity in Logic Programming. In *Fuzzy Logic and Soft Computing*, G. Chen, M. Ying, K.-Y. Cai (Eds.), Kluwer Acc. Pub., Norwell, 1999, pp. 19-31.

[Glo70] F.L. Goble. Grades of modality. *Logique et Analyse*, 51:323–334, 1970.

[Göd32] K. Gödel. Zum intuitionistischen aussgenkalkül. *Klasse*, 69:65–66, 1932.

[GHE03] L. Godo, P. Hájek and F. Esteva. A fuzzy modal logic for belief functions. *Fundamenta Informaticae* 57(2-4), 127-146, 2003.

[GR98] L. Godo, R. Rodríguez. A Fuzzy Modal Logic for Similarity Reasoning. In *Fuzzy Logic and Soft Computing*, Guoqing Chen, Mingsheng Ying and Kai-Yuan Cai eds., Kluwer, 1999, pp. 33-48.

[GR02] L. Godo and R. Rodríguez. Graded similarity-based semantics for nonmonotonic inferences. *Annals of Mathematics and Artificial Intelligence* 34, 89-105, 2002.

[Got01] S. Gottwald. *A Treatise on Many-valued Logics*, Studies in Logic and Computation 9, Research Studies Press Ltd., Baldock, UK, 2001.

[GH05] S. Gottwald and P. Hájek. Triangular norm based mathematical fuzzy logic. In Erich Peter Klement and Radko Mesiar, editors, *Logical, Algebraic, Analytic and Probabilistic Aspects of Triangular Norms*, pages 275-300. Elsevier, Amsterdam, 2005.

[Haj98] P. Hájek. *Metamathematics of Fuzzy Logic.*, volume 4 of *Trends in logic–Studia Logica Library.* Kluwer Academic Publishers, The Netherlands, 1998.

[Haj05] P. Hájek. Making fuzzy description logic more general. *Fuzzy Sets and Systems*, 154, 1-15, 2005.

[HGE95] P. Hájek, L. Godo, and F. Esteva. Fuzzy logic and probability. In *Proccedings of the 11th. Conference of Uncertainty in Artificial Intelligence*, pages 237–244. Morgan Kaufmann, 1995.

[HH96] P. Hájek and D. Harmancová. A many-valued modal logic. In *Proc. IPMU'96*, pages 1021–1024, 1996.

[Hal03] J. Halpern. *Reasoning about Uncertainty*, The MIT Press, 2003.

[HT06] G. Hansoul and B. Teheux. Completeness results for many-valued Lukasiewicz modal systems and relational semantics, 2006. Available at http://arxiv.org/abs/math/0612542.

[HK94] D. Harmanec and G.J. Klir. On the modal logic interpretation of dempster-sshafer theory of evidence. *International Journal Uncertainty Fuzzyness Knowledge Based Systems*, 9:941–951, 1994.

[Hil76] R. Hilpinen. Approximate truth and truthlikeness. In M. Przelecki, K. Szaniawski and R. Wojcicki (eds.), *Formal Methods in the Methodology of the Empirical Sciences*, pages 19–42, Dordrecht: Reidel, 1976.

[HM92] W. van der Hoek and J. J. Meyer. Modalities and (un-)certainties. *Lectures Notes for School Summer of Linköping'92*, May 1992.

[HR91] W. van der Hoek and M. de Rijke. Quantifiers and modal logic. ITLI publ. series LP-91-01, University of Amsterdam, Netherlands,1991.

[Hül01] E. Hüllermeier. Similarity-based inference as evidential reasoning. *Int. J. Approx. Reasoning* 26(2): 67-100, 2001.

[Jan03] V. Jani. Resemblance is a nearness. *Fuzzy Sets and Systems* 133 (2) 2003, pp. 171-173.

[Kla94] F. Klawonn. Fuzzy sets and vague environment. *Fuzzy Sets and Systems*, 66:207–221, 1994.

[Kla95] F. Klawonn. Similarity based reasoning. In *Proceedings of EU-FIT'95*, pages 34–38, Aachen (Germany), August 28-31, 1995.

[Kla03] F. Klawonn. Should fuzzy equality and similarity satisfy transitivity? Comments on the paper by M. De Cock and E. Kerre. *Fuzzy Sets and Systems* 133 (2) 2003, pp. 175-180.

[KC95] F. Klawonn and J.L. Castro. Similarity in fuzzy reasoning. *Mathware & Soft Computing*, (2):197–228, 1995.

[KGK95] F. Klawonn, J. Gebhardt, and R. Kruse. Fuzzy control on the basis of equality relations with an example from idle speed control. *IEEE Transactions on Fuzzy Systems*, 3(3):336–350, 1995.

[KK93] F. Klawonn and R. Kruse. Equality relations as a basis for fuzzy control. *Fuzzy Sets and Systems*, 54:147–156, 1993.

[KN96] F. Klawonn and V. Novák. The relation between inference and interpolation in the framework of fuzzy systems. *Fuzzy Sets and Systems*, 81:331–354, 1996.

[Kon97] B. Konikowska. A logic for reasoning about relative similarity. *Studia Logica*, 58:185–226, 1997.

[Kri59a] S. Kripke. A completeness theorem in modal logic. *Journal of Symbolic Logic*, 24:1–14, 1959.

[Kri59b] S. Kripke. Semantical analysis of modal logic. *Journal of Symbolic Logic*, 24:323–324, 1959.

[Leh98] D. Lehmann. Stereotypical reasoning: logical properties. *Logic Journal of the IGPL*, 6(1):49–58, 1998.

[Lew73] D. Lewis. *Contrafactuals*. Oxford Basil Blackwell, London, 1973.

[Lia98] C.-J. Liau. Possibilistic residuated implication logics with applications. *International Journal of Uncertainty, Fuzziness and Knowledge-based Systems*, 6(4):365–385, 1998.

[LL92] C.-J. Liau and B.I-Peng Lin. Qualitative modal logic and possibilistic reasoning. In B.Newmann, editor, *Proceedings of ECAI'92*, pages 43–47. John Willey & Sons ltd., 1992.

[LL95] C.-J. Liau and B.I-Peng Lin. A theoretical investigation into possibilistic reasoning. *Fuzzy Sets and Systems*, 75:355–363, 1995.

[LL96] C.-J. Liau and Bertrand I-Peng Lin. Possibilistic reasoning-a mini-survey and uniform semantics. *Artificial Intelligence*, 88:163–193, 1996.

[LR91] S. Lindström and W. Rabinowicz. Epistemic entrenchment with incomparabilities and relational belief revision. In Fuhrmann and Morreau, editors, *The Logic of Theory Change*, pages 93–126, Berlin, 1991. Springer-Verlag.

[Mak94] D. Makinson. General patterns in nonmonotnic reasoning. In D.M. Gabbay, C.J. Hogger, J.A. Robinson, and D. Nute, editors, *Handbook of Logic in Artificial Inteligence and Logic Programming*, volume 4 of *Nonmonotonic Reasoning and Uncertain Reasoning*, pages 35–110. Clarendon Press, Oxford, 1994.

[McD87] D. McDermott. A critic of pure reason. *Computational Intelligence*, 3(3):151–160, 1987.

[Mil74] D. Miller. On the comparison of false theories by their bases. *The British Journal for the Philosophy of Science*, 25(2):178–188, 1974.

[Min85] M. Minsky. A framework for representation knowledge. In R.J. Brachman and H.J. Levesque, editors, *Reading in Knowledge Representation*, pages 246–262. Morgan Kaufman, Los Altos, 1985.

[Nic70] J. Nicod. *Geometry and Induction*. Routledge Press, London, 1970.

[Nii87] I. Niiniluoto. *Truthlikeness*, volume 185 of *Synthese Library*. D. Reidel Publishing Company, 1rt. edition, 1987.

[Nov90] V. Novák. On the syntactico-semantical completeness of first-order fuzzy logic (I) and (II). *Kybernetika* (26): 47–66; 134–154, 1990.

[NPM99] V. Novák, I. Perfilieva, and J. Močkoř. *Mathematical Principles of Fuzzy Logic.* Kluwer, Dordrecht, 1999.

[Odd07] G. Oddie. Truthlikeness. The Stanford Encyclopedia of Philosophy (Spring 2007 Edition), Edward N. Zalta (ed.), URL = http://plato.stanford.edu/archives/spr2007/entries/truthlikeness/.

[Ost88] P. Ostermann. Many-valued modal propositional calculi. *Zeitschrift für Mathematische Logik und Grundlagen der Mathematik*, 34(4):343–354, 1988.

[Pan98] G. Panti. Multi-valued logics. In D. Gabbay and P. Smets, editors, *Quantified Representation of Uncertainty*, volume 1 of the *Handbook of Defeasible Reasoning and Uncertainty Management Systems*, pp. 25-74. Kluwer, 1998.

[Pav79] J. Pavelka. On the fuzzy logic I: Many valued rules and inference. *Math. Logik Grundlag. Math.*, (25): 45–52, 1979.

[Pea88] J. Pearl. *Probabilistic Reasoning in Intelligent Systems: Network of Plausible Inference*. Morgan Kauffman, Los Altos, Ca, 1988.

[RKC92] G. Resconi, G.J. Klir, and U.St. Clair. Hierarchical uncertainty metatheory based upon modal logic. *International Journal of General Systems*, (21): 23–50, 1992.

[RKCH93] G. Resconi, G.J. Klir, U.St. Clair, and D. Harmanec. On the integration of uncertainty theories. *International Journal of Uncertainty, Fuzziness and Knowledge-Based Systems*, 1(1):1–18, 1993.

[Rod02] R. O. Rodríguez. *Aspectos formales en el Razonamiento basado en Relaciones de Similitud Borrosas*, Ph. D. Thesis, Technical University of Catalonia (UPC), 2002.

[Rot91] H. Rott. A nonmonotonic conditional logic for belief revision. Part 1: Semantics and logic of simple conditionals. In Fuhrmann A. and M. Morreau, editors, *The Logic of Theory Change, Workshop, Lecture Notes in Artificial Intelligence, Volume 465*, Konstanz, FRG, October 1991. Springer Verlag.

[Rus87] E. Ruspini. The logical foundations of evidential reasoning. Technical Report 408, Artificial Inteligence Center, SRI International, Merlo Park, California, 1987.

[Rus91] E. Ruspini. On the semantics of fuzzy logic. *International Journal of Approximate Reasoning*, 5:45–88, 1991.

[Sch97] K. Schlechta. *Nonmonotonic Logics. Basic Concepts, Results, and Techniques*, Lecture Notes in Artifical Intelligence 1187, Springer, 1997.

[Ses01] M.I. Sessa. Translations and Similarity-based Logic Programming. *Soft Computing* 5(2), 2001.

[Ses02] M.I. Sessa. Approximate Reasoning by Similarity-based SLD Resolution. *Theoretical Computer Science*, 275, 2002, pp. 389-426.

[Suz97] N.-Y. Suzuki. Kripke frame with graded accesibility and fuzzy possible world semantics. *Studia Logica*, 59(2):249–269, 1997.

[Tar56] A. Tarski. Methodology of deductive sciences. In *Logics, Semantics, Metamathematics*. Oxford University Press, 1956.

[Thi93] H. Thiele. On the definition of modal operators in fuzzy logic. In IEEE Computer Society Press, editor, *Proceedings of the 23rd IEEE International Symposium on Multiple-Valued Logic*, pages 269–276, Sacramento, California, 1993.

[Tic74] P. Tichý. On Popper's definitions of verisimilitude. *The British Journal for the Philosophy of Science*, 25:155–160, 1974.

[Wes87] T. Weston. Approximate truth. *Journal of Philosophical Logic*, 16(4):203–227, 1987.

[Wil88] T. Williamson. First order logics for comparative similarity. *Notre Dame Journal of Formal Logic*, 29(4):457–481, 1988.

[Yin88] M.-S. Ying. On standard models of fuzzy modal logics. *Fuzzy Sets and Systems*, 26:357–363, 1988.

[Yin94] M.-S. Ying. A logic for approximate reasoning. *The Journal of Symbolic Logic*, 53(3):830–837, 1994.

[Zad65] L. Zadeh. Fuzzy sets. *Information and Control*, (8):338–353, 1965.

[Zad71] L. Zadeh. Similarity relations and fuzzy orderings. *Information Sciences*, 3:177–200, 1971.

[Zad86] L. Zadeh. Is probability theory sufficient for daeling with uncertainty in ia: A negative view. In L.N. Karnal and J.F. Lemmer, editors, *Uncertainty in Artificial Intelligence*, volume 9, pages 103–116. Elsevier Science Publishers, 1986.

[Zad94] L. Zadeh. Fuzzy logic, neural networks and soft computing. *Communications of the ACM*, 37(3):77–84, march 1994.

Logics of Similarity and their Dual Tableaux
A Survey*

Joanna Golińska-Pilarek[1]** and Ewa Orłowska[2]

[1] Institute of Philosophy, Warsaw University, Poland

National Institute of Telecommunications, Warsaw, Poland

[2] National Institute of Telecommunications, Warsaw, Poland

Abstract. We present several classes of logics for reasoning with information stored in information systems. The logics enable us to cope with the phenomena of incompleteness of information and uncertainty of knowledge derived from such an information. Relational inference systems for these logics are developed in the style of dual tableaux.

1 Introduction

Intuitively, similarity is a degree of resemblance which results by comparing the features of objects. Various theories of similarity aim at capturing the essence of similarity that remains invariant from one collection of objects to another. In this paper we present a survey of models of qualitative similarity inspired by the notion of rough set. The models are relevant for data structures referred to as information systems with incomplete information. Any such system consists of a collection of objects described in terms of their properties. A property is specified as a pair 'an attribute, a subsets of values of this attribute'. Such a form of properties is a manifestation of incompleteness of information. Instead of a single value of an attribute assigned to an object, as it is in relational database model, here we have a range of values. There are two fundamental intuitive interpretations of such a specification of properties, they will be discussed in some detail in Section 2. As every human concept, similarity is context dependent. We need to state in which context similarity should be decided. For that purpose, given a set of objects whose similarity is to be investigated, we choose and fix a collection of attributes meaningful and/or important for the objects under consideration. In information systems with incomplete information we define several types of similarity and dissimilarity in the form of binary relations in the family of objects. The distinguishing

---

* Partial support from the Polish Ministry of Science and Higher Education grant N N206 399134 is gratefully acknowledged.
** The author is a recipient of the 2007 Foundation for Polish Science Grant for Young Scientists.

feature of the concept of similarity considered in this paper is that the corresponding relations capture both a qualitative degree of similarity and the relevant context. In Section 2 we discuss in detail two classes of relations referred to as indistinguishability relations and distinguishability relations. The indistinguishability relations reflect degrees of similarity and distinguishability relations correspond to degrees of dissimilarity. Each of these relations is defined with respect to a chosen collection of attributes of the objects. We present modal logics characterized by the classes of relational systems with some of these relations. Next, we develop relational dual tableaux for these logics. The logical approaches to information systems with incomplete information can be found in [DEO02], [KON87], [KON94], [ORL83], [ORL88a], [VAK89], [VAK91a], and [VAK91b], among others.

Relational proof theory enables us to build proof systems for non-classical logics in a systematic modular way. First, deduction rules are defined for the common relational core of the logics. These rules constitute a core of all the relational proof systems. Next, for any particular logic some specific rules are designed and adjoined to the core set of rules. Hence, we need not implement each deduction system from the scratch, we should only extend the core system with a module corresponding to a specific part of a logic under consideration.

Relational formalization of non-classical logics originated in [ORL88]. The applications of relational dual tableaux to reasoning tasks in various non-classical logics can be found, among others, in [BUR06], [DEM96], [FRI95], [KON98], [MAC97], [MAC98a], [MAC98b], [ORL92], [ORL93], [ORL94], [ORL95], [BGO06], [GOO06], [MAC06]. The algebraic basis for a relational formalization of logics can be found in [TAR41] and [TAR87]. A correspondence theory for relational dual tableaux systems can be found in [MAC02].

Implementations of relational dual tableau systems are described, among others, in [DAL05], [FOR05], [FOR06], [FOO06]. The systems are available at http://www.logic.stfx.ca/reldt/ and http://www.di.univaq.it/TARSKI/transIt/. The present paper is based on [DEO02] and [ORG07].

2 Information systems

A formal model of an information system with incomplete information was introduced by Lipski in [LIP76] and [LIP79]. In this model information systems are collections of information items that have the form of descriptions of some objects in terms of their properties. An *information system* is a structure of the form $S = (\mathbb{OB}, \mathbb{AT}, (\mathbb{VAL}_a)_{a \in \mathbb{AT}}, f)$ where:

- $\mathbb{OB}$ is a non-empty set of objects;
- $\mathbb{AT}$ is a non-empty set of attributes;
- $\mathbb{VAL}_a$ is a non-empty set of values of the attribute a;

- f is a total function $\mathbb{OB} \times \mathbb{AT} \rightarrow \bigcup_{a \in \mathbb{AT}} \mathcal{P}(\mathbb{VAL}_a)$ such that for every $(x, a) \in \mathbb{OB} \times \mathbb{AT}$, $f(x, a) \subseteq \mathbb{VAL}_a$ (an information function).

Usually, instead of $(\mathbb{OB}, \mathbb{AT}, (\mathbb{VAL}_a)_{a \in \mathbb{AT}}, f)$ the more concise notation, namely $(\mathbb{OB}, \mathbb{AT})$, is used. With that short notation, each attribute $a \in \mathbb{AT}$ is considered as a mapping $a : \mathbb{OB} \rightarrow \mathcal{P}(\mathbb{VAL}_a)$ that assigns subsets of values to objects. An information system $(\mathbb{OB}, \mathbb{AT})$ is *total* (resp. *deterministic*) whenever for every $a \in \mathbb{AT}$ and for every $x \in \mathbb{OB}$, $f(x, a) \neq \emptyset$ (resp. $card(f(x, a)) \leq 1$, in that case x is said to be a *deterministic object*). If an information system is not deterministic, then it is said to be *nondeterministic*. In nondeterministic information systems descriptions of objects are tuples consisting of subsets of values of attributes. Similar models are also used in symbolic data analysis, see e.g. [DID87], [DID88], [PRE97] and in rough set-based data analysis, e.g., [ORL97b], [WAN98], and [WAN00].

Any set $a(x)$ can be viewed as a set of properties of an object x corresponding to attribute a. For example, if attribute a is 'colour' and $a(x)$ =green, then x possesses the property of 'being green'; if a is 'languages spoken', and if a person x speaks Polish (Pl), German (D), and French (F), then $a(x) = $ {Pl, D, F}. Similarly, set $\mathbb{VAL}_a - a(x)$ can be interpreted as a set of *negative* a-properties of object x. If both the set of objects and the set of attributes are finite, then we regard such a system as a data table with rows labelled by objects, and columns labelled by attributes; the entry (x, a) contains the value set $a(x)$ of attribute a for object x.

Any information system $S = (\mathbb{OB}, \mathbb{AT})$ contains also some implicit information about relationships among its objects. These relationships are determined by the properties of objects. Usually, they have the form of binary relations. They are referred to as *information relations derived from an information system*. There are two groups of information relations: the relations that reflect various forms of indistinguishability of objects in terms of their properties and the relations that indicate distinguishability of the objects. Below we present a list of the classes of atomic relations that generate a whole family of information relations.

Indistinguishability relations

These relations reflect various kinds of 'sameness' or 'similarity' of objects. Let $S = (\mathbb{OB}, \mathbb{AT})$ be an information system. For every $A \subseteq \mathbb{AT}$ and all $x, y \in \mathbb{OB}$ we define the following binary relations on $\mathbb{OB}$:

- the *strong* (resp. *weak*) *indiscernibility relation* $ind(A)$ (resp. $wind(A)$): $(x, y) \in ind(A)$ (resp. $(x, y) \in wind(A)$) iff for all (resp. for some) $a \in A$, $a(x) = a(y)$;

- the *strong* (resp. *weak*) *similarity relation* $sim(A)$ (resp. $wsim(A)$): $(x, y) \in sim(A)$ (resp. $(x, y) \in wsim(A)$) iff for all (resp. for some) $a \in A$, $a(x) \cap a(y) \neq \emptyset$;
- the *strong* (resp. *weak*) *forward inclusion relation* $fin(A)$ (resp. $wfin(A)$): $(x, y) \in fin(A)$ (resp. $(x, y) \in wfin(A)$) iff for all (resp. for some) $a \in A$, $a(x) \subseteq a(y)$;
- the *strong* (resp. *weak*) *backward inclusion relation* $bin(A)$ (resp. $wbin(A)$): $(x, y) \in bin(A)$ (resp. $(x, y) \in wbin(A)$) iff for all (resp. for some) $a \in A$, $a(y) \subseteq a(x)$;
- the *strong* (resp. *weak*) *negative similarity relation* $nim(A)$ (resp. $wnim(A)$): $(x, y) \in nim(A)$ (resp. $(x, y) \in wnim(A)$) iff for all (resp. for some) $a \in A$, $-a(x) \cap -a(y) \neq \emptyset$, where $-$ is the complement with respect to $\mathbb{VAL}_a$;
- the *strong* (resp. *weak*) *incomplementarity relation* $icom(A)$ (resp. $wicom(A)$): $(x, y) \in icom(A)$ (resp. $(x, y) \in wicom(A)$) iff for all (resp. for some) $a \in A$, $a(x) \neq -a(y)$.

If A is a singleton, then the respective strong and weak relations coincide. Intuitively, two objects are strongly A-indiscernible whenever all of their sets of a-properties determined by the attributes $a \in A$ are the same. Objects are weakly A-indiscernible whenever their properties determined by some members of A are the same. Objects are strongly A-similar (resp. weakly A-similar) whenever all (resp. some) of the sets of their properties determined by the attributes from A are not disjoint, in other words the objects share some properties. Strong (resp. weak) information inclusions hold between the objects whenever their all (resp. some) corresponding sets of properties are included in each other. Strong (resp. weak) negative similarity relation holds between objects whenever they share some negative properties with respect to all (resp. some) attributes. Strong (resp. weak) incomplementarity relation holds between objects whenever a-properties of one object do not coincide with negative a-properties of the other one, for all (resp. some) attributes.

Important applications of the information relations from the indiscernibility group are related to the representation of approximations of subsets of objects in information systems. If $R(A)$ is one of these relations, where A is a subset of $\mathbb{AT}$ and X is a subset of $\mathbb{OB}$, then the *lower $R(A)$-approximation of X*, $L(R(A))X$, and the *upper $R(A)$-approximation of X, $U(R(A))X$*, are defined as follows:

$L(R(A))X = \{x \in \mathbb{OB} : \text{for all } y \in \mathbb{OB}, \text{ if } (x, y) \in R(A), \text{ then } y \in X\}$;

$U(R(A))X = \{x \in \mathbb{OB} : \text{there is } y \in \mathbb{OB} \text{ such that } (x, y) \in R(A) \text{ and } y \in X\}$.

In the rough set theory (see [PAW91]), where a relation $R(A)$ is a strong indiscernibility relation, we obtain the following hierarchy of definability of sets. A subset X of $\mathbb{OB}$ is said to be:

- *A-definable* iff $L(ind(A))X = X = U(ind(A))X$;
- *roughly A-definable* iff $L(ind(A))X \neq \emptyset$ and $U(ind(A))X \neq \mathbb{OB}$;
- *internally A-indefinable* iff $L(ind(A))X = \emptyset$;
- *externally A-indefinable* iff $U(ind(A))X = \mathbb{OB}$;
- *totally A-indefinable* iff it is internally *A*-indefinable and externally *A*-indefinable.

The other application of the above information relations is related to modelling uncertain knowledge acquired from information about objects provided in an information system. Let X be a subset of $\mathbb{OB}$, we define sets of *A-positive* $(POS(A)X)$, *A-borderline* $(BOR(A)X)$ and *A-negative* $(NEG(A)X)$ *instances of X* as follows:

$$POS(A)X = L(ind(A))X;$$
$$BOR(A)X = U(ind(A))X - L(ind(A))X;$$
$$NEG(A)X = \mathbb{OB} - U(ind(A))X.$$

The elements of $POS(A)X$ can be seen as the members of X up to the properties from A. The elements of $NEG(A)X$ are not the members of X up to the properties from A.

Knowledge about a set X of objects that can be discovered from an information system can be modelled as $K(A)X = POS(A)X \cup NEG(A)X$. Intuitively, *A*-knowledge about X consists of those objects that are either *A*-positive instances of X or *A*-negative instances of X. We say that *A*-knowledge about X is:

- *complete* if $K(A)X = \mathbb{OB}$, otherwise *incomplete*;
- *rough* if $POS(A)X$, $BOR(A)X$, $NEG(A)X$ are non-empty;
- *pos-empty* if $POS(A)X = \emptyset$;
- *neg-empty* if $NEG(A)X = \emptyset$;
- *empty* if it is pos-empty and neg-empty.

Distinguishability relations

Let $S = (\mathbb{OB}, \mathbb{AT})$ be an information system. For every $A \subseteq \mathbb{AT}$ and all $x, y \in \mathbb{OB}$ the following binary relations on $\mathbb{OB}$ reflect differences or dissimilarities between objects:

- the *strong* (resp. *weak*) *diversity relation* $div(A)$ (resp. $wdiv(A)$): $(x, y) \in div(A)$ (resp. $(x, y) \in wdiv(A)$) iff for all (resp. for some) $a \in A$, $a(x) \neq a(y)$;
- the *strong* (resp. *weak*) *right orthogonality relation* $rort(A)$ (resp. $wrort(A)$): $(x, y) \in rort(A)$ (resp. $(x, y) \in wrort(A)$) iff for all (resp. for some) $a \in A$, $a(x) \subseteq -a(y)$;

- the *strong* (resp. *weak*) *left orthogonality relation* $lort(A)$ (resp. $wlort(A)$): $(x, y) \in lort(A)$ (resp. $(x, y) \in wlort(A)$) iff for all (resp. for some) $a \in A$, $-a(x) \subseteq a(y)$;
- the *strong* (resp. *weak*) *right negative similarity relation* $rnim(A)$ (resp. $wrnim(A)$): $(x, y) \in rnim(A)$ (resp. $(x, y) \in wrnim(A)$) iff for all (resp. for some) $a \in A$, $a(x) \cap -a(y) \neq \emptyset$;
- the *strong* (resp. *weak*) *left negative similarity relation*, $lnim(A)$ (resp. $wlnim(A)$): $(x, y) \in lnim(A)$ (resp. $(x, y) \in wlnim(A)$) iff for all (resp. for some) $a \in A$, $-a(x) \cap a(y) \neq \emptyset$;
- the *strong* (resp. *weak*) *complementarity relation* $com(A)$ (resp. $wcom(A)$): $(x, y) \in com(A)$ (resp. $(x, y) \in wcom(A)$) iff for all (resp. for some) $a \in A$, $a(x) = -a(y)$.

Intuitively, objects are strongly A-diverse (resp. weakly A-diverse) if all (resp. some) of the sets of their properties determined by members of A are different. The objects are strongly A-right orthogonal (resp. weakly A-right orthogonal) whenever all (resp. some) of the sets of their properties determined by attributes from A are disjoint. The objects are strongly A-left orthogonal (resp. weakly A-left orthogonal) whenever all (resp. some) of their a-properties, for $a \in A$, are exhaustive, i.e. $a(x) \cup a(y) = \mathbb{VAL}_a$. Two objects are right or left strongly (resp. weakly) A-negatively similar whenever some properties of one of them are not the properties of the other, for all (resp. some) attributes from A. The objects are strongly (resp. weakly) A-complementary whenever their respective sets of properties are complements of each other, for all (resp. some) attributes from A.

Distinguishability relations can be applied to modelling in a non-numerical way degrees of dissimilarity. Diversity relations are applied, among others, in the algorithms for finding the cores of sets of attributes. Let an information system $(\mathbb{OB}, \mathbb{AT})$ be given and let A be a subset of $\mathbb{AT}$. We say that an attribute $a \in A$ is *indispensable* in A whenever $ind(A) \neq ind(A - \{a\})$, that is there are some objects such that a is the only attribute from A that can distinguish between them. A *reduct* of A is a minimal subset A' of A such that every $a \in A'$ is indispensable in A' and $ind(A') = ind(A)$. The *core* of A is defined as $CORE(A) = \bigcap\{A' \subseteq \mathbb{AT} : A' \text{ is a reduct of } A\}$. For any pair x, y of objects we define the *discernibility set* $D_{xy} = \{a \in \mathbb{AT} : (x, y) \in div(\{a\})\}$. It is proved in [RSK91] that $CORE(A) = \{a \in A : \text{ there are } x, y \in \mathbb{OB} \text{ such that } D_{xy} = \{a\}\}$.

In the proposition below some of the properties satisfied by information relations derived from an information system are listed. We recall that a binary relation R on a set U is:

- a weakly reflexive relation whenever $\forall x, y \in U(xRy \rightarrow xRx)$;

- a tolerance relation whenever it is reflexive and symmetric;
- a 3-transitive relation whenever $\forall x, y, z, t \in U[(xRz \wedge zRt \wedge tRy) \rightarrow xRy]$.

For any property α of R by property co-α of R we mean that $-R$ has the property α.

Proposition 1.
For every information system $S = (\mathbb{OB}, \mathbb{AT})$, for every $A \subseteq \mathbb{AT}$, the following hold:

1. *$ind(A)$ is an equivalence relation;*
2. *$sim(A)$ and $nim(A)$ are weakly reflexive and symmetric;*
3. *if S is total, then $sim(A)$ is a tolerance relation;*
4. *$fin(A)$ and $bin(A)$ are reflexive and transitive;*
5. *$icom(A)$ is symmetric and if $A \neq \emptyset$, then $icom(A)$ reflexive; for every $a \in \mathbb{AT}$, $icom(a)$ is co-3-transitive;*
6. *$wind(A)$ is a tolerance relation and for every $a \in \mathbb{AT}$, $wind(a)$ is transitive;*
7. *$wsim(A)$ is a tolerance relation;*
8. *$wnim(A)$ is weakly reflexive and symmetric;*
9. *$wicom(A)$ is reflexive, symmetric and co-3-transitive;*
10. *$wfin(A)$ and $wbin(A)$ are reflexive; for every $a \in \mathbb{AT}$, $wfin(a)$ and $wbin(a)$ are transitive;*
11. *$div(A)$ is symmetric; if $A \neq \emptyset$, then $div(A)$ is irreflexive; for every $a \in \mathbb{AT}$, $div(a)$ is cotransitive;*
12. *$rort(A)$ is symmetric; if $A \neq \emptyset$, then $rort(A)$ is irreflexive;*
13. *$lort(A)$ is coweakly reflexive and symmetric;*
14. *$com(A)$ is symmetric and 3-transitive; if $A \neq \emptyset$, then $com(A)$ is irreflexive;*
15. *$rnim(A)$ and $lnim(A)$ are irreflexive for every $A \neq \emptyset$; for every $a \in \mathbb{AT}$, $rnim(a)$ and $lnim(a)$ are cotransitive;*
16. *$wdiv(A)$ is irreflexive, symmetric and cotransitive;*
17. *$wrort(A)$ is symmetric; if S is total, then $wrort(A)$ is irreflexive;*
18. *$wlort(A)$ is coweakly reflexive and symmetric;*
19. *$wcom(A)$ is irreflexive and symmetric; for every $a \in \mathbb{AT}$, $wcom(a)$ is 3-transitive;*
20. *$wrnim(A)$ and $wlnim(A)$ are irreflexive and cotransitive.*

The following proposition states some relationships between information relations of different kinds:

Proposition 2.
For every information system $S = (\mathbb{OB}, \mathbb{AT})$, for every $A \subseteq \mathbb{AT}$, and for all $x, y, z \in \mathbb{OB}$, the following hold:

1. *$(x, y) \in sim(A)$ and $(x, z) \in fin(A)$ imply $(z, y) \in sim(A)$;*

2. $(x,y) \in ind(A)$ *implies* $(x,y) \in fin(A)$;
3. $(x,y) \in fin(A)$ *and* $(y,x) \in fin(A)$ *imply* $(x,y) \in ind(A)$.

Observe that definitions of information relations include both information on which objects are related and with respect to which attributes they are related. Relations of that kind are referred to as *relative relations*, they are relative to a subset of attributes. It follows that the formal systems for reasoning about these relations should refer to the structures with relative relations. For that purpose we define a class of relative frames which have the form $(U, (R_P^1)_{P \in \mathcal{P}_{fin}(\text{Par})}, \ldots, (R_P^n)_{P \in \mathcal{P}_{fin}(\text{Par})})$, where the relations in each family $(R_P^i)_{P \in \mathcal{P}_{fin}(\text{Par})}$ are indexed with finite subsets of a non-empty set Par. Intuitively, the elements of Par are representations of the attributes of an information system. If Par is a singleton set, then the relative frame is just a usual frame and in such a case it will be referred to as a *plain frame*.

A modal approach to reasoning in information systems resulted in various modal systems which are now called information logics. The first logics of that family are defined in [ORL82] published later as [ORL83] and in [ORL84a], [ORL84b], and [ORL85]. We refer the reader to [DEO02] for a comprehensive survey of information logics and to [DEG00], [DES02], [BAL01], [DEO07] for some more recent developments. In information logics the elements of the universes of the models are thought of as objects in an information system. This interpretation is quite different from the usual interpretation postulated in modal logics, where the elements of a model represent states (or possible worlds) in which formulas may be true or false.

3   The classical relational logic RL

In this section we recall the relational logic RL and its proof system (originated in [ORL88]). The relational logic of binary relations, RL, is a logical counterpart to the class FRA of full relation algebras introduced by Tarski ([TAR41]). The formulas of RL-language are intended to represent statements saying that two objects are related. Relations are specified in the form of relational terms. Terms are built from relational variables and/or relational constants with relational operations. The operations are the Boolean operations of union ($\cup$), intersection ($\cap$), and complement ($-$) and the specific relational operations of composition ($P;Q = \{(x,y) : \exists z(xPz \wedge zQy)\}$) and converse ($P^{-1} = \{(x,y) : yPx\}$). The relational constants include 1 and 1' interpreted as the universal relation and the relation which is a reflexive relation and a neutral element of the composition of relations (i.e., $P;1' = P = 1';P$ for any relation P), respectively. RL-formulas are of the form xPy, where P is a relational term and x,y are object variables.

With the RL-language a class of RL-models is associated. An RL-*model* is a structure $\mathcal{M} = (U, m)$, where U is a non-empty set and m is a meaning function such that $m(1) = U \times U$, $m(1')$ is reflexive relation on U and a neutral element of the composition of relations, i.e., $R; m(1') = R = m(1'); R$ for every relation $R \subseteq U \times U$, $m(Q) \subseteq U \times U$, for every atomic relational term Q (i.e., Q is a relational variable or a relational constant), and m extends homomorphically to all compound relational terms in a standard way as follows: $m(-P) = (U \times U) - m(P)$, $m(P^{-1}) = m(P)^{-1}$, and $m(P \# Q) = m(P) \# m(Q)$, for $\# \in \{\cup, \cap, ;\}$.

A *valuation* in $\mathcal{M} = (U, m)$ is any function which assigns elements of U to object variables. A formula xQy is *satisfied* in $\mathcal{M}$ by a valuation v, $\mathcal{M}, v \models xQy$ for short, whenever $(v(x), v(y)) \in m(Q)$. A formula xQy is *true* in $\mathcal{M}$, $\mathcal{M} \models xQy$ for short, whenever it is satisfied by all the valuations in $\mathcal{M}$. A formula xQy is RL-*valid* whenever it is true in all RL-models.

$$(\cup) \; \frac{x(P \cup Q)y}{xPy, xQy} \qquad\qquad (-\cup) \; \frac{x-(P \cup Q)y}{x-Py \mid x-Qy}$$

$$(\cap) \; \frac{x(P \cap Q)y}{xPy \mid xQy} \qquad\qquad (-\cap) \; \frac{x-(P \cap Q)y}{x-Py, x-Qy}$$

$$(-) \; \frac{x--Py}{xPy}$$

$$(^{-1}) \; \frac{xP^{-1}y}{yPx} \qquad\qquad (-^{-1}) \; \frac{x-P^{-1}y}{y-Px}$$

$$(;) \; \frac{x(P;Q)y}{xPz, x(P;Q)y \mid zQy, x(P;Q)y} \quad z \text{ is any object variable}$$

$$(-;) \; \frac{x-(P;Q)y}{x-Pz, z-Qy} \quad z \text{ is a new object variable}$$

Fig. 1. Decomposition rules

The RL-proof system is in the style of dual tableau (see [GOL07]). The rules are of the form $\frac{\Phi}{\Phi_1 \mid ... \mid \Phi_n}$, where $\Phi, \Phi_1, \ldots, \Phi_n$, $n \geq 1$, are finite (possibly empty) sets of formulas. The rules satisfy the following semantic property: Φ is valid iff $\Phi_1, \ldots, \Phi_n$ are valid, where validity of a finite set of RL-formulas is understood as validity in first order logic of disjunction of its members. The rules are intended to reflect properties of relational operations and constants. There are two groups of rules: *decomposition* rules and *specific* rules. Given a formula, the decomposition rules of the system enable us to transform it into simpler formulas. The specific rules characterize relational constants. Some valid sets of formulas take the place of axioms. They are referred to as *axiomatic sets*. Given a formula, successive applications of the rules result in a proof tree, called RL-proof tree, whose nodes consist of finite sets of formulas. Each node includes all the formulas of its predecessor node, except of possibly those which have been transformed according to a rule. A node of the tree does not have successors whenever its set of formulas includes an axiomatic subset or if none of the rules is applicable to it. We say that a variable in a rule is *new* whenever it appears in a conclusion of the rule and does not appear in its premise. The decomposition and specific rules of RL-dual tableau are presented in Figures 1 and 2, respectively, where x, y, z are object variables, P, Q are relational terms, and T is an atomic relational term. The specific rules for constant $1'$ reflect the fact that relation $1'$ is the neutral element of the composition of relations.

$$(1'1) \quad \frac{xTy}{xTz, xTy \mid y1'z, xTy} \quad z \text{ is any object variable}$$

$$(1'2) \quad \frac{xTy}{x1'z, xTy \mid zTy, xTy} \quad z \text{ is any object variable}$$

Fig. 2. Specific rules

RL-*axiomatic* sets are those finite sets of RL-formulas that include one of the following subsets for any object variables x, y and for any relational term Q: $\{x1'x\}$ which reflects reflexivity of $1'$, $\{x1y\}$ which corresponds to the fact that 1 is the universal relation, or $\{xQy, x-Qy\}$ which says that $Q \cup -Q$ is the universal relation. A branch of an RL-proof tree is said to be *closed* whenever it contains a node with an RL-axiomatic set of formulas. An RL-proof tree is *closed* iff all of its branches are closed. An RL-formula xQy is RL-*provable* whenever there is a closed RL-proof tree for it, which is then referred to as its RL-*proof*. The following theorem states the relationships between RL-validity and RL-provability. A proof can be found in [ORG07].

Theorem 1 (Soundness and Completeness of RL).
Let φ be an RL-formula. Then the following conditions are equivalent:

- φ *is RL-provable;*
- φ *is RL-valid.*

It is known that although the deductive system of RL specifies $1'$ only as a reflexive relation which is a neutral element of the composition, the logic RL is also complete with respect to the so called standard models, referred to as RL*-models, where $1'$ is interpreted as the identity.

4   Relational dual tableaux for information logics NIL and IL with semantics of plain frames

The language of most popular information logics with semantics of plain frames is a multimodal langauge that consists of the symbols from the following pairwise disjoint sets:

- $\mathbb{V}$ - a set of propositional variables possibly augmented with a propositional constant D interpreted as a set of deterministic objects;
- $\{\leq, \geq, \sigma, \equiv\}$ - a set of relational constants, where $\leq, \geq, \sigma, \equiv$ are the abstract counterparts of the relations of inclusions, similarity, and indiscernibility derived from an information system;
- $\{\neg, \vee, \wedge, [\leq], [\geq], [\sigma], [\equiv]\}$ - a set of propositional operations.

The set of formulas of a logic L based on such a language is defined as the smallest set including a set $\mathbb{V}$ of propositional variables and closed with respect to all the propositional operations.

An L-*frame* is a relational system of the form $\mathcal{F} = (U, R_\leq, R_\geq, R_\sigma, R_\equiv)$, where $R_\leq, R_\geq, R_\sigma, R_\equiv$ are binary relations on U. In various information logics the frames satisfy some postulates. Typical conditions on relations in the frames of logics associated with information systems with incomplete information are among the following:

(I1) $R_\leq = (R_\geq)^{-1}$;
(I2) $R_\leq$ is reflexive and transitive;
(I3) R_σ is weakly reflexive and symmetric;
(I4) R_σ is reflexive and symmetric;
(I5) $R_\equiv$ is an equivalence relation;
(I6) If $(x,y) \in R_\sigma$, $(x,x') \in R_\leq$ and $(y,y') \in R_\leq$, then $(x',y') \in R_\sigma$, for all $x, x', y, y' \in U$;
(I7) If $(x,y) \in R_\sigma$ and $(x,z) \in R_\leq$, then $(z,y) \in R_\sigma$;
(I8) If $y \in D$ and $(x,y) \in R_\leq$, then $x \in D$;
(I9) If $x \in D$ and $(x,y) \in R_\sigma$, then $(x,y) \in R_\leq$;
(I10) If $(x,y) \in R_\equiv$, then $(x,y) \in R_\leq$;
(I11) If $x,y \in D$ and $(x,y) \in R_\sigma$, then $(x,y) \in R_\equiv$;
(I12) If $(x,y) \in R_\leq$ and $(y,x) \in R_\leq$, then $(x,y) \in R_\equiv$;
(I13) If $x \notin D$, then there is $y \in U$ such that $(x,y) \notin R_\leq$.

In this section we consider two information logics with semantics of plain frames: the logic NIL and the logic IL.

The set of relational constants of NIL is $\{\leq, \geq, \sigma\}$. $\mathbb{V}$ is a countably infinite set of propositional variables. The set of propositional operations is $\{\neg, \vee, \wedge, [\leq], [\geq], [\sigma]\}$. The set of NIL-formulas is defined as above. The NIL-models are the structures $(U, R_{\leq}, R_{\geq}, R_{\sigma}, m)$ such that U is a non-empty set and m is a meaning function satisfying the following conditions:

- $m(p) \subseteq U$, for every $p \in \mathbb{V}$;
- $m(\#) = R_{\#} \subseteq U \times U$, for $\# \in \{\leq, \geq, \sigma\}$;
- for all $x, y, z \in U$ conditions (I1), (I2), (I4), and (I6) are satisfied.

As usual in modal logics the relations $R_{\#}$ are referred to as the *accessibility relations*.

A NIL-formula φ is said to be satisfied in a NIL-model $\mathcal{M}$ by a state s, $\mathcal{M}, s \models \varphi$ for short, whenever the following conditions are satisfied:

$\mathcal{M}, s \models p$ iff $s \in m(p)$ for $p \in \mathbb{V}$;
$\mathcal{M}, s \models \varphi \vee \psi$ iff $\mathcal{M}, s \models \varphi$ or $\mathcal{M}, s \models \psi$;
$\mathcal{M}, s \models \varphi \wedge \psi$ iff $\mathcal{M}, s \models \varphi$ and $\mathcal{M}, s \models \psi$;
$\mathcal{M}, s \models \neg\varphi$ iff not $\mathcal{M}, s \models \varphi$;
$\mathcal{M}, s \models [\#]\varphi$ iff for every $s' \in U$, if $(s, s') \in R_{\#}$, then $\mathcal{M}, s' \models \varphi$;
$\mathcal{M}, s \models \langle\#\rangle\varphi$ iff there exists $s' \in U$ such that $(s, s') \in R_{\#}$ and $\mathcal{M}, s' \models \varphi$;

for any $\# \in \{\leq, \geq, \sigma\}$.

A NIL-formula φ is said to be *true* in a NIL-model $\mathcal{M} = (U, R_{\leq}, R_{\geq}, R_{\sigma}, m)$, $\mathcal{M} \models \varphi$, whenever for every $s \in U$, $\mathcal{M}, s \models \varphi$, and it is NIL-*valid* whenever it is true in all NIL-models.

In [DEM00] the following theorem is proved:

Theorem 2.
1. The logic NIL *is decidable.*
2. NIL-*satisfiability problem is* PSPACE-*complete.*

Moreover in [VAK87] the following is proved:

Theorem 3 (Informational representability of NIL).
For every NIL-*model* $(U, R_{\leq}, R_{\geq}, R_{\sigma}, m)$, *there is a total information system* $\mathcal{S}$ *such that the relations of forward inclusion, backward inclusion, and similarity derived from* $\mathcal{S}$ *coincide with* $R_{\leq}, R_{\geq}$, *and* R_{σ}, *respectively.*

The logic IL is intended to be a tool for reasoning about indiscernibility, similarity, and forward inclusion, and about relationships between them. The set of relational constants of IL is $\{\equiv, \leq, \sigma\}$. $\mathbb{V}$ is a countably infinite set of propositional variables endowed with the propositional constant D interpreted as a set of deterministic objects of an information system. The set of propositional operations is $\{\neg, \vee, \wedge, [\equiv], [\leq], [\sigma]\}$. The set of IL-formulas is defined as usual. The IL-models are the structures of the form $(U, R_{\equiv}, R_{\leq}, R_{\sigma}, D, m)$ such that U is a non-empty set and m is a meaning function satisfying the following conditions:

- $m(p) \subseteq U$, for every $p \in \mathbb{V}$;
- $m(\#) = R_\# \subseteq U \times U$, for $\# \in \{\equiv, \leq, \sigma\}$;
- $m(D) = D$;
- for all $x, y, z \in U$ conditions (I2), (I3), (I5) and (I7) - (I13) are satisfied.

The following theorem can be found in [DEO02]:

Theorem 4.
1. The logic IL *is decidable.*
2. IL-*satisfiability problem is* PSPACE-*hard.*

The logic RL serves as a basis for the relational formalisms for modal logics whose Kripke-style semantics is determined by frames with binary accessibility relations. Let L be a logic with semantic of plain frames. The relational logic RL$_L$ appropriate for expressing L-formulas is obtained from RL by expanding its language with relational constants representing the accessibility relations from the models of L-language and with propositional constants of L which will be interpreted appropriately as relations. The vocabulary of the relational logic RL$_L$ consists of the symbols from the following pairwise disjoint sets:

- $\mathbb{OV}_{RL_L}$ - a countable infinite set of object variables;
- $\mathbb{RV}_{RL_L}$ - a countable infinite set of relational variables;
- $\mathbb{RC}_{RL_L} = \{1, 1'\} \cup \{R : R$ is a relational constant of L$\} \cup \{C : C$ is a propositional constant of L$\}$ - a set of relational constants;
- $\{-, \cup, \cap, ;, ^{-1}\}$ - the countable set of relational operations.

For the sake of simplicity, we denote the relations of $\mathbb{RC}_{RL_L}$ corresponding to propositional constants of L with the same symbols as the corresponding relations in L-models.

Atomic terms, relational terms, and formulas are defined as in RL-logic.

An RL$_L$-model is an RL-model $\mathcal{M} = (U, m)$ such that:

- $m(C) = X \times U$, where $X \subseteq U$, for any propositional constant C of L;
- the domains of relations $m(C)$ satisfy the properties imposed on constants C in L-models;
- for all relational constants representing the accessibility relations of L, all the properties of these relations from L-models are assumed in RL$_L$-models.

As usual, if in a modal logic L there is finitely many accessibility relations, then in the RL$_L$-models we list explicitly these relations and we denote them with the same symbols as the corresponding constants in the language.

Following the notation of Section 3, the models of RL$_L$ such that $1'$ is interpreted as identity are referred to as RL$_L^*$-models.

The translation of L-formulas into relational terms starts with a one-to-one assignment of relational variables to the propositional variables and propositional constants. Let τ' be such an assignment. Then the translation τ of formulas is defined inductively as follows:

- $\tau(p) := \tau'(p); 1$, for every propositional variable and constant p;
- $\tau(\neg\varphi) := -\tau(\varphi)$;
- $\tau(\varphi \vee \psi) := \tau(\varphi) \cup \tau(\psi)$;
- $\tau(\varphi \wedge \psi) := \tau(\varphi) \cap \tau(\psi)$;
- $\tau(\varphi \rightarrow \psi) := -\tau(\varphi) \cup \tau(\psi)$;

and for every relational constant R of L:

- $\tau(\langle R \rangle \varphi) := R; \tau(\varphi)$;
- $\tau([R]\varphi) := -(R; -\tau(\varphi))$.

Hence, when passing from L-formulas to relational terms we replace propositional variables by relational variables and propositional operations by relational operations. The crucial point here is that the accessibility relation is 'taken out' of the modal operator and it becomes an argument of an appropriate relational operation. In particular, possibility operation is replaced by the relational composition of two terms: the relational term representing an accessibility relation and the term resulting from the translation of the formula which is an argument of the possibility operator. In this way to any formula φ of a modal logic there is associated a relational term $\tau(\varphi)$. The translation is defined so that it preserves validity of formulas, that is the following holds:

Theorem 5.
For every L-formula φ and for all object variables x and y the following conditions are equivalent:

1. *φ is L-valid;*
2. *$x\tau(\varphi)y$ is $\mathsf{RL_L}$-valid.*

Following these general principles of relational formalization of modal logics, the language of the relational logic $\mathsf{RL_{NIL}}$ appropriate for the logic NIL is RL-language with the set of relational constants $\mathsf{RC_{RL_{NIL}}} = \{R_\leq, R_\geq, R_\sigma, 1, 1'\}$. $\mathcal{M} = (U, R_\leq, R_\geq, R_\sigma, m)$ is an $\mathsf{RL_{NIL}}$-model whenever it is an RL-model such that $m(R_\#) = R_\#$, for $\# \in \{\leq, \geq, \sigma\}$, satisfying the conditions (I1), (I2), (I4), and (I6). The language of the relational logic $\mathsf{RL_{IL}}$ appropriate for the logic IL is RL-language with the set of relational constants $\mathsf{RC_{RL_{IL}}} = \{R_\leq, R_\equiv, R_\sigma, D, 1, 1'\}$. $\mathcal{M} = (U, R_\leq, R_\equiv, R_\sigma, m)$ is an $\mathsf{RL_{IL}}$-model whenever it is an RL-model such that $m(R_\#) = R_\#$, for $\# \in \{\leq, \equiv, \sigma\}$, satisfying the conditions (I2), (I3), (I5), (I7), (I10), (I2), and the following:

(I8') If $(y, z) \in D$ and $(x, y) \in R_\leq$, then $(x, z) \in D$;
(I9') If $(x, z) \in D$ and $(x, y) \in R_\sigma$, then $(x, y) \in R_\leq$;
(I11') If $(x, z), (y, z) \in D$ and $(x, y) \in R_\sigma$, then $(x, y) \in R_\equiv$;
(I13') If $(x, z) \notin D$, then there is $y \in U$ such that $(x, y) \notin R_\leq$.

In this way, constant D in $\mathsf{RL_{IL}}$-logic represents a right ideal relation which is a counterpart to a set D of IL.

By Theorem 5 we obtain the following:

Theorem 6.
For every formula φ of the logic NIL (resp. IL) and for all object variables x and y the following conditions are equivalent:

1. *φ is NIL-valid (resp. IL-valid);*
2. *$x\tau(\varphi)y$ is $\mathsf{RL_{NIL}}$-valid (resp. $\mathsf{RL_{IL}}$-valid).*

Dual tableau proof systems for the logics NIL and IL in their relational formalizations are constructed as follows. We add to the classical RL-dual tableau the rules corresponding to the conditions on relations that are assumed in the models of these logics. They can be constructed according to the constraint-rule correspondences presented in [MAC02]. The rules have the following forms:

$$(R \text{ ref}) \quad \frac{xRy}{x1'y, xRy} \qquad\qquad (R \text{ sym}) \quad \frac{xRy}{yRx, xRy}$$

$$(R \text{ wref}) \quad \frac{xRx}{xRy, xRx} \qquad\qquad (R \text{ tran}) \quad \frac{xRy}{xRz, xRy \mid zRy, xRy}$$

$$\qquad y \text{ is any object variable} \qquad\qquad z \text{ is any object variable}$$

$$(rI1 \subseteq) \quad \frac{xR_\leq y}{yR_\geq x} \qquad\qquad (rI1 \supseteq) \quad \frac{xR_\geq y}{yR_\leq x}$$

$$(rI6) \quad \frac{xR_\sigma y}{zR_\sigma t, xR_\sigma y \mid zR_\leq x, xR_\sigma y \mid tR_\leq y, xR_\sigma y}$$

$$\qquad z, t \text{ are any object variables}$$

$$(rI7) \quad \frac{xR_\sigma y}{zR_\sigma y, xR_\sigma y \mid zR_\leq x, xR_\sigma y} \qquad z \text{ is any object variable}$$

$$(rI8') \quad \frac{xDy}{zDy, xDy \mid xR_\leq z, xDy} \qquad z \text{ is any object variable}$$

$$\text{(rI9')} \quad \frac{xR_{\leq}y}{xDz, xR_{\leq}y \mid xR_{\sigma}z, xR_{\leq}y} \quad z \text{ is any object variable}$$

$$\text{(rI10)} \quad \frac{xR_{\leq}y}{xR_{\equiv}y, xR_{\leq}y} \qquad \text{(rI12)} \quad \frac{xR_{\equiv}y}{xR_{\leq}y, xR_{\equiv}y \mid yR_{\leq}x, xR_{\equiv}y}$$

$$\text{(rI11')} \quad \frac{xR_{\equiv}y}{xDz, xR_{\equiv}y \mid yDz, xR_{\equiv}y \mid xR_{\sigma}y, xR_{\equiv}y} \quad z \text{ is any object variable}$$

$$\text{(rI13')} \quad \frac{xDy}{xR_{\leq}z, xDy} \quad z \text{ is a new object variable}$$

The specific rules of the logics in question are as follows, where the rule(s) (rI#) corresponds to the condition (I#), for $\# \in \{1, \ldots, 7, 8', 9', 10, 11', 12, 13'\}$.

The specific NIL-rules are (rI1$\subseteq$), (rI1$\supseteq$), (rI6), and the following:

(rI2 ref) - the rule (R ref) for $R = R_{\leq}$;
(rI2 tran) - the rule (R tran) for $R = R_{\leq}$;
(rI4 ref) - the rule (R ref) for $R = R_{\sigma}$;
(rI4 sym) - the rule (R sym) for $R = R_{\sigma}$.

The specific IL-rules are (rI7), (rI8'), (rI9'), (rI10), (rI11'), (rI12), (rI13'), and the following:

(rI2 ref) - the rule (R ref) for $R = R_{\leq}$;
(rI2 tran) - the rule (R tran) for $R = R_{\leq}$;
(rI3 wref) - the rule (R wref) for $R = R_{\sigma}$;
(rI3 sym) - the rule (R sym) for $R = R_{\sigma}$;
(rI5 ref) - the rule (R ref) for $R = R_{\equiv}$;
(rI5 sym) - the rule (R sym) for $R = R_{\equiv}$;
(rI5 tran) - the rule (R tran) for $R = R_{\equiv}$.

Theorem 7 (Correspondence).
Let L *be an information logic satisfying some of (I1), ..., (I13). Then* RL$_L$-*models satisfy the condition (I#) iff the rule(s) (rI#) is (are)* RL$_L$-*correct, where* $\# \in \{1, \ldots, 7, 8', 9', 10, 11', 12, 13'\}$.

Proof.
By way of example we show the proposition for the conditions (I6) and (I12).

($\rightarrow$) Assume RL$_L$-models satisfy the condition (I6). Then the direction from the validity of the upper set to the validity of the bottom sets is obvious. Assume $X_1 = \{zR_{\sigma}t, xR_{\sigma}y\}$, $X_2 = \{zR_{\leq}x, xR_{\sigma}y\}$, and $X_3 = \{tR_{\leq}y, xR_{\sigma}y\}$

are RL_L-sets. Suppose $\{xR_\sigma y\}$ is not an RL_L-set, that is there exist an RL_L-model $\mathcal{M}$ and a valuation v in $\mathcal{M}$ such that $\mathcal{M}, v \not\models xR_\sigma y$. Since X_1, X_2, X_3 are RL_L-sets, the model $\mathcal{M}$ and the valuation v satisfy: $(v(z), v(t)) \in R_\sigma$, $(v(z), v(x)) \in R_\leq$, and $(v(t), v(y)) \in R_\leq$. By the condition (I6), $(v(x), v(y)) \in R_\sigma$, a contradiction.

Assume RL_L-models satisfy the condition (I12). Let $\{xR_\leq y, xR_\equiv y\}$ and $\{yR_\leq x, xR_\equiv y\}$ be RL_L-sets. Suppose $\{xR_\equiv y\}$ is not RL_L-set, that is there exist an RL_L-model $\mathcal{M} = (U, m)$ and $a, b \in U$ such that $(a, b) \notin R_\equiv$. Since $\{xR_\leq y, xR_\equiv y\}$ and $\{yR_\leq x, xR_\equiv y\}$ are L-sets, $\mathcal{M}$ satisfies also $(a, b) \in R_\leq$ and $(b, a) \in R_\leq$. Then by the condition (I12), $(a, b) \in R_\equiv$, a contradiction. The other direction is obvious.

($\leftarrow$) Assume that the rule (rI6) is RL_L-correct. Suppose that there exists an RL_L-model $\mathcal{M}$ in which the condition (I6) is not satisfied. Then there is a valuation v in $\mathcal{M}$ such that $\mathcal{M}, v \models zR_\sigma t$, $\mathcal{M}, v \models zR_\leq x$, $\mathcal{M}, v \models tR_\leq y$, and $\mathcal{M}, v \not\models xR_\sigma y$. By correctness of (rI6), $\{xR_\sigma y, z-R_\sigma t, z-R_\leq x, t-R_\leq y\}$ is an RL_L-set. Since $\mathcal{M}, v \not\models xR_\sigma y$, in the model $\mathcal{M}$ the following holds: $\mathcal{M}, v \models z-R_\sigma t$ or $\mathcal{M}, v \models z-R_\leq x$ or $\mathcal{M}, v \models t-R_\leq y$. Hence, $\mathcal{M}, v \not\models zR_\sigma t$ or $\mathcal{M}, v \not\models zR_\leq x$ or $\mathcal{M}, v \not\models tR_\leq y$, a contradiction.

Assume now that the rule (rI12) is RL_L-correct. Suppose that there exists an RL_L-model $\mathcal{M}$ in which the condition (I12) is not satisfied. Then there is a valuation v in $\mathcal{M}$ such that $\mathcal{M}, v \models xR_\leq y$, $\mathcal{M}, v \models yR_\leq x$, and $\mathcal{M}, v \not\models xR_\equiv y$. By correctness of (rI12), $\{xR_\equiv y, x-R_\leq y, y-R_\leq x\}$ is an RL_L-set. Since $\mathcal{M}, v \not\models xR_\equiv y$, in the model $\mathcal{M}$ the following holds: $\mathcal{M}, v \models x-R_\leq y$ or $\mathcal{M}, v \models y-R_\leq x$. Hence, $\mathcal{M}, v \not\models xR_\leq y$ or $\mathcal{M}, v \not\models yR_\leq x$, a contradiction.

$\square$

By the above proposition we obtain the following:

Proposition 3.
1. The NIL-rules are RL_{NIL}-correct;
2. The IL-rules are RL_{IL}-correct.

It is known that conditions (I12) and (I13) are not definable in the language of logic IL, hence the completeness proof for a Hilbert-style axiomatization requires a special technique. As it is shown above, in the case of relational formalization the rules corresponding to (I12) and (I13) can be explicitly given.

The completion conditions corresponding to the above rules are as follows:

Cpl(R ref) If $xRy \in b$, then $x1'y \in b$;

Cpl(R wref) If $xRx \in b$, then for every object variable y, $xRy \in b$;

Cpl(R sym) If $xRy \in b$, then $yRx \in b$;

Cpl(R tran) If $xRy \in b$, then for every object variable z, either $xRz \in b$ or $zRy \in b$;

Cpl(rI1 $\subseteq$) If $xR_{\leq}y \in b$, then $yR_{\geq}x \in b$;

Cpl(rI1 $\supseteq$) If $xR_{\geq}y \in b$, then $yR_{\leq}x \in b$;

Cpl(rI6) If $xR_{\sigma}y \in b$, then for all object variables z and t, either $zR_{\sigma}t \in b$ or $zR_{\leq}x \in b$ or $tR_{\leq}y \in b$;

Cpl(rI7) If $xR_{\sigma}y \in b$, then for every object variable z, either $zR_{\sigma}y \in b$ or $zR_{\leq}x \in b$;

Cpl(rI8') If $xDy \in b$, then for every object variable z, either $zDy \in b$ or $xR_{\leq}z \in b$;

Cpl(rI9') If $xR_{\leq}y \in b$, then for every object variable z, either $xDz \in b$ or $xR_{\sigma}z \in b$;

Cpl(rI10) If $xR_{\leq}y \in b$, then $xR_{\equiv}y \in b$;

Cpl(rI11') If $xR_{\equiv}y \in b$, then for every object variable z, either $xDz \in b$, $yDz \in b$ or $xR_{\sigma}y \in b$;

Cpl(rI12) If $xR_{\equiv}y \in b$, then either $xR_{\leq}y \in b$ or $yR_{\leq}x \in b$;

Cpl(rI13) If $xDy \in b$, then for some object variable z, $xR_{\leq}z \in b$.

The completeness of dual tableaux presented above can be proved similarly as the completeness of RL-proof system. Let b be an open branch of an RL_L-proof tree. The branch structure has the form $\mathcal{M}^b = (U^b, (R^b_{\#})_{\# \in \{\leq, \geq, \sigma, \equiv\}}, m^b)$, where $U^b = \mathbb{OV}_{RL_L}$, $m^b(R) = \{(x, y) \in U^b \times U^b : xRy \notin b\}$, for every relational constant R, $R^b_{\#} = m^b(R_{\#})$ for every $\# \in \{\leq, \geq, \sigma, \equiv\}$, and m^b extends to all the compound relational terms as in RL_L-models. Using the completion conditions, it is easy to prove that branch structures satisfy all the conditions that are assumed in the models of a given logic.

Proposition 4 (Branch Model Property).
Let L be an information logic satisfying some of the conditions (I1), ..., (I13). Then the branch structure $\mathcal{M}^b$ determined by an open branch b of an RL_L-proof tree is an RL_L-model.

Proof.
For example, let us prove that the branch structure $\mathcal{M}^b = (U^b, R^b_{\leq}, R^b_{\equiv}, R^b_{\sigma}, m^b)$ determined by an open branch b of an RL_{IL}-proof tree satisfies the condition (I12). Assume $(x, y) \in R^b_{\leq}$ and $(y, x) \in R^b_{\leq}$, that is $xR_{\leq}y \notin b$ and $yR_{\leq}x \notin b$. Suppose $(x, y) \notin R^b_{\equiv}$. Then $xR_{\equiv}y \in b$. By the completion condition Cpl(rI12), either $xR_{\leq}y \in b$ or $yR_{\leq}x \in b$, a contradiction. The proofs of the remaining cases are similar. □

Now, completeness of RL_L-logic can be proved as in RL-logic. Thus, we obtain the following:

Theorem 8 (Soundness and Completeness of RL$_{NIL}$ and RL$_{IL}$).
1. RL$_{NIL}$-*proof system is sound and complete;*
2. RL$_{IL}$-*proof system is sound and complete.*

Finally, by the above theorem and Theorem 6 we obtain the following:

Theorem 9 (Relational Soundness and Completeness of NIL and IL).
For every NIL *(resp.* IL*) formula φ and for all object variables x and y the following conditions are equivalent:*

1. φ *is* NIL-*valid (resp.* IL-*valid);*
2. $x\tau(\varphi)y$ *is* RL$_{NIL}$-*provable (resp.* RL$_{IL}$-*provable).*

Example
Let us consider the following NIL-formula ψ and IL-formula ϑ:

$$\psi := \varphi \rightarrow [\leq]\langle\geq\rangle\varphi;$$

$$\vartheta := [\leq]\varphi \rightarrow [\equiv]\varphi,$$

where $\langle\rangle = \neg[\,]\neg$. For the sake of simplicity, let us denote $\tau(\varphi)$ by φ. Then the relational translations of these formulas are:

$$\tau(\psi) = -\varphi \cup -(R_{\leq}; -(R_{\geq}; \varphi));$$

$$\tau(\vartheta) = --(R_{\leq}; -\varphi) \cup -(R_{\equiv}; -\varphi).$$

Figure 3 presents an RL$_{NIL}$-proof for the formula $x\tau(\psi)y$ which proves NIL-validity of ψ, and Figure 4 presents an RL$_{IL}$-proof for the formula $x\tau(\vartheta)y$ that proves IL-validity of ϑ.

$$x(-\varphi \cup -(R_{\leq}; -(R_{\geq}; \varphi)))y$$

$$\Big\downarrow (\cup)$$

$$x-\varphi y, x(-(R_{\leq}; -(R_{\geq}; \varphi)))y$$

$$\Big\downarrow (-;)\ \text{and}\ (-)$$

$$x-\varphi y, x-(R_{\leq}z, z(R_{\geq}; \varphi)y$$

$$(;)$$

$$x-R_{\leq}z, zR_{\geq}x, \dots \qquad\qquad x-\varphi y, x\varphi y, \dots$$
$$\qquad\qquad\qquad\qquad\qquad\qquad \text{closed}$$

$$\Big\downarrow (\text{r1} \supseteq)$$

$$x-R_{\leq}z, xR_{\leq}z, \dots$$
$$\text{closed}$$

Fig. 3. An RL$_{NIL}$-proof of $\varphi \rightarrow [\leq]\langle\geq\rangle\varphi$

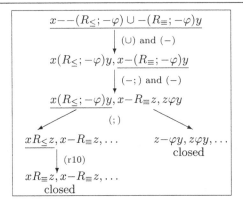

Fig. 4. An $\mathsf{RL}_{\mathsf{IL}}$-proof of $[\leq]\varphi \rightarrow [\equiv]\varphi$

5   Relational dual tableaux for information logics of relative frames

Let Par be a non-empty set of parameters intuitively interpreted as a set of attributes of an information system. A *relative frame* is a structure

$$\mathcal{F} = (U, (R_P^1)_{P \in \mathcal{P}_{fin}(\mathrm{Par})}, \ldots, (R_P^n)_{P \in \mathcal{P}_{fin}(\mathrm{Par})}),$$

where relations from $(R_P)_{P \in \mathcal{P}_{fin}(\mathrm{Par})}$ are indexed with finite subsets of the set Par.

Typically, these relations satisfy either of the following postulates for all $P, Q \in \mathcal{P}_{fin}(\mathrm{Par})$:

(S1) $R_{P \cup Q} = R_P \cap R_Q$;
(W1) $R_{P \cup Q} = R_P \cup R_Q$.

These conditions are referred to as *global* conditions, because they refer to a family of relations as a whole. Then the properties of relations listed in Proposition 1 will be called *local* conditions.

The characterization of a family of relative relations often requires special postulates for the relations indexed with the empty set. The typical condition for the relation $R_\emptyset$ is either of the following:

(S2) $R_\emptyset = U^2$;
(W2) $R_\emptyset = \emptyset$.

Conditions (S1) and (S2) reflect the behavior of strong relations, and conditions (W1) and (W2) reflect the behavior of weak relations.

Relations R_P, $P \subseteq$ Par, may also satisfy the usual properties of binary relations, e.g., reflexivity, transitivity, etc. We refer to them as *local* conditions.

Typically, information logics of relative frames are based on the following classes of frames:

- FS - the class of frames in which the families of relative relations satisfy conditions (S1) and (S2). The members of FS are called FS-*frames* or *relative frames with strong relations*.
- FW - the class of frames in which the families of relative relations satisfy conditions (W1) and (W2). The members of FW are called FW-*frames* or *relative frames with weak relations*.

Frames with indistinguishability and distinguishability relations listed below provide examples of members of the FS and FW families.

Frames with indistinguishability relations:

- FS−IND is the class of FS-frames $(U, (R_P)_{P \subseteq \mathrm{Par}})$ such that for every $p \in$ Par, $R_{\{p\}}$ is an equivalence relation. Consequently, for every $P \subseteq$ Par, R_P is an equivalence relation, since reflexivity, symmetry and transitivity are preserved under intersection. The members of FS−IND are called *strong indiscernibility frames*.
- FS−SIM is the class of FS-frames $(U, (R_P)_{P \subseteq \mathrm{Par}})$ such that for every $p \in$ Par, $R_{\{p\}}$ is weakly reflexive and symmetric. Consequently, for every $P \subseteq$ Par, R_P is weakly reflexive and symmetric. The members of FS−SIM are called *strong similarity frames*.
- FS−ICOM is the class of FS-frames $(U, (R_P)_{P \subseteq \mathrm{Par}})$ such that for every $p \in$ Par, $R_{\{p\}}$ is reflexive, symmetric and co-3-transitive. Consequently, for every $P \subseteq$ Par, R_P is reflexive and symmetric. The property of co-3-transitivity is not preserved under intersection. The members of FS−ICOM are called *strong incomplementarity frames*.
- FS−IN is the class of FS-frames $(U, (R_P)_{P \subseteq \mathrm{Par}}, (Q_P)_{P \subseteq \mathrm{Par}})$ with two families of relative relations such that for every $p \in$ Par, $R_{\{p\}}$ and $Q_{\{p\}}$ are reflexive and transitive, and $R_{\{p\}} = Q_{\{p\}}^{-1}$. Consequently, for every $P \subseteq$ Par, R_P and Q_P are reflexive and transitive, and $R_P = Q_P^{-1}$. The members of FS−IN are called *strong inclusion frames*.
- FW−IND is the class of FW-frames $(U, (R_P)_{P \subseteq \mathrm{Par}})$ such that for every $p \in$ Par, $R_{\{p\}}$ is an equivalence relation. Consequently, for every non-empty $P \subseteq$ Par, R_P is reflexive and symmetric. Transitivity is not preserved under union. The members of FW−IND are called *weak indiscernibility frames*.
- FW−SIM is the class of FW-frames $(U, (R_P)_{P \subseteq \mathrm{Par}})$ such that for every $p \in$ Par, $R_{\{p\}}$ is weakly reflexive and symmetric. Consequently, for every

$P \subseteq$ Par, R_P is weakly reflexive and symmetric. The members of FW$-$SIM are called *weak similarity frames*.

- FW$-$ICOM is the class of FW-frames $(U, (R_P)_{P \subseteq \text{Par}})$ such that for every $p \in$ Par, $R_{\{p\}}$ is reflexive, symmetric and co-3-transitive. Consequently, for every non-empty $P \subseteq$ Par, R_P is reflexive and symmetric and co-3-transitivity, since all these properties are preserved under union. The members of FW$-$ICOM are called *weak incomplementarity frames*.

- FW$-$IN is the class of FW-frames $(U, (R_P)_{P \subseteq \text{Par}}, (Q_P)_{P \subseteq \text{Par}})$ with two families of relative relations such that for every $p \in$ Par, $R_{\{p\}}$ and $Q_{\{p\}}$ are reflexive and transitive, and $R_{\{p\}} = Q_{\{p\}}^{-1}$. Consequently, for every $P \subseteq$ Par, $R_P = Q_P^{-1}$ and if $P \neq \emptyset$, then R_P and Q_P are reflexive. Transitivity is not preserved under union. The members of FW$-$IN are called *weak inclusion frames*.

Frames with distinguishability relations:

- FS$-$DIV is the class of FS-frames $(U, (R_P)_{P \subseteq \text{Par}})$ such that for every $p \in$ Par, $R_{\{p\}}$ is irreflexive, symmetric and cotransitive. Consequently, for every $P \subseteq$ Par, R_P is symmetric, and if $P \neq \emptyset$, then R_P is irreflexive. Cotransitivity is not preserved under intersection. The members of FS$-$DIV are called *strong diversity frames*.

- FS$-$RORT is the class of FS-frames $(U, (R_P)_{P \subseteq \text{Par}})$ such that for every $p \in$ Par, $R_{\{p\}}$ is coweakly reflexive and symmetric. Consequently, for every $P \subseteq$ Par, R_P is coweakly reflexive and symmetric. The members of FS$-$RORT are called *strong right orthogonality frames*.

- FS$-$COM is the class of FS-frames $(U, (R_P)_{P \subseteq \text{Par}})$ such that for every $p \in$ Par, $R_{\{p\}}$ is irreflexive, symmetric and 3-transitive. Consequently, for every $P \subseteq$ Par, R_P is symmetric and 3-transitive, and if $P \neq \emptyset$, then R_P is irreflexive. The members of FS$-$COM are called *strong complementarity frames*.

- FW$-$DIV is the class of FW-frames $(U, (R_P)_{P \subseteq \text{Par}})$ such that for every $p \in$ Par, $R_{\{p\}}$ is irreflexive, symmetric and cotransitive. Consequently, for every $P \subseteq$ Par, R_P is irreflexive, symmetric and cotransitive. Cotransitivity is preserved under union. The members of FW$-$DIV are called *weak diversity frames*.

- FW$-$RORT is the class of FW-frames $(U, (R_P)_{P \subseteq \text{Par}})$ such that for every $p \in$ Par, $R_{\{p\}}$ is coweakly reflexive and symmetric. Consequently, for every $P \subseteq$ Par, R_P is coweakly reflexive and symmetric. The members of FW$-$RORT are called *weak right orthogonality frames*.

- FW$-$COM is the class of FW-frames $(U, (R_P)_{P \subseteq \text{Par}})$ such that for every $p \in$ Par, $R_{\{p\}}$ is irreflexive, symmetric and 3-transitive. Consequently, for every $P \subseteq$ Par, R_P is irreflexive and symmetric. 3-transitivity is not preserved under union. The members of FW−COM are called *weak complementarity frames*.

The languages of information logics with semantics of relative frames (referred to as *Rare-logics*) are the multimodal languages with modal operators determined by relations indexed with finite subsets of a set Par.

L_{FS} *and* L_{FW} *logics*

As a first case study we present logics L_{FS} and L_{FW} based on FS-frames and FW-frames, respectively. The choice of modal operations usually depends on the global conditions assumed in the models. Typically, logic L_{FS} has the sufficiency operators in its language, and logic L_{FW} the necessity operators determined by the relational constants. We recall that satisfaction of a formula with sufficiency operator, $[T]\varphi$ by a state s in a model $\mathcal{M}$ is defined as follows: $\mathcal{M}, s \models [T]\varphi$ iff for every $s' \in U$, if $\mathcal{M}, s' \models \varphi$, then $(s, s') \in T$.

Let $L \in \{L_{FS}, L_{FW}\}$. An L-*model* is a structure $\mathcal{M} = (U, (R_P)_{P \in \mathcal{P}_{fin}(\text{Par})}, m)$ such that U is a non-empty set, R_P are binary relations on U indexed with finite subsets of Par, and m is a meaning function such that:

- $m(p) \subseteq U$, for any propositional variable p;
- $R_\emptyset = \begin{cases} U \times U, & \text{if } L = L_{FS} \\ \emptyset, & \text{if } L = L_{FW} \end{cases}$;
- $R_{\{p\}} \subseteq U \times U$, for every $p \in \text{Par}$;
- for all $P, Q \in \mathcal{P}_{fin}(\text{Par})$:

$$R_{P \cup Q} = \begin{cases} R_P \cap R_Q, & \text{if } L = L_{FS} \\ R_P \cup R_Q, & \text{if } L = L_{FW}. \end{cases}$$

If a Rare-logic L is based on any family of relations listed above being a subclass of FS or FW, then the appropriate local conditions should be assumed in the corresponding L-models.

The relational language corresponding to an L-language is an RL-language endowed with the set $\{R_P\}_{P \in \mathcal{P}_{fin}(\text{Par})}$ of relational constants. The set of relational terms and formulas are defined as in RL-logic.

The RL_L-models are structures of the form

$$\mathcal{M} = (U, (R_P)_{P \in \mathcal{P}_{fin}(\text{Par})}, m),$$

where (U, m) is an RL-model and R_P are binary relations on U satisfying the same conditions as in L-models.

As usual, we denote relations in the language and in the models with the same symbols.

The translation of L-formulas into relational terms of the logic RL_L starts, as usual, with a one-to-one assignment of relational variables to the propositional variables and then the translation τ is defined inductively as in Section 4. As in the case of modal logics with semantics of plain frames, we can prove that for every L-formula, L-validity is equivalent to RL_L-validity, for $L \in \{L_{FS}, L_{FW}\}$, that is the following can be proved:

Theorem 10.
For every L-formula φ and for all object variables x and y the following conditions are equivalent:

1. *φ is L-valid;*
2. *$x\tau(\varphi)y$ is RL_L-valid.*

Dual tableau systems for Rare-logics are constructed in a similar way as for information logics of plain frames. Namely, to the RL-proof system we add the rules corresponding to the global conditions assumed in a given logic. The rules corresponding to conditions (S1) and (W1) are of the following forms:

$$(\mathrm{rS1}\supseteq) \quad \frac{xR_{P\cup Q}y}{xR_Py \mid xR_Qy} \qquad (\mathrm{rS1}\subseteq) \quad \frac{x-R_{P\cup Q}y}{x-R_Py, x-R_Qy}$$

$$(\mathrm{rW1}\supseteq) \quad \frac{xR_{P\cup Q}y}{xR_Py, xR_Qy} \qquad (\mathrm{rW1}\subseteq) \quad \frac{x-R_{P\cup Q}y}{x-R_Py \mid x-R_Qy}$$

The rule corresponding to the condition (S2) has the following form:

$$(\mathrm{rS2}) \quad \frac{}{x-R_\emptyset y} \qquad x, y \text{ are any object variables}$$

The rule corresponding to the condition (W2) is:

$$(\mathrm{rW2}) \quad \frac{}{xR_\emptyset y} \qquad x, y \text{ are any object variables}$$

If some of the local conditions are imposed on relations in L-models, then we add the rules reflecting these properties. The examples of the rules corresponding to the local conditions can be found in Section 4.

The specific rules of relational proof systems for the logics L_{FS} and L_{FW} are:

- The specific $RL_{L_{FS}}$-rules: (rS2), (rS1$\supseteq$), and (rS1$\subseteq$);
- The specific $RL_{L_{FW}}$-rules: (rW2), (rW1$\supseteq$), and (rW1$\subseteq$).

Then the following theorem holds:

Theorem 11 (Correctness).
1. *The specific* $\mathsf{RL}_{\mathsf{L_{FS}}}$*-rules are* $\mathsf{RL}_{\mathsf{L_{FS}}}$*-correct;*
2. *The specific* $\mathsf{RL}_{\mathsf{L_{FW}}}$*-rules are* $\mathsf{RL}_{\mathsf{L_{FW}}}$*-correct.*

Proof.
By way of example we prove the $\mathsf{RL}_{\mathsf{L_{FS}}}$-correctness of the rule (rS2). Since all $\mathsf{RL}_{\mathsf{L_{FS}}}$-models satisfy the condition (S2), for every $\mathsf{RL}_{\mathsf{L_{FS}}}$-model $\mathcal{M}$ and for every valuation v in $\mathcal{M}$, $\mathcal{M}, v \models xR_\emptyset y$. Therefore, $\mathcal{M}, v \not\models x-R_\emptyset y$. Hence, the rule (rS2) is $\mathsf{RL}_{\mathsf{L_{FS}}}$-correct.   □

The completion conditions corresponding to the rules (rS1⊇), (rS1⊆), (rW1⊇), (rW1⊆), (rS2), and (rW2) are as follows:

Cpl(rS1⊇) If $xR_{P\cup Q}y \in b$, then either $xR_P y \in b$ or $xR_Q y \in b$;

Cpl(rS1⊆) If $x-R_{P\cup Q}y \in b$, then both $x-R_P y \in b$ and $x-R_Q y \in b$;

Cpl(rW1⊇) If $xR_{P\cup Q}y \in b$, then both $xR_P y \in b$ and $xR_Q y \in b$;

Cpl(rW1⊆) If $x-R_{P\cup Q}y \in b$, then either $x-R_P y \in b$ or $x-R_Q y \in b$;

Cpl(rS2) For all objects variables x and y, $x-R_\emptyset y \in b$;

Cpl(rW2) For all objects variables x and y, $xR_\emptyset y \in b$.

The branch structure determined by an open branch of an RL_L-proof tree is a structure $\mathcal{M}^b = (U^b, (R_P^b)_{P \in \mathcal{P}_{fin}(\mathrm{Par})}, m^b)$ satisfying the following conditions:

- $U^b = \mathbb{OV}_{\mathsf{RL_L}}$;
- $m^b(S) = \{(x,y) \in U^b \times U^b : xSy \notin b\}$, for every $S \in \mathbb{RV}_{\mathsf{RL_L}} \cup \{1, 1'\}$;
- $R_\emptyset^b = \{(x,y) \in U^b \times U^b : xR_\emptyset y \notin b\}$;
- $R_{\{p\}}^b = \{(x,y) \in U^b \times U^b : xR_{\{p\}}y \notin b\}$, for any $p \in \mathrm{Par}$;
- $R_{P\cup Q}^b$ is defined by the global condition (S1) or (W1), for all $P, Q \in \mathcal{P}_{fin}(\mathrm{Par})$, for example if L is a logic whose models are based on the FS-frames, then we put $R_{P\cup Q}^b \overset{\mathrm{df}}{=} R_P^b \cap R_Q^b$;
- m^b extends to all the compound relational terms as in RL-models.

As usual, valuation v^b in $\mathcal{M}^b$ is the identity valuation.

Proposition 5 (Branch Model Property).
Let $\mathsf{L} \in \{\mathsf{L_{FS}}, \mathsf{L_{FW}}\}$ *and let* b *be a complete branch of an* RL_L*-proof tree. Then* $\mathcal{M}^b$ *is an* RL_L*-model.*

Proof.
By way of example, we show that if L-models satisfy the condition (Si) (resp. (Wi)), $i \in \{1, 2\}$, then the branch model satisfies this condition as well. If conditions (S1) or (W1) are assumed, then these properties are satisfied due to the definition of the branch model. Assume that L-models satisfy the condition

(S2). By the completion condition Cpl(rS2), for all object variables $x, y \in U^b$, $x-R_\emptyset y \in b$. Therefore for all object variables $x, y \in U^b$, $xR_\emptyset y \notin b$, thus $(x, y) \in R_\emptyset^b$. Hence, the branch model satisfies the condition (S2). The proof for condition (W2) is similar. All the remaining conditions of $\mathsf{RL_L}$-models are clearly satisfied by $\mathcal{M}^b$.   □

If any local condition is assumed in $\mathsf{RL_L}$-models, then we also need to show that $\mathcal{M}^b$ satisfies them.

Next, we show the following:

Theorem 12 (Satisfaction in Branch Model Property).
Let $\mathsf{L} \in \{\mathsf{L_{FS}}, \mathsf{L_{FW}}\}$ *and let* $\mathcal{M}^b$ *be the branch model determined by an open branch b of an $\mathsf{RL_L}$-proof tree. Then for every $\mathsf{RL_L}$-formula φ, if $\mathcal{M}^b, v^b \models \varphi$, then $\varphi \notin b$.*

Proof.
By way of example consider logic $\mathsf{L_{FS}}$. Assume that the branch model satisfies a formula $xR_{P\cup Q}y$. By the definition of the branch model, $(x, y) \in R_P^b$ and $(x, y) \in R_Q^b$. Suppose $xR_{P\cup Q}y \in b$. Then by the completion condition Cpl(rS1⊇), either $xR_P y \in b$ or $xR_Q y \in b$. By the induction hypothesis, either $(x, y) \notin R_P^b$ or $(x, y) \notin R_Q^b$, a contradiction.   □

Thus, we obtain:

Theorem 13 (Soundness and Completeness of $\mathsf{RL_{L_{FS}}}$ and $\mathsf{RL_{L_{FW}}}$).
Let $\mathsf{L} \in \{\mathsf{L_{FS}}, \mathsf{L_{FW}}\}$ *and let φ be an $\mathsf{RL_L}$-formula. Then the following conditions are equivalent:*

1. φ *is* $\mathsf{RL_L}$-*provable;*
2. φ *is* $\mathsf{RL_L}$-*valid;*
3. φ *is* $\mathsf{RL_L^*}$-*valid.*

By the above theorem and Theorem 10 we obtain:

Theorem 14 (Relational Soundness and Completeness of Logics $\mathsf{L_{FS}}$ and $\mathsf{L_{FW}}$).
Let $\mathsf{L} \in \{\mathsf{L_{FS}}, \mathsf{L_{FW}}\}$ *and let φ be an L-formula. Then for all object variables x and y the following conditions are equivalent:*

1. φ *is* L-*valid;*
2. $x\tau(\varphi)y$ *is* $\mathsf{RL_L}$-*provable.*

The logic Rare-NIL

As a second case study we present a relative version of the logic NIL, Rare-NIL. Let Par be a non-empty set of parameters. The language of Rare-NIL consists of the following pairwise disjoint sets of symbols:

- $\mathbb{V}$ - a countable infinite set of propositional variables;
- $\{\leq_P\}_{P \in \mathcal{P}_{fin}(\mathrm{Par})}$, $\{\geq_P\}_{P \in \mathcal{P}_{fin}(\mathrm{Par})}$, $\{\sigma_P\}_{P \in \mathcal{P}_{fin}(\mathrm{Par})}$ - three families of relational constants;
- $\{\neg, \vee, \wedge\} \cup \{[T] : T$ is a relational constant$\}$ - a set of propositional operations.

A Rare-NIL-model is a structure

$$\mathcal{M} = (U, (R_P^{\leq})_{P \in \mathcal{P}_{fin}(\mathrm{Par})}, (R_P^{\geq})_{P \in \mathcal{P}_{fin}(\mathrm{Par})}, (R_P^{\sigma})_{P \in \mathcal{P}_{fin}(\mathrm{Par})}, m),$$

such that $(U, (R_P^{\#})_{P \in \mathcal{P}_{fin}(\mathrm{Par})}, m)$ is an $\mathsf{L_{FS}}$-model, for every $\# \in \{\leq, \geq, \sigma\}$, and the following conditions are satisfied, for every $P \in \mathcal{P}_{fin}(\mathrm{Par})$:

- $R_P^{\leq} = (R_P^{\geq})^{-1}$;
- $R_P^{\leq}$ is reflexive and transitive;
- R_P^{σ} is reflexive and symmetric;
- if $(x, y) \in R_P^{\sigma}$ and $(y, z) \in R_P^{\leq}$, then $(x, z) \in R_P^{\sigma}$.

Observe that the relations in a Rare-NIL-model are constrained in two ways. The three families of relations satisfy the global conditions (S1) and (S2) and, moreover, the local conditions analogous to the conditions in NIL-models.

In [DEO07] it is shown that Rare-NIL-satisfiability differs from NIL-satisfiability, namely we have the following:

Theorem 15.
1. Satisfiability problem of Rare-NIL is decidable;
2. Rare-NIL satisfiability is EXPTIME-complete.

The relational language corresponding to Rare-NIL-language is the RL-language endowed with the set $\{R_P^r\}_{P \in \mathcal{P}_{fin}(\mathrm{Par})}$, $r \in \{\leq, \geq, \sigma\}$ of relational constants. $\mathsf{RL_{Rare\text{-}NIL}}$-models are structures of the form

$$\mathcal{M} = (U, (R_P^{\leq})_{P \in \mathcal{P}_{fin}(\mathrm{Par})}, (R_P^{\geq})_{P \in \mathcal{P}_{fin}(\mathrm{Par})}, (R_P^{\sigma})_{P \in \mathcal{P}_{fin}(\mathrm{Par})}, m),$$

such that (U, m) is an RL-model, R_P^r are binary relations on U indexed with finite subsets of the set Par, and moreover, relations R_P^r satisfy all the conditions assumed in Rare-NIL-models.

Dual tableau for Rare-NIL is constructed as in the case of the previous logics. Namely, to the RL-proof system we add the rules corresponding to the global and local conditions assumed in this logic. More precisely, we add the following rules.

For $r \in \{\leq, \geq, \sigma\}$, and for all $P, Q \in \mathcal{P}_{fin}(\mathrm{Par})$, the rules corresponding to the global conditions are of the forms $(rS1\supseteq)$, $(rS1\subseteq)$, and $(rS2)$ for the relational constants $R_{P \cup Q}^r$ and $R_{\emptyset}^r$, respectively.

For $r \in \{\leq, \sigma\}$, and for every $P \in \mathcal{P}_{fin}(\text{Par})$, the rules corresponding to the local conditions are of the forms (rI1$\subseteq$), (rI1$\supseteq$), (rI2 ref), (rI2 tran) for the relational constants $R_P^{\leq}$ and $R_P^{\geq}$, and (rI4 ref), (rI4 sym), (rI6) for the relational constants R_P^{σ}.

By Theorems 7 and 11, it can be easily proved that all the specific RL$_{\text{Rare-NIL}}$-rules are RL$_{\text{Rare-NIL}}$-correct. The completeness can be proved by analogous reasoning as in the proof of the completeness of RL$_{\text{NIL}}$-dual tableau and RL$_{\text{LFS}}$-dual tableau. Thus we obtain:

Theorem 16 (Soundness and Completeness of RL$_{\text{Rare-NIL}}$).
For every RL$_{Rare\text{-NIL}}$*-formula φ the following conditions are equivalent:*

1. *φ is* RL$_{Rare\text{-NIL}}$*-provable;*
2. *φ is* RL$_{Rare\text{-NIL}}$*-valid.*
3. *φ is* RL$^*_{Rare\text{-NIL}}$*-valid.*

By the above theorem, Theorem 6, and Theorem 10 we obtain:

Theorem 17 (Relational Soundness and Completeness of Rare-NIL).
For every Rare-NIL-formula φ and for all object variables x and y the following conditions are equivalent:

1. *φ is Rare-NIL-valid;*
2. *$x\tau(\varphi)y$ is* RL$_{Rare\text{-NIL}}$*-provable.*

References

[BAL01] Ph. Balbiani, *Emptiness relations in property systems*, Lecture Notes in Computer Science 2561, Springer (2001), 15–34.

[BGO06] D. Bresolin, J. Golińska-Pilarek, and E. Orłowska, *Relational dual tableaux for interval temporal logics*, Journal of Applied Non-Classical Logics Vol. 16, No. 3-4 (2006), 251–277.

[BUR06] A. Burrieza, M. Ojeda-Aciego, and E. Orłowska, *Relational approach to order of magnitude reasoning*, Lecture Notes in Artificial Intelligence 4342 (2006), 105–124.

[DAL05] J. Dallien and W. MacCaull, *RelDT: A relational dual tableaux automated theorem prover*, Preprint, 2005.

[DEM96] S.Demri and E. Orłowska, *Logical analysis of demonic nondeterministic programs*, Theoretical Computer Science 166, 1996, 173-202.

[DEM00] S. Demri, *The nondeterministic information logic* NIL *is* PSPACE-*complete*, Fundamenta Informaticae 42 No. 3–4 (2000), 211–234.

[DEG00] S. Demri and D. Gabbay, *On modal logics characterized by models with relative accessibility relations: Part I.*, Studia Logica 65, No 3 (2000), 323–353.

[DEO02] S. Demri and E. Orłowska, *Incomplete Information: Structure, inference, complexity*, in: EATCS Monographs in Theoretical Computer Science, Springer (2002).

[DES02] S. Demri and U. Sattler, *Automata-theoretic decision procedures for information logics*, Fundamenta Informaticae 53, No 1 (2002), 1–22.

[DEO07] S. Demri and E. Orłowska, *Relative nondeterministic information logic is EXPTIME-complete*, Fundamenta Informaticae 75, No 1 (2007), to appear.

[DID87] E. Diday, *Introduction a l'approche symbolique en analyse des donnees*, in: Actes des journees symboliques numeriques pour l'apprentissage de connaissances a partir des donnes, Paris (1987).

[DID88] E. Diday and L. Roy, *Generating rules by symbolic data analysis and application to soil feature recognition*, in: Actes des 8emes Journees Internationales: Les systemes experts et leurs applications, Avignon (1988).

[FOR05] A. Formisano, E. Omodeo, and E. Orłowska, *A PROLOG tool for relational translation of modal logics: A front-end for relational proof systems*, in: B. Beckert (ed) TABLEAUX 2005 Position Papers and Tutorial Descriptions, Universität Koblenz-Landau, Fachberichte Informatik No 12, 2005, 1-10.

[FOR06] A. Formisano, M. Nicolosi Asmundo, *An efficient relational deductive system for propositional non-classical logics*, Journal of Applied Non-Classical Logics 16, No. 3–4 (2006), 367–408.

[FOO06] A. Formisano, E. Omodeo, and E. Orłowska, *An environment for specifying properties of dyadic relations and reasoning about them. II: Relational presentation of non-classical logics*, Lecture Notes in Artificial Intelligence 4342 (2006), 89–104.

[FRI95] M. Frias and E. Orłowska, *A proof system for fork algebras and its applications to reasoning in logics based on intuitionism*, Logique et Analyse 150-151-152, 1995, 239-284.

[GOL07] J. Golińska-Pilarek and E. Orłowska, *Tableaux and dual Tableaux: Transformation of proofs*, Studia Logica 85 (2007), 291–310.

[GOO06] J. Golińska-Pilarek and E. Orłowska, *Relational proof systems for spatial reasoning*, Journal of Applied Non-Classical Logics Vol. 16, No. 3-4 (2006), 409–431.

[KON87] B. Konikowska, *A formal language for reasoning about indiscernibility*, Bulletin of the Polish Academy of Sciences, Math. 35 (1987), 239–249.

[KON94] B. Konikowska, *A logic for reasoning about similarity*, in: H. Rasiowa and E. Orłowska (Eds.), *Reasoning with incomplete information*, Vol.58 of Studia Logica (1994), 185–226.

[KON98] B. Konikowska, Ch. Morgan, and E. Orłowska, *A relational formalisation of arbitrary finite-valued logics*, Logic Journal of IGPL 6 No 5, 1998, 755-774.

[LIP76] W. Lipski, *Informational systems with incomplete information*, Proceedings of the 3rd International Symposium on Automata, Languages and Programming, Edinburgh, Scotland (1976), 120–130.

[LIP79] W. Lipski, *On semantic issues connected with incomplete information databases*, ACM Transactions on Database Systems 4, No 3 (1979), 262–296.

[MAC97] W. MacCaull, *Relational proof theory for linear and other substructural logics*, Logic Journal of IGPL 5, 1997, 673-697.

[MAC98a] W. MacCaull, *Relational tableaux for tree models, language models and information networks*, in: E. Orłowska (ed) Logic at Work. Essays dedicated to the memory of Helena Rasiowa, Springer-Physica Verlag, Heidelberg, 1998a.

[MAC98b] W. MacCaull, *Relational semantics and a relational proof system for full Lambek Calculus*, Journal of Symbolic Logic 63, 2, 1998b, 623-637.

[MAC02] W. MacCaull and E. Orłowska, *Correspondence results for relational proof systems with applications to the Lambek calculus*, Studia Logica 71, 2002, 279-304.

[MAC06] W. MacCaull and E. Orłowska, *A logic of typed relations and its applications to relational databases*, Journal of Logic and Computation 16, No 6 (2006), 789–815.

[ORL82] E. Orłowska, *Semantics of vague concepts*, ICS PAS Reports 469 (1982), 20 pp.

[ORL83] E. Orłowska, *Semantics of vague concepts*, in: G. Dorn and P. Weingartner (eds), *Foundations of Logic and Linguistics. Problems and Solutions*, Selected contributions to the 7th International Congress of Logic, Methodology and Philosophy of Science, Salzburg (1983), Plenum Press, London/New York, 465–482.

[ORL84a] E. Orłowska, *Logic of indiscernibility relations*, Lecture Notes in Computer Science 208, Springer (1984), 177–186.

[ORL84b] E. Orłowska and Z. Pawlak, *Representation of Nondeterministic Information*, Theoretical Computer Science 29 (1984), 27–39.

[ORL85] E. Orłowska, *Logic of nondeterministic information*, Studia Logica 44 (1985), 93–102.

[ORL88a] E. Orłowska, *Kripke models with relative accessibility and their application to inferences from incomplete information*, in: G. Mirkowska and H. Rasiowa (eds.), *Mathematical Problems in Computation Theory*, Banach Center Publications 21 (1988), 329–339.

[ORL88] E. Orłowska, *Relational interpretation of modal logics*, in: Andreka, H., Monk, D., and Nemeti, I. (eds) Algebraic Logic, Colloquia Mathematica Societatis Janos Bolyai 54, North Holland, Amsterdam, 1988, 443-471.

[ORL92] E. Orłowska, *Relational proof systems for relevant logics*, Journal of Symbolic Logic 57, 1992, 1425-1440.

[ORL93] E. Orłowska, *Dynamic logic with program specifications and its relational proof system*, Journal of Applied Non-Classical Logic 3, 1993, 147-171.

[ORL94] E. Orłowska, *Relational semantics for non-classical logics: Formulas are relations*, in: Woleński, J. (ed) Philosophical Logic in Poland, Kluwer, 1994, 167-186.

[ORL95] E. Orłowska, *Temporal logics in a relational framework*, in: Bolc, L. and Szałas, A. (eds) Time and Logic-a Computational Approach, University College London Press, 1995, 249-277.

[ORL97b] E. Orlowska (ed), *Incomplete Information: Rough Set Analysis*, Physica Verlag, Heidelberg (1997).

[ORG07] E. Orłowska and J. Golińska-Pilarek, *Dual Tableaux and their Applications*, A draft of the book, 2007.

[PAW91] Z. Pawlak, *Rough Sets*, Kluwer, Dordrecht (1991).

[PRE97] S. Prediger, *Symbolic objects in formal concept analysis*, Preprint Nr. 1923, Technische Hohschule Darmstadt, Fachbereich Mathematik (1997).

[RSK91] C. Rauszer and A. Skowron, *The discernibility matrices and functions in information systems*, in: R. Słowiński (ed), *Intelligent decision support. Handbook of Applications and Advances in the Rough Set Theory*, Kluwer, Dordrecht (1991), 331–362.

[TAR41] A. Tarski, *On the calculus of relations*, The Journal of Symbolic Logic 6 (1941), 73-89.

[TAR87] A. Tarski and S. R. Givant, *A Formalization of Set Theory without Variables*, Colloquium Publications, vol. 41, American Mathematical Society, 1987.

[VAK87] D. Vakarelov, *Abstract characterization of some knowledge representation systems and the logic NIL of nondeterministic information*, in: Ph. Jorrand and V. Sgurev (eds.), *Artificial Intelligence: Methodology, Systems, Applications*, North-Holland, Amsterdam (1987), 255–260.

[VAK89] D. Vakarelov, *Modal logics for knowledge representation systems*, in: A. R. Meyer and M. Taitslin (eds.), *Symposuim on Logic Foundations of Computer Science, Pereslavl-Zalessky*, Lecture Notes in Computer Science, Vol. 363, Springer, Berlin (1989), 257–277.

[VAK91a] D. Vakarelov, *Logical analysis of positive and negative similarity relations in property systems*, in: M. de Glas and D. Gabbay (eds.), *First World Conference on the Fundamentals of Artificial Intelligence*, Paris, France (1991).

[VAK91b] D. Vakarelov, *A modal logic for similarity relations in Pawlak knowledge representation systems*, Fundamenta Informaticae 15 (1991), 61–79.

[WAN98] H. Wang, I. Düntsch and D. Bell, *Data reduction based on hyper relations*, in: R. Agrawal, P. Stolorz and G. Piatetsky-Shapiro (Eds), Proceedings of KDD98 (1998), 349–353.

[WAN00] H. Wang, I. Düntsch and G. Gediga, *Classificatory filtering in decision systems*, International Journal of Approximate Reasoning 23 (2000), 111–136.

Proximities in Statistics:
Similarity and Distance

Hans –J. Lenz

Institute of Statistics and Econometrics, Freie Universität Berlin, Germany

Abstract We review similarity and distance measures used in Statistics for clustering and classification. We are motivated by the lack of most measures to adequately utilize a non uniform distribution defined on the data or sample space.

Such measures are mappings from $O \times O \to R_+$ where O is either a finite set of objects or vector space like R^p and R_+ is the set of non-negative real numbers. In most cases those mappings fulfil conditions like symmetry and reflexivity. Moreover, further characteristics like transitivity or the triangle equation in case of distance measures are of concern.

We start with Hartigan's list of proximity measures which he compiled in 1967. It is good practice to pay special attention to the type of scales of the variables involved, i.e. to nominal (often binary), ordinal and metric (interval and ratio) types of scales. We are interested in the algebraic structure of proximities as suggested by Hartigan (1967) and Cormack (1971), information-theoretic measures as discussed by Jardine and Sibson (1971), and the probabilistic W-distance measure as proposed by Skarabis (1970). The last measure combines distances of objects or vectors with their corresponding probabilities to improve overall discrimination power. The idea is that rare events, i.e. set of values with a very low probability of observing, related to a pair of objects may be a strong hint to strong similarity of this pair.

1 Introduction

1.1 Frame of discernment

First we present some types of objects which are considered later, i.e. tupels, vectors or records, sets and probability distribution functions. Of course, there exists a unified view in form of sets embedded into a Cartesian space, but it is helpful to look at them separately.

Given a two-dimensional data space we can define several distances between two tupels.

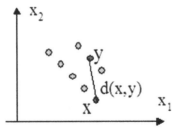

Fig.1: Distance d between two tupels

A slightly different situation is given when two sets are to be compared.

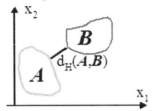

Fig.2: Distance d_H between two sets

It seems worthwhile considering a further case where two probability distributions are given.

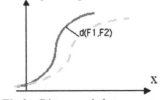

Fig.3: Distance d between two distribution functions

In the following we present some examples which will highlight some weakness of traditional proximity ("nearness") measures when prior information is available.

1.2 Examples

Our first example consists of a sample of five tupels $x_i \in R^2$, i=1,2,...,5 with $x_1^T = (1, 21)$; $x_2^T = (0, 20)$; $x_3^T = (1, 1)$; $x_4^T = (0, 0)$; $x_5^T = (1, 30)$. The Euclidean distance d_E is used as a distance measure, i.e. $d_E(x, y) = (x - y)^T (x - y)$ with x, $y \in R^2$. We can easily compute $d_E(x_1, x_2) \approx 1,4$; $d_E(x_3, x_4) \approx 1,4$; $d_E(x_2, x_5) \approx 10$.

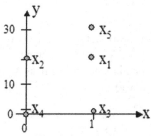

Fig. 4: Sample Space

Assume now that the data are normally distributed with X, $Y \sim N(0, 1)$. We observe that observations x_3, x_4 are equal or „near" to the centre $\mu^T = (0, 0)$ of the distribution. Their distance is $d_E(x_3, x_4) \approx 1{,}4$. The same distance is computed for the first two tupels x_1, x_2, which may be considered as outliers due to their very large second component. However, if we compare another "outlier pair", i.e. $(x_2,$ $x_5)$ we notice that the Euclidean distance d_E increases to $d_E(x_2, x_5) \approx 10$. To the best of the author's knowledge Skarabis (1970) was the first to point to this phenomenon.

We present a further example to stress the necessity for including probabilities of observations besides of the dissimilarities when comparing pairs of objects. We consider only one (Boolean) attribute and $n = 4$ objects: $x_1 = 1$; $x_2 = 1$; $x_3 = 2$; $x_4 = 2$. The semantic of the random variable X ("Behaviour in winter time") becomes important. $X=1$ is the code of "Take a bath in an icy lake in winter" while $X=2$ stands for "Take a warm coat". Assume that each observation x_i, $i = 1,2,3,4$, is linked to one and only one person. Pair wise comparisons of persons o_1, o_2 and o_3, o_4 by a Hamming distance $d_H(x_i, x_j) = |x_i - x_j|$, say, delivers $d_H(x_1, x_2) = d_H(x_3, x_4) = 0$. We induce that both pairs are equally similar. However, the probabilities of both values are generally very different due to $P(X=1) \ll P(X=2)$, i.e. only few people use to take a outdoor bath in the winter time but almost all wear warm clothes at winter time. It is exactly this low probability which makes the first pair more similar to each other than the second one. This effect motivated Skarabis (1970) to define a probability – based distance measure d_w which should fulfil $d_w(x_1, x_2) < d_w(x_3, x_4)$.

As a further example, take text mining which is mostly corresponding to a classification problem. As Frakes and Baeza-Yates (1992) point out words that occur extremely rarely are likely to be of no statistical relevance and thus may be dropped. Now assume one detects in two documents about movies the term "superkalifragilistic exialidocious". Such words are artificial, extremely low frequent but very informative because they give a strong hint to the movie "Mary Poppins" to which the documents may refer to. How can one incorporate such prior knowledge into a proximity measure?

2 Similarity and Distance measures

A common way to measure dissimilarity between objects or numeric vectors of measurements defined on a data space X is to use distance functions. A minimal characteristic is that a distance function d - as well as similarity function s – should have a non negative range $d(x,y) \geq 0$ and be self similar, i.e. $d(x,x) = 0$.

Def.1: A measurable function d: $X^2 \rightarrow R_{\geq 0}$ where X is an arbitrary set, is called a distance (metric) iff for all $x, y, z \in X$ we have:

        1. $d(x, y) = 0 \Leftrightarrow x = y$ (reflexive)
        2. $d(x, y) = d(y, x)$ (symmetric)
        3. $d(x, z) \leq d(x, y) + d(y, z)$ (triangle inequality).

In Def.1 we note that relaxing 3. by $d(x, z) \leq \max\{d(x, y), d(y, z)\} \leq d(x\,y) + d(y, z)$ leads to ultrametricity which is commonly used in science, cf. Murtagh (2007). Hartigan (1967) published a list of twelve possible proximity measures which are reprinted in Cormack (1971) and Cox and Cox (2001). His list includes metric, real-valued, symmetric real-valued, Euclidean distances and various kinds of complete or partial orderings as well as partitions of X^2. As these measures strongly depend on the underlying scales of the variables involved, we are going to present them accordingly, i.e. separated according to a nominal or even binary, ordinal and metric (ratio or interval) scale.

2.1 Nominal or Binary Scales

Sneath and Sokal (1973), Hubálek (1982) and Cox and Cox (2001) give a comprehensive table of similarity coefficients for binary data. Roughly speaking, similarities are derivable from related distances. Using a parametric measure of similarity one can represent most of those coefficient by one generalized formula. For this purpose we consider the following frequency table:

Object s Object r	1	0
1	a	b
0	c	d

Table 1: Frequency table of two binary attributes

We use the parametric similarity coefficient as used by Steinhausen and Langer (1977). Let $\lambda, \delta \in R, \lambda \geq 0, 0 \leq \delta \leq 1$ and $S_{r,s}^{\delta,\lambda} = (a + \delta d)/(a + \delta d + \lambda(b + c))$. For example, it follows the Jaccard-Tanimoto coefficient $S_{r,s}^{JT} = a/(a+b+c)$ for $\lambda=1$, $\delta=0$, the Rogers and Tanimoto coefficient $S_{r,s}^{RT} = (a+d)/(a+2(b+c)+d)$ for $\lambda=2$, $\delta=1$, the simple matching coefficient $S_{r,s}^{sm} = (a+d)/(a+b+c+d)$ for $\lambda=1, \delta=1$ etc.

2.2 Ordinal Scales

Variables are called ordinal scaled if the relational operators '=', '$\neq$', '<', and '>' are feasible. This implies that the operators 'min' and 'max' are applicable, too. There a three alternatives how to handle variables which have ordinal scales. First, reduce the ordinal scale to a nominal one. In this case one accepts a loss of (ordering) information. Second, one can use Gower's (1971) general similarity coefficient ("average possible similarity") $S_{r,s}^{G} = (\Sigma \omega_{rsi} \, s_{rsi})/ \Sigma \omega_{rsi}$, where s_{rsi} is the similarity between the rth and sth object based on the ith variable alone and ω_{rsi} is an indicator function with $\omega_{rsi} = 1$ if the rth and sth object can be compared on the ith variable $\omega_{rsi} = 0$ if not. Finally, one can use ranks instead of measurements for each variable $l = 1,2,\ldots,p$. The sample $(x_i)_{i=1,2,\ldots,n}$ is sorted in ascending order, i.e. $x_{[1]} \leq x_{[2]} \leq \ldots \leq x_{[n]}$. The rank r_i is the position of object i in the order statistic $(x_{[i]})_{i=1,2,\ldots,n}$, i.e. Rank$(x_i) = r_i = k$ if $x_i = x_{[k]}$. Let $y_{il} = r_{il}/n_l$ appropriately scaled ranks with $y_{il} \in [0,1]$ and n_l is the number of ranks. The "Canberra-Metric" applied on ranks is proposed, cf. Steinhausen and Langer (1977), which is scale-invariant.

$$d(y_i, y_j) = \sum_{l=1}^{p} \frac{|y_{il} - y_{jl}|}{y_{il} + y_{jl}} \qquad (1)$$

2.3 Metric Scales

If the measurements are metric scaled, i.e. ratio or interval scaled - dependent upon the existence of an absolute zero, one usually represents the measurement vectors $(x_1, x_2, \ldots, x_n)$ of a sample of size n as tupels ("points") in the p-dimensional space R^p of real numbers. Like in the qualitative case a lot of dissimilarity measures are proposed.

2.3.1 Distance Measures in Statistics

$$d_k(x,y) = (\sum_{l=1}^{p} |x_l - y_l|^k)^{1/k} \tag{2}$$

The most important parametric family of distance measures is the Minkowski metric which is defined as follows:

At least, three special cases are important:

$k=1$: Manhattan distance (city block distance) $d_1(x,y) = \sum_{l=1}^{p} |x_l - y_l|$

$k=2$: Euclidean distance $d_2(x,y) = \left(\sum_{l=1}^{p} (x_l - y_l)^2 \right)^{1/2}$

$k \to \infty$: maximum distance $d_\infty(x,y) = \max_{l=1,\ldots,p} |x_l - y_l|$.

These distances correspond to different kinds of neighbourhood which is illustrated in the following diagrams.

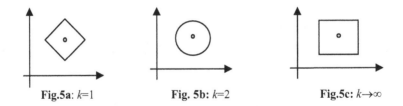

Fig.5a: $k=1$ **Fig. 5b**: $k=2$ **Fig.5c**: $k \to \infty$

The family of Minkowski metrics has the following main features:
- translation invariance, i.e. d_k is not affected by a translation
  $x \to x + c$, where $c \in R^p$ not scale invariant nor dimensional-free
- not sensitive to non-uniform probability distributions on R^p; invariant to orthogonal linear transformations.

Skipping further distance measures like Canberra metric, divergence coefficient, cosine distance etc., cf. Cox and Cox (2001) , we turn to the Mahalanobis distance (1936). The distance measure is dimension-free, invariant with respect to orthogonal transformations and is further scale-invariant.

Def. 2: Let $x, y \in R^p$ be random vectors and Σ the corresponding covariance

$$d_M(x,y) = \sqrt{(x-y)^T \Sigma^{-1} (x-y)} \tag{3}$$

matrix. Then

is called Mahalanobis distance.

This measure is influenced not only by the difference $(x - y)$, but by the variances and correlation of the corresponding variables, too. The covariance matrix is defined by $\sum_{XY} = \frac{1}{n-1}\sum_{l}(x_l - \mu)(y_l - \mu)^T$ and the mean vector by

$\mu = \frac{1}{n}\sum_{l} x_l$. Evidently, the Mahalanobis distance depends upon the distribution P_X on R^p only by the first two moments, i.e. the covariance matrix Σ and – indirectly - the mean μ.

Contrarily, the Kullback-Leibler divergence d_{KL} of two distributions P_1 and P_2 on R^p measures the mean information given observation $x \in R^p$ to separate P_1 and P_2, c.f. Kullback (1959).

Def. 3: Let P_1 and P_2 be two probability distributions with Radon-Nikodym densities $\frac{dP_i}{d\lambda_i} = p_i(x)$ for i=1,2. Then

$$d_{KL}(P_1, P_2) = \int (p_1(x) - p_2(x)) \log \frac{p_1(x)}{p_2(x)} d\lambda x \qquad (4)$$

is called Kullback-Leibler divergence. The Mahalanobis distance and the Kullback-Leibler measure are equivalent under the specific assumptions of Gaussian distributions and equal covariance matrices, cf. Skarabis (1971).

Lemma 1: Let the data space R^p with $x, y \sim N(\mu_i, \Sigma_i) \equiv P_i$ for i=1,2. Furthermore assume that $\Sigma_1 = \Sigma_2$. Then $d_{KL}(P_1, P_2) = (\mu_1 - \mu_2)^T \Sigma^{-1}(\mu_1 - \mu_2)$.

Instead of a distance measure it is often more convenient to use a similarity measure. It can be derived by any (non-linear) monotone non-increasing mapping. Analogue to distances one can define

Def. 4: A measurable function $s: X^2 \rightarrow R_{[0,1]}$ where X is an arbitrary set, is called a similarity measure iff for all x, y, z∈X

- $s(x,x) = 1$ (self-similarity)
- $s(x,y) = s(y,x)$ (symmetry)
- $s(x_i,y_j) = 1 \Rightarrow o_i = o_j$ (object identity)

- $s(x,z) \le s(x,y)\, s(y,z)\, /(s(x,y)+s(y,z))$ (analogue to triangle
  inequality)

As is well known it is difficult in some applications to establish symmetry as well as transitivity of s. As intuitively a great similarity means a small distance between two objects there exist a large set of transformations for switching from distances to similarity and vice versa, cf. Steinhausen and Langer (1977) and Borgelt (2006). For example, $d = 1 - s$ or $d = (1\text{-}s)^{1/2}$ may be such mappings.

2.3.2 Point wise Distance Measures

Another area of application of similarity or distance measures comes up when pairs of functions or probability distributions are to be compared. There exist two principles for deriving appropriate measures: One can make a point wise comparison ("supremum-norm") or one can use the area ("integral norm") between both functions. We start with the first group.

Assume that we have to compare a given distribution function F_0 with an empirical frequency distribution F_n which is defined by

$$F_n(x) = \frac{1}{n} \sum_{i=1}^{n} \begin{cases} 1 & \text{if } y_i \le x, \\ 0 & \text{otherwise.} \end{cases}$$

By definition both functions are monotonically non-decreasing. Then the Kolmogorov-Smirnov distance measure d_{KS} is given by

$d_{KS} = \sup|F_n(x) - F(x)| = \max\{D_n^-, D_n^+\}$ where $D_n^+ = \max(F_n(x) - F(x))$ and

$D_n^- = \max(\ F_n(x) - F_n(x)F(x))$. Fig. 6 illustrates the KS-measure for the case above.

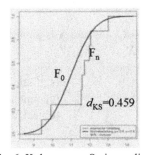

Fig. 6: Kolmogorov-Smirnov distance

Evidently, the distance is measured at one and only one point in the domain R, i.e.

arg sup $|F_n(x)-F(x)| \approx 0.459$.

Another idea is to measure the distance between two non empty point sets of some metric spaces. This approach was proposed for instance to discriminate between membership functions used in fuzzy logic, cf. Kruse and Meyer (1987). Let (X, d_X) be a metric space. We first define the distance between a point $x \in X$ and the non empty set $A \subseteq X$ by $d_h(x, A) = \inf_{a \in A} d_x(x, A)$. Then applying d_H to both non empty sets $A, B \subseteq X$ we get

Def.5: Let $A, B \subseteq X$. The distance measure
$$d_H(A,B) = max\{d^*(A,B), d^*(B,A)\} \qquad (5)$$
where $d^*(A, B) = \sup_{a \in A} d_H(a, B)$ is called Hausdorff metric.

There exists a draw back of d_H when being applied to two parameterised curves. As mentioned above d_H measures the distance between sets of some metric space. So it discards the parameterisation and is applied to the range or image set of both curves. This can lead to the nasty side effect of a low distance between two curves while they appear to be quite different from visual inspection as shown in fig. 6, cf. the distance value δ.

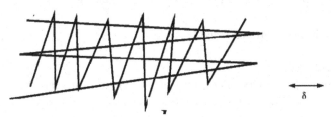

Fig. 7: Hausdorff metric d_H applied to two curves

In 1906 Frechét introduced a pseudo-metric which is more appropriate for functions with a finite number of parameters. The Fréchet distance can be illustrated as follows. Suppose a man is walking his dog and that he is constrained to walk on a curve and his dog on another curve on a plane. Let both the man and the dog control their speed independently. They are not allowed to go backwards. Then, the Fréchet distance of the curves is the minimal length of a leash that is necessary. More formally, we have, cf. Godan (1991):

Def.5: Let $f: A \to X$ and $g: B \to X$ be continuous mappings , (X, d_X) a metric space and let $A, B \subseteq R^d$ be homeomorphic to $[0,1]^d$ for fixed dimension $d \in N$. Let α: $A \to B$ be an orientation preserving homeomorphism. Then

$$d_F(f,g) = \inf_{\alpha} \sup_{x \in A} d_F(f(x), g(\alpha(x))) \qquad (6)$$

is called Fréchet distance of f, g.

As an example we take $d = 1$ and consider two (polygonal) curves. We use a linear function α. The Fréchet distance d_F is marked.

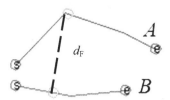

Fig. 8: Fréchet distance d_F

The following point wise distance measure receives a lot of attention in the asymptotic theory in Statistics. It is originated by Levy (1937) and is specially tailored to measure distances between not strictly but monotonically increasing functions, i.e. probability distribution functions.

Def. 6: Let F, G be continuous distribution functions. Then

$$d_L(F,G) = \inf\{\varepsilon \mid F(x-\varepsilon) - \varepsilon \leq G(x) \leq F(x+\varepsilon) + \varepsilon \ \textit{for all} \ x \in R\} \qquad (7)$$

$$(7)$$

is called Levy distance between F and G.

Rewriting (7) we get

$d_L(F,G) = \sup\inf\{\varepsilon > 0 : G(x - \varepsilon - \varepsilon \leq F(x) \leq G(x+\varepsilon) + \varepsilon\}$. It can be easily shown that

$\sqrt{2} \ d_L(F,G)$ is the maximum distance between F and G taken under an angle of $45°$, cf. Fig. 9.

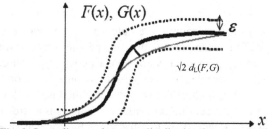

Fig. 9: Levy distance between distribution functions F, G

2.2.3 Distances based on Integral Norms

While the distance measures discussed so far measure the distance between two monotone increasing functions F and G "point wise" there exists a broad spectrum of competitors which make use of " integral norms".

Def.7: Let F be a proper distribution function with related density function f, F_n a sampled corresponding empirical distribution function and ψ a finite-parameter weighting function. Then an integral based distance is given by

$$d_{Int}(F,F_n) = \int_{\infty}^{\infty} \left[F_n(x) - F(x) \right]^2 \psi(x) f(x) dx \tag{8}$$

It is worthwhile considering at least two special cases:

Selecting the weighting function $\psi(x) = [F(x)(1-F(x))]^{-1}$ one gets the

Anderson - Darling distance $A^2 = n \int_R \dfrac{(F_n(x)-F(x))^2}{F(x)(1-F(x))} f(x) dx$, and using $\psi(x)=1$

the Cramér-von-Mises distance $Q = n \int_R (F_n(x) - F(x))^2 f(x) dx$.

3 W-Distance

Now, we come back to the example presented in the introductory section 1.2. The main message of the example was that two people who go swimming in an icy lake are more similar than a pair who is wearing warm winter clothes during winter time. Roughly speaking, two objects or people are more similar than another pair if their features coincide with values which have a low probability. Or the other way round: Observing rare values of objects is a stronger indication of similarity between a pair than to observe values which always happen. Evidently, the utilisation of such prior information should improve to determine an appropriate similarity or distance coefficient.

As proposed by Skarabis (1970) the first step is to construct a complete quasi order $(X^2, \prec\approx)$ based on a distance d and a probability distribution P, where X

$$\left(\begin{pmatrix} x_k \\ x_l \end{pmatrix}, \begin{pmatrix} x_i \\ x_j \end{pmatrix}\right) \in L_{d,P} \Leftrightarrow \begin{pmatrix} x_k \\ x_l \end{pmatrix} \prec\approx \begin{pmatrix} x_i \\ x_j \end{pmatrix}$$

$\subset R$ and $|X| < \infty$:

Having constructed $L_{d,P}$ appropriately, one can compute the predecessor set M_{ij} of each pair (x_i, x_j)

$$M_{ij} = \left\{ \begin{pmatrix} x_k \\ x_l \end{pmatrix} \in X^2 : \begin{pmatrix} x_k \\ x_l \end{pmatrix} \prec\approx \begin{pmatrix} x_i \\ x_j \end{pmatrix} \right\}$$

The distance of a pair wise observation $(x_i, x_j) \in X^2$ is measured by the probability of the set of all its ' $\prec\approx$ '- predecessors. We can now define the W-distance, a shorthand notation for a probability ("Wahrscheinlichkeit") based distance.

Def. 8: DEF.: Let $X \subset R$ and $|X| < \infty$. Then $d_W: (X^2, \prec\approx) \to R_{[0, 1]}$ with $d_W(x_i, x_j) = P_X(M_{ij})$ is called W-distance on X.

This measure has the following properties, cf. Skarabis (1970):

- symmetric: $d_W(x_i, x_j) = d_W(x_j, x_i)$
- normalized: $d_W(x_i, x_j) \leq 1$
- the triangle inequality not (generally) fulfilled – depending upon P_X
- dimension free.

3.1 Unordered Set X

We apply now the d_W to example no. 1 which is characterised by the triple (X, P_X, d_X). We let $X = \{1, 2\}$ where $1 \equiv$ „take a bath", and $2 \equiv$ „take a coat" (exclusive values). The distance d_X is simple indicator function, i.e. $d_X(x, y)=1$ if $x=y$ and $d_X(x, y)=0$ else. The probability distribution P_X on X is given by

$x \in X$	$x_1 = 1$	$x_2 = 2$
$P_X(x)$	0,01	0,99

Table 2: probability distribution P_X on X

$$L_1 = \left\{ \left[\begin{pmatrix} x_k \\ x_l \end{pmatrix}, \begin{pmatrix} x_i \\ x_j \end{pmatrix} \right] \in X^2 \times X^2 : x_i = x_j \text{ and } x_k = x_l \text{ and } P(x_i) \geq P(x_k) \right\}$$

$$L_2 = \left\{ \left[\begin{pmatrix} x_k \\ x_l \end{pmatrix}, \begin{pmatrix} x_i \\ x_j \end{pmatrix} \right] \in X^2 \times X^2 : x_i \neq x_j \text{ and } x_k, x_l \text{ any value} \right\}$$

Then the quasi order $(X^2, \prec \approx)$ can be determined as follows where $L_{d,P} = L_1 \cup L_2$.

The W-distance value for a pair who takes an icy bath is small and is given by

$$d_W(x_1, x_1) = P(M_{11}) = P_X\left(\left\{ \begin{pmatrix} x_1 \\ x_1 \end{pmatrix} \right\} \right) = \frac{1}{100^2} = 0,0001$$

Contrarily, the W-distance value for a pair who wears a warm coat in winter

$$d_W(x_2, x_2) = P(M_{22}) = P_X\left(\left\{ \begin{pmatrix} x_1 \\ x_1 \end{pmatrix}, \begin{pmatrix} x_2 \\ x_2 \end{pmatrix} \right\} \right) = \frac{1}{100^2} + \frac{99^2}{100^2} \cong 0,9802$$

time is high

By definition, all other pairs (x_i, x_j) with unequal observations, $x_i \neq x_j$, have $d_w(x_i, x_j) = 1$.

Moreover, due the small cardinality of X the sets $L_{d,P} = L_1 \cup L_2$ can be completely enumerated.

$$L_1 = \left\{ \left[\begin{pmatrix} x_1 \\ x_1 \end{pmatrix}, \begin{pmatrix} x_2 \\ x_2 \end{pmatrix} \right] \right\} \qquad L_2 = \left\{ \left[\begin{pmatrix} x_1 \\ x_2 \end{pmatrix}, \begin{pmatrix} x_1 \\ x_2 \end{pmatrix} \right] \right\}$$

Finally, the complete quasi order $(X^2, \prec \approx)$ is given by

$$\left\{ \begin{pmatrix} x_1 \\ x_1 \end{pmatrix}, \begin{pmatrix} x_2 \\ x_2 \end{pmatrix}, \begin{pmatrix} x_1 \\ x_2 \end{pmatrix} \right\}$$

One can summarize the computation of the W-distance for unordered sets X as follows:

$$d_W(x_i, x_j) = \begin{cases} \sum_{k \in pred(x_i)} P_X^2(x_k) & \text{for all } x_i = x_j \\ 1 & \text{for all } x_i \neq x_j \end{cases} \qquad (9)$$

where the set of predecessor pairs of x_i is given by $pred(x_i) = \{k \in N : P_X(x_k) \leq P_X(x_i)\}$
for all $i=1,2,\ldots,n$.

3.2 One-dimensional Metric Space X

We use as basic distance measure d a special form of a city block distance, i.e. $d(x, y) = |x - y|$ for all $x, y \in X=R$. Therefore such problems are described by the triple (R, P_X, d).

As done before a (complete) preorder $(R^2, \prec_\approx)$ is constructed for induced similarity of pairs (x, y) of observations, however, this time the information from the basic distance measure d as well as from the distribution P_X is utilized as follows:

The d_W-distance is given by

$$d_W(x_i, x_j) = P_X\left\{ \begin{pmatrix} x_k \\ x_l \end{pmatrix} : \begin{pmatrix} x_k \\ x_l \end{pmatrix} \prec_\approx \begin{pmatrix} x_i \\ x_j \end{pmatrix} \right\}$$

$$L_1 = \left\{ \left[\begin{pmatrix} x_k \\ x_l \end{pmatrix}, \begin{pmatrix} x_i \\ x_j \end{pmatrix} \right] \in X^2 \times X^2 : d_{kl} < d_{ij} \right\}$$

$$L_2 = \left\{ \left[\begin{pmatrix} x_k \\ x_l \end{pmatrix}, \begin{pmatrix} x_i \\ x_j \end{pmatrix} \right] \in X^2 \times X^2 : d_{kl} = d_{ij} \text{ and } P([x_k, x_l]) \leq P([x_i, x_j]) \right\}$$

We see that the W-distance is just the probability of the predecessor set of the current pair (x_i, x_j) including this pair itself. Because of the preorder $(X^2, \prec_\approx)$ we have again with $L_{d,P} = L_1 \cup L_2$.

$$\left(\begin{pmatrix} x_k \\ x_l \end{pmatrix}, \begin{pmatrix} x_i \\ x_j \end{pmatrix} \right) \in L_{d,P} \Leftrightarrow \begin{pmatrix} x_k \\ x_l \end{pmatrix} \prec_\approx \begin{pmatrix} x_i \\ x_j \end{pmatrix} .$$

Therefore the pair (x_k, x_l) is more similar to each other than this is the case for (x_i, x_j) if $\begin{pmatrix} x_k \\ x_l \end{pmatrix}, \begin{pmatrix} x_i \\ x_j \end{pmatrix} \in L_1$ or L_2. This means that either $d_{kl} < d_{ij}$ or if the basic (city block) distances are equal, i.e. $d_{kl} = d_{ij}$, then the inequality of probabilities, $P_X((x_k, x_l)) \leq P_X((x_i, x_j))$ becomes true.

We close with a final example. We consider the space $X=\{0,2,3\}\subset R$. Assume for simplicity that we can apply on X^2 the (basic) city block metric $d(x_i,x_j) = d_{ij} = |x_i - x_j|$. Then we determine the following distance matrix $D = (d_{ij})$ for all possible pairs of observations:

d_{ij}	0	2	3
0	0	2	3
2	2	0	1
3	3	1	0

Table 3: Basic Distance Matrix D

Assume that the following non uniform joint distribution P_{X^2} on X^2 is given:

p_{ij}	0	2	3
0	3/10	1/10	0
2	0	2/10	1/10
3	1/10	1/10	1/10

Table 4: P_{X^2} on X^2

We can compute in a straighforward manner the complete preorder $(X^2, \preceq_\approx)$ on X^2

$$\binom{3}{3} \preceq_\approx \binom{2}{2} \preceq_\approx \binom{0}{0} \preceq_\approx \binom{2}{3} \preceq_\approx \binom{3}{2} \preceq_\approx \binom{2}{0} \preceq_\approx \binom{0}{2} \preceq_\approx \binom{0}{3} \preceq_\approx \binom{3}{0}$$

From D and P_{X^2} we can easily derive distances like $d_W((3,3)) = 1/10 < d_W((2,2)) = 2/10 < d_W((2,3))=1$. The last inequality is true because tupel $(2,2) \neq (2,3)$ and therefore $\left(\binom{2}{2}, \binom{2}{3} \right) \in L_1$.

3.3 W-distance in X^p

We turn finally to the case where all observations x_i, $i=1,2,\ldots,n$, are p-tupels, not necessarily real vectors. A response or measurement vector gets relative to a prototype a small distance value if all its components are relatively small. Therefore we can define the W-distance analogue to the univariate case for all

$$d_W(x_i, x_j) = P_X \left\{ \binom{x_k}{x_l} : \binom{x_k}{x_l} \preceq_\approx \binom{x_i}{x_j} \right\}$$

pairs of p-tupels, $(x_i, x_j)^T \in X^p \times X^p$:

As Skarabis (1970) proposed we can construct a complete preorder ($X^p \times X^p$, $\prec\approx$) in order to determine the set of predecessors:

$$\left(\begin{pmatrix} x_k \\ x_l \end{pmatrix}, \begin{pmatrix} x_i \\ x_j \end{pmatrix}\right) \in L_{d,P} \Leftrightarrow \begin{pmatrix} x_k \\ x_l \end{pmatrix} \prec\approx \begin{pmatrix} x_i \\ x_j \end{pmatrix}$$

If we define for each vector x_i its l-th element by $x_{i\ l}$, $l = 1,2,...,p$, we can consider component-wise W- distances $d_{ij}^l(x_{il}, x_{jl})$ for all $l=1,2,...,p$. Of course, the basic distance used to construct d_W strongly depends upon the scale of measurements, i.e. nominal, ordinal or metric. Aggregation of the W-distances $d_{ij}^l(x_{il}, x_{jl})$ is performed by multiplication as Skarabis (1971) proposed.

$$L_{d,P} = \left\{ \left[\begin{pmatrix} x_k \\ x_l \end{pmatrix}, \begin{pmatrix} x_i \\ x_j \end{pmatrix} \right] \in X^{2p} \times X^{2p} : \prod_{l=1}^{p} d_{kl}^l \le \prod_{l=1}^{p} d_{ij}^l \right\}$$

Evidently, other combination rules can be thought of.

References

Borgelt, Ch., Prototype-based Classification and Clustering, Habilitationsschrift, Otto-von-Guericke-Universität Magdeburg, Magdeburg, 2005

Cormack, R.M. , A review of classification (with Discussion), J.R.Stat. Soc., A, 31, 321-367

Cox, T.F. and Cox, M.A.A., Multidimensional Scaling, 2nd. Ed., Chapman & Hall, Boca Raton etc., 2001

Frakes, W.B. and Baeza-Yates, R., Information Retrieval: Data Structures and Algorithms, Prentice Hal, Upper Saddle River, 1992

Godan, M., Über die Komplexität der Bestimmung der Ähnlichkeit von geometrischen Objekten in höheren Dimensionen, Dissertation, Freie Universität Berlin, 1991

Gower, J., A general coefficient of similarity and some of its properties, Biometrics, 27, 857-874

Hartigan, J.A., Representation of similarity matrices by trees, J.Am.Stat.Assoc., 62, 1140-1158, 1967

Hubálek, Z., Coefficients of association and similarity based on binary (presence-absence) data; an evaluation, Biol. Rev., 57, 669-689

Kruse, R. and Meyer, K.D., Statistics with Vague Data. D. Reidel Publishing Company, Dordrecht, 1987

Kullback, S., Information Theory and Statistics, Wiley, New York etc., 1959

Jardine, N. and Sibson, R., Mathematical Taxonomy, Wiley, London, 1971

Mahalanobis, P.C., On the Generalized Distance in Statistics. In: Proceedings Natl. Inst. Sci. India, 2, 49-55, 1936

Murtagh, F., Identifying and Exploiting ultrametricity. In: *Advances in Data Analysis*, Decker, R. and Lenz, H.-J. (eds.), Springer, Heidelberg, 2007

Skarabis, H., Mathematische Grundlagen und praktische Aspekte der Diskrimination und Klassifikation, Physika-Verlag, Würzburg, 1970

Sneath, P.H.A. and Sokal, R.R., Numerical Taxonomy, Freeman and Co., San Francisco, 1973

Similarity Relations and Independence Concepts

Frank Klawonn[†] and Rudolf Kruse[‡]

[†] Department of Computer Science, University of Applied Sciences,
Wolfenbüttel, Germany
[‡] Department of Computer Science, Otto-von-Guericke University, Magdeburg,
Germany

Abstract This paper addresses the definition of independence concepts in the context of similarity relations. After motivating the need for independence concepts basic ideas from similarity relations and their connections to fuzzy systems are reviewed. Three different independence notions are discussed and investigated in the framework of similarity relations. The results show that there are significant differences for independence concepts in a probabilistic setting and in the framework of similarity relations.

1 Introduction

Similarity is a very fundamental concept used in approximate and cased-based reasoning. There are many different ways to model similarity. In this paper we mainly focus on similarity as a dual concept to the notion of distance. When dealing with a real-valued attribute a distance function is an elementary notion, easy to define and to comprehend. As long as only a single variable is considered, the distance must take a context dependent scaling into account. However, when attribute vectors are used, it is usually not sufficient to aggregate the distances of the single attributes in an independent fashion. The overall distance or similarity of two elements that are described by the same vector of attributes, but with different values, crucially depends on the interaction and dependencies between the attributes. Within probability theory the notion of independence is a well defined and experienced concept. In other fields, related to but different from probability theory, like possibility theory (Bouchon-Meunier et al., 2004; De Cooman, 1997) or belief functions (Yaghlane et al., 2002) the definition of independence becomes difficult.

In this paper, we discuss the notion of independence in the context of distance-based similarity measures. To better illustrate the underlying questions and consequences, we use an interpretation of fuzzy systems based on similarity relations. We show that the concept of independence for similarity relations is crucial, but it is not at all obvious, how to define it. Certain definitions lead also to unusual properties like asymmetric independence.

The paper is organized as follows. Section 2 motivates the use and importance of independence considerations within modelling imperfect knowledge, especially in combination with data available for training or tuning model parameters. Section 3 briefly reviews basic ideas from similarity relations and explains their connection to fuzzy systems. General considerations about modelling independence under different aspects are discussed in section 4. The application of the considerations to similarity relations is investigated in section 5, before we come to the final conclusions in section 6.

2 Modelling Imperfect Knowledge Enhanced by Data

Classical two-valued logic and standard deduction system are designed to model crisp facts and perfect knowledge. Although this is suitable for certain   applications,   in knowledge-based systems it is very often desirable to include imperfect knowledge. It would take too much space to discuss all facets of imperfect and uncertain knowledge. A main characteristic is that numbers or weights are assigned to propositions, events or statements. Of course, the meaning of the numbers is crucial and determines how to operate with the imperfect knowledge and the assigned weights or numbers. Probability theory provides the most popular model. It provides only an abstract framework that leaves space for an interpretation. The frequentistic view of probabilities is probably the most common one. The numbers or weights – in this context they are called probabilities – represent relative frequencies of events in experiments that are assumed to be be repeatable "arbitrarily often" in an "independent" manner. Although this seems to be appealing and intuitive, it has certain problems and limitations. Other interpretations in terms of subjective probabilities within a framework of rational betting behaviours (see for instance (O'Hagan and Forster, 2004)) or in a game-theoretic setting (Shafer, 2006) put a stronger emphasis on the evaluation of knowledge and experience that does not have to be based on observations in terms of counting relative frequencies.

Other examples are belief functions within Dempster-Shafer theory (Shafer, 1976) or within the transferable belief model (Smets and Kennes, 1994), possibility theory (Dubois and Prade, 2001) or preferences. In all these models, the interpretation of the weights or numbers determines how to operate with them. Fuzzy systems are an example where the the interpretation of the weights – in this case degrees of membership – is not straightforward in most cases and sometimes the choice of operations looks very heuristic or even arbitrary.

Any interpretation of probabilities or degrees of membership makes certain assumptions about rational behaviour concerning the specification of the weights. Here, the term weight is used, since, depending on the interpretation, these numerical values might represent probabilities, confidence or truth degrees and the term "'weight"' is neutral without referring to a specific interpretation. Even though the underlying justification for assuming a certain rational behaviour might be plausible, in most cases human experts are very often unable to specify the required weights in a consistent way, when the application becomes more complex. Human experts can often provide important prior or meta information on structures, dependencies and qualitative judgements. However, when exact quantifications are needed, the experts might not be able to specify unique values.

Therefore, it is very common to couple expert knowledge with data, so that the structural model information is provided by the expert, whereas the fine tuning of the model is carried out based on the available data. A very common way to handle this estimation of the model parameters is to formulate an optimization problem where the model parameters should be determined in such a way that the model fits[1] best to the data. Figure 1 illustrates this approach. The model parameters must be tuned in such a way that the given input data produce the desired output data with minimal error. Difficulties arise here, when there is no analytical or obvious way to optimize the model parameters parameters in case of a large number of variables. For more complex models this is almost always the case. Then parameter optimization can become an extremely complex or almost impossible task.

It is interesting to note that at least certain models have found a way out of this problem. Graphical models (for overviews see for instance (Borgelt and Kruse, 2002; Cowell et al., 2003; Cox and Wermuth, 1996)) and specifically Bayesian networks describe the dependence or independence structure of variables in the form of of an acyclic and directed graph. In this way a probability distribution over a high-dimensional variable space can be decomposed into a number of marginal and conditional distributions over low-dimensional spaces. Figure 2 illustrates the graphical structure of a Bayesian network. Given the dependency or model structure, the parameters of the Bayesian network are not learned according to the strategy illustrated in

---

[1] Fitting the model should also include model validation by techniques like cross-validation or the minimum description length principle (see for instance Grünwald (2007)) in order to avoid overfitting.

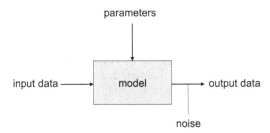

Figure 1. Open loop system for learning as an optimization problem.

Figure 1 to optimize the input-output behaviour[2] of the Bayesian network
with respect to the given data. Instead, the Bayesian network learns or estimates the low-dimensional probability distributions from the data. In this
sense, the dependence or independence structure of the Bayesian network
allows local computations of the parameters without taking their influence
on the whole model into account.

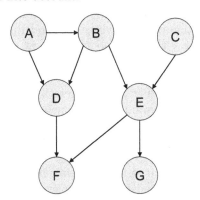

Figure 2. A Bayesian network for local learning.

The graphical structure of the Bayesian network specifies (conditional)
independencies of variables. Therefore, using the information about independence or conditional independence can lead to efficient and simplified
parameter learning schemes. The remaining part of this paper explains
the difficulties that arise, when similar ideas are applied in the context of
similarity relations.

---

[2]For a Bayesian network there are even no specific input or output variables, even
though it can be used in this way.

3   Similarity Relations and Fuzzy Systems

Here, we focus on a specific type of similarity relation. A very common definition of a similarity relation $s : X \times X \to [0,1]$ on a set X, where $s(x,y)$ expresses the similarity between elements x and y, requires the following properties:

 (a) Reflexivity: $s(x,x) = 1$
 (b) Symmetry: $s(x,y) = s(y,x)$
 (c) Transitivity: $s(x,y) * s(y,z) \le s(x,z)$

where $*$ is a suitable t-norm[3]. Besides the name similarity relation (Zadeh, 1971; Ruspini, 1991), depending on the choice of the operation $*$, s is also called an indistinguishability operator (Trillas and Valverde, 1984), fuzzy equality (relation) (Höhle and Stout, 1991; Klawonn and Kruse, 1993), fuzzy equivalence relation (Thiele and Schmechel, 1995) or proximity relation (Dubois and Prade, 1994). Reflexivity is an obvious property. Symmetry is very often, though not always, a canoncial property as well. Whether transitivity is required for similarity relations is sometimes questioned (De Cock and Kerre, 2003; Klawonn, 2003). However, in this paper we want to focus on similarity relations that satisfy a specific type of transitivity, namely transitivity with respect to the Łukasiewicz t-norm defined as $\alpha * \beta = \max\{\alpha + \beta - 1, 0\}$.

A similarity relation with respect to the Łukasiewicz t-norm can be viewed as a dual concept to a metric. In the following, we only consider similarity relations with respect to the Łukasiewicz t-norm and will not mention this fact explicitly each time. Such a similarity relation induces a (pseudo-)metric $\delta_s(x,y) = 1 - s(x,y)$ bounded by one and vice versa, any (pseudo-)metric δ_s bounded by one induces a similarity relation by $s_\delta(x,y) = 1 - \delta(x,y)$. The restriction that the metric is bounded by one is more or less neglectable, since any metric δ can be bounded by one, simply by defining $\bar{\delta}(x,y) = \min\{\delta(x,y), 1\}$ without affecting small distances that are usually of main interest.

When dealing with real numbers real numbers metric distances is an elementary concept leading to the canonical metric $\delta(x,y) = |x - y|$.

Extensionality is a very simple concept to take similarity between elements into account during a reasoning process. Extensionality means that similar elements should lead to similar results. The extensionality property we need here, is the extensionality of sets. For an ordinary set M we have

---

[3]A t-norm is an associative and commutative operation on the unit interval that is nondecreasing in its arguments and has one as a unit element. For example, the product or the minimum are t-norms.

the trivial property

$$x \in M \wedge x = y \ \Rightarrow \ y \in M. \tag{1}$$

When we replace equality by similarity, this simple property translates to: If element x belongs to the set M and x and y are similar to a certain degree, then y should also belong to M to a certain degree. Since similarity is a matter of degree, the property that y belongs to M should also be a matter of degree. Therefore, it is necessary to let M be a fuzzy set, i.e. elements do not simply belong or do not belong to M, but have a membership degree to M. A fuzzy set $\mu : X \rightarrow [0,1]$ is said to be extensional with respect to the similarity relation s on X, if it satisfies

$$\mu(x) * s(x,y) \ \leq \ \mu(y)$$

for all $x, y \in X$. This extensionality property is an extension of the simple property (1) for equality to similarity relations. In the presence of a similarity relation intending to model indistinguishability between elements, a (fuzzy) set should be consistent, i.e. extensional with respect to the given similarity relation. When we refer to an element x in the presence of a similarity relation, we might actually refer to x or a similar element. The (fuzzy) set of elements similar to x is the extensional hull of the set $\{x\}$, i.e. the smallest extensional fuzzy set containing x, i.e. the fuzzy set that contains x and all elements similar to x:

$$\mu_x(y) \ = \ s(x,y).$$

More generally, the extensional hull $\hat{\mu}$ of a fuzzy set μ is the smallest extensional fuzzy set containing μ given by

$$\hat{\mu}(y) \ = \ \bigvee_{x \in X} (\mu(x) * s(x,y))$$

which can be read as

$$y \in \mu \ \Leftrightarrow \ (\exists x \in X)(x \in \mu \wedge x \approx y).$$

The extensional hull of an ordinary set is the extensional hull of its indicator function and can be understood as the (fuzzy) set of points that are similar to at least one element in the set.

As an example consider the similarity relation $s(x,y) = 1 - \min\{|x-y|, 1\}$ on the real numbers. The extensional hulls of a single point and an interval are shown in Figure 3.

It is noteworthy that these extensional hulls lead to triangular and trapezoidal fuzzy sets that are very common in fuzzy systems. Extensional hulls

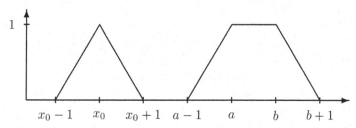

Figure 3. The extensional hulls of the point x_0 and of the interval $[a, b]$.

of points with respect to the similarity relation

$$s(x, y) = 1 - \min\{|x - y|, 1\}$$

always have a support of length two. In order to maintain the degrees of similarity (and the membership degrees), when changing the measurement unit (seconds instead of hours, miles instead of kilometres,...), we have to take a scaling into account:

$$s(x, y) = 1 - \min\{c \cdot |x - y|, 1\}$$

When we take a closer look at the concept of similarity relations, we can even introduce a more general concept of scaling. Similarity relations can be used to model indistinguishability. There are two kinds of indistinguishability, we have to deal with in typical similarity-based reasoning applications.

Enforced indistinguishability is caused by limited precision of measurement instruments, (imprecise) indirect measurements, noisy data, ...

Intended indistinguishability means that the human expert is not interested in more precise values, since a higher precision would not really lead to improved results.

Both kinds of indistinguishability might need a local scaling as the following example of designing an air conditioning system shows.

temperature (in °C)	scaling factor	interpretation
< 15	0.00	exact value meaningless (much too cold)
15-19	0.25	too cold, but not too far away from the desired temperature, regulation need not be too sensitive
19-23	1.50	very sensitive, near the optimal value
23-27	0.25	too warm, but not too far away from the desired temperature, regulation need not be too sensitive
> 27	0.00	exact value meaningless (much too hot)

When we apply these different scaling factors to our temperature domain, this has the following consequences, when we consider the similarity relation induced by the scaled distance. In order to determine how dissimilar two temperatures are, we do note compute their difference directly, but in the scaled domain, where the range up to 15 is shrunk to a single point, the range between 15 and 19 is shrunk by the factor 0.25, the range between 19 and 23 is stretched by the factor 1.5 and so on. The following table shows the scaled distances of some example values for the temperature.

pair of values	scal. factor	transformed distance	similarity degree
(x,y)	c	$\delta(x,y) = \lvert c \cdot x - c \cdot y \rvert$	$s(x,y) = 1 - \min\{\delta(x,y),1\}$
(13,14)	0.00	0.000	1.000
(14,14.5)	0.00	0.000	1.000
(17,17.5)	0.25	0.125	0.875
(20,20.5)	1.50	0.750	0.250
(21,22)	1.50	1.500	0.000
(24,24.5)	0.25	0.125	0.875
(28,28.5)	0.00	0.000	1.000

Figures 4 and 5 show examples of extensional hulls of single points.

The idea of piecewise constant scaling functions can be extended to arbitrary scaling functions in the following way (Klawonn, 1994). Consider an integrable scaling function $c : R \to [0, \infty)$, where c is a function $c(x)$, not a constant like c before. If we assume that we have for small values $\varepsilon > 0$ that the transformed distance between x and $x + \varepsilon$ is given by

$$\delta(x, x + \varepsilon) \approx c(x) \cdot \varepsilon,$$

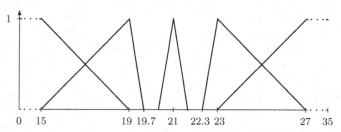

Figure 4. The extensional hulls of the points 15, 19, 21, 23 and 27.

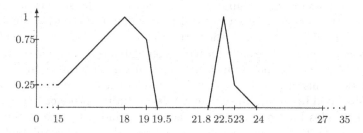

Figure 5. The extensional hulls of the points 18.5 and 22.5.

then the transformed distance induced by the scaling function c can be computed by

$$\delta(x,y) \;=\; \left| \int_x^y c(s)\,ds \right|.$$

This idea of scaling functions can exploited to derive a simplified learning scheme for fuzzy rule-based systems (Klawonn, 2006). The fuzzy sets in the body of a rule represent extensional hulls of single points and the fuzzy rule-based system constructs an interpolating function based on these nodes or sampling points, taking the underlying similarity relation into account. In this sense, the body of a fuzzy rule is nothing else than a single value including the similar values in terms of the similarity relation. Prototype-based fuzzy clustering (for an overview see for instance (Höppner et al., 1999)) is based on very similar ideas. A cluster is represented by a single point – the prototype – and the membership degree of a data point to the cluster decreases with increasing distance to the cluster. Specialized algorithms as proposed in (Klawonn and Kruse, 1997; Keller and Klawonn, 2000; Borgelt,

2005) use even a scaling concept for the attributes. However, these scalings are carried out more or less independently on the single variables. Some fuzzy clustering algorithms (Gustafson and Kessel, 1979; Gath and Geva, 1989) take also dependencies between the variables into account and use in addition to the scaling a rotation in order to compute similarities or distances.

Considering fuzzy rule-based systems in the context of similarity-based reasoning, a body of a rule represents a point in the – usually – multidimensional input space. When a concrete (multidimensional) measured input is given, the similarity of the measured value to the value representing the body of the rule must be determined. This is usually done by first determining the membership degrees of each variable value to the corresponding fuzzy set. These membership degrees correspond to the similarities of the values of the single variables. In order to compute the overall similarity degree – the degree to which the corresponding fuzzy rule is applicable – these membership degrees are normally aggregated by a suitable operation, usually a t-norm like the product or the minimum. In terms of the similarity relations this means that the similarity relations on the single variables are aggregated to an overall similarity relation on the product space of the variables. This kind of aggregation requires an independence assumption for the similarity relations, since it is assumed that the overall similarity can be derived solely from knowing the similarity degree of each variable without referring to single values.

In order to illustrate that this assumption is unrealistic in many cases, we consider a typical control task. The aim is to balance an inverted pendulum that is fixed on a cart that can be driven forward and backward to fulfil the task (see Figure 6). As input variables we use the deviation of the angle of the pendulum from the upright position e and the angle velocity Δe.

With this simple example, we can easily demonstrate the dependency between the similarity relation on the variables e and Δe. Let us first consider the situation on the left hand side of Figure 6. The inverted pendulum is almost in an upright position. In this case, it is very important to have a more or less precise value of Δe in order to know whether the inverted pendulum tends to fall down to the right, will overshoot to the left or remain more or less stable in its current position. This means that the similarity relation on the domain of the variable Δe must be fine granular.

The situation on the right hand side of Figure 6 is completely different. The inverted pendulum has fallen down almost completely and a strong control reaction has to be carried out in order to get it closer to the upright position. In this case, the actual value of Δe does not matter much at all. This means that a very coarse similarity relation on Δe would be sufficient.

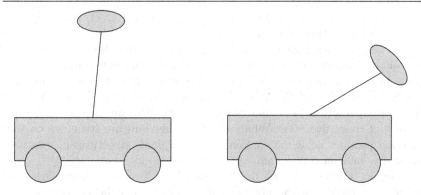

Figure 6. Balancing an inverted pendulum.

In other words, the similarity on Δe depends on the value of the variable e. When e is small, a refined similarity relation, distinguishing more between values, is needed on the domain of the variable Δe than in the case, when e is large.

Although this simple example clarifies in an intuitive manner that interaction between similarity relations should not be ignored, it does, however, not provide a formal definition what dependence or independence of similarity relations means. The following section discusses the notion of independence from a more general point of view in order to apply it in Section 5 to the context of similarity relations.

4 Independence Concepts

In this section we take a more general view on the formal concept of independence, before we apply it to similarity relations in the following section. We consider the notion of independence in a more general framework of product spaces. Independence involves (at least) two variables or domains. The variables can be considered separately or in combination. Independence intuitively refers to the property that it is sufficient to measure the variables separately and then to combine the results of these marginal measurements. For instance, in probability theory independence of two random variables X and Y means the following. If we want to know the probability $P(X \in A, Y \in B)$ for two combined events, i.e. Borel-measurable sets A and B, in the case of independence we can first compute the marginal probabilities $p_A = P(X \in A)$ and $p_B = P(Y \in B)$ and then combine these two probabilities (by the product). However, when the variables are dependent, we cannot deduce the joint distribution $P_{X,Y}(X \in A, Y \in B)$ knowing only p_A and p_B for all Borel-measurable sets A and B.

The general view that we take here is the following. We have two sets, each of them endowed with a structure for modelling uncertainty or similarity. In the case of probability theory this structure would be a σ-algebra together with a probability measure. In the context of modelling similarity it would simply be a similarity relation. We also consider the cartesian product of these two sets. What would be the resulting structure on the cartesian product when we combine the (marginal) structures on the two sets in an "independent" manner?

Category theory provides one framework to formalize these ideas. A formal introduction of the notion of a category would be far beyond the scope of this paper. Therefore, we give a more informal description of the underlying concepts. A category can be considered as a class of objects and morphisms between the objects. Very often, the objects are sets with an additional structure (for instance, algebraic structures like groups, topological spaces, measure spaces or probability spaces). In this case the morphism are structure preserving mappings between the elements, homomorphisms in the case of algebraic structures, continuous mappings for topological spaces or measurable mappings for measure spaces. Such categories are called concrete categories (Adamek et al., 1990). The product $X = X_1 \times X_2$ together with two projections (morphisms) $\pi_i : X \to X_i$ $(i = 1, 2)$ of two objects X_1 and X_2 in a category is characterized by the following property. For any object Y and two morphisms $f_i : Y \to X_i$ $(i = 1, 2)$ there is a morphism f such that the diagram in Figure 7 commutes, i.e. $\pi_i \circ f = f_i$ $(i = 1, 2)$ holds. It can be shown that the product or product space X in a category is unique up to isomorphism in case of its existence.

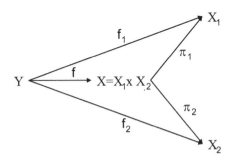

Figure 7. The product space as a limit in a category.

If product structures in the sense of category theory are available, one possible definition of independence is the following. A structure (probability measure or similarity relation) on a product space is considered to be composed of independent components, if the product of its projections yields the same structure on the product space.

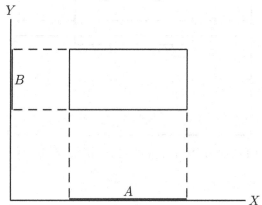

Figure 8. Reconstructing the original structure from its projections.

Figure 8 illustrates this concept in the context of sets without structure. A subset of a Cartesian product space can be reconstructed by its projections, if and only if it is a rectangle.

In the case of a probability measure on the product space $X \times Y$, this independence property is equivalent to $P(A \times B) = P(A \times Y) \cdot P(X \times B)$.

Another formalization of independence is the following one: No matter at which point the projection is carried out, the projection will always be the same. Figure 9 illustrates this idea for sets without structure. It means that for a given subset $S \subset X \times Y$ of a product space, the sets $\{y \in Y \mid (x_0, y)\}$ are either empty or identical independent of the choice of x_0. The same applies to the projection sets $\{x \in X \mid (x, y_0)\}$.

In the probabilistic setting, this means that $P(Y|X = x_0)$ is independent of the choice of x_0 and vice versa, $P(X|Y = y_0)$ is independent of the choice of y_0. In the case of probability this leads again to the classical definition of independence.

Note that this definition contains two parts: $P(Y|X = x_0)$ does not depend on any x_0 means that Y is independent of X, whereas $P(X|Y = y_0)$ is independent of the choice of y_0 says that X is independent of Y. In the context of probability theory we can only have both properties or none of the two properties. In the next section we will see that this is not the case for similarity relations.

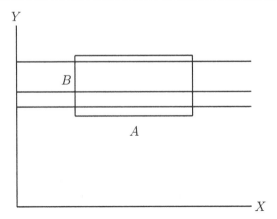

Figure 9. Projections at different positions.

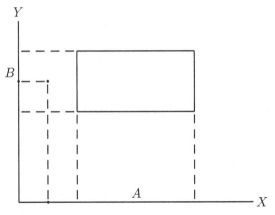

Figure 10. Deriving information from the projections.

Another possible notion of independence is the following one: The complete information for every point in the product space can be reconstructed from the projections. Figure 10 illustrates this idea for sets without structure.

In a probabilistic setting this can be viewed as a more general independence concept, at least when cumulative distribution functions are considered. Using copulas[4] (see for instance (Nelsen, 1999)), arbitrary two-dimensional cumulative distribution functions can be constructed. In this

---

[4]A copula is a cumulative distribution function $C : [0, 1]^n \to [0, 1]$ with uniform distributions on the unit interval as its one-dimensional marginal distributions.

sense, independence would hold for any two cumulative distribution functions.

5 Similarity Relations and Independence

Since fuzzy rule-based systems usually use multiple inputs, it is necessary to combine the similarity relations on the single domains to an overall similarity relation in the product space. The canonical similarity relation on a product space – at least in the sense of category theory – is given by

$$s((x_1, \ldots, x_p), (x_1', \ldots, x_p')) = \min_{i \in \{1, \ldots, p\}} \{s_i(x_i, x_i')\}.$$

In terms of fuzzy rule-based systems this means that for a single rule, the membership degrees of an input would be combined using the minimum.

Assume there is a similarity relation v (or any other structure) on a product space $X \times Y$ with

$$\pi_X(v) = s, \quad \pi_X(v)(x_1, x_2) = \bigvee_{y \in Y} v((x_1, y), (x_2, y))$$

$$\pi_Y(v) = t$$

where s and t are the projections of v onto X and Y, respectively. What is the meaning of s and t being independent?

The first definition of independence in the previous section based on category theory means that s and t are independent, if and only if $v = \min\{s, t\}$ holds.

The second definition was asymmetric and leads indeed to an asymmetric property for similarity relations. To see this, consider the product space $[0.5, 1] \times [0.5, 1]$ and the metric defined by the transformation

$$t(x, y) : [0.5, 1] \times [0.5, 1] \to [0.5, 1] \times [0.25, 1], \quad (x, y) \mapsto (x, xy)$$

The distance between two points (x_1, y_1) and (x_2, y_2) is the (product space metric) distance between the transformed points

$$\max\{t(x_1, y_1), t(x_2, y_2)\}.$$

- $\delta((x_1, y_1), (x_2, y_2)) = \max\{|x_1 - x_2|, |x_1 y_1 - x_2 y_2|\}$
- $\delta_X(x_1, x_2) = |x_1 - x_2| = \delta^{(y)}(x_1, x_2)$
- $\delta_Y(y_1, y_2) = |y_1 - y_2|$
- $\delta^{(x)}(y_1, y_2) = x|y_1 - y_2|$

This example shows that the similarity relation (or, dually, the metric) on X is independent of the similarity relation on Y, but not vice versa.

Finally, let us consider the last independence definition of the previous chapter. For similarity relations this independence notion means that there is a function

$$h : [0,1] \times [0,1] \rightarrow [0,1]$$

satisfying

$$h(1,1) \;=\; 1 \quad \text{and} \quad h(\alpha, \alpha') * h(\beta, \beta') \leq h(\alpha * \alpha', \beta * \beta')$$

such that

$$v((x,y),(x',y')) \;=\; h(s(x,x'), t(y,y')).$$

holds.

Although this independence notion is weaker than the first one, it does not lead to independence in all cases as in the probabilistic setting with copulas. Consider the product space $[0.5,1] \times [0.5,1]$ and the metric defined by the transformation

$$t(x,y) : [0.5,1] \times [0.5,1] \rightarrow [0.25,1], \quad (x,y) \mapsto xy$$

The metric is

$$\delta((x_1,y_1),(x_2,y_2)) \;=\; |x_1 y_1 - x_2 y_2|.$$

We obtain

$$
\begin{aligned}
\delta((0.8, 0.5), (0.9, 0.6)) &= 0.14 \\
\delta((0.8, 0.8), (0.9, 0.9)) &= 0.17 \\
\delta_X(0.8, 0.9) &= 0.1 \\
\delta_Y(0.5, 0.6) &= 0.1 \\
\delta_Y(0.8, 0.9) &= 0.1
\end{aligned}
$$

This example shows that we cannot reconstruct the first two different similarity degrees (or, dually, the distances) in the product space based only on the similarities in the projection spaces, since the latter ones are all identical.

6 Conclusions

In this paper, we have discussed the need for independence concepts for similarity relations and have investigated different approaches that lead to surprising and different results, especially when compared to the probabilistic setting. Further research is needed to make use of the independence concepts within applications of similarity-based reasoning. Especially, tests for independence need to be developed outside of the scope of statistics.

Bibliography

J. Adamek, H. Herrlich, and G.E. Strecker. *Abstract and Concrete Categories: The Joy of Cats.* Wiley, Chichester, 1990.

C. Borgelt. *Prototype-based Classification and Clustering.* PhD thesis, University of Magdeburg, 2005.

C. Borgelt and R. Kruse. *Graphical Models – Methods for Data Analysis and Mining.* Wiley, Chichester, 2002.

B. Bouchon-Meunier, G. Coletti, and C. Marsala. Independence and possibilistic conditioning. *Annals of Mathematics and Artificial Intelligence*, 35:107–123, 2004.

R.G. Cowell, A.P. Dawid, S.L. Lauritzen, and D.J. Spiegelhalter. *Probabilistic Networks and Expert Systems.* Springer, Berlin, 2003.

D.R. Cox and N. Wermuth. *Multivariate Dependencies: Models, Analysis and Interpretation.* Chapman & Hall/CRC, Boca Raton, 1996.

M. De Cock and E.E. Kerre. Why fuzzy t-equivalence relations do not resolve the poincaré paradox, and related issues. *Fuzzy Sets and Systems*, 133:175–180, 2003.

G. De Cooman. Possibility theory III: possibilistic independence. *International Journal of General Systems*, 25:353–371, 1997.

D. Dubois and H. Prade. Possibility theory, probability theory and multiple-valued logics: A clarification. *Annals of Mathematics and Artificial Intelligence*, 32:35–66, 2001.

D. Dubois and H. Prade. Similarity-based approximate reasoning. In J.M. Zurada, R.J. Marks II, and C.J. Robinson, editors, *Computational Intelligence Imitating Life*, pages 231–256. IEEE Press, New York, 1994.

I. Gath and A.B. Geva. Unsupervised optimal fuzzy clustering. *IEEE Trans. on Pattern Analysis and Machine Intelligence*, 11:773–781, 1989.

P.D. Grünwald. *The Minimum Description Length Principle.* MIT Press, Cambridge, MAssachusetts, 2007.

D.E. Gustafson and W.C. Kessel. Fuzzy clustering with a fuzzy covariance matrix. In *IEEE CDC*, pages 761–766, San Diego, 1979.

U. Höhle and L.N. Stout. Foundations of fuzzy sets. *Fuzzy Sets and Systems*, 40:257–296, 1991.

F. Höppner, F. Klawonn, R. Kruse, and T. Runkler. *Fuzzy Cluster Analysis.* Wiley, Chichester, 1999.

A. Keller and F. Klawonn. Fuzzy clustering with weighting of data variables. *Uncertainty, Fuzziness and Knowledge-Based Systems*, 8:735–746, 2000.

F. Klawonn. Should fuzzy equality and similarity satisfy transitivity? *Fuzzy Sets and Systems*, 133:175–180, 2003.

F. Klawonn. Reducing the number of parameters of a fuzzy system using scaling functions. *Soft Computing*, 10:749–756, 2006.

F. Klawonn. Fuzzy sets and vague environments. *Fuzzy Sets and Systems*, 66:207–221, 1994.

F. Klawonn and R. Kruse. Equality relations as a basis for fuzzy control. *Fuzzy Sets and Systems*, 54:147–156, 1993.

F. Klawonn and R. Kruse. Constructing a fuzzy controller from data. *Fuzzy Sets and Systems*, 85:177–193, 1997.

R.J. Nelsen. *An Introduction to Copulas*. Springer, Berlin, 1999.

A. O'Hagan and J. Forster. *Kendall's Advanced Theory of Statistics, Volume 2B: Bayesian Inference*. Arnold, London, 2004.

E.H. Ruspini. On the semantics of fuzzy logic. *Intern. Journ. of Approximate Reasoning*, 5:45–88, 1991.

G. Shafer. The game-theoretic framework for probability. In B. Bouchon-Meunier, J. Gutierrez-Rios, and L. Magdalena, editors, *Proceedings of the 11th International Conference on Information Processing and Management of Uncertainty in Knowledge-Based Systems*, pages 3–10, Paris, 2006. Éditions E.D.K.

G. Shafer. *A Mathematical Theory of Evidence*. Princeton University Press, Princeton, 1976.

P. Smets and R. Kennes. The transferable belief model. *Artificial Intelligence*, 66:191–234, 1994.

H. Thiele and N. Schmechel. The mutual defineability of fuzzy equivalence relations and fuzzy partitions. In *Proc. Intern. Joint Conference of the Fourth IEEE International Conference on Fuzzy Systems and the Second International Fuzzy Engineering Symposium*, pages 1383–1390, Yokohama, 1995.

E. Trillas and L. Valverde. An inquiry into indistinguishability operators. In H.J. Skala, S. Termini, and E. Trillas, editors, *Aspects of Vagueness*, pages 231–256. Reidel, Dordrecht, 1984.

B.B. Yaghlane, P. Smets, and K. Mellouli. Independence concepts for belief functions. In B. Bouchon-Meunier, J. Gutierrez-Rios, and L. Magdalena, editors, *Technologies for constructing intelligent systems 2: tools*, pages 45–58. Physica, Heidelberg, 2002.

L.A. Zadeh. Similarity relations and fuzzy orderings. *Information Sciences*, 3:177–200, 1971.

Imprecision and Structure in Modelling Subjective Similarity

Thomas Sudkamp

Department of Computer Science, Wright State University, Dayton, OH, USA

Abstract Similarity measures based on feature matching have been designed for modelling subjective similarity judgements. In this paper, the taxonomic presence-absence feature representation is extended to assess the similarity of objects whose attributes are described by partial satisfaction of predicates or by fuzzy sets. The principle of minimum specificity is used to obtain possibilistic bounds on the combination of similarity assessments. A priority hierarchy and bipolarity are incorporated into similarity measurement to utilize inter-attribute relationships in modelling similarity judgements.

1 Introduction

Similarity is one of the most versatile concepts in both human and computational reasoning. The preeminence of similarity in psychological modelling was noted by Sloman and Rips (Sloman and Rips, 1998) who asserted, "Explanation in psychology has at its disposal a few key concepts that it wields to account for a host of phenomena. Frequency is one such concept, saliency another, similarity is a third ... but the greatest of these is similarity." In formal and computational information analysis, similarity provides the basis for selecting alternatives in case-based reasoning, analogical reasoning, and decision theory, and is used in recommender systems to predict interests or actions based on a profile of previous decisions. Each of the preceding applications requires a quantitative assessment of the similarity of the objects in the underlying problem domain. The assessment may be obtained from an analysis of the properties of objects or by a subjective judgement made by an observer.

In computational reasoning, similarity values are often obtained using a similarity measure. A similarity measure is a mapping $S : U \times U \rightarrow I$, where U is the universe and I is a real-valued interval whose values indicate the similarity of the objects of U. Frequently I is taken to be the interval $[0, 1]$ in which case values 0 and 1 indicate minimal and maximal similarity between objects. Similarity measures used in psychological domains are referred to as models since they are designed to model subjective similarity judgements.

Similarity measures may be defined axiomatically or may be obtained constructively by a direct analysis of the properties of the objects in the domain. Constructive approaches are frequently based on feature matching or on an embedding of the domain objects in a metric space. The former approach, which has its roots in taxonomic classification, considers objects to be described by a set of attributes and similarity is determined by a comparison of the number common and distinct features. When objects are associated with points in a metric space, similarity information may be obtained directly from the distance function—the closer the points in the space, the more similar the corresponding objects.

The axiomatic approach begins by postulating mathematical properties that intuitively capture the notion of similarity. The axioms frequently include properties such as reflexivity, symmetry, and various versions of transitivity. Any function that satisfies the axioms is considered to an acceptable similarity measure. Following this approach, Tversky (Tversky, 1977) developed the contrast model from the premise that similarity can be modelled as a function of feature comparisons that is monotonic and satisfies several independence conditions. The seminal paper by Dubois and Prade (Dubois and Prade, 1982) provided axioms suitable for the determination of similarity of objects when the features are defined by fuzzy attributes. Another axiomatic approach to similarity assessment is provided by t-equivalences, which are built from t-norms and their related implication operators (Trillas and Valverde, 1984; De Baets and Mesiar, 2002).

Similarity judgements are affected by the objective, context, and focus of the observer. Consequently models should be sufficiently flexible to incorporate these factors into the analysis. The objective of a similarity judgement may be prescriptive, descriptive, or predictive. Relevance and focus determine the set of features used in the assessment. The context consists of external factors not explicitly in the representation of the objects that may affect a subjective assessment of similarity. For example, price may be considered as a feature in comparing potential purchases. A purchaser who considers two automobiles whose prices differ by $100 to be completely similar based on the price attribute, may consider the prices of two televisions whose costs differ by $100 to be significantly dissimilar.

The variety of approaches that have been proposed to measure similarity indicates that similarity is not an intrinsic property of objects, but rather takes place within a framework that is influenced by the focus, context, and the objective. In this paper we will be concerned with modelling similarity judgments between single objects. The measurement of similarity in scenarios with multiple interacting objects is used in analogical reasoning and relies more heavily on preserving inter-object relationships than on simple feature matching (Gentner, 1983; Hofstader, 1995; French, 1995). The importance of relations in similarity judgements, however, is not limited to those between domain items. Relationships between attributes may also affect the assessment of object similarity. In Section 5 we incorporate priority relationships between attributes into commonality based similarity assessment.

In this paper we will consider the extension of presence-absence feature matching models when feature values are represented by partial truth values or by fuzzy sets. These techniques will be used to establish bounds for the aggregation of similarity values with different foci. This is followed by the incorporation of inter-object feature relationships and bipolarity into similarity assessment. The paper begins with a review of standard methods employed in computational similarity analysis.

2 Similarity Measures

The classical approaches to similarity assessment are based on the commonality of attributes of objects or on proximity when the objects are embedded in a metric space. In either case, the domain objects are described by a set of attributes or features $A_1, \ldots, A_n$, where each attribute A_i has an associated set of values $\{a_{i,1}, \ldots, a_{i,m_i}\}$. With this representation, an object X can be represented by an n-dimensional vector $X = [x_1, x_2, \ldots, x_n]$ where $x_t \in A_t$. For the purposes of similarity assessment, an object is considered to be completely characterized by the attributes that it possesses.

Basing similarity on proximity is accomplished by associating a real number with each attribute value (Boyce, 1969). With this association, an object X defined by n attributes is represented by a vector $[v(x_1), v(x_2), \ldots, v(x_n)] \in R^n$, where $v(x_t)$ is the numeric value associated with the tth attribute of X. The fundamental assumption behind proximity based similarity assessment is that similarity behaves as an inverse of distance; the similarity of objects decreases as the distance between the associated points increases.

In proximity-based similarity assessment, the distance is frequently measured by a Minkowski metric

$$d_r(X, Y) = \left(\sum_{i=1}^n |v(x_i) - v(y_i)|^r \right)^{1/r},$$

where $r \geq 1$. The corresponding similarity is

$$S(X,Y) = 1 - d_r(X,Y)/max_d,$$

where max_d is the maximum distance between two objects in the domain. The Manhattan distance,

$$d(X,Y) = \frac{1}{n}\sum |v(x_i) - v(y_i)|, \tag{1}$$

has been proposed as a measure of taxonomic resemblance (Cain and Harrison, 1958) when the objects are represented by real-valued vectors.

Experimental results have called into question the validity of all of the metric axioms for modelling subjective similarity judgements. Krumhansl (Krumhansl, 1978) cites studies in which similarity judgements do not support the minimality property, $d(X,Y) \geq d(X,X)$. To account for the discrepancy between minimality and human similarity judgement, she proposed a *distance-density* model that incorporates the distribution of the domain objects into a distance based similarity model.

Experiments have also shown that subjective similarity judgements are not necessarily symmetric (Tversky, 1977; Rosh, 1975). In a similarity statement "X is like Y", the comparison between a subject and a referent is inherently asymmetric. Even when the comparison is phrased in a symmetric manner, the more prototypical of the objects being compared often takes on the role of the referent. The inadequacy of the triangle inequality for modelling similarity judgements was considered in detail in (Tversky and Gaiti, 1982). Moreover, the fundamental assumption of proximity-based similarity assessment, that similarity measures and dissimilarity measures behave as inverses, has been shown not to be justified for subjective similarity judgements. Experiments have demonstrated that judgements of similarity and dissimilarity use different subsets of features: similarity judgements focus on the common features while the mismatching features have a greater influence on dissimilarity judgements (Gregson, 1975; Tversky, 1977).

Due to the divergence between subjective similarity judgements and proximity based measures, we will use feature matching as the basis for the similarity measures considered in this paper. In the similarity measure proposed by Jaccard for taxonomic classification, objects are defined by attributes that assume one of two possible values: present or absent (Jaccard, 1908). Figure 1 illustrates two feature vectors with presence-attribute feature values, where p and a stand for present and absent respectively. There are four possible outcomes for the comparison of attributes: (p,p), (p,a), (a,p), and (a,a). For simplicity we let $|X \cap Y|$, $|X \cap \overline{Y}|$, $|\overline{X} \cap Y|$, $|\overline{X} \cap \overline{Y}|$ denote the number of attributes that are present in both X and Y (called

A$_1$									A$_i$												A$_n$
X	a	p	p	a	p	p	p	a	a	a	p	a	p	p	p	a	a	p	a	a	a	p
Y	a	p	a	a	a	p	a	p	a	p	p	a	a	p	a	a	a	a	a	a	a	p

Figure 1. Feature Matching

positive matches), present in X and absent in Y, absent in X and present in Y, and absent in X and Y (called negative matches).

Using the preceding notation, the *Jaccard index* can be written

$$S(X,Y) = |X \cap Y|/(|X \cap Y| + |X \cap \overline{Y}| + |\overline{X} \cap Y|). \qquad (2)$$

The Jaccard index considers only positive matches, incorporating negative matches produces

$$S(X,Y) = \frac{(|X \cap Y| + |\overline{X} \cap \overline{Y}|)}{|U|}, \qquad (3)$$

which has been referred to as the *simple matching coefficient* (Sokal and Sneath, 1963).

The *ratio model* of similarity

$$S(X,Y) = \frac{f(X \cap Y)}{f(X \cap Y) + \alpha f(X \cap \overline{Y}) + \beta f(Y \cap \overline{X})}. \qquad (4)$$

is a parameterized generalization of the Jaccard index where α and β are constants greater than or equal to 0. The function f is typically taken to be the cardinality, but may be any set function $f : 2^U \rightarrow [0, \infty)$ that is additive over disjoint sets.

Like the ratio model, Tversky's *contrast model* uses weights to indicate the importance of the types of feature relationships. In the contrast model, the similarity of X and Y is given by

$$S(X,Y) = \theta f(X \cap Y) - \alpha f(X \cap \overline{Y}) - \beta f(Y \cap \overline{X}), \qquad (5)$$

where θ, α, β are constants and the set function f is the same as in the ratio model. The weights reflect the relative salience of the features being compared or the directionality of a comparison. The selection of weights in the contrast and ratio models can be used to produce non-symmetric similarity functions that model the directionality in subjective judgements.

A general strategy for constructing similarity measures from the sets of positive matches, negative matches, and mismatches was presented in (De Baets et al., 2001; De Baets and De Meyer, 2003), which also classified these measures based on their boundary behaviour, reflexivity, and monotonicity.

The ratio model, contrast model, and the similarity measures studied in (De Baets et al., 2001; De Baets and De Meyer, 2003) assign weights to the types of matching relationships. An alternative approach is to assign weights to the attributes themselves. In taxonomic classification it has been suggested that the significance of a feature should be affected by the frequency of its occurrence in the population (Gambaryan, 1965; Sneath, 1965). In Section 5 we will assign weights to attributes to model priorities between features.

3   Feature Matching and Imprecision

Taxonomic classification uses attribute values that represent the presence or absence of a feature. In more general problems, the domains of the attributes are not restricted to two values. To maintain the presence-absence dichotomy used in the similarity models, Tversky proposed converting numeric values to suitable two-valued representations. In addition to multiple valued and numeric attributes, subjective similarity judgements introduce the possibility that an attribute may be partially satisfied by an object. This is modelled by permitting attribute values to be fuzzy membership values or entire fuzzy sets. The presence-absence matching paradigm can be extended to attributes whose values may represent partial satisfaction of a predicate or fuzzy sets over a family of linguistic terms. Extensions of feature matching similarity assessment to fuzzy attributes have been proposed by Santini and Jain (Santini and Jain, 1999) and Tolinas et al. (Tolinas et al., 2001). These approaches used fuzzy set operations to compute the cardinalities for the sets $X \cap Y$, $X \cap \overline{Y}$, $\overline{X} \cap Y$, $\overline{X} \cap \overline{Y}$. The method employed by Santini and Jain preserved the law of contradiction while the latter work used the standard conjunction and complementation operations to obtain the partial membership values in the preceding four sets.

One of the computational advantages of feature matching models is that each attribute is compared individually. The resulting similarity value is obtained by summing the weighted number of each type of match and nonmatch. The independent comparison of corresponding features allows us to consider the extension of matching to partial membership and fuzzy sets on single attributes. Two feature values that completely match will be assigned value 1, and 0 will indicate that there is no matching between the values.

Partial membership values describe the degree to which a fuzzy predicate subcell   1   2   3   4   5   6   7   8   9   10

p	p	p	p	p	p	p	a	a	a

Figure 2. Binary representation of partial membership

is satisfied. For example, a fuzzy predicate such as "near the airport" may be used as an attribute describing hotels. The value 1 for this attribute indicates complete satisfaction of the predicate, 0 no satisfaction, and values between 0 and 1 represent partial satisfaction.

The intuition for the presence-absence representation of a partial degree of satisfaction is given in Figure 2. To represent a partial degree of satisfaction, the "cell" for the feature is divided into subcells. A p in subcell i indicates that the feature is present to at least degree i/t, where t is the number of subcells. In Figure 2 the first seven of the ten subcells receive the binary attribute p indicating that the object satisfies the feature to degree .7. For determining the degree of matching, the initial α portion of the subcell (rather than an arbitrary portion) must be assigned value p when an object satisfies the attribute to degree α. The remainder of the subcells are assigned a.

The comparison of features that have partial membership values is illustrated in Figure 3. The shaded regions in the cells indicate that the feature is satisfied to degree α by X and to degree β by Y. The contribution of the attribute to the four types of feature combination is

set	membership
$\|X \cap Y\|$	$\min(\alpha, \beta)$
$\|X \cap \overline{Y}\|$	$\max(\alpha - \beta, 0)$,
$\|\overline{X} \cap Y\|$	$\max(\beta - \alpha, 0)$, and
$\|\overline{X} \cap \overline{Y}\|$	$\min(1 - \alpha, 1 - \beta)$.

Assessing the similarity of partial truth values uses both positive and negative matches. If the membership values are both α, then the features should completely match. Thus the degree of matching of features with membership values α and β is $1 - |\alpha - \beta|$. The presence-absence comparison for partial membership produces the same extension of the contrast model as proposed by Santini and Jain (Santini and Jain, 1999).

A subjective judgement may also produce a fuzzy set as an attribute value. Consider the feature *Height* described by linguistic terms such as *tall*,

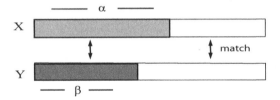

Figure 3. Partial satisfaction matching

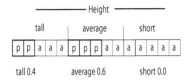

Figure 4. Fuzzy set matching

average, and *short*. A subjective evaluation of a person's height may produce
a fuzzy set $.4/tall + .6/average + 0/short$. The technique for determining
the degree of match of a single membership value can be repeated for each
term in the fuzzy set. The attribute cell is subdivided into regions for each
of the linguistic terms as in Figure 4. Each of the subregions will contribute
a maximum of $1/r$ to the degree of matching of the features, where r is the
number of linguistic terms. Consider an attribute defined by a linguistic
term set $T_1, \ldots, T_r$. If the values of the attribute for objects X and Y are
$\alpha_1/T_1 + \cdots + \alpha_r/T_r$ and $\beta_1/T_1 + \cdots + \beta_r/T_r$, respectively, then the degree
of matching of the attribute is

$$\sum_{i=1}^{r} \frac{1 - |\alpha_i - \beta_i|}{r} = 1 - \frac{1}{r} \sum_{i=1}^{r} |\alpha_i - \beta_i|.$$

Comparing the fuzzy set in Figure 4 with a fuzzy set $.1/tall + .6/average
+ .3/short$ produces a match of .8.

4   Combination of Subjective Similarity Assessments

The initial step in feature-based similarity assessment is the selection of
a set features. To accomplish this task, Tversky noted that the modeler

must extract and compile "a limited list of relevant features on the basis of which we perform the required task." A similarity judgement, however, may not utilize all of the relevant features. For example, features such as price, year of manufacture, make, model, price, transmission type, milage, upholstery, clear-coat finish, etc., may be relevant for the comparison of automobiles. A statement of the form, "based on the price, year, and milage, these automobiles are extremely similar," explicitly denotes the focus of the particular comparison.

In this section we consider combining similarity judgements from different observers. The judgements may be obtained from human assessment or generated from sensors. In either case, we do not assume that the assessments utilize the full set of features. The possibilistic principle of minimal specificity is used for representing and combining similarity assessments: the similarity measure indicates possible matches rather than assured matches. The simple matching coefficient (3) will be used as the underlying similarity measure.

We let $S_i(X, Y)$ represent the similarity returned by observation i and the focus of the observation is denoted F_i. The possibilistic interpretation of $S(X, Y) = \alpha$ indicates that X and Y may agree on $(100 \cdot \alpha)\%$ of the features and that the remainder of the features are known not to match. Thus incomplete information is included as a potential match in possibilistic similarity assessment.

The regions with different levels of shading in the corresponding vectors in Figure 5 indicate assured mismatch when $S_1(X, Y) = \alpha$ and $S_2(X, Y) = \beta$. The clear segments labelled α and β represent the areas of known or potential feature matching.

The top two vectors illustrate a combination of similarity that produces the minimal assured mismatch (maximal possibility). This occurs when the area of mismatch of S_2 is a subset of that of S_1 or vice versa. The amount mismatch assured by both of these similarities is $\max(1 - \alpha, 1 - \beta)$ so the possible degree of similarity is $\min(\alpha, \beta)$.

The maximal assured mismatch occurs when the mismatches from S_1 and S_2 have the minimal set of features in common. This is illustrated in the lower pair of vectors in Figure 5. The resulting possible matching is $\max(\alpha + \beta - 1, 0)$. Denoting the combination of similarity assessments by $\otimes$, $S_1 \otimes S_2 \in [\max(\alpha + \beta - 1, 0), \min(\alpha, \beta)]$ when $S_1(X, Y) = \alpha$ and $S_2(X, Y) = \beta$. That is, to be consistent with the information in the individual judgements, the combination must yield a value between the Lukasïewicz and minimum t-norms of the component similarities.

Using the properties of t-norms, the preceding argument can be generalized to produce consistency constraints for the combination of multiple

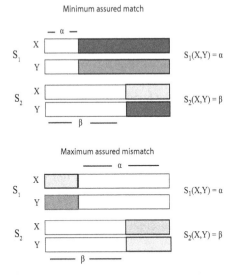

Figure 5. Combination of similarity

similarity judgements. The bounds produced by the combination of similarity assessments $S_1(X,Y) = \alpha$, $S_2(X,Y) = \beta$, and $S_3(X,Y) = \gamma$ are $[\max(\alpha + \beta + \gamma - 2, 0), \min(\alpha, \beta, \gamma)]$. If we let the constant α denote the interval $[\alpha, \alpha]$, then the operation $\otimes$ can be thought of as an interval function that satisfies

   i) identity: $1 \otimes S(X,Y) = S(X,Y)$, $0 \otimes S(X,Y) = 0$

   ii) commutativity: $S_1(X,Y) \otimes S_2(X,Y) = S_2(X,Y) \otimes S_1(X,Y)$

   iii) associativity: $(S_1(X,Y) \otimes S_2(X,Y)) \otimes S_3(X,Y) = S_1(X,Y) \otimes (S_2(X,Y) \otimes S_3(X,Y))$

In terms of combination of the similarity information, associativity and commutativity imply that the resulting bounds are independent of the order in which the individual similarities are combined.

When the foci F_1 and F_2 of similarity assessments S_1 and S_2 are disjoint, the combination reduces to the single value

$$S_1 \otimes S_2(X,Y) = \alpha + \beta - 1,$$

since the mismatching regions must necessarily be disjoint. Consequently, the lower bound for the possibility is achieved.

5   Priority in Similarity Assessment

With the appropriate selection of parameters, the contrast and ratio models have successfully modelled human similarity judgements in a number of domains. In complex domains with multiple interacting objects, psychological research has demonstrated that similarity assessment uses both relational structure and object features. Experiments in Goldstone, Medin, and Gentner (Goldstone et al., 1991) showed that increasing the relational similarity of two scenarios had a greater impact on similarity than increasing common features. Other studies have shown that relational commonality was more compelling than attribute matching (Ratterman and Gentner, 1987).

The role of relations in similarity assessment is particularly important in generating and understanding analogies. Consider the common analogy that compares an atom to the solar system. The corresponding objects, the sun with the atom's nucleus and planets with electrons, have little or no attribute similarity. However, the analogical similarity is obtained from the mutual satisfaction of the relations LARGER(sun,planet), CENTER(sun), ORBITS(planet,sun), and LARGER(nucleus,electron), CENTER(nucleus), ORBITS(electron,nucleus). In response to these observations, structure mapping theory (Markam and Gentner, 1993; Holyoak and Thagard, 1997) and the copycat architecture (Hofstader, 1995; French, 1995) were developed to emphasize relational pairings that identify consistent structural parallels between the domains for determining scenario similarity.

Gentner and Medina (Gentner and Medina, 1998) distinguished three types of similarity based on the roles played by relational and object similarity. *Analogical* similarity occurs when there is significant relational overlap between the items being compared and little object similarity. The challenge in analogical reasoning is determining the appropriate mapping between objects in the base domain and the target domain. *Literal* similarity requires both relational and object similarity. Comparing a doll to a person provides an example of *mere-appearance* similarity, which considers only object descriptions and not relations.

The importance of relations in similarity assessment is not restricted to inter-object relationships. Certain types of relations between attributes may be significant in determining the relative similarities of objects. In this section we use weights and a partition of the set of attributes to incorporate priority into feature matching for literal similarity.

The models introduced in Section 3 considered all attributes to be of equal significance. However, in judging relative similarity some attributes may play a more important role than others. If the objective is to compare vehicles based on their suitability for large families, the type of vehicle (SUV,

station wagon, sedan, etc) and price are more significant than the presence
of a CD player or the type of upholstery. The primary consideration in
assessing the relative similarity of vehicles is determined by their agreement
on the high priority features. The lower priority items affect the relative
similarity only when the high priority features do not differentiate between
the two. We will incorporate priority into similarity assessment by assigning
weights to attribute priority classes.

The properties of priorities and the motivation for selecting the weights
will be illustrated by considering the relative similarities of three objects X,
Y, and Z. If there are more matches between X, Y than X, Z among high
priority attributes, then $S(X, Y) > S(X, Z)$ regardless of the relationships
between lower priority attributes. If X, Y and X, Z have the same degree
of matching on the high priority attributes, then the relationship between
the relative similarities $S(X, Y)$ and $S(X, Z)$ are determined by the degree
to which the lower priority attributes agree.

The process of creating weights that satisfy the preceding conditions
begins by partitioning the set of attributes into priority classes $P_0, P_1, \ldots, P_r$
in which the attributes in P_i have higher priority than those in P_t, $t = 0, \ldots, i - 1$. We will construct a weight w_i for priority class P_i to insure
that the aforementioned properties of priority are enforced. The weights
for P_0 and P_1 are 0 and 1, respectively. The set P_0 consists of attributes
that are not deemed to be relevant to the objective while P_1 contains the
relevant attributes of lowest priority. The weights for the remainder of the
priority classes are obtained iteratively. For $i = 2, \ldots, r$ let

$$w_i = 1 + \sum_{t=1}^{i-1} w_t |P_t|. \tag{6}$$

The similarity is determined by

$$S(X, Y) = \frac{\sum_{i=1}^{r} m(x_i, y_i) w_i}{\sum_{i=1}^{r} w_i} \tag{7}$$

where $m(x_i, y_i)$ is the degree of matching of the attribute values x_i and y_i.
When there is single priority class, the priority evaluation reduces to the
simple matching coefficient (3). The assignment of weights to differentiate priorities is in the spirit of "order of magnitude" qualitative reasoning
(Raiman, 1991; Hadj Ali et al., 2001; Parsons, 2003) with lower priorities
being considered negligible with respect to those of higher priority.

Example: Consider a similarity assessment in which the features are partitioned into five priority classes as shown in the table below. Columns 1 and 2 give the priority class and the number of features in the class. The column labelled 'level total' gives the maximal contribution of the features in class P_i to the similarity, while 'total' gives the maximal contribution of features in the set $\bigcup_{t=1}^{i} P_i$.

Priority Class	$|P_i|$	w_i	level total	total
P_0	1	0	0	0
P_1	2	1	2	2
P_2	3	3	9	11
P_3	2	12	24	35
P_4	2	36	72	107

The partition and weights given above are used to demonstrate the role of priority in relative similarity comparisons.

Priority	X, Y matches	X, Z matches	X, Y matches	X, Z matches
P_4	1	2	1	1
P_3	2	0	1	2
P_2	3	0	3	0
P_1	2	0	2	0
P_0	1	0	1	0

In the first case, X, Z has one more match of highest priority than X, Y. However, X, Y has every possible lower priority match while X, Z has none. The similarity values are $S(X, Y) = .66 < S(X, Z) = .67$. In the second example, X, Y and X, Z have the same number of highest priority matches. The relative similarities, $S(X, Y) = .55 < S(X, Z) = .56$, are determined by the second level matches. The difference between priorities, and consequently the difference in the resulting similarity values, can be set at any desired level by increasing the constant term added in (6).   □

6   Bipolarity in Similarity Assessment

The priority hierarchy described in the preceding section recognizes differences in significance of matching features but does not distinguish between features that do not match. However, the effect of some mismatching features may be negligible with regard to a similarity judgment but others may completely disqualifying. The need for bipolarity in similarity modelling in demonstrated using the prototype theory of conceptualization.

Three prevalent theories of conceptualization and categorization in cognitive science are the defining-characteristic view, prototype theory, and exemplar theory. The classical view of conceptualization holds that concepts are specified by criteria or rules that provide necessary and sufficient conditions for category membership. The defining-characteristic view is a refinement of the classical approach that adds flexibility by distinguishing between defining and characteristic attributes (Rips et al., 1973; Armstrong et al., 1983). The prototype approach to categorization posits an ideal or most typical member of the concept (Rosch and Mervis, 1975; Lynch et al., 2000). Membership of an object in the category is determined by similarity to the prototype. The exemplar approach uses similarity to previously known examples of the concept to determine category membership (Brooks, 1978; Nosofsky, 1992).

In judging the similarity of an object to a prototype, the impact of a feature mismatch is not necessarily the complement of a match of the same feature. Consider a prototype for the concept 'vehicle suitable for large family' and the feature 'seats at least five'. Matching this feature does not ensure that the concept is satisfied. However, a vehicle that does not match the prototype for this feature is completely precluded from belonging to the category.

The difference between matching and mismatching necessitates that the two types of information be accumulated and aggregated separately. The effects of feature matches are additive; a match simply increases the numerator of the similarity measure. Because of the additivity, there is no feature whose match can ensure the maximal similarity is attained; a similarity value 1 occurs only when all relevant features match.

Mismatches, however, act as constraints on similarity. As demonstrated by the 'suitable vehicle' concept, a single mismatching feature may be sufficient to indicate that there is no similarity between the concept prototype and the object. In addition, mismatching constraints are not additive but rather 'maxitive'. If a mismatch of attribute A_i provides a constraint of degree α and A_j a constraint of degree β, then the combined constraint is $\max(\alpha, \beta)$. The dichotomy between matches and mismatches is similar to that between positive and negative aspirations in bipolar preference modelling (Benferhat et al., 2006).

To add bipolarity to similarity modelling, two partitions of the set of attributes are constructed. The partition $P_0, P_1, \ldots, P_r$ provides the priority hierarchy to calculate the similarity from the matching features. A second partition, $N_0, N_1, \ldots, N_s$, is used to compute the constraints imposed by the features that do not match. Each set N_i has an associated weight v_i that indicates the degree of the constraint on similarity when the object and the prototype differ on an attribute in N_i. The weights satisfy $v_0 = 0 < v_1 < \cdots < v_s$. The set N_0 contains attributes that do not place any constraint on the similarity assessment when the values of the two objects do not match. The similarity constraint obtained from the feature mismatches is

$$N(X,Y) = \max\{(1 - m(x_i, y_i))v_i \mid i = 1, \ldots, n\}, \tag{8}$$

where, as before, $m(x_i, y_i)$ is the degree to which features x_i and y_i match. The constraint in (8) is an example of a weighted dissimilarity measure (Dubois et al., 1988).

The constraint function N yields a possibility measure $\hat{N}$ on the set $A = \{A_1, \ldots, A_n\}$ of attributes. Intuitively, the argument for the measure $\hat{N} : 2^A \to [0,1]$ is the set of mismatching attributes and the value is the maximal constraint. From (8), it is clear that $\hat{N}$ satisfies the axioms for possibility measures:

   i) $\hat{N}(\emptyset) = 0$

   ii) $\hat{N}(U \cup V) = \max(\hat{N}(U), \hat{N}(V))$.

Conversely, a set of weights for a similarity constraint function can be obtained from any possibility measure over 2^A using the possibility distribution associated with the possibility measure (Zadeh, 1978).

The total similarity obtained by combining the positive and negative feature matches is

$$S_{bi}(X,Y) = \max(S(X,Y) - N(X,Y), 0). \tag{9}$$

The following example illustrates the utilization of both matching and mismatching features in the bipolar evaluation of similarity.

Example: The sets P_i and weights w_i are the same as in the previous example. The sets N_i and weights v_i are

Constraint class	$|N_i|$	v_i
N_0	3	0
N_1	2	.1
N_2	2	.3
N_3	2	1.0

The bipolar similarity evaluation is illustrated using the matches and mismatches described below. In the example, six of the ten features match and the remaining four do not.

Priority	X,Y matches	Constraint	X,Y mismatches
P_4	2	N_3	0
P_3	1	N_2	1
P_2	2	N_1	1
P_1	0	N_0	2
P_0	1		

The matching features produce a similarity of .84 and the maximum constraint is .3. Consequently, the resulting similarity is .54. □

7 Conclusion

This paper generalized feature-based similarity measures to add flexibility in modelling subjective judgements. The presence-absence taxonomic feature paradigm was extended to attributes that take partial membership or fuzzy sets as values. Priority and bipolarity were added to model inter-object relationships and constraints in similarity assessment. The next step is to determine if this added flexibility can be used to explain differences between the similarity models and the results of psychological experimentation.

Bibliography

S. Armstrong, L. Gleitman, and H. Gleitman. What some concepts might not be. *Cognition*, 813:263–308, 1983.

S. Benferhat, D. Dubois, S. Kaci, and H. Prade. Bipolar possibility theory in preference modeling: Representation, fusion, and optimal solutions. *Information Fusion*, 7:135–150, 2006.

A. J. Boyce. Mapping diversity: A comparative study of some numerical methods. In A. J. Cole, editor, *Numerical Taxonomy*, pages 1–31. Academic Press, London, 1969.

L. Brooks. Nonanalytic concept formation and memory for instances. In E. Rosch and B. B. Lloyd, editors, *Cognition and Categorization*, pages 169–211. Lawrence Erlbaum, Hillsdale, NJ, 1978.

A. J. Cain and G. A. Harrison. An analysis of the taxonomist's judgement of affinity. *Proc. Zool. Soc. Lond.*, 131:85–98, 1958.

B. De Baets and H. De Meyer. Transitivity-preserving fuzzification schemes for cardinality-based similarity measures. *European Journal of Operational Research*, 160:726–740, 2003.

B. De Baets and R. Mesiar. Metrics and t-equalities. *Journal of Mathematical Analysis and Applications*, 267:531–547, 2002.

B. De Baets, H. De Meyer, and H. Naessens. A class of rational cardinality-based similarity measures. *Journal of Computational and Applied Mathematics*, 132:51–69, 2001.

D. Dubois and H. Prade. A unifying view of comparison indices in a fuzzy set-theoretic framework. In Ronald R. Yager, editor, *Fuzzy Set and Possibility Theory Recent Developments*, pages 3–13. Pergamon Press, New York, NY, 1982.

D. Dubois, H. Prade, and C. Testemale. Weighted fuzzy pattern matching. *Fuzzy Sets and Systems*, 28:313–331, 1988.

R. French. *The Subtlety of Sameness*. MIT Press, 1995.

P. Gambaryan. Taxonomic analysis of the genus pinus l. *Izvest. Akad. Nauk Armen. SRR, Biol. Nauki*, 18(8):75–81, 1965.

D. Gentner. Structure mapping: A theorical view for analogy. *Cognitive Science*, 7:155–170, 1983.

D. Gentner and J. Medina. Similarity and the development of rules. In S. A. Sloman and L. J. Rips, editors, *Similarity and Symbols in Human Thinking*, pages 177–211. MIT Press, Cambridge, Massachusetts, 1998.

R. L. Goldstone, D. L. Medin, and D. Gentner. Relational similarity and the non-independence of features in similarity judgements. *Cognitive Psychology*, 23:222–262, 1991.

R. M. Gregson. *Psychometrics of Similarity*. Academic Press, New York, 1975.

A. Hadj Ali, D. Dubois, and H. Prade. Implementing fuzzy reasoning with closeness and neglibility relations. In *Proceedings of the 9th IFSA World Congress*, pages 363–368, Vancouver, July 2001.

D. Hofstader. *Fluid Concepts and Creative Analogy*. Harper Collins, 1995.

K. J. Holyoak and P. Thagard. The analogical mind. *American Psychologist*, 51(1):35–44, 1997.

P. Jaccard. Nouvelles recherches sur la distribution florale. *Bulletin de la Societe de Vaud des Sciences Naturelles*, 44:223, 1908.

C. L. Krumhansl. Concerning the applicability of geometric models to similarity data: The interrelationship between similarity and spatial density. *Psychological Review*, 85(5):445–463, 1978.

E. B. Lynch, J. D. Coley, and D. L. Medin. Tall is typical: Central tendency, ideal dimensions and graded category structure among tree experts. *Memory and Cognition*, 28:41–50, 2000.

A. B. Markam and D. Gentner. Structural alignment during similarity comparisons. *Cognitive Psychology*, 25:431–467, 1993.

R. Nosofsky. Exemplars, prototypes, and similarity rules. In A. Healy, S. Kosslyn, and R. Shriffin, editors, *From Learning Theory to Connectionist Theory: Essays in Honor of William K. Estes*, pages 149–167. Lawrence Erlbaum, Hillsdale, NJ, 1992.

S. Parsons. Qualitative probability and order of magnitude reasoning. *International Journal of Uncertainty, Fuzziness, and Knowledge-Based Systems*, 11(3):373–390, 2003.

O. Raiman. Order of magnitude reasoning. *Artificial Intelligence*, 51(1): 11–38, 1991.

M. J. Ratterman and D. Gentner. Analogy and similarity: Determinants of accessibility and inferential soundnesss. In *Proceedings of the 9th Annual Conference of the Cognitive Science Society*, pages 23–25, 1987.

L. Rips, E. Shoben, and E. Smith. Semantic distance and the verification of semantic relations. *J. of Verbal Learning and Verbal Behaviour*, 12: 1–20, 1973.

R. Rosch and C. B. Mervis. Family resemblances: Studies in the internal structure of categories. *Cognitive Psychology*, 7:382–439, 1975.

E. Rosh. Cognitive reference points. *Cognitive Psychology*, 7(5):532–547, 1975.

S. Santini and R. Jain. Similarity measures. *IEEE Transactions on Pattern Analysis and Machine Intelligence*, 21(9):871–883, 1999.

S. A. Sloman and L. J. Rips. *Similarity and Symbols in Human Thinking*. MIT Press, Cambridge, MA, 1998.

P. H. A. Sneath. The application of numerical taxonomy to medical problems. In *Mathematics and Computer Science in Biology and Medicine*, pages 81–91. Her Majesty's Stationery Office, London, 1965.

R. R. Sokal and P. H. Sneath. *Principles of Numerical Taxonomy*. Freeman, San Francisco, CA, 1963.

Y. Tolinas, S. Panas, and L. Tsoukalas. Generalized fuzzy indices for similarity matching. *Fuzzy Sets and Systems*, 120(2):255–270, 2001.

E. Trillas and L. Valverde. An inquiry into indistinguishability operators. In H. Skala, S. Termini, and E. Trillas, editors, *Aspects of Vagueness*, pages 231–256. Reidel, New York, 1984.

A. Tversky. Features of similarity. *Psychol. Rev.*, 84:327–352, 1977.

A. Tversky and I. Gaiti. Similarity, separability, and the triangle inequality. *Psychological Review*, 89(2):123–154, 1982.

L. A. Zadeh. Fuzzy sets as a basis for a theory of possibility. *Fuzzy Sets and Systems*, 1(1):3–28, 1978.

Defensive Forecasting: How to Use Similarity to Make Forecasts That Pass Statistical Tests

Glenn Shafer*

Rutgers Business School and Royal Holloway, University of London

Abstract Defensive forecasting first identifies a betting strategy that succeeds if probabilistic forecasts are inaccurate and then makes forecasts that will defeat this strategy. Both the strategy and the forecasts are based on the similarity of the current situation to previous situations.

The theory of defensive forecasting uses the game-theoretic framework for probability, in which game theory replaces measure theory. In this framework, a classical theorem such as the law of large numbers is proven by a betting strategy that multiplies the capital it risks by a large factor if the theorem's prediction fails. Theorems proven in this way apply not only to the classical case where complete probability distributions are given, but also to cases where only point predictions are made. Defensive forecasting is possible because the strategies are specified explicitly.

1 Introduction

Defensive forecasting, introduced by Vovk et al. (2005b), first identifies a betting strategy that succeeds if probabilistic forecasts are inaccurate and then makes forecasts that will defeat this strategy. Both the strategy and the forecasts are based on the similarity of the current situation to previous situations.

The theory of defensive forecasting uses the game-theoretic framework for probability, in which game theory replaces measure theory. In this framework, introduced by Shafer and Vovk (2001), a classical theorem such as

---

*The author thanks Volodya Vovk for his advice on the exposition as well as for his central role in the work reviewed. He also thanks Hans-J. Lenz and Giacomo Della Riccia for their invitation to present this work at the 2006 ISSEK Invitational Workshop on Preferences and Similarities in Udine, Italy. Mr. Te-Chien Lo, at Rutgers Business School, helped with the final document.

the law of large numbers is proven by a betting strategy that multiplies
the capital it risks by a large factor if the theorem's prediction fails. Theorems proven in this way apply not only to the classical case where complete
probability distributions are given, but also to cases where only point predictions are made. Defensive forecasting is possible because the strategies
are specified explicitly.

It is well known that probabilities can be estimated consistently using
a random sample (see, e.g., Stone, 1977). But such estimation is based
on a strong assumption: past and future observations are independently
drawn from the same probability distribution. Defensive forecasting, in
contrast, gives probabilities that pass statistical tests without using any
advance knowledge about how reality will behave.

1.1 Dawid's Counterexample

At first glance, it seems implausible that we can give probability forecasts
that cannot possibly be defeated by a betting opponent. The intuition that
this is impossible can be formalized using the following betting protocol,
in which Reality successively decides the outcomes of a sequence of events.
Just before Reality announces the outcome of the nth event ($y_n = 1$ if the
event happens, $y_n = 0$ if it fails), Forecaster gives a probability p_n for its
happening, and his betting opponent, Skeptic, sets the stakes s_n for a bet
for or against its happening. We assume that this is a perfect-information
protocol: each player sees the other player's moves as they are made.

PROTOCOL 1. PROBABILITY FORECASTING
  FOR $n = 1, 2, \dots$:
    Forecaster announces $p_n \in [0, 1]$.
    Skeptic announces $s_n \in \mathbb{R}$.
    Reality announces $y_n \in \{0, 1\}$.
    Skeptic's profit := $s_n(y_n - p_n)$.

If $s_n > 0$, Skeptic is betting on the event; he gets $s_n(1 - p_n)$ if it happens
and loses $s_n p_n$ if it fails. If $s_n < 0$, he is betting against the event; he gets
$-s_n p_n$ if it fails and loses $-s_n(1 - p_n)$ if it happens.

Working together, Skeptic and Reality can refute Forecaster spectacularly. When Forecaster gives a low probability, Skeptic bets on the event and
Reality makes it happen; when Forecaster gives a high probability, Skeptic
bets against the event and Reality makes it fail. This idea was formalized in
1985 by A. P. Dawid, whose studies of probability forecasting were seminal
for game-theoretic probability (Dawid, 1986), in a discussion of an article
by David Oakes (see Dawid, 1985, and Oakes, 1985). As Dawid explained,

if Reality follows the strategy

$$y_n := \begin{cases} 1 & \text{if } p_n < 0.5 \\ 0 & \text{if } p_n \geq 0.5, \end{cases}$$

and Skeptic follows the strategy

$$s_n := \begin{cases} 1 & \text{if } p_n < 0.5 \\ -1 & \text{if } p_n \geq 0.5, \end{cases}$$

then Skeptic makes a profit of at least 0.5 on every round: $1 - p_n$ when $p_n < 0.5$ and p_n when $p_n \geq 0.5$.

Surprisingly, Dawid's counterexample to the possibility of good probability forecasting is not as watertight as it first appears. The weak point of Skeptic's and Reality's strategy is that it requires them to be able to tell whether p_n is exactly equal to 0.5 and to switch their moves with infinite abruptness (discontinuously) as p_n shifts from 0.5 to something ever so slightly less. Because the idea of an infinitely abrupt shift lives in an idealized mathematical world, we should be wary about drawing practical conclusions from it.

To show that Dawid's counterexample depends on the artificiality of the mathematical idealization, it suffices to show that it disappears when we hobble Skeptic and Reality in small ways that are reasonable or inconsequential in practice. This has been done in two different ways:

1. We can hobble Skeptic a bit by requiring that he follow a strategy that makes his bet a continuous function of the forecast p_n. This is not a practical impediment, because a continuous function can change with any degree of abruptness short of infinite. It can easily be shown—I reproduce in §3.2 below the proof given in Vovk et al. (2005b)—that Forecaster can beat any continuous strategy. And as I explain in §3.3, there are continuous strategies for Skeptic that make a lot money unless Forecaster's probabilities perform well. In particular, Skeptic has continuous strategies that make a lot of money unless Forecaster is well calibrated, in the sense that about 30% of the events for which p_n is near 0.3 will happen, about 40% of the events for which p_n is near 0.4 will happen, etc. By playing against and beating a continuous strategy for Skeptic that makes money if Forecaster does not perform well, Forecaster is sure to perform well no matter what Reality does. This may seem surprising, but Forecaster's play turns out to be quite natural. To guarantee calibration, for example, he always chooses a value of p_n where he has been fairly well calibrated so far, so that

Reality cannot make his calibration much worse, no matter whether she puts y_n equal to 1 or 0; see §3.3.

2. Alternatively, we can hobble Skeptic and Reality by allowing Forecaster to make the exact value of p_n slightly indeterminate. Forecaster announces a probability distribution rather than an exact value for p_n, leaving the exact value to be determined by a random drawing from the probability distribution after Skeptic and Reality make their moves. In this case, Forecaster can beat any strategy for Skeptic, even it if is not continuous. Vovk and Shafer (2007) gave a direct proof of this, building on earlier work by Foster and Vohra (1998) and others, and the result follows easily from the result concerning continuous strategies for Skeptic (Vovk, 2007c).

The idea of getting good forecasts by playing against strategies for Skeptic turns out to be very productive. It works not only when we give probabilities for a sequence of events but also when we merely make point predictions for a sequence of quantities (see Vovk et al., 2005a, and Vovk, 2006a). Its success requires, however, that we sees all the preceding outcomes $y_1, \ldots, y_{n-1}$ before forecasting y_n.

1.2   Key Points

The following points are key to understanding the success and scope of defensive forecasting:

- The empirical meaning of a theory that gives probabilities for a sequence of events lies in the predictions it makes very confidently. We can also say that the theory's meaning is captured by statistical tests, which reject the theory when something to which it gives very small probability happens. These ideas have a venerable history (Shafer and Vovk, 2005; Shafer, 2005).

- Statistical testing can alternatively be understood in betting terms, because the happening of a particular event with very small probability is equivalent to a betting strategy multiplying the capital it risks by a large factor. This is Ville's theorem. I state it more precisely in §2.1.

- This game-theoretic notion of testing generalizes from the case where complete probability distributions are given to the case where only some quantities are predicted. I discuss a very simple example in §2.5. Numerous examples are given in Shafer and Vovk (2001).

- If two or more betting strategies risk the same amount of money, then their average, which also risks that same amount of money, will multiply it by a large factor if any of the strategies being averaged do so. So we can combine game-theoretic tests by averaging; see §2.2 for details.

- In many cases, we can average enough betting strategies to obtain one that is quasi-universal, in the sense that it multiplies the capital risked by a large factor whenever our probabilistic predictions fail in a way that is important to us; see §3.1 for details.

Defensive forecasting plays against a quasi-universal strategy.

1.3   Does Reality Play Strategically?

At least since the work of Wald (1950), scholars have been familiar with the idea of a game against nature. In Wald's games, nature is a player, but not a player like others. She does not play strategically. She ignores the other players, either choosing all her moves at the outset or choosing them at random. It is often thought that good prediction is possible in spite of Dawid's counterexample only because of this neutrality on the part of nature.

The protocols in used by defensive forecasting and other applications of game-theoretic probability do not, in contrast, rule out strategic play by Reality. This novelty may confuse some readers. Do the success of defensive forecasting and the validity of other results in game-theoretic probability depend on allowing nature to play strategically?

No. The protocols for defensive forecasting make no assumption about how Reality chooses her moves simply because no such assumption is needed in order to prove that defensive forecasting works. The mathematical propositions that underlie defensive forecasting and other applications of game-theoretic probability are propositions about what players other than Reality can achieve in the worst case. Propositions 2 and 3, for example, each assert that Skeptic has a strategy that achieves a certain goal regardless of how Forecaster and Reality move. Propositions 4 and 5 each assert that Forecaster has a strategy that achieves a certain goal regardless of how Reality moves.

In many domains where defensive forecasting and other game-theoretic techniques can be used—in engineering, for example—no one would hesitate to assume that Reality does not move strategically. But there are other applications, especially in business and economics, where the reality we play against includes competitors and other counterparties who may indeed be playing against us strategically. See Vovk and Shafer (2002, 2003), Shafer (2005), Wu and Shafer (2007) for examples in which an investor plays the role of Skeptic while a financial market, which determines the returns on his investments, plays the roles of Forecaster and Reality. The financial market is not a single person, but the prices it sets are influenced by many people who are very intent on taking advantage of the investor.

2   Game-Theoretic Probability

Since Emile Borel's proof of the strong law of large numbers in 1909, mathematicians have understood that measure theory can provide a rigorous foundation for the classical theorems of probability. Defensive forecasting is made possible by the realization that game theory provides an equally rigorous and even more general foundation. Within the game-theoretic framework, a classical probability theorem becomes a theorem asserting the existence of a betting strategy that multiplies the capital it risks by a large factor unless outcomes satisfy a given condition. If complete probability distributions are given and we are allowed to buy any random variable for its expected value, the game-theoretic theorems can be thought of as a way of restating the corresponding measure-theoretic theorems. But the game-theoretic theorems also apply when only some variables are priced and offered for sale.

The game-theoretic framework has its roots in work by Jean Ville in the 1930s (Ville, 1939). Ville worked under the assumption that complete probability distributions are given, and for the most part he considered only the case where we seek betting strategies that multiply the capital risked by an infinite factor (achieving this corresponds to the happening of an event of zero probability, rather than merely the happening of an event of small probability). Moreover, he spelled out his reasoning fully only for the case where outcomes are binary. But explained fully the idea of proving theorems by constructing betting strategies.

In §2.1, I review Ville's theorem, which establishes the equivalence between the happening of an event of small probability and the success of a betting strategy. In §2.2, I review how Ville thought about martingales in the binary probability protocol. In §2.3, I discuss a martingale that Ville used to prove the strong law of large numbers in the special case of his binary protocol in which successive events are independent and all have the same probability p.

I then turn to the generalization to the case where no joint probability distribution for what we may observe is given. In §2.4, I return to the probability forecasting protocol we considered in §1.1. I discuss the weak and strong law of large numbers for this protocol, and as an illustration, I sketch a very simple proof of the weak law. In §2.5, I discuss a protocol in which predictions m_n of quantities y_n are interpreted as prices at which Skeptic can buy or sell the y_n, and I explain how we can obtain laws of large numbers even in this case.

2.1 Ville's Theorem

Ville considered only the infinitary case, where the game continues for an infinite number of rounds and Skeptic tries to become infinitely rich, because he conceived his work as a critique of Richard von Mises's notion of a collective (von Mises, 1919, 1928, 1931); the title of his book was *Étude critique de la notion de collectif*. For von Mises, an event has a probability p only in the context of an infinite sequence of events whose limiting frequency of occurrence is p, and which obeys the further condition that any reasonable rule for selecting a subsequence will produce one with the same limiting frequency. This latter condition, von Mises thought, would keep a gambler from getting rich by betting on some of the events and not others. Ville showed by example that von Mises's condition is inadequate, inasmuch as it does not rule out the gambler's getting rich by varying his bet. Ville then showed that ruling out an arbitrary strategy's making a gambler infinitely rich, even if that strategy does vary how much and on what side to bet, is just the same as ruling out the happening of an arbitrary event of probability zero.

Unfortunately, Ville's work was largely overlooked, in general because of the eclipse of the French school of probability after World War II, and in particular because of the success of Joseph L. Doob's reformulation of Ville's notion of a martingale in measure-theoretic terms (Doob, 1953). Discussions of von Mises's frequentism still usually overlook Ville's emendation of it, and Ville's theorem is still not well known.

In order to state Ville's theorem, consider a sequence $Y_1, Y_2, \ldots$ of binary random variables with a joint probability distribution P. Suppose, for simplicity, that P assigns every finite sequence $y_1, \ldots, y_n$ of 0s and 1s positive probability, so that its conditional probabilities for Y_n given values of the preceding variables are always unambiguously defined. Following Ville, consider a gambler who begins with $1 and is allowed to bet as he pleases on each round, provided that he never risks more than he has. (The condition that he never risks more than he has is needed to guarantee that the initial capital of $1 represents the total capital he risks. If he were allowed to borrow in order to make larger bets, he would be risking more.) We can formalize this with the following protocol, where betting on Y_n is represented as buying some number s_n (possibly zero or negative) of tickets that cost $\$P(Y_n = 1 | Y_1 = y_1, \ldots, Y_{n-1} = y_{n-1})$ and pay $\$Y_n$.

PROTOCOL 2. VILLE'S BINARY PROBABILITY PROTOCOL

   $\mathcal{K}_0 := 1$.

   FOR $n = 1, 2, \ldots$:

      Skeptic announces $s_n \in \mathbb{R}$.

      Reality announces $y_n \in \{0, 1\}$.

      $\mathcal{K}_n := \mathcal{K}_{n-1} + s_n(y_n - P(Y_n = 1 | Y_1 = y_1, \ldots, Y_{n-1} = y_{n-1}))$.

Restriction on Skeptic: Skeptic must choose the s_n so that his capital is always nonnegative ($\mathcal{K}_n \geq 0$ for all n) no matter how Reality moves.

The sequence $\mathcal{K}_0, \mathcal{K}_1, \ldots$ is Skeptic's capital process. Along with all the other protocols considered in this article, this is a perfect-information sequential protocol; moves are made in the order listed, and each player sees the other player's moves as they are made.

Notice the limited role played by the probability distribution P. Its only role is to gives prices at which Skeptic can buy tickets. (We can think of it as a strategy for Forecaster, who does not appear in the game because his strategy is fixed.) Reality is not required to select Y_n's value y_n randomly according to the conditional probability $P(Y_n = 1 | Y_1 = y_1, \ldots, Y_{n-1} = y_{n-1})$.

Infinite horizon, zero probability Versions of Ville's theorem hold whenever a complete probability distribution P is given for outcomes $y_1, y_2, \ldots$, but for simplicity, let us consider only Protocol 2, where the outcomes are binary. The theorem says that Skeptic's getting infinitely rich in this protocol is equivalent to an event of zero probability happening, in the following sense:

1. When Skeptic follows a strategy that gives s_n as a function of $y_1, \ldots, y_{n-1}$,

$$P(\mathcal{K}_0, \mathcal{K}_1, \ldots \text{ is unbounded}) = 0. \tag{1}$$

2. If A is a measurable subset of $\{0, 1\}^\infty$ with $P(A) = 0$, then Skeptic has a strategy that guarantees

$$\lim_{n \to \infty} \mathcal{K}_n = \infty$$

whenever $(y_1, y_2, \ldots) \in A$.

We can summarize these two statements by saying that Skeptic's being able to multiply his capital by an infinite factor is equivalent to the happening of an event with probability zero.

Infinite horizon, small probability Practical applications require that we consider small probabilities rather than zero probabilities. In this case, we can use the following finitary version of Ville's theorem, which is proven in Shafer and Vovk (2001, chapter 8).

1. When Skeptic follows a strategy that gives s_n as a function of $y_1, \ldots, y_{n-1}$,

$$P \left(\sup_{n=0,1,\ldots} \mathcal{K}_n \geq \frac{1}{\delta} \right) \leq \delta \qquad (2)$$

   for every $\delta > 0$. (Although Ville was the first to establish Equation (2), it is now sometimes called *Doob's inequality*.)

2. If A is a measurable subset of $\{0,1\}^\infty$ with $P(A) \leq \delta$, then Skeptic has a strategy that guarantees

$$\liminf_{n \to \infty} \mathcal{K}_n \geq \frac{1}{\delta}$$

   whenever $(y_1, y_2, \ldots) \in A$.

We can summarize these results by saying that Skeptic's being able to multiply his capital by a factor of $1/\delta$ or more is equivalent to the happening of an event with probability δ or less.

Finite horizon, small probability If we assume that the game is played only for a fixed number of rounds N instead of being continued indefinitely, then the preceding statements simplify to the following:

1. When Skeptic follows a strategy that gives s_n as a function of $y_1, \ldots, y_{n-1}$,

$$P \left(\max_{0 \leq n \leq N} \mathcal{K}_n \geq \frac{1}{\delta} \right) \leq \delta \qquad (3)$$

   for every $\delta > 0$.

2. If A is a subset of $\{0,1\}^N$ with $P(A) < \delta$, then Skeptic has a strategy that guarantees

$$\mathcal{K}_N > \frac{1}{\delta}$$

   whenever $(y_1, \ldots, y_N) \in A$.

2.2 Martingales in Ville's Picture

Consider again Ville's binary probability protocol (Protocol 2 on p. 8), but now suppose that Skeptic begins with capital α not necessarily equal to 1, and drop the requirement that he keep his capital nonnegative.

PROTOCOL 3. VILLE'S BINARY PROBABILITY PROTOCOL AGAIN
Parameters: real number α, positive probability distribution P on $\{0,1\}^\infty$
$\quad \mathcal{K}_0 := \alpha$.
$\quad$ FOR $n = 1, 2, \ldots$:
$\quad\quad$ Skeptic announces $s_n \in \mathbb{R}$.
$\quad\quad$ Reality announces $y_n \in \{0, 1\}$.
$\quad\quad \mathcal{K}_n := \mathcal{K}_{n-1} + s_n(y_n - \mathrm{P}(Y_n = 1 | Y_1 = y_1, \ldots, Y_{n-1} = y_{n-1}))$. $\quad$ (4)

Recall the meaning of the assumption that the probability distribution P is positive: for every sequence $y_1, \ldots, y_n$ of 0s and 1, $\mathrm{P}(Y_1 = y_1, \ldots, Y_n = y_n) > 0$.

A strategy for Skeptic in Protocol 3 is a rule that specifies, for each n and each possible sequence of prior moves $y_1, \ldots, y_{n-1}$ by Reality, a move s_n for Skeptic. When such a strategy is fixed and α is given, Skeptic's capital $\mathcal{K}_n$ becomes a function of Reality's moves $y_1, \ldots, y_n$. Ville was the first to call the sequence of functions $\mathcal{K}_0, \mathcal{K}_1, \ldots$ a *martingale*.

In Protocol 3, knowing the capital process $\mathcal{K}_0, \mathcal{K}_1, \ldots$ produced by a strategy for Skeptic is equivalent to knowing the strategy and the initial capital α. You can find $\mathcal{K}_0, \mathcal{K}_1, \ldots$ from α and the strategy, and you can find α and the strategy from $\mathcal{K}_0, \mathcal{K}_1, \ldots$. This equivalence was Ville's justification for calling a capital process a martingale; before his work, "martingale" was a name for a gambler's strategy, not a name for his capital process. The name stuck; now we call capital processes martingales even in protocols where the strategy cannot be recovered from them.

Let us call a martingale $\mathcal{K}_0, \mathcal{K}_1, \ldots$ a *scoring martingale* if $\mathcal{K}_0 = 1$ and $\mathcal{K}_n$ is always nonnegative—i.e., $\mathcal{K}_n(y_1, \ldots, y_n) \geq 0$ for all n and all $y_1, \ldots, y_n$. Let us call a strategy for Skeptic that produces a scoring martingale when it starts with unit capital a *scoring strategy*. When Skeptic plays a scoring strategy starting with $\mathcal{K}_0 = 1$, he can be sure that $\mathcal{K}_n \geq 0$ for all n no matter how Reality plays. He may be risking the entire initial unit of capital, but he is not putting any other capital—his own or anyone else's—at risk.

Our basic principle for relating Protocol 2 and its probability distribution P to the empirical world is to predicts that a scoring martingale will be bounded. This prediction can be used in two ways:

Prediction. The prediction that a particular scoring martingale $\mathcal{K}_n$ is bounded can imply other predictions that are interesting in their own right. It is easy to give examples. In §2.3, we will look at a scoring martingale whose being bounded, as predicted with probability one by (1), implies the strong law of large numbers. In §2.4, we will look at a scoring martingale whose being bounded by $1/\delta$, as predicted with probability δ by (3), implies the weak law of large numbers.

Testing. The actual values of a scoring martingale test the validity of the probability distribution P. The larger these "scores" are, the more strongly P is refuted.

Ville used scoring martingales in both ways.

Equation (4), the rule for updating the capital in Protocol 3, implies that $\mathcal{K}_{n-1}$ is the expected value at time $n-1$ of the future value of $\mathcal{K}_n$:

$$\mathrm{E}(\mathcal{K}_n|y_1,\ldots,y_{n-1}) = \mathcal{K}_{n-1}(y_1,\ldots,y_{n-1}). \qquad (5)$$

Because its left-hand side is equal to

$$\mathcal{K}_n(y_1,\ldots,y_{n-1},1)\frac{\mathrm{P}(y_1,\ldots,y_{n-1},1)}{\mathrm{P}(y_1,\ldots,y_{n-1})} + \mathcal{K}_n(y_1,\ldots,y_{n-1},0)\frac{\mathrm{P}(y_1,\ldots,y_{n-1},0)}{\mathrm{P}(y_1,\ldots,y_{n-1})},$$

Equation (5) is equivalent to

$$Q(y_1,\ldots,y_{n-1},1) + Q(y_1,\ldots,y_{n-1},0) = Q(y_1,\ldots,y_{n-1}), \qquad (6)$$

where Q is the function on finite strings of 0s and 1s defined by

$$Q(y_1,\ldots,y_n) = \mathcal{K}_n(y_1,\ldots,y_n)\mathrm{P}(y_1,\ldots,y_n).$$

Equation (6) is necessary and sufficient for a nonnegative function Q on finite strings of 0s and 1s to define a probability measure on $\{0,1\}^\infty$. So a nonnegative martingale with respect to P is the same thing as the ratio of a probability measure Q to P—i.e., a likelihood ratio with P as denominator.

Doob imported Ville's notion of a martingale into measure-theoretic probability, where the gambling picture is not made explicit, by taking Equation (5) as the definition of a martingale. Game-theoretic probability goes in a different direction. It uses Ville's definition of a martingale in more general forecasting games, where the forecasts are given by a player in the game, not by a probability distribution P for Reality's moves. In these games, martingales are not likelihood ratios. They are simply capital processes for Skeptic.

One very important property of martingales that Ville used, which does carry over to the more general games studied in game-theoretic probability, is this: an average of scoring strategies produces the same average of the scoring martingales. In order to avoid any confusion, let me spell out what this means in the case where we are taking a simple average of two strategies and also in the general case where we are averaging a class of strategies.

Simplest case. Suppose the scoring strategies $\mathcal{S}^1$ and $\mathcal{S}^2$ recommend moves $s_n^1(y_1, \ldots, y_{n-1})$ and $s_n^2(y_1, \ldots, y_{n-1})$, respectively, on the nth round of the game. The average of $\mathcal{S}^1$ and $\mathcal{S}^2$—call it $\mathcal{S}$—recommends the move

$$s_n(y_1, \ldots, y_{n-1}) = \frac{1}{2}\left(s_n^1(y_1, \ldots, y_{n-1}) + s_n^2(y_1, \ldots, y_{n-1})\right)$$

on the nth round of the game. If we write $\mathcal{K}_n^1$, $\mathcal{K}_n^2$, and $\mathcal{K}_n$ for the corresponding scoring martingales, then

$$\mathcal{K}_n(y_1, \ldots, y_n) = \frac{1}{2}\left(\mathcal{K}_n^1(y_1, \ldots, y_n) + \mathcal{K}_n^2(y_1, \ldots, y_n)\right)$$

for all n and all $y_1, \ldots, y_n$.

General case. In general, consider strategies $\mathcal{S}^\xi$, where the index ξ ranges over a set Ξ. We may average these strategies with respect to a probability distribution μ on Ξ, obtaining a strategy $\mathcal{S}$ with moves

$$s_n(y_1, \ldots, y_{n-1}) = \int_\Xi s_n^\xi(y_1, \ldots, y_{n-1})\mu(d\xi),$$

provided only that this integral always converges. The corresponding scoring martingales then average in the same way:

$$\mathcal{K}_n(y_1, \ldots, y_n) = \int_\Xi \mathcal{K}_n^\xi(y_1, \ldots, y_n)\mu(d\xi).$$

These assertions are true because the increment $\mathcal{K}_n - \mathcal{K}_{n-1}$ is always linear in Skeptic's move s_n. This linearity is a feature of all the protocols considered in Shafer and Vovk (2001).

2.3 Ville's Constant Probability Game

Ville studied some strategies for Skeptic in the special case of the preceding protocol in which $P(Y_n = 1 | Y_1 = y_1, \ldots, Y_{n-1} = y_{n-1})$ is always equal to p. In order to give the reader a glimpse of Ville's methods, I will now review the scoring martingale he used to prove the strong law of large numbers for this special case: Skeptic can become infinitely rich unless Reality makes the relative frequency of 1s converge to p.

Under the assumption that $P(Y_n = 1 | Y_1 = y_1, \ldots, Y_{n-1} = y_{n-1})$ is always equal to p, our protocol looks like this.

PROTOCOL 4. FORECASTING WITH A CONSTANT PROBABILITY p
Parameter: real number p satisfying $0 < p < 1$
$\mathcal{K}_0 := 1$.
FOR $n = 1, 2, \ldots$:
    Skeptic announces $s_n \in \mathbb{R}$.
    Reality announces $y_n \in \{0, 1\}$.
    $\mathcal{K}_n := \mathcal{K}_{n-1} + s_n(y_n - p)$.

This protocol represents what classical probability calls independent Bernoulli trials: successive events that are independent and all have the same probability.

The scoring martingale Ville used to prove the strong law of large numbers for this protocol is

$$\mathcal{K}_n(y_1, \ldots, y_n) := \frac{r_n!(n - r_n)!}{(n+1)!} p^{-r_n} q^{-(n-r_n)}, \tag{7}$$

where q is equal to $1 - p$ and r_n is the number of 1s among $y_1, \ldots, y_n$:

$$r_n := \sum_{i=1}^{n} y_i$$

(see Ville, 1939, p. 52; Ville, 1955, and Robbins, 1970). To confirm that (7) is a scoring martingale, it suffices to notice that it is a likelihood ratio with P as the denominator. In fact,

$$p^{r_n} q^{n-r_n} = P(y_1, \ldots, y_n)$$

and

$$\frac{r_n!(n - r_n)!}{(n+1)!} = \int_0^1 \xi^{r_n}(1 - \xi)^{n-r_n} d\xi = Q(y_1, \ldots, y_n), \tag{8}$$

where Q is the probability distribution obtained by averaging probability distributions under which the events $y_i = 1$ are independent and all have a probability ξ possibly different from p.

Proposition 1. *A classical strong law of large numbers. With probability one,*

$$\lim_{n \to \infty} \frac{r_n}{n} = p. \tag{9}$$

Sketch of Proof Because (7) is a scoring martingale, Ville's theorem (Equation (1)) says that, with probability one, there is a constant C such that

$$\frac{r_n!(n-r_n)!}{(n+1)!}p^{-r_n}q^{-(n-r_n)} < C \qquad (10)$$

for $n = 0, 1, \ldots$. One can deduce (9) from (10) using Stirling's formula. ∎

The reader may verify that (7) is Skeptic's capital process when he follows the strategy that prescribes the moves

$$s_n(y_1, \ldots, y_{n-1}) := \frac{1}{pq}\left(\frac{r_{n-1}+1}{n+1} - p\right)\mathcal{K}_{n-1}(y_1, \ldots, y_{n-1}). \qquad (11)$$

The ratio $(r_{n-1}+1)/(n+1)$ is close to the relative frequency of 1s so far, $r_{n-1}/(n-1)$. Roughly speaking, the strategy (11) bets that y_n will be 1 when the relative frequency is more than p, 0 when the relative frequency is less than p. So whenever the relative frequency diverges from p, Reality must move it back towards p to keep Skeptic from increasing his capital.

The rate of convergence of $r_n/n - p$ to zero implied by (10) is $\sqrt{(\log n)/n}$ Ville (1955). Using other scoring martingales (obtained by averaging $\xi^{r_n}(1-\xi)^{n-r_n}$ as in (8), but with respect to distributions concentrated around p rather than the uniform distribution), Ville also derived the faster convergence asserted by the law of the iterated logarithm (Shafer and Vovk, 2001, chapter 5).

We can also use martingale methods to prove other classical theorems, including the weak law of large numbers (Shafer and Vovk, 2001, chapter 6) and the central limit theorem (Shafer and Vovk, 2001, chapter 7). Rather than pursue this path here, I will now step outside classical probability theory, into more general protocols like the probability forecasting protocol of §1.1. In these protocols, martingale methods allow us to prove theorems analogous to the classical theorems, but we must express them directly in game-theoretic terms. Instead of saying that something happens with probability one, we say that if it does not happen, Skeptic will multiply the capital he risks by an infinite factor. Instead of saying that something happens with the high probability $1 - \delta$, we say that if it does not happen, Skeptic will multiply the capital he risks by the large factor $1/\delta$.

2.4 The Probability Forecasting Game

As a first step outside classical probability, let us return to the protocol we considered in §1.1, in which probability forecasts are made by a player, Forecaster, rather than by a probability distribution P. For the sake of variety, let us consider the weak law of large numbers rather than the strong law. Accordingly, I now assume that the game has a fixed finite horizon: it ends after a large but finite number of rounds, N.

PROTOCOL 5. FINITE-HORIZON PROBABILITY FORECASTING
Parameter: natural number N
  $\mathcal{K}_0 := 1$.
  FOR $n = 1, \ldots, N$:
    Forecaster announces $p_n \in [0, 1]$.
    Skeptic announces $s_n \in \mathbb{R}$.
    Reality announces $y_n \in \{0, 1\}$.
    $\mathcal{K}_n := \mathcal{K}_{n-1} + s_n(y_n - p_n)$.

Our study of this protocol will focus on

$$S_n := \sum_{i=1}^{n}(y_i - p_i).$$

The weak law of large numbers says that if N is sufficiently large, the relative frequency of 1s, $(1/N)\sum_{n=1}^{N} y_n$, should be close to the average probability forecast, $(1/N)\sum_{n=1}^{N} p_n$. This means S_N/N should be close to zero.

The weak law can be formulated and proven for Protocol 5 as follows:

Proposition 2. A game-theoretic weak law of large numbers. *There exists a scoring martingale that will exceed $1/\delta$ unless*

$$\left|\frac{S_N}{N}\right| \le \frac{1}{\sqrt{N\delta}}. \tag{12}$$

Proof. Consider the strategy for Skeptic that prescribes the move

$$s_n = \frac{2S_{n-1}}{N}.$$

This produces the capital process

$$\mathcal{K}_n = 1 + \frac{1}{N}\left(S_n^2 - \sum_{i=1}^{n}(y_i - p_i)^2\right),$$

which is a scoring martingale: $\mathcal{K}_n \ge 0$ for $n = 1, \ldots, N$ because $(y_i - p_i)^2 \le 1$ for each i. For the same reason, the hypothesis $\mathcal{K}_N \le 1/\delta$ implies (12). $\square$

When ϵ and δ are small positive numbers, and N is extremely large, so that

$$N \geq \frac{1}{\epsilon^2 \delta},$$

Proposition 2 implies that we can be as confident that $|S_N/N| \leq \epsilon$ as we are that Skeptic will not multiply his capital by the large factor $1/\delta$. The martingale in the proof appears in measure-theoretic form in Kolmogorov's 1929 proof of the weak law (Kolmogorov, 1929).

A positive probability distribution P on $\{0,1\}^N$ can serve as a strategy for Forecaster in Protocol 5, prescribing

$$p_n := \mathrm{P}(Y_n = 1 | Y_1 = y_1, \ldots, Y_{n-1} = y_{n-1}).$$

When such a strategy is imposed, Protocol 5 reduces to a finite-horizon version of Ville's binary protocol, Proposition 2 says that there is a scoring martingale in this finite-horizon protocol that will exceed $1/\delta$ unless

$$\left| \frac{1}{N} \sum_{n=1}^{N} (y_n - \mathrm{P}(Y_n = 1 | Y_1 = y_1, \ldots, Y_{n-1} = y_{n-1})) \right| \leq \frac{1}{\sqrt{N\delta}}, \qquad (13)$$

and by Ville's theorem, this implies that

$$\mathrm{P}\left(\left| \frac{1}{N} \sum_{n=1}^{N} (y_n - \mathrm{P}(Y_n = 1 | Y_1 = y_1, \ldots, Y_{n-1} = y_{n-1})) \right| \leq \frac{1}{\sqrt{N\delta}} \right) \geq 1 - \frac{1}{\delta}.$$

When $\mathrm{P}(Y_n = 1 | Y_1 = y_1, \ldots, Y_{n-1} = y_{n-1})$ is always equal to p, we are in a finite-horizon version of Protocol 3, and we get

$$\mathrm{P}\left(\left| \frac{1}{N} \sum_{n=1}^{N} y_n - p \right| \leq \frac{1}{\sqrt{N\delta}} \right) \geq 1 - \frac{1}{\delta},$$

the elementary version of the classical weak law usually derived using Chebyshev's inequality.

Protocol 5 does not require Forecaster to follow a strategy defined by a probability distribution for $y_1, \ldots, y_N$. He can use information from outside the game to decide how to move, or he can simply follow his whims. So instead of having a classical probability distribution, we are in what A. P. Dawid called the *prequential framework* (Dawid, 1984). In this framework, we cannot say that (13) has probability at least $1 - 1/\delta$, because we have no probability distribution, but Proposition 2 has the same intuitive meaning as such a probability statement. We consider Skeptic's multiplying his capital by $1/\delta$ or more against a good Forecaster unlikely in the same way as we consider the happening of an event unlikely when it is given probability δ or less by a valid probability distribution.

Although I have focused on the weak law here, it is also straightforward to prove the strong law for the probability forecasting protocol (Protocol 5, but with the game played for an infinite number of rounds instead of only N rounds). Kumon and Takemura have given a proof using a modified form of Ville's martingale (7) (Kumon and Takemura, 2007). In Shafer and Vovk (2001, chapter 3), Vovk and I gave an alternative proof using a martingale extracted from Kolmogorov's 1930 proof of the strong law (Kolmogorov, 1930b).

2.5   The Bounded Forecasting Game

In order to illustrate the point that game-theoretic probability generalizes classical probability, I now ask the reader to consider a protocol where Forecaster's task on each round is to give not a probability for an event but a prediction of a bounded quantity. To fix ideas, I assume that the quantity and the prediction are always in the interval from 0 to 100.

PROTOCOL 6. FINITE-HORIZON BOUNDED FORECASTING
Parameter: natural number N
   $\mathcal{K}_0 := 1$.
   FOR $n = 1, \ldots, N$:
      Forecaster announces $m_n \in [0, 100]$.
      Skeptic announces $s_n \in \mathbb{R}$.
      Reality announces $y_n \in [0, 100]$.
      $\mathcal{K}_n := \mathcal{K}_{n-1} + s_n(y_n - m_n)$.

As it turns out, the game-theoretic treatment of Protocol 6 is scarcely different from that of Protocol 5. Setting

$$S_n := \sum_{i=1}^{n}(y_i - m_i),$$

we reason almost as before.

Proposition 3. A weak law for bounded forecasting. *There exists a scoring martingale that will exceed $1/\delta$ unless*

$$\left| \frac{S_N}{N} \right| \leq \frac{100}{\sqrt{N\delta}}. \tag{14}$$

Proof. Consider the strategy for Skeptic that prescribes the move

$$s_n = \frac{2S_{n-1}}{10000N}.$$

This produces

$$\mathcal{K}_n = 1 + \frac{1}{10000N}\left(S_n^2 - \sum_{i=1}^{n}(y_i - m_i)^2\right),$$

which is nonnegative because $(y_i - m_i)^2 \leq 10000$ for each i. For the same reason, the hypothesis $\mathcal{K}_N \leq 1/\delta$ implies (14). $\square$

The proofs of the strong law for the infinite-horizon version of Protocol 5 that we just cited, in Kumon and Takemura (2007) and Shafer and Vovk (2001, chapter 3), also apply to the infinite-horizon version of Protocol 6.

3 Defensive Forecasting

I now turn from strategies for Skeptic, which test Forecaster, to strategies for Forecaster, which seek to withstand such tests. Forecaster engages in *defensive forecasting* when he plays in order to defeat a particular strategy for Skeptic.

As it turns out, Forecaster can defeat any particular strategy for Skeptic, provided only that each move prescribed by the strategy varies continuously with respect to Forecaster's previous move. Forecaster wants to defeat more than a single strategy for Skeptic. He wants to defeat simultaneously all the scoring strategies Skeptic might use. But as we will see, Forecaster can often amalgamate the scoring strategies he needs to defeat by averaging them, and then he can play against the average. Defeating the average may be good enough, because when any one of the scoring strategies rejects Forecaster's validity, the average will generally reject as well, albeit less strongly.

I begin this section, in §3.1, with an overview of related work on prediction. Then I explain defensive forecasting in the case of binary forecasting, leaving the reader to consult other expositions for other protocols (see Vovk et al., 2005a; Vovk, 2006b). In §3.2, I review the simple proof that Forecaster can defeat any continuous strategy for Skeptic in the binary case. In §3.3, I explain how to average strategies for Skeptic to test for the calibration of binary probability forecasts, and in §3.4, I explain how resolution can also be achieved.

There is much more to say about defensive forecasting, much of it in recent papers by Vovk (2005, 2006a,b,c,d, 2007a,b,c). I cannot begin to summarize this work here, but I should mention that probabilities produced by defensive forecasting can often be used in decision problems, where calibration and resolution often suffice to guarantee that decisions derived from them are optimal in the same sense as decisions derived from classical probabilities.

3.1 Context

Although the names "Forecaster," "Skeptic," and "Reality" may not have been used systematically prior to Shafer and Vovk (2001), a good deal of prior work on probabilistic prediction can be understood in terms of averaging strategies in a game in which, for successive values of n, Forecaster predicts the value of y_n, Skeptic then bets on the value of y_n, and Reality then determines the value of y_n.

This work can be classified into the four cells of a 2×2 table based to these two distinctions:

Forecast-based vs. test-based. Work is *forecast-based* if it involves averaging or otherwise amalgamating strategies for Forecaster. Work is *test-based* if it amalgamates strategies for Skeptic and then seeks a strategy for Forecaster that is optimal against the resulting strategy for Skeptic.

Universalizing vs. amalgamating. Work is *universalizing* if it seeks to amalgamate all possible strategies for a particular player, thus obtaining a strategy that is universal for that player. Universal strategies are usually not computable. Work is (merely) *amalgamating* if it attempts only to amalgamate a more manageable class of strategies of the player concerned, which may be sufficient in practice.

Defensive forecasting is test-based and merely amalgamating.

A substantial amount of work has been done in each of the four cells.

Forecast-based and universalizing. The only work in this cell of which I am aware is that of Ray Solomonoff, who has argued for decades that it is possible to average all computable strategies for Forecaster, thus obtaining a universal strategy that will be successful regardless of Reality's behavior (Solomonoff, 2003). Solomonoff's universal strategy is only semi-computable, and it is not clear that useful approximations can be implemented.

Forecast-based and amalgamating. An immense amount of work falls in this cell, including all the work on Bayesian prediction (Bernardo and Smith, 2000) and prediction with expert advice (Cesa-Bianchi and Lugosi, 2006; Vovk, 1999). All this work seeks to improve strategies for Forecaster (probability distributions for Reality's moves $y_1, y_2, \dots$) by averaging or otherwise amalgamating them. Averaging strategies for Forecaster can be effective asymptotically because the average will eventually behave like the strategy in the average that best matches the behavior of Reality. Whether this happens in practice depends on how many rounds the prediction game runs and how close Reality's behavior is to any of the strategies being averaged.

Test-based and universalizing. The best known work in this cell is that of Leonid Levin and Peter Gács. Their work has roots in a celebrated 1966 article by Martin-Löf (1966), which established the existence of universal tests in the case of Bernoulli trials. In the early 1970s, Levin generalized Martin-Löf's result beyond the binary case and showed that the amalgamation of individual tests can be carried out by averaging (Levin, 1973, 1976). Levin established the existence of a "neutral" probability distribution, one that defeats the universal test (Levin, 1976, 1984), and this result has been developed further by Gács (2005). The result is interesting to those who study randomness, because it asserts the existence of a probability distribution with respect to which any sequence $y_1, y_2, \dots$ is random.

Test-based and amalgamating. This includes work on well-calibrated randomized forecasting by Foster and Vohra (1998), Sandroni et al. (2003), and more recent work on well-calibrated deterministic calibration by Kakade and Foster (2004).

Defensive forecasting goes beyond the other test-based amalgamating work primarily because it uses the game-theoretic framework and can therefore defend against any strategy by Skeptic, not just strategies that test calibration and resolution. This is analogous to the difference between von Mises, who was concerned only with frequencies, and Ville, who considered all properties of probabilities. The added power of the game-theoretic framework may be of limited importance in the binary case, where calibration and resolution are most important. But it is key for the generalization to other forecasting games.

3.2 Defeating a Continuous Strategy for Skeptic

In this section, I repeat a simple proof, first given in Vovk et al. (2005b), showing that Forecaster can defeat any particular fixed strategy for Skeptic, provided that each move prescribed by the strategy varies continuously with respect to Forecaster's previous move

Consider a strategy $\mathcal{S}$ for Skeptic in Protocol 1, the binary forecasting protocol we studied in §1.1. Write

$$\mathcal{S}(p_1, y_1, \ldots, p_{n-1}, y_{n-1}, p_n) \qquad (15)$$

for the move that $\mathcal{S}$ prescribes on the nth round of the game. At the beginning of the nth round, just before Forecaster makes his move p_n, the earlier moves $p_1, y_1, p_1, \ldots, p_{n-1}, y_{n-1}$ are known and therefore fixed, and so (15) becomes a function of p_n only, say

$$\mathcal{S}_n(p_n).$$

This defines a function $\mathcal{S}_n$ on the interval $[0, 1]$. If $\mathcal{S}_n$ is continuous for all n and all $p_1, y_1, \ldots, p_{n-1}, y_{n-1}$, let us say that $\mathcal{S}$ is *forecast-continuous*.

When we fix the strategy $\mathcal{S}$, Skeptic no longer has a role to play in the game, and we can omit him from the protocol.

PROTOCOL 7. BINARY PROBABILITY FORECASTING AGAINST A FIXED TEST
Parameter: Strategy $\mathcal{S}$ for Skeptic
   $\mathcal{K}_0 := \alpha.$
   FOR $n = 1, 2, \ldots$:
      Forecaster announces $p_n \in [0, 1]$.
      Reality announces $y_n \in \{0, 1\}$.
      $\mathcal{K}_n := \mathcal{K}_{n-1} + \mathcal{S}_n(p_n)(y_n - p_n).$

Proposition 4. *If the strategy $\mathcal{S}$ is forecast-continuous, Forecaster has a strategy that ensures $\mathcal{K}_0 \geq \mathcal{K}_1 \geq \mathcal{K}_2 \geq \cdots$.*

Proof. By the intermediate-value theorem, the continuous function $\mathcal{S}_n$ is always positive, always negative, or else satisfies $\mathcal{S}_n(p) = 0$ for some $p \in [0, 1]$. So Forecaster can use the following strategy:

- if $\mathcal{S}_n$ is always positive, take $p_n := 1$;

- if $\mathcal{S}_n$ is always negative, take $p_n := 0$;

- otherwise, choose p_n so that $\mathcal{S}_n(p_n) = 0$.

This guarantees that $\mathcal{S}_n(p_n)(y_n - p_n) \leq 0$, so that $\mathcal{K}_n \leq \mathcal{K}_{n-1}$. $\square$

If the reader finds it confusing that the notation $\mathcal{S}_n(p_n)$ leaves the dependence on the earlier moves $p_1, y_1, p_1, \ldots, p_{n-1}, y_{n-1}$ implicit, he or she may wish to think about the following alternative protocol, which leaves Skeptic in the game and has him announce the function $\mathcal{S}_n$ just before Forecaster makes his move p_n:

PROTOCOL 8. SKEPTIC CHOOSES A STRATEGY ON EACH ROUND

$\mathcal{K}_0 := \alpha.$
FOR $n = 1, 2, \ldots$:
    Skeptic announces continuous $\mathcal{S}_n : [0,1] \to \mathbb{R}$.
    Forecaster announces $p_n \in [0,1]$.
    Reality announces $y_n \in \{0,1\}$.
    $\mathcal{K}_n := \mathcal{K}_{n-1} + \mathcal{S}_n(p_n)(y_n - p_n).$

Protocol 8 gives Skeptic a little more flexibility than Protocol 7 does; it allows Skeptic to take into account information coming from outside the game as well as the previous moves $p_1, y_1, \ldots, p_{n-1}, y_{n-1}$ when he decides on $\mathcal{S}_n$. But it still requires that $\mathcal{S}_n(p_n)$ depend on p_n continuously, and it still makes sure that Forecaster knows $\mathcal{S}_n$ before he makes his move p_n. (Like all protocols in this article, Protocol 8 is a perfect-information protocol; the players move in sequence and see each other's moves as they are made.) So the proof and conclusion of Proposition 4 still hold: Forecaster has a strategy that ensures $\mathcal{K}_0 \geq \mathcal{K}_1 \geq \mathcal{K}_2 \geq \cdots$.

As I argued in (1.1), the requirement that $\mathcal{S}_n$ be continuous does not restrict the practical significance of the result, because a continuous function can change with arbitrarily great abruptness. This is consistent with the views of L. E. J. Brouwer, who argued that the idealized concept of computability for real-valued functions (idealized because real numbers are already idealized objects) should include the requirement of continuity (Brouwer, 1918; Martin-Löf, 1970). Notice also that the strategies for Skeptic used in §2 to establish classical results in probability theory (as well as all those used in Shafer and Vovk, 2001) are continuous. Finally, as I noted in §1.1, we can get a version of Proposition 4 even if we permit Skeptic to be discontinuous, provided we allow Forecaster to randomize his forecasts a little (Vovk and Shafer, 2007; Vovk, 2007c).

3.3 Calibration

I now exhibit a forecast-continuous strategy $\mathcal{S}$ for Skeptic in Protocol 7 that multiplies Skeptic's capital by a large factor whenever Forecaster's probabilities fail to be well calibrated. According to Proposition 4, Forecaster can give probabilities that are well calibrated by playing against $\mathcal{S}$.

This subsection follows closely the more general exposition in Vladimir Vovk's "Non-asymptotic calibration and resolution" (Vovk, 2006a).

Goal Leaving aside Skeptic for a moment, consider binary forecasting with Forecaster and Reality alone:

PROTOCOL 9. FORECASTER & REALITY
>   FOR $n = 1, \ldots, N$:
>   Forecaster announces $p_n \in [0, 1]$.
>   Reality announces $y_n \in \{0, 1\}$.

If a forecaster is doing a good job, we expect about 30% of the events to which he gives probabilities near 30% to happen. If this is true not only for 30% but also for all other probability values, then we say the forecaster is *well calibrated*. Here are two ways to apply this somewhat fuzzy concept to the probabilities $p_1, \ldots, p_N$ and outcomes $y_1, \ldots, y_N$.

1. For a given $p \in [0, 1]$, divide the p_n into those we consider near p and those we consider not near. Write $\sum_{n:p_n \approx p} 1$ for the number in the group we consider near p. Divide this group further into those for which y_n is equal to 0 and those for which y_n is equal to 1. Write $\sum_{n:p_n \approx p} y_n$ for the number in the latter group. Thus the fraction of 1s on those rounds where p_n is near p is

$$\frac{\sum_{n:p_n \approx p} y_n}{\sum_{n:p_n \approx p} 1}. \tag{16}$$

We say the forecasts are well calibrated at p if (16) is approximately equal to p. We say the forecasts are well calibrated overall if they are well calibrated at p for every p for which the denominator of (16), the number of p_n near p, is large.

2. Alternatively, instead of dividing the p_n sharply into those we consider near p and those we consider not near, we can introduce a continuous measure $K(p_n, p)$ of similarity, a function such as the *Gaussian kernel*

$$K(p_n, p) := e^{-\gamma(p_n - p)^2} \tag{17}$$

(with $\gamma > 0$), which takes the value 1 when p_n is exactly equal to p, a value close to 1 when p_n is near p, and a value close to 0 when p_n is far from p. Then we say the forecasts are well calibrated if

$$\frac{\sum_{n=1}^{N} K(p_n, p) y_n}{\sum_{n=1}^{N} K(p_n, p)} \approx p \tag{18}$$

for every p for which the denominator is large.

The second approach, making the closeness of p_n and p continuous, fits here, because Skeptic can enforce (18) using a forecast-continuous strategy.

Recall that a *kernel* on a set on Z is a function $K : Z^2 \to \mathbb{R}$ that satisfies two conditions:

- It is symmetric: $K(p, p') = K(p', p)$ for all $p, p' \in Z$.

- It is positive definite: $\sum_{i=1}^{m} \sum_{j=1}^{m} \lambda_i \lambda_j K(z_i, z_j) \geq 0$ for all real numbers $\lambda_1, \ldots, \lambda_m$ and all elements $z_1, \ldots, z_m$ of Z.

The Gaussian kernel (17) is a kernel on $[0, 1]$ in this sense. It also satisfies $0 \leq K(p, p') \leq 1$ for all $p, p' \in Z$. And as I have already noted, $K(p, p')$ is 1 when $p = p'$, close to 1 when p' is near p, and close to 0 when p' is far from p. Our reasoning in this section works when K is any kernel on $[0, 1]$ satisfying these conditions.

The goal that (18) hold for all p for which $\sum_{n=1}^{N} K(p_n, p)$ is large is fuzzy on two counts: "$\approx p$" is fuzzy, and "large" is fuzzy. But reasonable interpretations of these two fuzzy predicates lead to the following precise goal.

GOAL
$$\left| \sum_{n=1}^{N} K(p_n, p)(y_n - p_n) \right| \leq \sqrt{N} \qquad (19)$$

Heuristic Proposition 1. Under reasonable interpretations of "$\approx p$" and "large," (19) implies that (18) holds for all p for which $\sum_{n=1}^{N} K(p_n, p)$ is large.

Explanation Condition (18) is equivalent to

$$\frac{\sum_{n=1}^{N} K(p_n, p)(y_n - p)}{\sum_{n=1}^{N} K(p_n, p)} \approx 0. \qquad (20)$$

We are assuming that $K(p_n, p)$ is small when p is far from p_n. This implies that

$$\frac{\sum_{n=1}^{N} K(p_n, p)(p_n - p)}{\sum_{n=1}^{N} K(p_n, p)} \approx 0$$

when $\sum_{n=1}^{N} K(p_n, p)$ is large. So (20) holding when $\sum_{n=1}^{N} K(p_n, p)$ is large is equivalent to

$$\frac{\sum_{n=1}^{N} K(p_n, p)(y_n - p_n)}{\sum_{n=1}^{N} K(p_n, p)} \approx 0 \qquad (21)$$

holding when $\sum_{n=1}^{N} K(p_n, p)$ is large. If we take $\sum_{n=1}^{N} K(p_n, p)$ being large to mean that

$$\sum_{n=1}^{N} K(p_n, p) \gg \sqrt{N},$$

then this condition together with (19) implies

$$\frac{\left| \sum_{n=1}^{N} K(p_n, p)(y_n - p_n) \right|}{\sum_{n=1}^{N} K(p_n, p)} \ll 1,$$

which is a reasonable interpretation of (21).   ∎

Betting strategy and forecasting algorithm In order to derive a strategy for Forecaster that guarantees the goal (19) in Protocol 9, let us imagine that Skeptic is allowed to enter the game and bet, as in Protocol 8.

Our strategy for Forecaster will be to play against the following forecast-continuous strategy for Skeptic.

K29 BETTING STRATEGY

$$\mathcal{S}_n(p) = \sum_{i=1}^{n-1} K(p, p_i)(y_i - p_i)$$

We call this strategy for Skeptic the K29 betting strategy because it is modeled on the martingale that is used in Kolmogorov (1929) to prove the weak law of large numbers (see §2.4).

According to the proof of Proposition 4, playing against the K29 betting strategy means using the following algorithm to choose p_n for $n = 1, \ldots, N$.

K29 FORECASTING ALGORITHM

- If the equation

$$\sum_{i=1}^{n-1} K(p, p_i)(y_i - p_i) = 0 \tag{22}$$

  has at least one solution p in the interval $[0, 1]$, set p_n equal to such a solution.

- If $\sum_{i=1}^{n-1} K(p, p_i)(y_i - p_i) > 0$ for all $p \in [0, 1]$, set p_n equal to 1.

- If $\sum_{i=1}^{n-1} K(p, p_i)(y_i - p_i) < 0$ for all $p \in [0, 1]$, set p_n equal to 0.

Why the forecasting algorithm works   Why does the K29 forecasting algorithm work? I will give a formal proof that it works and then discuss its success briefly from an intuitive viewpoint.

Proposition 5. *Suppose Forecaster plays in Protocol 9 using the K29 algorithm with a kernel K satisfying $K(p, p) \leq 1$ for all $p \in [0, 1]$. Then (19) will hold no matter how Reality chooses $y_1, \ldots, y_N$.*

Proof. Mercer's theorem says that for any kernel K on $[0, 1]$, there is a mapping Φ (called a *feature mapping*) of $[0, 1]$ into a Hilbert space H such that

$$K(p, p') = \Phi(p) \cdot \Phi(p') \tag{23}$$

for all p, p' in $[0, 1]$, where $\cdot$ is the dot product in H (Mercer, 1909; Schölkopf and Smola, 2002).

Under the K29 betting strategy, Skeptic's moves are

$$s_n = \sum_{i=1}^{n-1} K(p_n, p_i)(y_i - p_i).$$

Proposition 4 says that when Forecaster plays the K29 forecasting algorithm against this strategy, Skeptic's capital does not increase. So

$$0 \geq K_N - K_0 = \sum_{n=1}^{N} s_n(y_n - p_n) = \sum_{n=1}^{N} \sum_{i=1}^{n-1} K(p_n, p_i)(y_n - p_n)(y_i - p_i)$$

$$= \frac{1}{2} \sum_{n=1}^{N} \sum_{i=1}^{N} K(p_n, p_i)(y_n - p_n)(y_i - p_i) - \frac{1}{2} \sum_{n=1}^{N} K(p_n, p_n)(y_n - p_n)^2$$

$$= \frac{1}{2} \left\| \sum_{n=1}^{N} (y_n - p_n)\Phi(p_n) \right\|^2 - \frac{1}{2} \sum_{n=1}^{N} \|(y_n - p_n)\Phi(p_n)\|^2 .$$

Hence

$$\left\| \sum_{n=1}^{N} (y_n - p_n)\Phi(p_n) \right\|^2 \leq \sum_{n=1}^{N} \|(y_n - p_n)\Phi(p_n)\|^2 . \tag{24}$$

From (24) and the fact that

$$\|\Phi(p)\| = \sqrt{K(p,p)} \leq 1,$$

we obtain

$$\left\| \sum_{n=1}^{N} (y_n - p_n)\Phi(p_n) \right\| \leq \sqrt{N}. \tag{25}$$

Using (23), the Cauchy-Schwartz inequality, and then (25), we obtain

$$\left| \sum_{n=1}^{N} K(p_n, p)(y_n - p_n) \right| = \left| \left(\sum_{n=1}^{N} \Phi(p_n)(y_n - p_n) \right) \cdot \Phi(p) \right|$$

$$\leq \left\| \sum_{n=1}^{N} \Phi(p_n)(y_n - p_n) \right\| \|\Phi(p)\| \leq \sqrt{N}.$$

$\square$

Additional insight about the success of the K29 forecasting algorithm can be gleaned from Equation (22):

$$\sum_{i=1}^{n-1} K(p, p_i)(y_i - p_i) = 0.$$

In practice, this equation usually has a unique solution in $[0, 1]$, and so this solution is Forecaster's choice for p_n. Because $K(p, p_i)$ is small when p and

p_i are far apart, the main contribution to the sum comes from terms for which p_i is close to p. So the equation is telling us to look for a value of p such that $y_i - p_i$ average to zero for i such that p_i is close to p. This is precisely what calibration requires. So we can say that on each round, the algorithm *chooses as p_n the probability value where calibration is the best so far.*

The pertinence of this formulation becomes clear when we recognize that Forecaster's calibration cannot be rejected because of what Reality does on a single round of the forecasting game. A statistical test of calibration (such as the K29 betting strategy) can reject calibration (multiply its initial capital by a large factor) only as a result of a trend involving many trials. To reject calibration at p, we must see many rounds with p_i near p, and the relative frequency of 1s for these p_i must diverge substantially from p. The K29 formulation avoids any such divergence by always putting the next p_n at values of p where no trend is emerging—where, on the contrary, calibration is excellent so far.

This is only natural. In general, we avoid choices that have worked out poorly in the past. The interesting point here is that this is sufficient to avoid rejection by a statistical test. Forecaster can make sure he is well calibrated by acting as if the future will be like the past, regardless of what Reality does on each round.

More to say   Calibration is only one probabilistic property of the forecasts $p_1, \ldots, p_N$ in Protocol 8 that we might demand in order to count Forecaster as a good probability forecaster. For example, we might demand that the relative frequency of 1s on rounds for which p_i is close to p converge to p at the rate described by the law of the iterated logarithm. This demand can also be satisfied using Proposition 4. Because violation of the law of the iterated logarithm is an event of small probability in classical probability, Ville's theorem tells us that there is a strategy for Skeptic that multiplies the capital risked by a large factor if the law is violated. Such a strategy is constructed in Shafer and Vovk (2001, Chapter 5), and Proposition 4 tells us that Forecaster will satisfy the law of the iterated logarithm by playing against it.

There is much more to say. For example:

- Proposition 4 does more than prevent Skeptic from multiplying the capital he risks by a large factor: it prevents him from making any money at all. This means that defensive forecasts do even better, with respect to tests being defended against, than classical probability theory expects. Rejection by these tests is avoided for certain, not merely with high probability.

- Forecaster's strategy on each round n does not depend on the horizon N. So if the game is played indefinitely, the goal (calibration in the case of the K29 forecasting algorithm) is achieved for every N.

See Vovk (2006a) for a more comprehensive discussion.

3.4 Resolution

Probability forecasting is usually based on more information than the success of previous forecasts for the various probability values. If rainfall is more common in April than May, for example, then a weather forecaster should take this into account. It should rain on 30% of the April days for which he gives rain a probability of 30% and also on 30% of the May days for which he gives rain a probability 30%. This property is stronger than mere calibration, which requires only that it rain on 30% of all the days for which the forecaster says 30%. It is called *resolution*.

To see that defensive forecasting can achieve resolution as well as mere calibration, we consider a protocol in which Reality provides auxiliary information x_n that Skeptic and Forecaster can use in making their moves:

PROTOCOL 10. FORECASTING WITH AUXILIARY INFORMATION x_n
Parameter: natural number N, set $textbfX$
$\quad \mathcal{K}_0 := \alpha.$
$\quad$ FOR $n = 1, \ldots, N$:
$\qquad$ Reality announces $x_n \in textbfX$.
$\qquad$ Skeptic announces continuous $S_n : [0,1] \to \mathbb{R}$.
$\qquad$ Forecaster announces $p_n \in [0,1]$.
$\qquad$ Reality announces $y_n \in \{0,1\}$.
$\qquad \mathcal{K}_n := \mathcal{K}_{n-1} + S_n(p_n)(y_n - p_n).$

In this context, we need a kernel $K : ([0,1] \times textbfX)^2 \to [0,1]$ to measure the similarity of (p,x) to (p',x'). We may choose it so that $K((p,x)(p',x'))$ is 1 when $(p,x) = (p',x')$, close to 1 when (p,x) is near (p',x'), and close to 0 when (p,x) is far from (p',x'). Once we have chosen such a kernel, we may say that the forecasts have good resolution if

$$\frac{\sum_{n=1}^{N} K((p_n, x_n)(p,x))y_n}{\sum_{n=1}^{N} K((p_n, x_n)(p,x))} \approx p$$

for every pair (p,x) for which the denominator is large.

This is a straightforward generalization of calibration, and the entire theory that I have reviewed for calibration generalizes directly. In the generalization, the K29 betting strategy is

$$\mathcal{S}_n(p) = \sum_{i=1}^{n-1} K((p, x_n), (p_i, x_i))(y_i - p_i),$$

and K29 forecasting algorithm achieves good resolution by playing against it. The K29 forecasting strategy is again very natural. It chooses p_n to satisfy

$$\sum_{i=1}^{n-1} K((p_n, x_n), (p_i, x_i))(y_i - p_i) = 0$$

In other words, it chooses p_n so that we already have good resolution for (p_i, x_i) near (p_n, x_n). This is analogous to the practice of varying one's actions with the situation in accordance with past experience in different situations. If x is the friend I am spending time with and p is our activity, and experience tells me that bowling has been the most enjoyable activity with Tom, bridge with Dick, and tennis with Harry, then this is how I will choose in the future. See Vovk (2006a) for details.

Bibliography

José M. Bernardo and Adrian F. M. Smith. *Bayesian Theory*. Wiley, Chichester, 2000.

L. E. J. Brouwer. Begründung der Mengenlehre unabhängig vom logischen Satz vom ausgeschlossenen Dritte. Erster Teil. Allgemeine Mengelehre. *Koninklijke Nederlandse Akademie van Wetenschschappen Verhandelingen*, 5:1–43, 1918.

Nicolò Cesa-Bianchi and Gábor Lugosi. *Prediction, Learning, and Games*. Cambridge University Press, Cambridge, 2006.

A. Philip Dawid. Statistical theory: The prequential approach (with discussion). *Journal of the Royal Statistical Society. Series A*, 147:278–292, 1984.

A. Philip Dawid. Self-calibrating priors do not exist: Comment. *Journal of the American Statistical Association*, 80:340–341, 1985. This is a contribution to the discussion in Oakes (1985).

A. Philip Dawid. Probability forecasting. In Samuel Kotz, Norman L. Johnson, and Campbell B. Read, editors, *Encyclopedia of Statistical Sciences*, volume 7, pages 210–218. Wiley, New York, 1986.

Joseph L. Doob. *Stochastic Processes*. Wiley, New York, 1953.

Dean P. Foster and Rakesh V. Vohra. Asymptotic calibration. *Biometrika*, 85:379–390, 1998.

Peter Gács. Uniform test of algorithmic randomness over a general space. *Theoretical Computer Science*, 341:91–137, 2005.

Sham Kakade and Dean Foster. Deterministic calibration and Nash equilibrium. In John Shawe-Taylor and Yoram Singer, editors, *Proceedings of the Seventeenth Annual Conference on Learning Theory*, volume 3120 of *Lecture Notes in Computer Science*, pages 33–48, Heidelberg, 2004. Springer.

Andrei N. Kolmogorov. Sur la loi des grands nombres. *Atti della Reale Accademia Nazionale dei Lincei, Serie VI, Rendiconti*, 9:470–474, 1929.

Andrei N. Kolmogorov. Sur la loi forte des grands nombres. *Comptes rendus hebdomadaires des séances de l'Académie des Sciences*, 191:910–912, 1930b.

Masayuki Kumon and Akimichi Takemura. On a simple strategy weakly forcing the strong law of large numbers in the bounded forecasting game. *Annals of the Institute of Statistical Mathematics*, 2007. Forthcoming, doi:10.1007/s10463-007-0125-5.

Leonid A. Levin. On the notion of a random sequence. *Soviet Mathematics Doklady*, 14:1413–1416, 1973.

Leonid A. Levin. Uniform tests of randomness. *Soviet Mathematics Doklady*, 17:337–340, 1976. The Russian original in: Доклады АН СССР 227(1), 1976.

Leonid A. Levin. Randomness conservation inequalities; information and independence in mathematical theories. *Information and Control*, 61:15–37, 1984.

Per Martin-Löf. The definition of random sequences. *Information and Control*, 9:602–619, 1966.

Per Martin-Löf. *Notes on Constructive Mathematics*. Almqvist & Wiksell, Stockholm, 1970.

James Mercer. Functions of positive and negative type, and their connection with the theory of integral equations. *Philosophical Transactions of the Royal Society of London. Series A, Containing Papers of a Mathematical or Physical Character*, 209:415–446, 1909.

David Oakes. Self-calibrating priors do not exist (with discussion). *Journal of the American Statistical Association*, 80:339–342, 1985.

Herbert Robbins. Statistical methods related to the law of the iterated logarithm. *Annals of Mathematical Statistics*, 41:1397–1409, 1970.

Alvaro Sandroni, Rann Smorodinsky, and Rakesh Vohra. Calibration with many checking rules. *Mathematics of Operations Research*, 28:141–153, 2003.

Bernhard Schölkopf and Alexander J. Smola. *Learning with Kernels*. MIT Press, Cambridge, MA, 2002.

Glenn Shafer. From Cournot's principle to the erfficient market hypothesis, November 2005. Working Paper # 15, www.probabilityandfinance.com. An abridged version appeared in *Augustin Cournot: Modelling Economics*, edited by J.-P. Touffut, Edward Elgar, 2007.

Glenn Shafer and Vladimir Vovk. The origins and legacy of Kolmogorov's *Grundbegriffe*, Working Paper 4, www.probabilityandfinance.com, October 2005. An abridged version, emphasizing the period before 1933, appeared as "The sources of Kolmogorov's *Grundbegriffe*" in *Statistical Science*, 26:70–98, 2006.

Glenn Shafer and Vladimir Vovk. *Probability and Finance: It's Only a Game*. Wiley, New York, 2001.

Ray Solomonoff. The universal distribution and machine learning. *The Computer Journal*, 46, 2003.

Charles J. Stone. Consistent nonparametric regression (with discussion). *Annals of Statistics*, 5:595–645, 1977.

Jean-André Ville. *Étude critique de la notion de collectif*. Gauthier-Villars, Paris, 1939. This differs from Ville's dissertation, which was defended in March 1939, only in that a 17-page introductory chapter replaces the dissertation's one-page introduction. For a translation into English of the passages where Ville spells out an example of a sequence that satisfies von Mises's conditions but can still be beat by a gambler who varies the amount he bets, see www.probabilityandfinance.com/misc/ville1939.pdf.

Jean-André Ville. Notice sur les travaux scientifiques de M. Jean Ville, 1955. Prepared by Ville when he was a candidate for a position at the University of Paris and archived by the Institut Henri Poincaré in Paris.

Richard von Mises. Grundlagen der Wahrscheinlichkeitsrechnung. *Mathematische Zeitschrift*, 5:52–99, 1919.

Richard von Mises. *Wahrscheinlichkeitsrechnung, Statistik und Wahrheit*. Springer, Vienna, 1928. Second edition 1936, third 1951. A posthumous fourth edition, edited by his widow Hilda Geiringer, appeared in 1972. English editions, under the title *Probability, Statistics and Truth*, appeared in 1939 and 1957.

Richard von Mises. *Wahrscheinlichkeitsrechnung und ihre Anwendung in der Statistik und theoretischen Physik*. Deuticke, Leipzig and Vienna, 1931.

Vladimir Vovk. On-line regression competitive with reproducing kernel Hilbert spaces, Working Paper 11, www.probabilityandfinance.com, January 2006a.

Vladimir Vovk. Non-asymptotic calibration and resolution, Working Paper 13, www.probabilityandfinance.com, July 2006b.

Vladimir Vovk. Competitive on-line learning with a convex loss function, Working Paper 14, www.probabilityandfinance.com, September 2005.

Vladimir Vovk. Competing with wild prediction rules, Working Paper 16, www.probabilityandfinance.com, January 2006c.

Vladimir Vovk. Predictions as statements and decisions, Working Paper 17, www.probabilityandfinance.com, June 2006d.

Vladimir Vovk. Leading strategies in competitive on-line prediction, Working Paper 18, www.probabilityandfinance.com, August 2007a.

Vladimir Vovk. Defensive forecasting for optimal prediction with expert advice, Working Paper 20, www.probabilityandfinance.com, August 2007b.

Vladimir Vovk. Continuous and randomized defensive forecasting: unified view, Working Paper 21, www.probabilityandfinance.com, August 2007c.

Vladimir Vovk. Derandomizing stochastic prediction strategies. *Machine Learning*, 35:247–282, 1999.

Vladimir Vovk and Glenn Shafer. The game-theoretic capital asset pricing model, Working Paper 1, www.probabilityandfinance.com, March 2002. An abridged version will appear in the *International Journal of Approximate Reasoning*.

Vladimir Vovk and Glenn Shafer. A game-theoretic explanation of the $\sqrt{dt}$ effect, Working Paper 5, www.probabilityandfinance.com, January 2003.

Vladimir Vovk and Glenn Shafer. Good randomized sequential probability forecasting is always possible, Working Paper 7, www.probabilityandfinance.com, September 2007. An abridged version appeared in *Journal of the Royal Statistical Society, Series B*, 67:747–764, 2005.

Vladimir Vovk, Ilia Nouretdinov, Akimichi Takemura, and Glenn Shafer. Defensive forecasting for linear protocols, Working Paper 10, www.probabilityandfinance.com, February 2005a. An abridged version appeared in *Algorithmic Learning Theory: Proceedings of the 16th International Conference, ALT 2005, Singapore, October 8-11, 2005*, edited by Sanjay Jain, Simon Ulrich Hans, and Etsuji Tomita, www-alg.ist.hokudai.ac.jp/ thomas/ALT05/alt05.jhtml on pp. 459–473 of *Lecture Notes in Computer Science*, Volume 3734, Springer-Verlag, 2005.

Vladimir Vovk, Akimichi Takemura, and Glenn Shafer. Defensive forecasting, Working Paper 8, www.probabilityandfinance.com, January 2005b. An abridged version appeared in *Proceedings of the Tenth International Workshop on Artificial Intelligence and Statistics*, www.gatsby.ucl.ac.uk/aistats/.

Abraham Wald. *Statistical Decision Functions*. Wiley, New York, 1950.

Wei Wu and Glenn Shafer. Testing lead-lag effects under game-gheoretic efficient market hypotheses, Working Paper 23, www.probabilityandfinance.com, November 2007.

Comparing decisions on the basis of a bipolar typology of arguments

Leila Amgoud[†] and Henri Prade[†]

[†] IRIT, CNRS and Université de Toulouse, France

Abstract Arguments play two types of roles w.r.t. decision, namely helping to select an alternative, or to explain a choice. Until now, the various attempts at formalizing argument-based decision making have relied only on one type of arguments, in favor of or against alternatives. The paper [1] proposes a systematic typology that identifies eight types of arguments, some of them being weaker than others. First the setting emphasizes the *bipolar* nature of the evaluation of decision results by making an explicit distinction between prioritized *goals* to be pursued, and prioritized *rejections* that are stumbling blocks to be avoided. This is the basis for an argumentative framework for decision. Each decision is *supported* by arguments emphasizing its positive consequences in terms of goals certainly satisfied, goals possibly satisfied, rejections certainly avoided and rejections possibly avoided. A decision can also be *attacked* by arguments emphasizing its negative consequences in terms of certainly or possibly missed goals, or rejections certainly or possibly led to by that decision. The proposed typology partitions the set of alternatives into four classes, giving thus a *status* to decisions, which may be *recommended*, *discommended*, *controversial* or *neutral*. This typology is also helpful from an explanation point of view for being able to use the right type of arguments depending on the context. The paper also presents a preliminary investigation on *decision principles* that can be used for comparing decisions. Three classes of principles can be considered: *unipolar*, *bipolar* or *non-polar* principles depending on whether i) only arguments pro or only arguments cons, or ii) both types, or iii) an aggregation of them into a meta-argument are used.

---

[1]This paper is a revised version of a contribution which previously appeared in the electronic proceedings of the 11th International Workshop on Non-Monotonic Reasoning held in the Lake District area of the UK in 2006. A preliminary version also appeared in a 2005 deliverable of the 6th PCRDT ASPIC (Argument Service Platform With Integrated Components) project.

1   Introduction

Decision making, often viewed as a form of reasoning toward action, has raised the interest of many scholars including philosophers, economists, psychologists, and computer scientists for a long time. Any decision problem amounts to select the best option(s) among different alternatives.

The decision problem has been considered from different points of view. *Classical* decision theory, as developed by economists, has focused mainly on identifying *criteria* for comparing different alternatives. The inputs of this approach are a set of *feasible* actions, and a function that assesses the value of their consequences when the actions are performed in a given state. The output is a preference relation between actions. A decision criterion, such as the classical expected utility Savage (1954), should then be justified on the basis of a set of postulates to which the preference relation between actions should obey. Such an approach does not provide arguments supporting (or attacking) the proposed decisions, nor is interested in the way these decisions may be executed in practice. Moreover, the candidate actions are supposed to be feasible.

More recently, some researchers in AI have advocated the need for a new approach in which the different aspects that may be involved in a decision problem (such as the goals of the agent, the feasibility of an action, its consequences, the conflicts between goals, the alternative plans for achieving the same goal, etc) can be explicitly handled. In Bratman (1987); Bratman et al. (1988), it has been argued that this can be done by representing the cognitive states, namely agent's beliefs, desires and intentions (thus the so-called *BDI* architecture). The decision problem is then to select among the conflicting desires a consistent and feasible subset that will constitute the intentions. The above line of research takes its inspiration in the work of philosophers who have advocated practical reasoning Raz (1978). Practical reasoning mainly deals with the adoption, filling in, and reconsideration of intentions and plans. Moreover, it allows reasoning about individual actions using for instance the well-known *practical syllogism* Walton (1996):

- G is a goal for agent a
- Doing action A is sufficient for agent a to carry out goal G
- Then, agent a ought to do action A

In this setting, a candidate action may be rejected because it would lead to the violation of other important goals, or to other bad consequences, etc.

In this paper, we are concerned with an argumentative counterpart of classical decision theory. Humans use arguments for supporting, attacking or explaining choices. Indeed, each potential choice has usually pros and cons of various strengths. Adopting such an approach in a decision support system would have some obvious benefits. On the one hand, not only would the user be provided with a "good" choice (if any), but also with the reasons underlying this recommendation, in a format that is easy to grasp. On the other hand, argumentation-based decision making is expected to be more akin with the way humans deliberate and finally make or understand a choice. This argumentative view of decision has not been much considered until recently even if the idea of basing decisions on arguments pros and cons is very old and was already somewhat formally stated by Benjamin Franklin (1887) more than two hundred years ago.

Articulating decisions on the basis of arguments is relevant for different decision problems or approaches such as decision under uncertainty, multiple criteria decisions, or rule-based decisions. In general, in practical domains, decisions are usually to be made under incomplete or uncertain information, and the potential results of candidate decisions may be evaluated from different criteria. Moreover, there may exist some expertise under the form of decision rules that associate possible decisions with given contexts. Thus, the different types of decision problems interfere, and consequently a unified argumentation-based model may be still more worth developing.

Whatever the decision problem is, the basic idea is that candidate decisions may lead to positively or negatively assessed results. This gives birth to arguments in favor of (pros) or against (cons) a decision in a given context. Different attempts at formalizing argument-based decision making can be found in the literature Fox and Das (2000); Fox et al. (1992); Bonet and Geffner (1996); Brewka and Gordon (1994); Amgoud and Prade (2004); Dubois and Fargier (2005); Amgoud et al. (2005). These works do not much discuss the nature of arguments in a decision analysis, and usually rely on one type of argument that may be in favor of or against alternatives.

This paper emphasizes the *bipolar* nature of the evaluation of decision results, by making an explicit distinction between *goals* having a positive flavor, and rejections, with a negative flavor, that are stumbling blocks to be avoided. This, for instance, applies to criteria scales where the positive grades (associated with positive results) are separated from the negative ones (associated with negative results) by a neutral value.

The paper proposes a systematic typology that identifies eight types of arguments. Some of them are weaker than others, since they rather reflect the existence of examples or counter-examples as supporting or challenging possible choices. In the proposed framework, each decision is *supported* by arguments emphasizing its positive features in terms of goals certainly satisfied, goals possibly satisfied, rejections certainly avoided and rejections possibly avoided. The possibility that a goal may be reached or that a rejection may be avoided is assessed in practice by the existence of relevant known examples. A decision can also be *attacked* by arguments emphasizing its negative features in terms of certainly or possibly missed goals, or rejections certainly or possibly led to by that decision. The richness of the proposed typology makes it possible to partition the set of alternatives into four classes, giving thus a *status* to decisions, which may be *recommended, discommended, controversial* or *neutral*. Each class may be refined into subclasses taking advantage of the strengths of the different types of arguments.

The aim of this paper is also to present a general discussion and a first and preliminary study of the different classes of argument-based decision principles. In the following, we argue that three main classes of principles can be distinguished:

1. *Unipolar principles* that focus only on one type of arguments when comparing choices (either arguments pros or arguments cons);
2. *Bipolar principles* that take into account both types of arguments but still keeping the distinction between the two types;
3. *Non-polar principles* that consist of aggregating the two types of arguments into a meta-argument and compare pairs of choices on the basis of their meta-arguments.

Note that, the use of suffix "polar" here refers to the dichotomy between arguments pros and arguments cons (and not to the bipolar structure induced by goals and rejections).

2   A general framework for decision making

Solving a decision problem amounts to defining a pre-ordering, usually a complete one, on a set $\mathcal{D}$ of possible choices (or decisions), on the basis of the different consequences of each decision. Argumentation can be used for defining such a pre-ordering. An argumentation-based decision process can be decomposed into the following steps:

1. Constructing arguments in *favor/against* each decision in $\mathcal{D}$.
2. Evaluating the strength of each argument.
3. Comparing decisions on the basis of their arguments.
4. Defining a pre-ordering on $\mathcal{D}$.

In Amgoud et al. (2005), an argumentation-based decision framework is defined as follows:

Definition 2.1 (Argumentation-based decision framework). An *argumentation-based decision framework* is a tuple $<\mathcal{D}, \mathcal{A}, \succeq, \rhd_{Princ}>$ where:

- $\mathcal{D}$ is a set of all possible choices.
- $\mathcal{A}$ is a set of arguments.

- $\succeq$ is a (partial or complete) pre-ordering on $\mathcal{A}$.
- $\triangleright_{Princ}$ (for principle for comparing decisions), defines a (partial or complete) pre-ordering on $\mathcal{D}$, defined on the basis of $\mathcal{A}$.

The *output* of the framework is a (complete or partial) pre-ordering $\triangleright_{Princ}$, on $\mathcal{D}$. $d_1 \triangleright_{Princ} d_2$ means that the decision d_1 is *at least as preferred as* the decision d_2 w.r.t. the decision *principle Princ*.

Notation: Let A, B be two arguments of $\mathcal{A}$, and $\succeq$ be a pre-order (maybe partial) on $\mathcal{A}$. $A \succeq B$ means that A is at least as 'strong' as B. $\succ$ and $\approx$ will denote respectively the strict ordering and the relation of equivalence associated with the preference between arguments, defined as follows:

- $A \succ B$ iff $A \succeq B$ and not $(B \succeq A)$ (meaning that A is strictly stronger than B),
- $A \approx B$ iff $A \succeq B$ and $B \succeq A$ (meaning that A is as strong as B).

Different definitions of $\succeq$ or different definitions of $\triangleright_{Princ}$ may lead to different decision frameworks that may not return the same results.

3 Logical language

In what follows, let $\mathcal{L}$ be a propositional language. From $\mathcal{L}$ we can distinguish the four following sets:

1. The set $\mathcal{D}$ gathers all the possible *alternatives*, or *decisions*. These candidate actions are assumed to be feasible. Elements of $\mathcal{D}$ are supposed to be represented by literals.
2. The set $\mathcal{K}$ represents the *background knowledge* that is assumed to be consistent. Elements of $\mathcal{K}$ are formulas of $\mathcal{L}$.
3. The set $\mathcal{G}$ gathers the *goals* of an agent. A goal represents what the agent wants to achieve, and has thus a positive flavor. This base is assumed to be consistent too, i.e. an agent is not allowed to have contradictory goals. Note that a goal may be expressed in terms of a logical combination of constraints on criteria values, and does not necessarily refer to one criterion.
4. The set $\mathcal{R}$ gathers the *rejections* of an agent. A rejection represents what the agent wants to avoid. Clearly rejections express negative preferences. The set $\{\neg r \mid r \in \mathcal{R}\}$ is assumed to be consistent since acceptable alternatives should satisfy $\neg r$ due to the rejection of r. However, note that if r is a rejection, this does not necessarily mean that $\neg r$ is a goal. For instance, in case of choosing a medical drug, one may have as a goal the immediate availability of the drug, and as a rejection its availability only after at least two days. As it can be guessed on this example, if g is a goal only r such that $r \vdash \neg g$

can be a rejection, and conversely. This means that rejection can be more specific than the negation of goals. Moreover, recent cognitive psychology studies Cacioppo et al. (1997) have confirmed the cognitive validity of this distinction between goals and rejections.

Definition 3.1. A *decision problem* is a tuple $\mathcal{T} = \langle \mathcal{D}, \mathcal{K}, \mathcal{G}, \mathcal{R} \rangle$.

4   A new typology of arguments

When solving a decision problem, there may exist several alternative solutions. Each alternative may have arguments in its favor (called PROS), and arguments against it (called CONS). In the following, an argument is associated with an alternative, and always either refers to a goal or to a rejection.

Arguments PROS point out the existence of good consequences or the absence of bad consequences for a given alternative. More precisely, we can distinguish between two types of good consequences, namely the guaranteed satisfaction of a goal when $\mathcal{K} \cup \{d\} \vdash g$, and the possible satisfaction of a goal when $\mathcal{K} \cup \{d\} \not\vdash \neg g$, with $d \in \mathcal{D}$ and $g \in \mathcal{G}$. Note that this latter situation corresponds to the existence of an interpretation that satisfies $\mathcal{K}$, d, and g. This leads to the following definition:

Definition 4.1 (Types of positive arguments PRO). Let $\mathcal{T}$ be a decision problem. A *positively expressed argument in favor of* an alternative d is a pair $A = \langle d, g \rangle$ such that:
1. $d \in \mathcal{D}$, $g \in \mathcal{G}$, $\mathcal{K} \cup \{d\}$ is consistent
2.
   - $\mathcal{K} \cup \{d\} \vdash g$ (arguments of Type SPP), or
   - $\mathcal{K} \cup \{d\} \not\vdash \neg g$ (arguments of Type WPP)

The consistency of $\mathcal{K} \cup \{d\}$ means that d is applicable in the context $\mathcal{K}$, in other words that we cannot prove from $\mathcal{K}$ that d is impossible. This means that impossible alternatives w.r.t. $\mathcal{K}$ have been already taken out when defining the set $\mathcal{D}$.

Note that SPP arguments are stronger than WPP ones since $(\mathcal{K} \cup \{d\} \vdash g)$ entails $(\mathcal{K} \cup \{d\} \not\vdash \neg g)$. SPP stands for "Strong Positive PROS", whereas WPP is short for "Weak Positive PROS". Clearly, WPP arguments have interest only when the corresponding SPP do not exist. From a practical point of view, SPP arguments will be generally expressed by only exhibiting a minimal subset S of $\mathcal{K}$ such that $S \cup \{d\} \vdash g$, while a WPP argument corresponds to the existence of (at least) one known case where g was satisfied while d was applied. This means that together with $\mathcal{K}$, the agent stores a case memory of already experienced choices. Let $A_{SPP}(d)$ (resp. $Arg_{WPP}(d)$) be the set of all arguments of type SPP (resp. WPP) in favor of d in the sense of the above definition. The following inclusion holds:

Property 1. Let $d \in \mathcal{D}$. Then $A_{SPP}(d) \subseteq Arg_{WPP}(d)$.

Similarly, there are two forms of absence of bad consequences that lead to arguments PROS: the first one amounts to avoid a rejection for sure, i.e. $\mathcal{K} \cup \{d\} \vdash \neg r$, and the second form corresponds only to the possibility of avoiding a rejection ($\mathcal{K} \cup \{d\} \not\vdash r$), which can be testified in practice by the existence of a counter-example case assuring that $\mathcal{K} \wedge d \wedge \neg r$ is consistent (with $r \in \mathcal{R}$). This leads to the following definition:

Definition 4.2 (Types of negative arguments PROS). Let $\mathcal{T}$ be a decision problem. A *negatively expressed argument in favor of* an alternative is a pair $A = \langle d, r \rangle$ such that:
1. $d \in \mathcal{D}$, $r \in \mathcal{R}$, $\mathcal{K} \cup \{d\}$ is consistent
2. $\quad$ • $\mathcal{K} \cup \{d\} \vdash \neg r$ (arguments of Type SNP), or
   $\quad$ • $\mathcal{K} \cup \{d\} \not\vdash r$ (arguments of Type WNP)

Here again, SNP arguments are stronger than WNP ones since $\mathcal{K} \cup \{d\} \vdash \neg r$ entails $\mathcal{K} \cup \{d\} \not\vdash r$. SNP stands for "Strong Negative PROS", while WNP means "Weak Negative PROS". Let $A_{SNP}(d)$ (resp. $Arg_{WNP}(d)$) be the set of all arguments of type SNP (resp. WNP) in favor of d.

Property 2. Let $d \in \mathcal{D}$. Then $A_{SNP}(d) \subseteq Arg_{WNP}(d)$.

Arguments CONS highlight the existence of bad consequences for a given alternative, or the absence of good ones. As in the case of arguments PROS, there are a strong form and a weak form of both situations. Namely, negatively expressed arguments CONS are defined either by exhibiting a rejection that is necessarily satisfied, or a rejection that is possibly satisfied. Formally:

Definition 4.3 (Types of negative arguments CONS). Let $\mathcal{T}$ be a decision problem. A *negatively expressed argument against* an alternative d is a pair $A = \langle d, g \rangle$ such that:
1. $d \in \mathcal{D}$, $r \in \mathcal{R}$, $\mathcal{K} \cup \{d\}$ is consistent
2. $\quad$ • $\mathcal{K} \cup \{d\} \vdash r$ (arguments of Type SNC), or
   $\quad$ • $\mathcal{K} \cup \{d\} \not\vdash \neg r$ (arguments of Type WNC)

Let $A_{SNC}(d)$ (resp. $Arg_{WNC}(d)$) be the set of all arguments of type SNC (resp. WNC) against d, where C stands for Cons.

Property 3. Let $d \in \mathcal{D}$. Then $A_{SNC}(d) \subseteq Arg_{WNC}(d)$.

Lastly, the absence of positive consequences can also be seen as an argument against (CONS) an alternative. A strong form and a weak form of positively expressed arguments against an alternative can be defined as follows:

Definition 4.4 (Types of arguments CONS). Let $\mathcal{T}$ be a decision problem. A *positively expressed argument against* an alternative is a pair $A = \langle d, g \rangle$ such that:

1. $d \in \mathcal{D}$, $g \in \mathcal{G}$, $\mathcal{K} \cup \{d\}$ is consistent
2.
   - $\mathcal{K} \cup \{d\} \vdash \neg g$ (arguments of Type SPC), or
   - $\mathcal{K} \cup \{d\} \not\vdash g$ (arguments of Type WPC)

Let $A_{SPC}(d)$ (resp. $Arg_{WPC}(d)$) be the set of all arguments of type SPC (resp. WPC) against d.

Property 4. Let $d \in \mathcal{D}$. Then $A_{SPC}(d) \subseteq Arg_{WPC}(d)$.

Let us consider positively expressed arguments for instance. Observe that for a given alternative d and a fixed goal g, all the types of arguments cannot take place at the same time. Formally,

Property 5. SPP and WPC (resp. SPC and WPP, and SPP and SPC) arguments are mutually exclusive.

In the first two cases, this is due to the opposite characteristic conditions of the definitions. The last exclusion is due to the consistency of $\mathcal{K} \cup \{d\}$, and thus g and $\neg g$ cannot be obtained simultaneously. Taking into account the subsumptions between weak and strong forms of arguments, the following result holds:

Property 6. Let $d \in \mathcal{D}$ and $g \in \mathcal{G}$. There are only three possible situations w.r.t a positively expressed argument linking d and g, namely: i) there is an SPP argument, ii) there is an SPC argument, iii) there are both an WPP and an WPC argument.

The above property reflects the three possible epistemic status of a knowledge base ($\mathcal{K} \cup \{d\}$) w.r.t. a proposition (here g), which may be true, false, or having an unknown truth status. In the latter case, emphasizing either a WPP argument, or a WPC argument is a matter of optimism vs. pessimism Amgoud and Prade (2006). Since WPP and WPC arguments are somewhat neutralizing each other, we will not consider them in the decision status classification that we introduce now.

Status	Sub-status	Combination
Recom.	Strongly	$\langle A_{SPP}(d) \neq \emptyset, A_{SNP}(d) \neq \emptyset, A_{SNC}(d) = \emptyset, A_{SPC}(d) = \emptyset \rangle$
	Only	$\langle A_{SPP}(d) \neq \emptyset, A_{SNP}(d) = \emptyset, A_{SNC}(d) = \emptyset, A_{SPC}(d) = \emptyset \rangle$
	Weakly	$\langle A_{SPP}(d) = \emptyset, A_{SNP}(d) \neq \emptyset, A_{SNC}(d) = \emptyset, A_{SPC}(d) = \emptyset \rangle$
Discom.	Strongly	$\langle A_{SPP}(d) = \emptyset, A_{SNP}(d) = \emptyset, A_{SNC}(d) \neq \emptyset, A_{SPC}(d) \neq \emptyset \rangle$
	Only	$\langle A_{SPP}(d) = \emptyset, A_{SNP}(d) = \emptyset, A_{SNC}(d) \neq \emptyset, A_{SPC}(d) = \emptyset \rangle$
	Weakly	$\langle A_{SPP}(d) = \emptyset, A_{SNP}(d) = \emptyset, A_{SNC}(d) = \emptyset, A_{SPC}(d) \neq \emptyset \rangle$
Neutral		$\langle A_{SPP}(d) = \emptyset, A_{SNP}(d) = \emptyset, A_{SNC}(d) = \emptyset, A_{SPC}(d) = \emptyset \rangle$
Controv.		$\langle A_{SPP}(d) \neq \emptyset, A_{SNP}(d) \neq \emptyset, A_{SNC}(d) \neq \emptyset, A_{SPC}(d) \neq \emptyset \rangle$
		$\langle A_{SPP}(d) \neq \emptyset, A_{SNP}(d) \neq \emptyset, A_{SNC}(d) \neq \emptyset, A_{SPC}(d) = \emptyset \rangle$
		$\langle A_{SPP}(d) \neq \emptyset, A_{SNP}(d) \neq \emptyset, A_{SNC}(d) = \emptyset, A_{SPC}(d) \neq \emptyset \rangle$
		$\langle A_{SPP}(d) \neq \emptyset, A_{SNP}(d) = \emptyset, A_{SNC}(d) \neq \emptyset, A_{SPC}(d) \neq \emptyset \rangle$
		$\langle A_{SPP}(d) \neq \emptyset, A_{SNP}(d) = \emptyset, A_{SNC}(d) \neq \emptyset, A_{SPC}(d) = \emptyset \rangle$
		$\langle A_{SPP}(d) \neq \emptyset, A_{SNP}(d) = \emptyset, A_{SNC}(d) = \emptyset, A_{SPC}(d) \neq \emptyset \rangle$
		$\langle A_{SPP}(d) = \emptyset, A_{SNP}(d) \neq \emptyset, A_{SNC}(d) \neq \emptyset, A_{SPC}(d) \neq \emptyset \rangle$
		$\langle A_{SPP}(d) \neq \emptyset, A_{SNP}(d) = \emptyset, A_{SNC}(d) = \emptyset, A_{SPC}(d) \neq \emptyset \rangle$
		$\langle A_{SPP}(d) = \emptyset, A_{SNP}(d) \neq \emptyset, A_{SNC}(d) = \emptyset, A_{SPC}(d) \neq \emptyset \rangle$

Table 1. Decision status

5   Decision status

In the previous section, we have shown that each decision may be supported by two types of strong arguments, and attacked by two other types of strong arguments. In summary, given a decision $d \in \mathcal{D}$, we will have the following sets of arguments:

- $A_{SPP}(d) =$ those arguments which capture the goals that are reached when applying d in context $\mathcal{C}$
- $A_{SNP}(d) =$ those arguments which capture the rejections that are avoided when applying d in context $\mathcal{C}$
- $A_{SNC}(d) =$ those arguments which capture the rejections that are not avoided when applying d in context $\mathcal{C}$
- $A_{SPC}(d) =$ those arguments which capture the goals that are missed when applying d in context $\mathcal{C}$

Note that when a given set is empty, for instance $A_{SPP}(d) = \emptyset$, this does not mean at all that decision d cannot lead to any goal, but rather we cannot be certain that a goal is reached as some information is missing. The above types of arguments supporting or attacking a choice d give birth to four main different *statuses* for that decision: *recommended, discommended, neutral* and *controversial* (see Table 1 for the straightforward formal definitions).

Recommended choices are those choices that have only arguments in favor of them and no arguments against them (whatever their type). Discommended choices are those choices that have no arguments in favor of them and only arguments against them. Regarding neutral choices, they have neither arguments in favor of them, nor arguments against. Choices that have at the same time arguments in favor of them and arguments against are said controversial. As shown in Table 1, there are 9 situations in which a choice is controversial.

Property 7. Let $d \in \mathcal{D}$. Then d is either fully recommended, or fully discommended, or controversial or neutral.

Note that one may give priority to SPP and SNC arguments, which directly state that a goal is reached, or a rejection is not missed respectively. SNP and SPC arguments that are "only indirectly" in favor of or against a choice can be used for refining the two first types of arguments. For instance, in Table 1, a choice that has both SPP and SNP arguments in favor of it is strongly recommended, whereas a choice with only SPP arguments in favor of it is only recommended.

This classification of choices is of interest from a persuasion or explanation perspective, since e.g recommended choices are more easily arguable than controversial ones. This does not mean that recommended choices are always better than any other as we shall see in the next section.

6   Principles for comparing decisions

In the following we are interested in discussing possible choices for $\triangleright_{Princ}$. The relation $\succeq$ is assumed to be given. It may be either a partial or a complete preorder. This preorder may account for the certainty of the pieces of knowledge involved in the argument and/or to the importance of the goal to which the argument pertains. However, this will not be detailed in the following.

Comparing choices on the basis of the sets of PROS or CONS arguments that are associated with them is a key step in an argumentative decision process. Depending on what sets are considered and how they are handled, one can roughly distinguish between three categories of principles:

Unipolar principles: are those that only refer to either the arguments PROS or the arguments CONS.

Bipolar principles: are those that reason on both types of arguments at the same time.

Non-polar principles: are those where arguments PROS and arguments CONS a given choice are aggregated into a unique *meta-argument*. It results that the negative and positive polarities disappear in the aggregation.

Below we present the main principles that can be thought of for each category. In what follows, $Arg_{Pro}(d) = A_{SPP}(d) \cup A_{SNP}(d)$, and $Arg_{Cons}(d) = A_{SNC}(d) \cup A_{SPC}(d)$. Moreover, the function `Result` returns for a given set of arguments, all the goals/rejections involved in those arguments.

6.1 Unipolar principles

In this section we present basic criteria for comparing decisions on the basis of only arguments PROS. Note that similar ideas apply to arguments CONS. Even if focusing on only one type of arguments is losing a part of the information, it may reflect natural, although somewhat extreme, attitudes. Pessimism privileges negative points, while pure optimism may only retain the good points only.

We start by presenting those criteria that do not involve the strength of arguments, then their respective refinements when strength is taken into account.

A first natural criterion consists of preferring the decision d_1 over d_2 if for each argument $<d_2, g>$, there exists an argument $<d_1, g>$, while the reverse is not true. Formally:

Definition 6.1. Let $d_1, d_2 \in \mathcal{D}$.
$d_1 \vartriangleright d_2$ iff `Result`$(Arg_{Pro}(d_2)) \subseteq$ `Result`$(Arg_{Pro}(d_1))$.

This *partial* preorder is refined by the following *complete* preorder in terms of cardinality, i.e preferring the decision that has more arguments PROS.

Definition 6.2 (Counting arguments PROS). Let $d_1, d_2 \in \mathcal{D}$.
$d_1 \vartriangleright d_2$ iff $|Arg_{Pro}(d_1)| \geq |Arg_{Pro}(d_2)|$.

When the strength of arguments is taken into account in the decision process, one may think of preferring a choice that has a dominant argument, i.e. an argument PROS that is preferred to any argument PROS the other choices.

Definition 6.3. Let $d_1, d_2 \in \mathcal{D}$.
$d_1 \vartriangleright d_2$ iff $\exists A \in Arg_{Pro}(d_1)$ such that $\forall B \in Arg_{Pro}(d_2), A \succeq B$.

The above definition relies heavily on the relation $\succeq$ that compares arguments. Thus, the properties of this criterion depends on those of $\succeq$. Namely, it can be checked that the above criterion works properly only if $\succeq$ is a complete preorder.

Property 8. If the relation $\succeq$ is a complete preorder, then $\rhd$ is also a complete preorder.

Note that the above relation may be found to be too restrictive, since when the strongest arguments in favor of d_1 and d_2 have equivalent strengths (in the sense of $\approx$), d_1 and d_2 are also seen as equivalent. However, we can refine the above definition by ignoring the strongest arguments with equal strengths, by means of the following *strict preorder*.

Definition 6.4. Let d_1, $d_2 \in \mathcal{D}$, and $\succeq$ a complete preorder.
Let $(P_1, \ldots, P_r)$, $(P'_1, \ldots, P'_s)$ be the vectors of arguments PROS the decisions d_1 and d_2 respectively. Each of these vectors is assumed to be decreasingly ordered w.r.t $\succeq$ (e.g. $P_1 \succeq \ldots \succeq P_r$). Let $v = \min(r, s)$.
$d_1 \rhd d_2$ iff:

- $P_1 \succ P'_1$, or
- $\exists\, k \leq v$ such that $P_k \succ P'_k$ and $\forall\, j < k$, $P_j \approx P'_j$, or
- $r > v$ and $\forall\, j \leq v$, $P_j \approx P'_j$.

Note that in all the above criteria, the two types of arguments PROS are considered as having the same importance. Thus, reasoning with goals is as important as reasoning with rejections. However, this may be debatable, since one may prefer arguments ensuring that a goal is reached to an argument that shows that a rejection is avoided, since the latter is the least thing that can be expected. On the basis of this new source of preference between arguments, the above criteria can be further reformulated by processing separately the two sets of arguments. More precisely, we can apply the above definitions only for the set of arguments of type SPP, and only in case of ties to apply again the same definitions on SNP arguments. We may even a different criterion on the set SNP of arguments.

Another point that is worth discussing is the impact of possible dependencies between goals (or rejections) on the decision criteria. Namely, assume that two goals are, for instance, redundant, i.e they are logically equivalent giving $\mathcal{K}$. Applying the cardinality-based criterion may lead to privilege decisions reaching redundant goals. This maybe debatable although allowing for redundancy is clearly a way of stressing the importance of a goal (or a rejection). Note that not all the above criteria are sensible to redundancy, for instance the first one (Definition 6.1).

Till now, we have only discussed decision criteria based on arguments PROS. However, the counterpart criteria when arguments CONS are considered can also be defined. Thus, the counterpart criterion of the one defined in Definition 6.1 is the following partial preorder:

Definition 6.5. Let $d_1, d_2 \in \mathcal{D}$. $d_1 \vartriangleright d_2$ iff
$\texttt{Result}(Arg_{Cons}(d_1)) \subseteq \texttt{Result}(Arg_{Cons}(d_2))$.

Similarly, it refinement in terms of cardinality is given by the following complete preorder:

Definition 6.6 (Counting arguments CONS). Let $d_1, d_2 \in \mathcal{D}$.
$d_1 \vartriangleright d_2$ iff $|Arg_{Cons}(d_1)| \leq |Arg_{Cons}(d_2)|$.

The criteria that take into account the strengths of arguments have also their counterparts when handling arguments CONS.

Definition 6.7. Let $d_1, d_2 \in \mathcal{D}$.
$d_1 \vartriangleright d_2$ iff $\exists B \in Arg_{Cons}(d_2)$ such that $\forall A \in Arg_{Cons}(d_1), B \succeq A$.

As in the case of arguments PROS, when the relation $\succeq$ is a complete preorder, the above relation is also a complete preorder, and can be refined into the following strict one.

Definition 6.8. Let $d_1, d_2 \in \mathcal{D}$.
Let $(C_1, ..., C_r)$, $(C'_1, ..., C'_s)$ be the vectors of arguments CONS the decisions d_1 and d_2. Each of these vectors is assumed to be decreasingly ordered w.r.t $\succeq$ (e.g. $C_1 \succeq ... \succeq C_r$). Let $v = \min(r, s)$.
$d_1 \succ d_2$ iff:
- $C'_1 \succ C_1$, or
- $\exists k \leq v$ such that $C'_k \succ C_k$ and $\forall j < k, C_j \approx C'_j$, or
- $v < s$ and $\forall j \leq v, C_j \approx C'_j$.

Finally, it may be also worth distinguishing between SNC and SPC arguments, and to privilege those which are SNC since they are the most striking ones. Similar ideas given in the case of arguments PROS apply.

6.2 Bipolar principles

Let's now define some principles where both types of arguments (PROS and CONS) are taken in account when comparing decisions. Generally speaking, we can conjunctively combine the criteria dealing with arguments PROS with their counterpart handling arguments CONS. For instance, the criterion given in Definition 6.2 can be combined with that given in Definition 6.6 into the following one:

Definition 6.9. Let d_1, $d_2 \in \mathcal{D}$.
$d_1 \rhd d_2$ iff

    1. $|Arg_{Pro}(d_1)| \geq |Arg_{Pro}(d_2)|$, and
    2. $|Arg_{Cons}(d_1)| \leq |Arg_{Cons}(d_2)|$.

However, note that unfortunately this is no longer a complete preorder. Similarly, the criteria given respectively in Definition 6.3 and Definition 6.7 can be combined into the following one:

Definition 6.10. Let d_1, $d_2 \in \mathcal{D}$.
$d_1 \rhd d_2$ iff:

- $\exists~A \in Arg_{pros}(d_1)$ such that $\forall~B \in Arg_{pros}(d_2)$, $A \succeq B$.
- $\not\exists~A' \in Arg_{Cons}(d_1)$ such that $\forall~B' \in Arg_{Cons}(d_2)$, $A \succeq B$.

This means that one prefers a decision which has at least one supporting argument which is better than any supporting argument of the other decision, and also which has not a very strong argument against it.
Note that the above definition can be also refined in the same spirit as Definitions 6.4 and 6.8.

Another family of bipolar decision criteria applies the *Franklin principle* which is a natural extension to the bipolar case of the idea underlying Definition 6.4. This criterion consists, when comparing pros and CONS a decision, of ignoring pairs of arguments pros and CONS which have the same strength. After such a simplification, one can apply any of the above bipolar principles. In what follows, we will define formally the Franklin simplification.

Definition 6.11 (Franklin simplification). Let $d \in \mathcal{D}$.
Let $P = (P_1, ..., P_r)$, $(C = C_1, ..., C_m)$ be the vectors of the arguments PROS and CONS the decision d. Each of these vectors is assumed to be decreasingly ordered w.r.t $\succeq$ (e.g. $P_1 \succeq ... \succeq P_r$).
The *result of the simplification* is $P' = (P_{j+1}, ..., P_r)$, $C' = (C_{j+1}, ..., C_m)$ such that:

- $\forall~1 \leq i \leq j$, $P_i \approx C_i$ and $(P_{j+1} \succ C_{j+1}$ or $C_{j+1} \succ P_{j+1})$
- If $j = r$ (resp. $j = m$), then $P' = \emptyset$ (resp. $C' = \emptyset$).

6.3   Non-polar principles

In some applications, the arguments in favor of and against a decision are aggregated into a unique *meta-argument* having a unique strength. Thus, comparing two decisions amounts to compare the resulting meta-arguments. Such a view is well in agreement with current practice in multiple principles decision making, where each decision is evaluated according to different principles using the same scale (with a positive and a negative part), and an aggregation function is used to obtain a global evaluation of each decision.

Definition 6.12 (Aggregation criterion). Let d_1, $d_2 \in \mathcal{D}$. Let $<P_1, \ldots, P_n>$ and $<C_1, \ldots, C_m>$ (resp. $<P_1', \ldots, P_l'>$ and $<C_1', \ldots, C_k'>$) the vectors of the arguments PROS and CONS the decision d_1 (resp. d_2). $d_1 \rhd d_2$ iff $h(P_1, \ldots, P_n, C_1, \ldots, C_m) \succeq h(P_1', \ldots, P_l', C_1', \ldots, C_k')$, where h is an *aggregation function*.

A simple example of this aggregation attitude is computing the difference of the number of arguments PROS and CONS.

Definition 6.13. Let d_1, $d_2 \in \mathcal{D}$.
$d_1 \rhd d_2$ iff $|Arg_{Pros}(d_1)| - |Arg_{Cons}(d_1)| \geq |Arg_{Pros}(d_2)| - |Arg_{Cons}(d_2)|$.

This has the advantage to be again a complete preorder, while taking into account both PROS and CONS arguments.

7 Conclusion

The paper has proposed an argumentation-based framework for decision making. The framework emphasizes clearly the bipolar nature of the consequences of choices by distinguishing goals to be pursued from rejections to be avoided. This bipolar setting gives birth to two kinds of arguments for each choice: arguments in favor of that choice and arguments against it. Moreover, we have shown that there are four types of arguments PROS a choice (resp. against a choice), and some of them are stronger than others. The different types of arguments allow us to give a unique status to each choice (recommended, discommended, neutral or controversial). We have also proposed different criteria for comparing pairs of choices. The proposed approach is very general and includes as particular cases already studied argumentation-based decision principles Fox and Das (2000); Amgoud and Prade (2004); Dubois and Fargier (2005). Besides, the richness of the different possible behaviors when arguing a decision in this framework should be compared to the actual practice of humans as studied in cognitive psychology.

8 Acknowledgments

This work was supported by the Commission of the European Communities under contract IST-2004-002307, ASPIC project "Argumentation Service Platform with Integrated Components".

Bibliography

L. Amgoud and H. Prade. Explaining qualitative decision under uncertainty by argumentation. In *21st Conference on Artificial Intelligence, AAAI 2006*, pages 219–224, 2006.

L. Amgoud and H. Prade. Using arguments for making decisions. In *Proceedings of the 20th Conference on Uncertainty in Artificial Intelligence*, pages 10–17, 2004.

L. Amgoud, J-F. Bonnefon, and H. Prade. An argumentation-based approach to multiple criteria decision. In *Proceedings of the 8th European Conference on Symbolic and Quantitative Approaches to Reasoning with Uncertainty, ECSQARU'2005*, pages 269–280, 2005.

B. Bonet and H. Geffner. Arguing for decisions: A qualitative model of decision making. In F. Jensen eds. E. Horwitz, editor, *Proc. 12th Con. on Uncertainty in Artificial Intelligence (UAI'96)*, pages 98–105, Portland, Oregon, 31 juillet-4 août 1996.

M. Bratman. *Intentions, plans, and practical reason.* Harvard University Press, Massachusetts., 1987.

M. Bratman, D. Israel, and M. Pollack. *Plans and resource bounded reasoning.*, volume 4. Computational Intelligence., 1988.

G. Brewka and T. Gordon. How to buy a Porsche: An approach to defeasible decision making. In *Working Notes of the AAAI-94 Workshop on Computational Dialectics*, pages 28–38, 1994.

J.T. Cacioppo, W.L. Gardner, and G.G. Bernston. Beyond bipolar conceptualizations and measures: The case of attitudes and evaluative space. *Personality and Social Psychology Review*, 1, 1:3–25, 1997.

D. Dubois and H. Fargier. On the qualitative comparison of sets of positive and negative affects. In *Proceedings of ECSQARU'05*, 2005.

J. Fox and S. Das. *Safe and Sound. Artificial Intelligence in Hazardous Applications.* AAAI Press, The MIT Press, 2000.

J. Fox, P. Krause, and S. Ambler. Arguments, contradictions and practical reasoning. In *Proceedings of the 10th European Conference on AI, ECAI'92*, pages 623–627, 1992.

B. Franklin. *Letter to J. B. Priestley, 1772, in The Complete Works, J. Bigelow, ed.* New York: Putnam, 1887.

J. Raz. Practical reasoning. *Oxford, Oxford University Press*, 1978.

L. J. Savage. *The Foundations of Statistics.* Dover, New York, 1954. Reprinted by Dover, 1972.

D. Walton. *Argument schemes for presumptive reasoning*, volume 29. Lawrence Erlbaum Associates, Mahwah, NJ, USA, 1996.

A Snapshot on Reasoning with Qualitative Preference Statements in AI

Carmel Domshlak

Faculty of Industrial Engineering and Management, Technion, Israel

Abstract Preference elicitation is a well-known bottleneck in decision analysis and decision automation tasks, especially in applications targeting lay users that cannot be assisted by a professional decision analyst. Focusing on the ordinal preferences of the users, here we discuss the principles that appear to underly various frameworks developed in the AI research for interpretation and formal reasoning about sets of qualitative preference statements.

1. Introduction

The ability to make decisions and to assess potential courses of action is a corner-stone of numerous AI applications, including expert systems, autonomous agents, decision-support systems, recommender systems, configuration software, and constrained optimization applications (e.g, see [13, 14, 32, 37]). To make good decisions, we must be able to assess and compare different alternatives. Sometimes, this comparison is performed implicitly, as it is done in some recommender systems. However, explicit information about *decision-maker preferences* should be communicated to the decision-support system.

At first view, the conceptual foundations to support such decision-aid tools should be abound—the field of decision theory and its companion methodology of decision analysis deal with making decisions and evaluating their quality. As developed over some 50 years, these disciplines have provided many powerful ideas and techniques, which exert major influences over the biological, cognitive, and social sciences.

Unfortunately, in spite of these remarkable achievements, the tools of traditional decision theory have not proven fully adequate for supporting recent attempts in artificial intelligence (AI) to automate the process of decision making. While there are several reasons for such a gap between theory and practice (e.g., see an excellent discussion of this issue by Luce and Raiffa [35] back in 1957), we believe that the Achilles heel of the traditional decision theory is the *amount* and *form of the information* that the decision maker needs to communicate regarding her preferences.

In classical decision theory and decision analysis a utility function is used to represent the decision-maker's preferences. Utility functions are a powerful form of knowledge representation. They provide a quantitative measure of the desirability of different outcomes, capture attitude toward risk, and support decision making under uncertainty. However, the process of obtaining the type of information required to generate a good utility function is time-consuming and requires considerable effort on the part of the user. In some applications, this effort is necessary and/or possible, e.g., when uncertainty plays a key role, and when the decision-maker and the decision analyst are able and willing to engage in the required preference elicitation process. One would expect to see such effort invested when medical or important business decisions are involved. However, there are many applications where either uncertainty is not a crucial factor, or the user cannot be engaged for a lengthy period of time (e.g., in on-line product recommendation systems), or the preference elicitation process cannot be supported by a human decision analyst and must be performed by a software system (e.g., due to replicability or mass marketing aims). In many such cases, direct elicitation of a good (even ordinal) utility function is not a realistic option; the traditional approach provides little help for decision makers who (for these or other reasons) exhibit discomfort with numerical evaluation of lotteries and/or outcomes. This shortcoming has been precisely formulated by Doyle and Thomason [21]: "Traditional decision theory provides an account of the information that, in principle, suffices for making a rational decision. In practice, however, the decision maker might have never considered the type of choice in question and so might not happen to possess this information."

But if direct eliciting of a good utility function is not a realistic option in our application, then what is? When a utility function cannot be or need not be obtained, we may resort to other, more *qualitative* forms of information communicating user preferences. Ideally, this qualitative information should be easily obtainable from the user by non-intrusive means. That is, we should be able to generate it from natural and relatively simple statements about preferences obtained from the user, and this elicitation process should be amenable to automation. In addition, automated reasoning with this information should be both semantically reasonable and computationally efficient.

In this paper we aim at sketching a general scheme for reasoning about user preferences that unifies treating this cognitive paradigm with the way other cognitive and computational paradigms are treated in the AI research. We then try to identify the limitations of such a general scheme, pointing on some of its shortcomings that unavoidably should be addressed in practice. Both the general scheme, as well as bypasses of its shortcomings, are then illustrated on two principle methodologies and their instances.

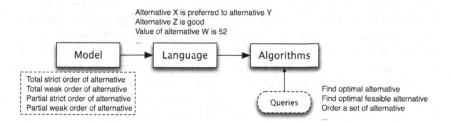

Figure 1: The AI approach to reasoning about preferences.

2. The AI approach: Models + Languages + Algorithms

In many senses, reasoning about user preferences bare similarity to many other problems faced by the AI research, and thus we may try dealing with user preferences in a way AI aims at treating other cognitive and computational paradigms. The general scheme underlying the AI approach has three major components:

1. **mathematical models** to concretize, understand, and classify various cognitive paradigms,

2. **languages** for describing models conveniently,

3. **algorithms** for answering queries about these models as efficiently as possible.

To allow a system to reason about user preferences, the user should *realize* to herself her preferences as an instance of the model, and *communicate* this model instance in the (agreed-upon) language to the system. Figure 1 illustrates this scheme along with some examples for models, language(s), and queries about user preferences the system may have to answer.

On the positive side, the foundations of decision theory suggest that we can restrict ourselves to models constituting (possibly partial, possibly weak) *orderings* over the space of alternatives[1].

While the concept of model in preferential reasoning is rather clear, the choice of language is *much* more open, and this due to numerous reasons. Suppose we adopt a language lying closest possible to our model of user preferences, that is, the language of pairwise comparisons between possible alternatives. The good news are that this type of information poses no ambiguity on its interpretation

---

[1]When reasoning under certainty, the alternatives constitute concrete outcomes of the decisions, while in reasoning under uncertainty, the alternatives constitute, e.g., lotteries over such outcomes. In this paper we restrict ourselves to discussing reasoning under certainty, and thus the former perspective suffices.

(and later we'll show that these *are* good news). Thus, if the number of generally acceptable alternatives is small, then adopting such a language appears appealing. This language, however, do not "scale" well to applications in whose the number of acceptable alternatives is larger than trivial. As an example, imagine yourself sending your web-agent to look for a used car for you on the web. Even if there are only some 100 car configurations that you are ready to accept, specifying an ordering over 100 alternatives is not a walk in the park. Typically, however, we have no such strict "threshold" on acceptability, and thus we'll have to specify an ordering over a sea of manufactured, used, and sold car configurations.

So what are other alternatives for qualitative preference specification languages? While explicit ordering specification as above might be infeasible due to both time and cognitive effort required from the user[2], our everyday practice shows that users are capable of providing *generalizing* statements of preference such as

- "I like ecologically friendly cars",

- "For a sport car, I prefer red color over black color",

- "This car would be better in red".

Assuming the preferences of the users are not entirely unsystematic, one would expect a relatively compact set of guidelines *structuring* (at least the core of) the user's preferences. Given that, it is only natural to assume that by such generalizing statements of preference the user will aim at communicating to the system exactly these guidelines.

Note also that generalizing statements refer not (only) to alternatives, but to the *properties* of the alternatives. To do anything with statements over properties, both the user and *the system* should consider the alternatives Ω not as monolithic entities, but as compound objects drawn from some combinatorial space. This property-based perspective is typically natural to the users — when choosing a used car to buy, we implicitly consider each car as a composition of its model, age, color, number of previous owners, accidents history, etc. And targeting this perception of the users, the systems also represent and keep track of the objects of users' interest in terms of this or another attribution $\mathbf{X} = \{X_1, \ldots, X_n\}$, by that effectively abstracting the alternatives' space Ω to $\mathcal{X} = \times Dom(X_i)$.

Taking now a closer look at the general scheme depicted in Figure 1, it appears that the scheme complicates when facing the realm of real users. The lessons learnt in the areas of psychology, philosophical logic, AI, and information systems indicate at least four major obstacles to operationalising this scheme in practice as is:

---

[2]To illustrate the potential cognitive issues with ordering realization, recall yourself choosing a car from a lot of say 20 cars standing for sale.

1. Incompleteness and noise in model specification.

2. System's uncertainty about the semantics the user puts into her statements.

3. Language constraints stemming from system's design decisions.

4. Potential intractability of reasoning about the model on the basis of the user statements.

The first problem is not at all specific to generalizing-statements-based languages, and we have already discussed it above[3]. In contrast, the next three problems are inherited from the necessity to adopt this or another *compact* preference specification language.

Let us first illustrate the issue of uncertainty in statements' interpretation. Here and in what follows, we assume the user provides the system with a qualitative *preference expression*

$$S = \{s_1, \ldots, s_m\} = \{\langle \varphi_1 \ominus_1 \psi_1 \rangle, \cdots, \langle \varphi_m \ominus_m \psi_m \rangle\}, \tag{1}$$

consisting of a set of *preference statements* $s_i = \varphi_i \ominus_i \psi_i$, where φ_i, ψ_i are logical formulas over $\mathbf{X}$, $\ominus_i \in \{\succ, \succeq, \sim\}$, and $\succ$, $\succeq$, and $\sim$ have the standard semantics of strong preference, weak preference, and preferential equivalence, respectively.

First, consider an "instance comparison" statement "$\mathbf{x}$ is better than $\mathbf{x}'$", where $\mathbf{x}, \mathbf{x}' \in \mathcal{X}$. The interpretation of this statement poses no serious difficulties because it explicitly compares between complete descriptions of two alternatives. However, this is the exception, rather than the rule. Most of the preference statements that we use in our everyday activities (e.g., "I prefer compact cars to SUVs") have this or another *generalizing* nature. As such, these statements typically mention only a subset of attributes. This creates an ambiguity with respect to the actual referents of these statements. Several proposals on how to interpret generalizing preference statements have been made both in philosophy and AI. However, there is no agreed-upon solution to this problem (e.g., see [5, 22, 27]), and the inherent uncertainty about the message that such a statement aims to communicate makes developing such a solution very questionable. Having said that, different existing proposals are not entirely tangential. Specifically, all these proposals suggest to interpret generalizing preference statements as indirectly comparing between *sets* of alternatives from Ω, while possibly disagreeing on what what sets of alternatives are actually compared by each statement separately, and/or by a multi-statement preference expression as a whole.[4]

Next, as if interpreting preference statements over $\mathbf{X}$ is not complicated enough already, note that

---

[3]A very thorough overview of lessons learnt on this matter in psychology and philosophical logic can be found, e.g., in [28].

[4]For an excellent survey of this topic, we refer the reader to [28].

- The attributes **X** and their domains effectively constitute the *maximal alphabet for any language* that can be used to provide the system with an information about Ω. In particular, the users have to communicate their preferences to the system also only in terms of **X**.

- The attribution **X** is typically fixed by the system to be used by all its users. Moreover, this attribution typically serves various components of the system, and often the attribution is selected to optimize system components other than this dealing with reasoning about user preferences. (This situation is typical to the choice of schema attributes of most database systems.)

- The attribution **X** is just one out of many possible attributions of the physical alternatives Ω, and as such it does not necessarily correspond to the *criteria* affecting preferences of a user over Ω.

To stress the latter point, suppose that a used-cars catalog maintains in its records the model and the color of the cars as a pair of attributes $X, X' \in \mathbf{X}$. Suppose that a user of the system likes Porsche Cayenne, likes green color, and yet strongly dislikes green Porsche Cayenne, providing a statement capturing the latter piece of information. In this case, the user articulates her preferences over a *combination of a particular pair of values of X and X'*, and no single attribute directly maintained by the system captures this preference-related criterion. On the positive side, however, if the user *does* articulate some preference information in terms of **X**, then the implicit preference-related criteria behind this information obviously have *some* encoding in terms of **X** (as it in fact happens in this "green Porsche Cayenne" example).

3. Independence-based Preference Modeling

Probably one of the best-known instantiations of the general scheme as in Figure 1 these days is this of CP-nets [7], along with its various extensions and derivatives [11, 12, 6, 19, 18, 38, 33, 44, 43]. Here we use this tool for representing and reasoning about preferences to illustrate both the different elements of the general scheme, as well as how the problematic issues discussed in the previous section may pop up in its concrete instantiations.

In terms of Eq. 1, the **language** underlying CP-nets corresponds to sets of (conditional) preference statements for values of variables **X**; each statement expresses user's preference over a single variable. For instance, in the statement "if the car is a sports car, I prefer black to red as its color", the addressed variable corresponds to the exterior color of the car. Formally, the expressions supported by CP-nets are

$$S \subseteq \{\mathbf{y} : x_i \succ x_j \mid X \in \mathbf{X}, \mathbf{Y} \subseteq \mathbf{X} \setminus \{X\}, x_i, x_j \in Dom(X), \mathbf{y} \in Dom(\mathbf{Y})\}$$
$$(2)$$

Reasoning about the ordering induced by such an expression on Ω requires a commitment to a concrete logical interpretation of these natural language statements. While different interpretations are feasible, the CP-nets adopt the *ceteris paribus* (all else equal) semantics for statement interpretation [28]. In this conservative semantics, a statement "I prefer $X = x_1$ to $X = x_2$" means that given any two alternatives that are identical except for the value of X, the user prefers the one assigning x_1 to X to the one assigning x_2. If these two alternatives differ on some other attribute as well, then they cannot be compared based on this preference statement alone. Conditional statements have the same semantics, except that they are restricted to comparisons between elements that satisfy the condition. Thus, "I prefer $X = x_1$ to $X = x_2$ given that $Y = y_1$" is interpreted exactly as above, but only for objects that satisfy $Y = y_1$.

The **model** underlying the CP-nets language is this of *strict partial orders*. Clearly, each preference statement as in Eq. 2 induces such a preference ordering over Ω. The "global" preference (ordering) relation specified by a collection of such statements (that is, by a CP-net) corresponds to the transitive closure of the union of these "local" preference relations. If the user provides us with consistent information about her preferences, then the binary relation induced by the TCP-net on Ω is a strict partial order. Note that this order is rarely complete, and thus typically not all pairs of alternatives are comparable with respect to a CP-net.

Having specified the model and the language, we shall now proceed with discussing reasoning **algorithms** for various queries with respect to CP-nets. All these algorithms exploit an *intermediate graphical representation* of preference expressions. Given an expression S as in Eq. 1, it is represented by an annotated graph. The nodes of the graph correspond to the attributes $\mathbf{X}$ and the edges provide information about direct preferential dependencies between the variables; there is an edge from X to X' implies that user preference over values of X' vary with values of X. Each node X in a CP-net is annotated with a conditional preference table (CPT) describing the user's preference order over $Dom(X)$ for every possible value assignment to the immediate predecessors of X (denoted $Pa(X)$). Figure 2 depicts a CP-net over four variables—binary E, C, T and ternary F. The graph shows that the preference over values of C depends on F's value, while the preference over values of T depends on the value of both F and E. Actual preferences are provided in CPTs. For example, when $F = f_0$, we prefer C to be *false*.

The structure of the CP-net graph plays an important role in determining the consistency of preference specification and in reasoning about preference, although the user need not be aware of this structure [7]. While not all preference expressions representable as CP-nets are consistent [15], the latter *is* the case, e.g., for acyclic CP-nets [7]. Note that the latter property of the CP-nets can be recognized in time linear in $|\mathbf{X}|$ —this is probably the simplest example for queries that can be efficiently answered, at least for some sub-classes of statements as in Eq. 1.

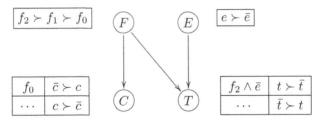

Figure 2: A schematic example of a TCP-net.

A more striking illustration of algorithmic exploiting of the structure induced by the preference expressions comes in processing three other important queries:

- *optimization*—finding a preferentially-optimal alternative from Ω, that is, finding an alternative o such that $S \not\models o' \succ o$ for any $o' \in \Omega$,

- *dominance testing*—for a pair of given alternatives $o, o' \in \Omega$, determining whether preference expression S entails $o \succ o'$ (denoted as $S \models o \succ o'$), and

- *ordering*—given a subset $\Omega' \subseteq \Omega$, order Ω' in a non-increasing order of preference communicated by S (that is, if some o comes before o' on this ordering, then we have $S \not\models o' \succ o$).

In preferential reasoning, all these three queries typically constitute NP-hard problems [33]. Surprisingly, optimization for acyclic CP-nets can be solved in time linear in $|\mathbf{X}|$ by a simple, top-down traversal of the graph [7]. The situation with dominance testing is not as sharp—while NP-hard in general even for acyclic CP-nets, this query still can be answered efficiently for boolean attributes $\mathbf{X}$ and certain topologies of the CP-net's graph [7]. Finally, the situation is most intriguing with the ordering query. As this query corresponds to sorting a given set of alternative, and pairwise comparison between alternative is a basic operation of any sorting procedure, at first view, it seems that ordering is at least as hard as dominance testing. This, however, is not precisely so. To order a pair of alternatives $o, o' \in \Omega$ consistently with S it is sufficient to know only that $o \not\succ o'$ or $o' \not\succ o$. Note that this information is weaker than knowing the precise preference relationship between o and o' with respect to S. While obtaining the latter knowledge would unavoidably require answering dominance queries, turns out that (i) answering its weaker counterpart can be done in time linear in $|\mathbf{X}|$ for any acyclic CP-net over any finite-domain attributes $\mathbf{X}$ [7], and (ii) this procedure can be used to sort any set of alternative $\Omega' \subseteq \Omega$ in time $O(|\mathbf{X}| \cdot |\Omega'| \log |\Omega'|)$ [8].

At the big picture, the CP-nets framework constitutes an instance of direct logical reasoning about S, and, of course, other proposals for such frameworks can be found in the literature. More specifically, the CP-nets framework corresponds to what we call here *independence-based methodology*, roughly characterized by the following three steps.

1. One defines certain *preferential independence* conditions on **X**, and provides a "representation theorem" stating that under these conditions the preference model can be compactly specified using certain (hopefully, intuitive) language. Some of such foundational representation theorems come from the classical works on measurement and multi-criteria decision theories [31, 29, 23], while some other (e.g., those underlying the CP-nets tool) come from the research in AI (e.g., see [7, 44, 2]).

2. Next, one possibly defines some additional preferential independence conditions on **X** under which the model is not only compactly specifiable, but can also be reasoned about efficiently (at least for some queries of interest).

3. Finally, the system poses restrictions on the form of allowable preference expressions, so that they are constrained to a sufficiently simple language for which the conditions from above are fulfilled.

Unfortunately, all independence-based methodologies for direct logical reasoning about preferences are limited by severe trade-offs between computational efficiency and semantic expressiveness (i.e., the richness of the supported preference expressions) [7, 33, 24, 44]. In attempt to escape these trade-offs as much as possible at least for optimization and ordering queries, several works in AI (e.g., see [4, 10, 9, 25, 34, 36]) suggested compiling the information carried by S into an ordinal utility function

$$U : \mathcal{X} \mapsto \mathbb{R} \qquad (3)$$

consistent with (what we believe S tells us about) P, that is requiring

$$\forall \mathbf{x}, \mathbf{x}' \in \mathcal{X}. \ U(\mathbf{x}) \geq U(\mathbf{x}') \Rightarrow P \not\models \mathbf{x}' \succ \mathbf{x}. \qquad (4)$$

The consistency requirement posed on U by Eq. 4 says that ordering a set of alternatives from $\mathcal{X}$ in a non-increasing order of values provided to these alternatives by U will never put alternative $\mathbf{x}$ before alternative $\mathbf{x}'$ if our interpretation of the user's expression S implies that the user strictly prefers $\mathbf{x}'$ to $\mathbf{x}$. The task of constructing such a utility function U from S is called *ordinal utility revelation*.

Observe that specifying a utility function U as in Eq. 3 can be expensive due to the fact that $|\mathcal{X}| = O(2^n)$. Thus, previous works on ordinal utility revelation suggested to stick here as well to the independence-based methodology (e.g., see [1, 6, 9, 25, 26, 32, 36]); in case of ordinal utility revelation, the first two steps of the above methodology are as follows.

1. One defines certain *preferential independence* conditions on **X**, and provides a "representation theorem" stating that under these conditions U can be compactly *represented*.

2. Next, one possibly defines some additional preferential independence conditions on **X** under which a utility function U consistent with S is not only compactly representable, but also can be efficiently *generated* from S [25, 36, 9].

Considering the first step, note that any function U as in Eq. 3 can be represented in a generalized additive form [23, 1]:

$$U(\mathbf{x}) = \sum_{i=1}^{k} u_i(\mathbf{x}[i]) \tag{5}$$

where each sub-function u_i depends on some subset of variables $\mathbf{X}[i] \subseteq \mathbf{X}$, and $\mathbf{x}[i]$ is the restriction of a complete assignment $\mathbf{x} \in \mathcal{X}$ to the attributes in $\mathbf{X}[i]$. Note that u_i can be selected to be any function that maps a (partial) assignment to a real value. The generality of Eq. 5 is immediate since we may have $k = 1$ and $\mathbf{X}[1] = \mathbf{X}$, which means that one can effectively select a function $u_1(\mathbf{x})$ that assigns an arbitrary utility to each possible complete assignment $\mathbf{x} \in \mathcal{X}$.

While by itself this generality of Eq. 5 has no practical implications, Eq. 5 allows us to generalize the core assumptions of previous works on ordinal utility revelation — each concrete instance of the independence-based methodology corresponds to some independence conditions on **X** that guarantee existence of U (i) satisfying Eq. 4 and (ii) having a *compact* decomposition in terms of Eq. 5 (that is, defined by a small number k of small attribute subsets). An additional key property of all previous works is that attribute subsets $\mathbf{X}[1], \ldots, \mathbf{X}[k]$ decomposing U are assumed to be *known* to the system.Finally, to our knowledge, all the works on independence-based ordinal utility revelation (except for the approach suggested in [26]) assume that the user's preference expression is consistent, that is, the user makes no mistakes in specifying her preferences. In practice, however, this assumption is not necessarily reasonable.

4. Unstructured Preference Modeling

In short, the independence-based methodologies for multi-attribute preference revelation are parametrized by the *structure* that user preferences induce on **X**, and thus are applicable only when such *compact structure exists* and is *known* to the system. In Section 2, however, we have discussed already the limited power of **X** to provide the "ultimate alphabet" for preference specification. The attributes **X** do not necessarily correspond to the criteria affecting preference of each individual user over Ω, and thus, even if user preferences are compactly structured, they should not necessarily be compactly structured *over* **X**.

Having in mind the "lessons learnt" from exploring the independence-based methodology for a few decades, let us try sketching the "universal instance" of the general information-processing scheme as in Figure 1. The vision here is threefold.

1. The user should be able to provide preference expressions S while being as little constrained in her language as possible.

2. The preference-model revelation machinery should be completely non-parametric, that is free of any explicit assumptions about the structure of the user preference ordering.

3. Both the process of model revelation and reasoning with the revealed model should be computationally efficient, including the case where user preferences pose no significant independence structure on **X** whatsoever.

While possibly not formalized precisely this way, this vision is obviously not new. For instance, while listing open problems in the area, Doyle [20] addresses the problem of language constraints and fixed attribution, and writes: "Can one recast the underlying set [of attributed alternatives] in terms of a different span of dimensions such that the utility function becomes linear? If so, can one find new linearizing dimensions that also mean something to human interpreters?" The same questions were considered by Shoham in the scope of his work on utility distributions [39, 40]. In an attempt to provide a unified view on probabilities and utilities, Shoham showed that, in principle, such a set of linearizing dimensions (called, in [39, 40], factors) exist for *any* utility function, and that this set of dimensions may have to be exponentially larger than the original set of attributes. However, the result of Shoham is more foundational than operational. The connection between the attributes and the particular set of factors proposed in [39, 40] is not generally natural, and thus it is rather unclear how to perform preference elicitation with respect to this set of factors. Likewise, no efficient computational scheme for reasoning about this, potentially very large, set of factors has been suggested until these days.

It is possible, of course, that the "universal methodology" as above is simply utopia. Some recent results, however, provide a positive evidence that, at least getting close to, this utopia *is* possible. In particular, a recently suggested by Domshlak and Joachims [16, 17] framework for ordinal utility revelation appears to satisfy to a large degree all the desiderata of the "universal methodology" as above. Connecting some ideas from knowledge representation, machine learning, and philosophical logic, this frameworks is based on a high-dimensional preference decomposition, and a specific adaptation of certain standard techniques for high-dimensional continuous optimization. Here we briefly outline the basic knowledge-representation idea underlying this proposal, referring the reader for details and computational solutions to [17].

Suppose the user provides the system with a preference expression S, and the task of the system to suggest an ordinal utility function U satisfying Eq. 3-4. In general case, the system is not provided with any information about the independence structure the user preferences induce on $\mathbf{X}$. In fact, the system cannot even assume that a significant such independence structure on $\mathbf{X}$ exists. The basic idea underlying the framework in [17] is simple: If no useful preferential independence information in the original representation space $\mathcal{X}$ is provided, the only escape is to switch to a different space in which no such independence information is required. But what this "different space" can be?

Assuming here that the attributes $\mathbf{X}$ are all binary-valued, let us schematically map the alternatives $\mathcal{X}$ into a new, higher dimensional space $\mathcal{F}$ using a certain mapping

$$\Phi : \mathcal{X} \mapsto \mathcal{F} = \mathbb{R}^{4^n} . \tag{6}$$

Specifically, the mapping Φ connections between the dimensions of $\mathcal{X}$ and $\mathcal{F}$ as follows. Let $\mathbf{F} = \{\mathfrak{f}_1, \cdots, \mathfrak{f}_{4^n}\}$ be a labeling of the dimensions of $\mathcal{F}$, and

$$\mathscr{D} = \bigcup_{i=1}^{n} Dom(X_i) = \{x_1, \overline{x_1}, \cdots, x_n, \overline{x_n}\} ,$$

be the union of attribute domains in $\mathbf{X}$. Let val : $\mathbf{F} \to 2^{\mathscr{D}}$ be a bijective mapping from the dimensions of $\mathcal{F}$ onto the power set of $\mathscr{D}$, uniquely associating each dimension $\mathfrak{f}_i$ with a subset $\mathsf{val}(\mathfrak{f}_i) \subseteq \mathscr{D}$, and vice versa. Let $\mathsf{Var}(\mathfrak{f}_i) \subseteq \mathbf{X}$ denote the subset of attributes "instantiated" by $\mathsf{val}(\mathfrak{f}_i)$. For example, if $\mathsf{val}(\mathfrak{f}_i) = \{x_2, \overline{x}_3, x_{17}\}$, then $\mathsf{Var}(\mathfrak{f}_i) = \{X_2, X_3, X_{17}\}$. Given that, for each $\mathbf{x} \in \mathcal{X}$ and $\mathfrak{f}_i \in \mathbf{F}$, we set:

$$\Phi(\mathbf{x})[i] = \begin{cases} 1, & \mathsf{val}(\mathfrak{f}_i) \neq \emptyset \land \mathsf{val}(\mathfrak{f}_i) \subseteq \mathbf{x} \\ 0, & \text{otherwise} \end{cases} \tag{7}$$

That is, geometrically, Φ maps each n-dimensional vector $\mathbf{x} \in \mathcal{X}$ to the 4^n-dimensional vector in $\mathcal{F}$ that uniquely encodes the set of all projections of $\mathbf{x}$ onto the subspaces of $\mathcal{X}$.

Considering the semantics of the transformation Φ, recall the pitfalls of the system-level fixing of the attribution $\mathbf{X}$, along with the example of green Porsche discussed in Section 2. In that example, the user articulates her preferences over a *combination of a particular pair of values of two attributes* $X, X' \in \mathbf{X}$, and no single attribute in $\mathbf{X}$ can directly capture the user's utility alone. However, as we also already suggested in Section 2, (i) if such a complex preference is articulatable in terms of the attributes $\mathbf{X}$, then it has to correspond to this or another set of value assignments to a subset of $\mathbf{X}$, and (ii) the evaluation of *any* abstracted alternative $\mathbf{x} \in \mathcal{X}$ with respect to such a complex preference corresponds to a single value assignment to a subset of $\mathbf{X}$, and that is, to a *single dimension of* $\mathcal{F}$. This means that there are not only dimensions in $\mathcal{F}$ that capture the utilities of "Porsche" and "green", but there is also a dimension that directly captures the utility of "green Porsche". This correspondence between complex preferences and individual dimensions of $\mathcal{F}$ makes the semantics of $\mathcal{F}$ very attractive. In addition, it can be shown that any preference ordering over alternatives $\mathcal{X}$ can be captured by a *linear* real-valued function from $\mathcal{F}$ (to which the alternatives in $\mathcal{X}$ are transformed using Φ.)

Now, let us dedicate a few words to interpretation of preference expressions S suggested in [17]. Assuming here that the referents of the statements in S correspond to propositional logic formulas over $\mathbf{X}$, consider an arbitrary comparative statement $\varphi \succ \psi$. Let $\mathbf{X}_\varphi \subseteq \mathbf{X}$ (and similarly $\mathbf{X}_\psi$) be the variables involved in φ, and $M(\varphi) \subseteq Dom(\mathbf{X}_\varphi)$ be the set of all φ's models in the subspace of $\mathcal{X}$ defined by $\mathbf{X}_\varphi$. For instance, if $\mathbf{X} = \{X_1, \dots, X_{10}\}$, and $\varphi = X_1 \vee X_2$, then $\mathbf{X}_\varphi = \{X_1, X_2\}$, and $M(\varphi) = \{x_1 x_2, \overline{x_1} x_2, x_1 \overline{x_2}\}$. In [17], the statement $\varphi \succ \psi$ is compiled into a set of constraints on the space of (candidate) linear, real-valued functions from $\mathcal{F}$. Specifically, $\varphi \succ \psi$ is compiled into a set of $|M(\varphi)| \times |M(\psi)|$ constraints

$$\forall \mathbf{m}_\varphi \in M(\varphi), \forall \mathbf{m}_\psi \in M(\psi). \sum_{f_i : \mathrm{val}(f_i) \in 2^{\mathbf{m}_\varphi}} w_i > \sum_{f_j : \mathrm{val}(f_j) \in 2^{\mathbf{m}_\psi}} w_j \qquad (8)$$

where $2^{\mathbf{m}}$ denotes the set of all non-empty value subsets of the local model $\mathbf{m}$. For example, statement $(X_1 \vee X_2) \succ (\neg X_3)$ (e.g., "It is more important that the car is powerful or fast than not having had an accident") is compiled into

$$w_{x_1} + w_{x_2} + w_{x_1 x_2} > w_{\overline{x_3}}$$
$$w_{x_1} + w_{\overline{x_2}} + w_{x_1 \overline{x_2}} > w_{\overline{x_3}} \qquad (9)$$
$$w_{\overline{x_1}} + w_{x_2} + w_{\overline{x_1} x_2} > w_{\overline{x_3}}$$

The constraint system $\mathfrak{C}$ resulting from such compilation of a user expression S defines the space of solutions for the framework in [17]. (The reader is referred to [17] for a thorough discussion on why this approach constitutes a least committing interpretation of preference statement.) Note, however, that solving $\mathfrak{C}$ poses numerous complexity issues. First, though this constraint system is linear, it is linear in the exponential space $\mathbb{R}^{4^n}$. Second, the very description size of $\mathfrak{C}$, and, in fact, of each individual constraint in $\mathfrak{C}$, can be exponential in n. Interestingly, Domshlak and Joachims show that these complexity complexity issues can be overcome by using some duality techniques from optimization theory [3] and Reproducing Kernel Hilbert Spaces (RKHS) [30, 42, 41]. At the very bottom line[5], these techniques allow for computing a solution for $\mathfrak{C}$ (corresponding to the desired ordering function $U : \mathcal{F} \mapsto \mathbb{R}$), and subsequently computing the values of U on $\mathcal{X}$ without requiring any explicit computation in $\mathbb{R}^{4^n}$.

5. Summarizing Discussion

The goal of this paper was mainly to provide a personal perspective of the author on the way user preferences are (or should be) modeled and reasoned about by general purpose systems such as these considered by the AI research. One important thing implied by this perspective is that the general model/language/algorithms scheme can be arguably instantiated in lots of ways, and each such proposal will unavoidably be open for (not less arguable) critique from this or another angle. If so, then the only real evidence for/against this or another concrete proposal will have to come from the experience with these proposals in practice. Unfortunately, here we observe a paradoxical deadlock situation suggesting the "chicken-and-egg" metaphor.

On the one hand, it is only natural to assume that reasoning about user's preference expressions is useful in many applicative domains (e.g., in online catalog systems). On the other hand, to our knowledge, no application these days allows its users to express any but trivial (e.g., "bag-of-word") preference expressions. It seems that the real-world players wait for the research community to come up with a concrete suggestion on how natural-language style preference expressions should be treated, while the research community waits for the real-world to provide it with the data essential to make the former decision. It is clear that this deadlock situation should somehow be resolved, and we believe that now this should be a primary goal for both sides.

Acknowledgments

My personal perspective on preferences in AI outlined here resulted (directly or indirectly) from numerous discussions I had on the topic with Ronen Brafman, Thorsten Joachims, Craig Boutilier, Hector Geffner, and many other colleagues and friends. This, however, does not imply that any of them necessarily agree with this perspective as a whole, or any of its parts.

---

[5]Presenting the computational machinery here is simply infeasible, and thus the reader is referred to [17].

References

[1] F. Bacchus and A. Grove. Graphical models for preference and utility. In *Proceedings of the Eleventh Annual Conference on Uncertainty in Artificial Intelligence*, pages 3–10, San Francisco, CA, 1995. Morgan Kaufmann Publishers.

[2] S. Benferhat, D. Dubois, S. Kaci, and H. Prade. Bipolar possibility theory in preference modeling: Representation, fusion and optimal solutions. *Information Fusion*, 7:135–150, 2006.

[3] D. Bertsekas, A. Nedic, and A. Ozdaglar. *Convex Analysis and Optimization*. Athena Scientific, 2003.

[4] J. Blythe. Visual exploration and incremental utility elicitation. In *Proceedings of the National Conference on Artificial Intelligence (AAAI)*, pages 526–532, 2002.

[5] C. Boutilier. Toward a logic for qualitative decision theory. In *Proceedings of the Third Conference on Knowledge Representation (KR–94)*, pages 75–86, Bonn, 1994.

[6] C. Boutilier, F. Bacchus, and R. I. Brafman. UCP-networks: A directed graphical representation of conditional utilities. In *Proceedings of Seventeenth Conference on Uncertainty in Artificial Intelligence*, pages 56–64, 2001.

[7] C. Boutilier, R. Brafman, C. Domshlak, H. Hoos, and D. Poole. CP-nets: A tool for representing and reasoning about conditional *ceteris paribus* preference statements. *Journal of Artificial Intelligence Research*, 21:135–191, 2004.

[8] R. Brafman and C. Domshlak. Database preference queries revisited. Technical Report TR2004-1934, Cornell University Computing and Information Science, 2004.

[9] R. Brafman and C. Domshlak. Graphically structured value-function compilation. *Artificial Intelligence*, 2008. in press.

[10] R. Brafman, C. Domshlak, and T. Kogan. Compact value-function representations for qualitative preferences. In *Proceedings of the Twentieth Annual Conference on Uncertainty in Artificial Intelligence*, pages 51–58, Banff, Canada, 2004.

[11] R. I. Brafman and Y. Dimopoulos. Extended semantics and optimization algorithms for cp-networks. *Computational Intelligence (Special Issue on Preferences in AI and CP)*, 20(2):218–245, 2004.

[12] G. Brewka. Logic programming with ordered disjunction. In *Proceedings of Eighteenth National Conference on Artificial Intelligence*, pages 100–105, Edmonton, Canada, 2002. AAAI Press.

[13] U. Chajewska, L. Getoor, J. Norman, and Y. Shahar. Utility elicitation as a classification problem. In *Proceedings of the Fourteenth Annual Conference on Uncertainty in Artificial Intelligence*, pages 79–88, San Francisco, CA, 1998. Morgan Kaufmann Publishers.

[14] J. D'Ambrosio and W. Birmingham. Preference-directed design. *Journal of Artificial Intelligence in Engineering Design, Analysis, and Manufacturing*, 9:219–230, 1995.

[15] C. Domshlak and R. Brafman. CP-nets - reasoning and consistency testing. In *Proceedings of the Eighth International Conference on Principles of Knowledge Representation and Reasoning*, pages 121–132, Toulouse, France, April 2002.

[16] C. Domshlak and T. Joachims. Unstructuring user preferences: Efficient non-parametric utility revelation. In *Proceedings of the Twenty First Annual Conference on Uncertainty in Artificial Intelligence*, Edinburgh, Scotland, 2005.

[17] C. Domshlak and T. Joachims. Efficient and non-parametric reasoning over user preferences. *User Modeling and User-Adapted Interaction*, 17(1-2):41–69, 2007. Special issue on Statistical and Probabilistic Methods for User Modeling.

[18] C. Domshlak, S. Prestwich, F. Rossi, K. B. Venable, and T. Walsh. Hard and soft constraints for reasoning about qualitative conditional preferences. *Journal of Heuristics*, 12(4-5):263–285, 2006.

[19] C. Domshlak, F. Rossi, K. B. Venable, and T. Walsh. Reasoning about soft constraints and conditional preferences: Complexity results and approximation techniques. In *Proceedings of the Eighteenth International Joint Conference on Artificial Intelligence*, pages 215–220, Acapulco, Mexico, 2003.

[20] J. Doyle. Prospects for preferences. *Computational Intelligence (Special Issue on Preferences in AI)*, 20(2):111–136, 2004.

[21] J. Doyle and R. H. Thomason. Background to qualitative decision theory. *AI Magazine*, 20(2):55–68, 1999.

[22] J. Doyle and M. Wellman. Representing preferences as ceteris paribus comparatives. In *Proceedings of the AAAI Spring Symposium on Decision-Theoretic Planning*, pages 69–75, March 1994.

[23] P. C. Fishburn. *The Foundations of Expected Utility*. Reidel, Dordrecht, 1982.

[24] J. Goldsmith, J. Lang, M. Truszczynski, and N. Wilson. The computational complexity of dominance and consistency in CP-nets. In *Proceedings of the Nineteenth International Joint Conference on Artificial Intelligence*, pages 144–149, Edinburgh, Scotland, 2005.

[25] V. Ha and P. Haddawy. A hybrid approach to reasoning with partially elicited preference models. In *Proceedings of the Fifteenth Annual Conference on Uncertainty in Artificial Intelligence*, Stockholm, Sweden, July 1999. Morgan Kaufmann.

[26] P. Haddawy, V. Ha, A. Restificar, B. Geisler, and J. Miyamoto. Preference elicitation via theory refinement. *Journal of Machine Learning Research*, 4:317–337, 2003.

[27] S. O. Hansson. Preference logic. In D. M. Gabbay and F. Guenthner, editors, *Handbook of Philosophical Logic*, volume 4, pages 319–394. Kluwer, 2 edition, 2001.

[28] S. O. Hansson. *The Structure of Values and Norms*. Cambridge University Press, 2001.

[29] R. L. Keeney and H. Raiffa. *Decision with Multiple Objectives: Preferences and Value Tradeoffs*. Wiley, 1976.

[30] G. Kimeldorf and G. Wahba. Some results on tchebycheffian spline functions. *Journal of Mathematical Analysis and Applications*, 33:82–95, 1971.

[31] D. H. Krantz, R. D. Luce, P. Suppes, and A. Tversky. *Foundations of Measurement*. New York: Academic, 1971.

[32] P. La Mura and Y. Shoham. Expected utility networks. In *Proceedings of the Fifteenth Annual Conference on Uncertainty in Artificial Intelligence*, pages 367–373, Stockholm, Sweden, 1999. Morgan Kaufmann Publishers.

[33] J. Lang. Logical preference representation and combinatorial vote. *Annals of Mathematics and Artificial Intelligence*, 42(1-3):37–71, 2004.

[34] G. Linden, S. Hanks, and N. Lesh. Interactive assessment of user preference models: The automated travel assistant. In *Proceedings of the Sixth International Conference on User Modeling*, pages 67–78, 1997.

[35] R. D. Luce and H. Raiffa. *Games and Decisions*. Wiley, 1957.

[36] M. McGeachie and J. Doyle. Utility functions for ceteris paribus preferences. *Computational Intelligence*, 20(2):158–217, 2004. (Special Issue on Preferences in AI).

[37] H. Nguyen and P. Haddawy. The decision-theoretic video advisor. In *Proceedings of the Fifteenth Annual Conference on Uncertainty in Artificial Intelligence*, pages 77–80, Madison, WI, 1999.

[38] F. Rossi, K. B. Venable, and T. Walsh. mCP nets: Representing and reasoning with preferences of multiple agents. In *Proceedings of the Nineteenth National Conference on Artificial Intelligence*, pages 729–734, San Jose, CL, 2004.

[39] Y. Shoham. Conditional utility, utility independence, and utility networks. In *Proceedings of the Thirteenth Annual Conference on Uncertainty in Artificial Intelligence*, pages 429–436, San Francisco, CA, 1997. Morgan Kaufmann Publishers.

[40] Y. Shoham. A symmetric view of probabilities and utilities. In *Proceedings of the Fifteenth International Joint Conference on Artificial Intelligence*, pages 1324–1329, 1997.

[41] V. Vapnik. *Statistical Learning Theory*. Wiley, Chichester, GB, 1998.

[42] G. Wahba. *Spline Models for Observational Data*, volume 59 of *CBMS-NSF Regional Conference Series in Applied Mathematics*. SIAM, 1990.

[43] N. Wilson. Consistency and constrained optimisation for conditional preferences. In *Proceedings of the Sixteenth European Conference on Artificial Intelligence*, pages 888–894, Valencia, 2004.

[44] N. Wilson. Extending CP-nets with stronger conditional preference statements. In *Proceedings of the Nineteenth National Conference on Artificial Intelligence*, pages 735–741, San Jose, CL, 2004.

Learning Preference Models from Data: On the Problem of Label Ranking and Its Variants*

Eyke Hüllermeier[†] and Johannes Fürnkranz[‡]

[†] FB Mathematik und Informatik, Philipps-Universität Marburg, Germany
[‡] FB Informatik, TU Darmstadt, Germany

Abstract The term "preference learning" refers to the application of machine learning methods for inducing preference models from empirical data. In the recent literature, corresponding problems appear in various guises. After a brief overview of the field, this work focuses on a particular learning scenario called label ranking, where the problem is to learn a mapping from instances to rankings over a finite number of labels. Our approach for learning such a ranking function, called ranking by pairwise comparison (RPC), first induces a binary preference relation from suitable training data, using a natural extension of pairwise classification. A ranking is then derived from this relation by means of a ranking procedure. This paper elaborates on a key advantage of such an approach, namely the fact that our learner can be adapted to different loss functions by using different ranking procedures on the same underlying order relations. In particular, the Spearman rank correlation is minimized by using a simple weighted voting procedure. Moreover, we discuss a loss function suitable for settings where candidate labels must be tested successively until a target label is found. In this context, we propose the idea of "empirical conditioning" of class probabilities. A related ranking procedure, called "ranking through iterated choice", is investigated experimentally.

1 Introduction

Recently, the topic of *preferences* has attracted considerable attention in Artificial Intelligence (AI) research, notably in fields such as agents, non-monotonic reasoning, constraint satisfaction, planning, and qualitative decision theory Doyle (2004). Preferences provide a means for specifying desires in a declarative way, which is a point of critical importance for AI.

---

*Extended version of the conference paper Hüllermeier and Fürnkranz (2005).

In fact, consider AI's paradigm of a rationally acting (decision-theoretic) agent: The behavior of such an agent has to be driven by an underlying preference model, and an agent recommending decisions or acting on behalf of a user should clearly reflect that user's preferences. Therefore, the formal modeling of preferences can be considered an essential aspect of autonomous agent design.

Drawing on past research on knowledge representation and reasoning, AI offers qualitative and symbolic methods for treating preferences that can reasonably complement traditional approaches that have been developed for quite a while in fields such as economic decision theory. Needless to say, however, the acquisition of preferences is not always an easy task. Therefore, not only are modeling languages and representation formalisms needed, but also methods for the automatic learning, discovery and adaptation of preferences. For example, computerized methods for discovering the preferences of individuals are useful in e-commerce and various other fields where an increasing trend toward personalization of products and services can be recognized.

It is hence hardly surprising that methods for learning and predicting preferences in an automatic way are among the very recent research topics in disciplines such as machine learning, knowledge discovery, and recommender systems. In these fields, several approaches have been subsumed under the terms of ranking and preference learning. In Section 2, we distinguish between *object ranking problems*, where the task is to order a set of objects according to a preference function, and *label ranking problems*, where the task is to assign a permutation of a fixed set of class labels to a given object. We observe that there are two principal approaches to address these preference learning tasks. One possibility is to try to learn a *utility function* which in turn induces the sought ranking. The underlying assumption is that the observed preferences are based on a hidden numerical preference model which produces a numerical score for each object or label. The second approach is to model a *binary preference relation* that, instead of evaluating *single* objects, allows for comparing *pairs* of alternatives. The assumption here is that a total order of all alternatives can be derived from pairwise preferences between these alternatives. In a learning context, this approach is complicated by the fact that preferences learned from data are not necessarily correct and, hence, may be inconsistent (e.g., violate transitivity).

Among the four problem types that can be obtained by applying the two modeling approaches to the two learning tasks, this paper will focus of the fourth option, which appears to be the most recent one considered in the literature. More specifically, the learning scenario that we will consider in this paper consists of a collection of training examples which are associated with a finite set of decision alternatives. Following the common notation of supervised learning, we shall refer to the latter as *labels*. However, contrary to standard classification, a training example is not assigned a single label, but a set of *pairwise preferences* between labels (which neither has to be complete nor entirely consistent), each one expressing that one label is preferred to another. The goal is to use pairwise preferences from training examples for predicting a total order, a *ranking*, of all possible labels for a new training example. The *ranking by pairwise comparison* (RPC) algorithm, to be introduced and investigated in this paper, works in two phases. First, pairwise preferences are learned from suitable training data, using a natural extension of so-called *pairwise classification*. Then, a ranking is derived from a set of such preferences by means of a *ranking procedure*.

The goal of this paper is to show that, by using suitable ranking functions, our approach can easily be customized to different performance tasks, that is, to different loss functions for rankings. In fact, the need for a ranking of class labels may arise in different learning scenarios. In this work, we are particularly interested in two types of practically motivated learning problems, one in which the complete ranking is relevant and one in which the predicted ranking serves the purpose of reducing the search effort for finding the single target label.

The remainder of the paper is organized as follows: We start with an overview of preference learning and a systematic presentation of ranking problems in Section 2. Subsequently, our pairwise approach to label ranking will be presented in Section 3. In Section 4, the aforementioned variants of the label ranking problem are discussed and compared in more detail. The ranking procedures suitable for the two types of problems are then discussed in Sections 5 and 6, respectively. Experimental results are presented in Section 7. The paper ends with some concluding remarks in Section 8.

2   Preference Learning

In this section, we will motivate preference learning as a theoretically interesting and practically relevant subfield of machine learning. Moreover, we will give a systematic overview of existing approaches in this field.

When talking about preference learning, two questions immediately arise: First, whose preferences are to be learned? And second, in which way are the preferences formalized, i.e., what kind of model is to be inferred?

Regarding the first question, one can basically distinguish between learning the preferences of a *single* individual and learning those of a *group* of individuals (or, more generally, agents or instances). Both types of problems are relevant. When attempting to personalize a web search engine, for example, one is preliminary interested in the preferences of a particular user. On the other hand, in collaborative filtering one tries to predict the preferences of any client on the basis of the preferences of other clients. Note that this presupposes a connection between individuals which allows one to model dependencies. In fact, learning the preferences of a group of individuals only makes sense if these individuals' preferences are not completely independent of each other. (Otherwise, one actually faces multiple instances of the first type of problem, namely learning the preferences of each of the individuals separately.) In collaborative filtering, such a connection is established on the basis of a client's *preference profile*, which allows one to distinguish similar clients from dissimilar ones.

In the following, we shall more formally distinguish two types of learning problems, namely *learning from object preferences* and *learning from label preferences*. The corresponding scenarios are roughly in agreement with the above distinction between learning the preferences of a single individual and those of a group of individuals: When learning object preferences, only a single preference relation is considered. Here, the focus is on the objects, which are characterized through attributes. When learning label preferences, one tries to induce many preference relations simultaneously. Here, the individuals are represented through attributes, while the objects are considered as unrelated items. A more formal definition of these learning scenarios will be given in Sections 2.1 and 2.2 below.

Regarding the second question, there are two approaches for dealing with preferences that prevail the literature on choice and decision theory. These are based, respectively, on the two perhaps most natural ways for expressing preferences, namely by *evaluating* individual alternatives, or by *comparing* (pairs of) competing alternatives. In the latter approach, binary relations are employed in order to express (comparative) preferences in a qualitative way. The basic relation, often denoted $\succeq$, is interpreted as a weak preference, i.e., $a \succeq b$ means that "alternative a is at least as good as alternative b".

The second approach is more inclined to numerical representations of preferences via *utility* or *value functions*. A utility function $f(\cdot)$ assigns an abstract utility degree to each alternative under consideration and thus induces a preference relation $\succeq$ by virtue of $a \succeq b \Leftrightarrow f(a) \geq f(b)$. Obviously, the numerical approach provides stronger information than the relational one but is also more restrictive and more demanding from a modeling point of view. Advantages and disadvantages of these two approaches, from a learning point of view, will be discussed in Sections 2.3 and 2.4.

The two answers to the above two questions, respectively, give rise to

	modeling utility functions	modeling pairwise preferences
object ranking	comparison training Tesauro (1989)	learning to order things Cohen et al. (1998)
label ranking	constraint classification Har-Peled et al. (2002)	**this work** Fürnkranz and Hüllermeier (2003)

Table 1. Four different approaches to learning from preference information together with representative references.

the four combinations shown in Table 1. Despite their differences in the underlying models, all these approaches assume the same type of training information. This information is of the relational type, that is, a single piece of information specifies that one entity (object or label) is preferred to some other entity.

Before discussing these four settings in more detail, let us note that the term "preference" should not be taken literally and instead always be interpreted in a wide sense. Thus, $a \succ b$ can indeed mean that alternative a is more liked by a person than b, but also, for example, that a is an algorithm that outperforms b on a certain problem, that a is an event which is more probable than b, or that a is a student finishing her studies before b.

2.1 Learning from Object Preferences

The most frequently studied problem in learning from preferences is to induce a *ranking function* $r(\cdot)$ that is able to order any subset $\mathcal{O}$ of an underlying class $\mathcal{X}$ of objects. That is, $r(\cdot)$ assumes as input a subset $\mathcal{O} = \{x_1 \ldots x_n\} \subseteq \mathcal{X}$ of objects and returns as output a permutation τ of $\{1 \ldots n\}$. The interpretation of this permutation is that object x_i is preferred to x_j whenever $\tau(i) < \tau(j)$. The objects themselves are typically characterized by a finite set of features as in conventional attribute-value learning. The training data consists of a set of exemplary pairwise preferences. This scenario is also known as "learning to order things" Cohen et al. (1998).

As an example consider the problem of learning to rank query results of a search engine Joachims (2002); Radlinski and Joachims (2005). The training information is provided implicitly by the user who clicks on some of the links in the query result and not on others. This information can be turned into binary preferences by assuming that the selected pages are preferred over nearby pages that are not clicked on Joachims et al. (2005).

2.2 Learning from Label Preferences

In this learning scenario, the problem is to predict, for any instance x (e.g., a person) from an instance space $\mathcal{X}$, a preference relation $\succ_x \subseteq \mathcal{L} \times \mathcal{L}$ among a finite set $\mathcal{L} = \{\lambda_1 \ldots \lambda_m\}$ of labels or alternatives, where $\lambda_i \succ_x \lambda_j$ means that, for the input x, label λ_i is preferred to label λ_j. More specifically, as we are especially interested in the case where $\succ_x$ is a total strict order,[1] the problem is to predict a permutation of $\mathcal{L}$.

The training information consists of a set of instances for which (partial) knowledge about the associated preference relation is available. More precisely, each training instance x is assumed to be associated with only a *subset* of all pairwise preferences which, moreover, can be conflicting. Therefore, this setting covers the typical situation in practice where only incomplete preference information is known. In particular, a ranking model can be learned from standard *classification* data in which each instance is associated with only a single label λ^*: Considering this label as the maximally preferred one gives rise to the set of $(m-1)$ preferences $\{\lambda^* \succ \lambda \mid \lambda \in \mathcal{L}\}$.

2.3 Learning Utility Functions

As mentioned above, one natural way to represent preferences is to evaluate individual alternatives by means of a (real-valued) utility function. In the object preferences scenario, such a function is a mapping $f : \mathcal{X} \to \mathbb{R}$ that assigns a utility degree $f(x)$ to each object x and, hence, induces a total order on $\mathcal{X}$. In the label preferences scenario, a utility function $f_i : \mathcal{X} \to \mathbb{R}$ is needed for each of the labels λ_i, $i = 1 \ldots m$. Here, $f_i(x)$ is the utility assigned to alternative λ_i by instance x. To obtain a ranking for x, the alternatives are ordered according to these utility scores, i.e., $\lambda_i \succeq_x \lambda_j \Leftrightarrow f_i(x) \geq f_j(x)$.

If the training data would offer the utility scores directly, preference learning would reduce to a regression problem (up to a monotonic transformation of the utility values). This information can rarely be assumed, however. Instead, only constraints derived from comparative preference information of the form "This object (or label) should have a higher utility score than that object (or label)" are usually given. Thus, the challenge for

---

[1] Needless to say, these are strong assumption that will often not be satisfied in practice; we shall come back to this issue in the concluding remarks in Section 8.

the learner is to find a function (from an underlying hypothesis space) that is as much as possible in agreement with all constraints.

For object ranking approaches, this idea has first been formalized in Tesauro (1989) under the name *comparison training*. Here, the author proposed a symmetric neural-network architecture that can be trained with representations of two states and a training signal that indicates which of the two states is preferable. The elegance of this approach comes from the property that one can replace the two symmetric components of the network with a single network, which can subsequently provide a real-valued evaluation of single states. Similarly, training data in the form of pairwise comparisons of objects is used in Haddawy et al. (2003) to train a neural network. The network learns a function that takes two objects as input and outputs either 0 or 1, depending on whether or not the first object is preferred to the second one. The structure of the network is not arbitrary, but is chosen in a way that allows one to combine domain knowledge about partial preferences between the feature-based state descriptions of the objects. This work is based on an earlier approach proposed in Wang (1994).

Similar ideas have also been investigated for training other types of classifiers, in particular support vector machines. We already mentioned Joachims (2002), where "click-through data" was analyzed in order to rank documents retrieved by a search engine according to their relevance. Earlier, an algorithm for training SVMs from pairwise preference relations between objects was proposed in Herbrich et al. (1998).

For the case of label ranking, a corresponding method for learning the functions $f_i(\cdot)$, $i = 1 \ldots m$, from training data has been proposed in the framework of *constraint classification*, introduced as an extension of standard classification in Har-Peled et al. (2002, 2003). The learning method proposed in this work constructs two training examples for each preference $\lambda_i \succ \lambda_j$, where the original N-dimensional training examples are mapped into a $(m \times N)$-dimensional space. The positive example copies the original training vector into the components $((i - 1)N + 1) \ldots iN$ and its negation into the components $((j - 1)N + 1) \ldots jN$ of a vector in the new space. The remaining entries are filled with 0, and the negative example has the same elements with reversed signs. In this $(m \times N)$-dimensional space, the learner tries to find a separating hyperplane. For classifying a new example x_0, the labels are ordered according to the response resulting from multiplying x_0 with the i-th N-element section of the hyperplane vector.

2.4   Learning Preference Relations

It has already been noted that *observed* preferences are usually of the relational type, since utility scores are difficult to elicit. For example, it is very hard to ensure a consistent scale even if all utility evaluations are performed by the same user, let alone if utility scores are elicited from different users which may not have a uniform scale of their scores Cohen et al. (1998). In Pyle (1999), the author claims that it is easier for a human to determine an order between several items if one makes pairwise comparisons between the individual items and then adds up the wins for each item, instead of trying to order the items right away.

For the *learning* of preferences, one may bring up a similar argument. It will typically be easier to learn a separate theory for each individual preference that compares two objects or two labels and determines which one is better. This technique essentially reduces the problem of learning preferences to a binary classification task. The learner is trained to predict for each pair of objects/labls which one is preferable. In Pyle (1999), a very similar technique called *pairwise ranking* is proposed in order to facilitate human decision-making in ranking problems. Of course, every learned utility function that assigns a score to a set of labels $\mathcal{L}$ induces such a binary preference relation on these labels.

Note that the preference relation induced by a utility function is necessarily a total order, whereas the converse is not true: not every learned binary preference relation induces a total order that can be represented by a utility function. The point is that the learned preference relation does not necessarily have the typical properties of order relations, for example, it is not necessarily transitive. In fact, to obtain a ranking (total strict order) of the items, one has to apply a *ranking procedure* that takes a binary preference relation as input and produces a ranking as output. The simplest approach is *ranking by scoring*: A score, such as the number of pairwise comparisons in which an item is preferred, is derived from the binary relation, and the items are then ordered according to their scores. For alternative (more complex) combination schemes see e.g. Wu et al. (2004); Hüllermeier and Fürnkranz (2004).

For object ranking problems, the pairwise approach has been pursued in Cohen et al. (1998). This paper proposes to solve object ranking problems by learning a binary preference predicate $Q(x, x')$, which predicts whether x is preferred to x' or vice versa. A final ordering is found in a second phase by deriving a ranking that is maximally consistent with these predictions (in the sense of violating as few as possible binary preferences).

For label ranking problems, the pairwise approach has been introduced by the authors in Fürnkranz and Hüllermeier (2003). The key idea, that we shall describe in more detail below, is to learn, for each pair of labels (λ_i, λ_j), a binary predicate $\mathcal{M}_{ij}(x)$ that predicts whether $\lambda_i \succ_x \lambda_j$ or $\lambda_j \succ_x \lambda_i$ for an input x. In order to rank the labels for a new object, predictions for all pairwise label preferences are obtained and a ranking that is maximally consistent with these preferences is derived. This approach is a natural extension of pairwise classification, i.e., the idea to tackle a multi-class classification problem by learning separate theories for each pair of classes.

3   Ranking by Pairwise Comparison

As mentioned above, the idea of pairwise learning is well-known in the context of classification Fürnkranz (2002), where it allows one to transform a multi-class classification problem, i.e., a problem involving $m > 2$ classes $\mathcal{L} = \{\lambda_1 \ldots \lambda_m\}$, into a number of *binary* problems. To this end, a separate model (base learner) $\mathcal{M}_{ij}$ is trained for each *pair* of labels $(\lambda_i, \lambda_j) \in \mathcal{L}$, $1 \leq i < j \leq m$; thus, a total number of $m(m-1)/2$ models is needed. $\mathcal{M}_{ij}$ is intended to separate the objects with label λ_i from those having label λ_j.

At classification time, a query x is submitted to all learners, and each prediction $\mathcal{M}_{ij}(x)$ is interpreted as a vote for a label. If classifier $\mathcal{M}_{ij}$ predicts λ_i, this is counted as a vote for λ_i. Conversely, the prediction λ_j would be considered as a vote for λ_j. The label with the highest number of votes is then proposed as a prediction.

The above procedure can be extended to the case of preference learning in a natural way Fürnkranz and Hüllermeier (2003). A preference information of the form $\lambda_i \succ_x \lambda_j$ is turned into a training example (x, y) for the learner $\mathcal{M}_{ab}$, where $a = \min(i, j)$ and $b = \max(i, j)$. Moreover, $y = 1$ if $i < j$ and $y = 0$ otherwise. Thus, $\mathcal{M}_{ab}$ is intended to learn the mapping that outputs 1 if $\lambda_a \succ_x \lambda_b$ and 0 if $\lambda_b \succ_x \lambda_a$:

$$x \mapsto \begin{cases} 1 & \text{if} \quad \lambda_a \succ_x \lambda_b \\ 0 & \text{if} \quad \lambda_b \succ_x \lambda_a \end{cases} \tag{1}$$

The mapping (1) can be realized by any binary classifier. Alternatively, one might of course employ a classifier that maps into the unit interval $[0, 1]$ instead of $\{0, 1\}$. The output of such a "soft" binary classifier can usually be interpreted as a probability or, more generally, a kind of confidence in the classification. Thus, the closer the output of $\mathcal{M}_{ab}$ to 1, the stronger the preference $\lambda_a \succ_x \lambda_b$ is supported.

A preference learner composed of an ensemble of soft binary classifiers (which can be constructed on the basis of training data in the form of instances with associated partial preferences) assigns a *valued preference relation* $\mathcal{R}_x$ to any (query) instance $x \in \mathcal{X}$:

$$\mathcal{R}_x(\lambda_i, \lambda_j) = \left\{ \begin{array}{ll} \mathcal{M}_{ij}(x) & \text{if} \quad i < j \\ 1 - \mathcal{M}_{ij}(x) & \text{if} \quad i > j \end{array} \right. \tag{2}$$

for all $\lambda_i \neq \lambda_j \in \mathcal{L}$. Given a preference relation of that kind, the next question is how to derive an associated ranking τ_x. This question is non-trivial, since a relation $\mathcal{R}_x$ does not always suggest a unique ranking in an unequivocal way. In fact, the problem of inducing a ranking from a (valued) preference relation has received a lot of attention in several research fields, e.g., in fuzzy preference modeling and (multi-attribute) decision making Fodor and Roubens (1994). Besides, in the context of our application, it turned out that the *ranking procedure* used to transform a relation $\mathcal{R}_x$ into a ranking τ_x is closely related to the definition of the quality of a prediction and, hence, to the intended purpose of a ranking. In other words, risk minimization with respect to different loss functions might call for different ranking procedures.

The approach introduced in this section, referred to as *ranking by pairwise comparison* (RPC), consists of two steps and can be summarized as follows:

- First, a valued preference relation (2) is derived by training an ensemble of (soft) binary classifiers, and then

- a ranking of the labels $\mathcal{L}$ is obtained by means of a suitable ranking procedure.

4 Ranking Error versus Position Error

In Section 3, we introduced the problem of predicting a ranking of class labels in a formal way, but without discussing the semantics of a predicted ranking. In fact, one should realize that a ranking can serve different purposes. Needless to say, this point is of major importance for the evaluation of a predicted ranking.

In this paper, we are especially interested in two types of practically motivated performance tasks. In the first setting, which is probably the most obvious one, the *complete ranking* is relevant, i.e., the positions assigned to all of the labels. As an example, consider the problem of learning to predict the best order in which to supply a certain set of stores (route of a truck), depending on external conditions like traffic, weather, purchase order quantities, etc.

In case the complete ranking is relevant, the quality of a prediction should be quantified in terms of a distance measure between the predicted and the true ranking. We shall refer to any deviation of the predicted ranking from the true one as a *ranking error*.

To motivate the second setting, consider a fault detection problem which consists of identifying the cause for the malfunctioning of a technical system. If it turned out that a predicted cause is not correct, an alternative candidate must be tried. A ranking then suggests a simple (trial and error) search process, which successively tests the candidates, one by one, until the correct cause is found Alonso et al. (2004). In this scenario, where labels correspond to causes, the existence of a single target label (instead of a target ranking) is assumed. Hence, an obvious measure of the quality of a predicted ranking is the number of futile trials made before that label is found. A deviation of the predicted target label's position from the top-rank will subsequently be called a *position error*.

The main difference between the two types of error is that an evaluation of a full ranking (ranking error) attends to all positions. For example, if the two highest ranks of the true ranking are swapped in the predicted ranking, this is as bad as the swapping the two lowest ranks.

Note that the position error is closely related to the conventional (classification) error, i.e., the incorrect prediction of the top-label. In both cases, we are eventually concerned with predictions for the top-rank. In our setting, however, we not only try to maximize the number of correct predictions. Instead, in the case of a misclassification, we also look at the position of the target label. The higher this position, the better the prediction. In other words, we differentiate between "bad" predictions in a more subtle way.

5 Minimizing the Ranking Error

The quality of a model $\mathcal{M}$, induced by a learning algorithm from a set of data $\mathcal{D}$, is commonly expressed in terms of its *expected loss* or *risk*

$$\mathbb{E}\left(D(y, \mathcal{M}(x))\right), \tag{3}$$

where $\mathcal{M}(x)$ denotes the prediction made by the learning algorithm for the instance x, and y is the true outcome. The expectation $\mathbb{E}$ is taken over $\mathcal{X} \times \mathcal{Y}$, where $\mathcal{Y}$ is the output space (e.g., the set $\mathcal{L}$ of classes in classification).[2] $D(\cdot)$ is a (real-valued) loss or distance function $\mathcal{Y} \times \mathcal{Y} \to \mathbb{R}$.

In the context of label ranking, $\mathcal{Y}$ can formally be defined by the class $\mathcal{S}_m$ of all permutations of $\{1 \ldots m\}$. A frequently used distance measure on

---

[2] The existence of a probability measure over $\mathcal{X} \times \mathcal{Y}$ must of course be assumed.

this class is the sum of squared rank distances:

$$D(\tau', \tau) \stackrel{\text{df}}{=} \sum_{i=1}^{m} \left(\tau'(i) - \tau(i) \right)^2 \qquad (4)$$

for all $\tau, \tau' \in \mathcal{S}_m$. The measure (4) is closely related to the well-known *Spearman rank correlation*, a similarity measure which is obtained by the linear transformation

$$1 - \frac{6D(\tau, \tau')}{m(m^2 - 1)} \in [-1, 1].$$

Given a distance measure $D(\cdot)$ for rankings, the risk minimizing prediction for an instance x is

$$\hat{\tau}_x = \arg \min_{\tau \in \mathcal{S}_k} \sum_{\tau \in \mathcal{S}_m} D(\tau, \tau') \cdot \mathbb{P}(\tau' \,|\, x), \qquad (5)$$

where $\mathbb{P}(\tau \,|\, x)$ is the conditional probability of a ranking (permutation) given x.

RPC can yield a risk minimizing prediction for the loss function (4). To this end, the predictions of the binary classifiers have to be combined by weighted voting, i.e., the alternatives λ_i are evaluated by means of the sum of weighted votes

$$S(\lambda_i) = \sum_{\lambda_j \neq \lambda_i} \mathcal{R}_x(\lambda_i, \lambda_j) \qquad (6)$$

and ranked according to these evaluations:

$$\lambda_{\tau_x(1)} \succ_x \lambda_{\tau_x(2)} \succ_x \ldots \succ_x \lambda_{\tau_x(m)} \qquad (7)$$

with τ_x satisfying $S(\lambda_{\tau_x(i)}) \geq S(\lambda_{\tau_x(i+1)})$, $i = 1 \ldots m-1$.[3] This is a particular type of "ranking by scoring" strategy, with the scoring function given by (6).

Formally, we can show the following result, which provides a theoretical justification for the voting procedure (6). The proof of this theorem can be found in Hüllermeier and Fürnkranz (2005).

Theorem 5.1. *Using the "ranking by scoring" procedure outlined above, RPC is a risk minimizer with respect to (4) as a loss function. More precisely, given that*

$$\mathcal{M}_{ij}(x) = \mathbb{P}(\lambda_i \succ_x \lambda_j) = \sum_{\tau \,:\, \tau(j) < \tau(i)} \mathbb{P}(\tau \,|\, x),$$

---

[3]Ties can be broken arbitrarily.

the expected distance ($p(\cdot)$ is a probability distribution on $\mathcal{S}_m$)

$$E(\tau') = \sum_{\tau \in \mathcal{S}_m} p(\tau) \cdot D(\tau', \tau) = \sum_{\tau \in \mathcal{S}_m} p(\tau) \sum_{i=1}^{m} (\tau'(i) - \tau(i))^2$$

becomes minimal by choosing τ' such that $\tau'(i) \leq \tau'(j)$ whenever $S(\lambda_i) \geq S(\lambda_j)$, where $S(\lambda_i)$ is given by (6).

6 Minimizing the Position Error

Despite the fact that (4) is a reasonable loss function for rankings, it is not always appropriate. In particular, it assumes that the *complete* ranking is relevant for the quality of a prediction, which is not the case in connection with the fault detection scenario outlined in Section 4. Here, only the prefix of a ranking τ_x is considered, up to the position of the target label λ_x, while the rest of the prediction is of no importance (since the search procedure stops if λ_x has been found). In this case, the loss function only depends on the rank of λ_x.

More specifically, we define the *position error* as $\tau_x^{-1}(\lambda_x)$, i.e., by the position of the target label λ_x in the ranking τ_x. To compare the quality of rankings for problems involving different numbers of labels, it is useful to employ a *normalized position error* which is defined as

$$\frac{\tau_x^{-1}(\lambda_x) - 1}{m - 1} \in \{0, 1/(m-1), \ldots, 1\}. \tag{8}$$

What kind of ranking procedure should be used in order to minimize the risk of a predicted ranking with respect to the position error as a loss function? Intuitively, the candidate labels λ should now be ordered according to their probability $\mathbb{P}(\lambda = \lambda_x)$ of being the target label. Especially, the top-rank (first position) should be given to the label $\lambda_{\top}$ for which this probability is maximal. Regarding the second rank, recall the fault detection metaphor, where the second hypothesis for the cause of the fault is only tested in case the first one turned out to be wrong. In this setting, the second rank should not simply be given to the label with the second highest probability according to the measure $\mathbb{P}_1(\cdot) = \mathbb{P}(\cdot)$. Instead, it must be assigned to the label that maximizes the *conditional* probability $\mathbb{P}_2(\cdot) = \mathbb{P}(\cdot \mid \lambda_x \neq \lambda_{\top})$, i.e., the probability of being the target label *given that the first proposal was incorrect*.

At first sight, passing from $\mathbb{P}_1(\cdot)$ to $\mathbb{P}_2(\cdot)$ might appear meaningless from a ranking point of view, since standard probabilistic conditioning (dividing all probabilities by $1 - \mathbb{P}(\lambda_\top)$ and setting $\mathbb{P}(\lambda_\top) = 0$) does not change the order of the remaining labels. One should realize, however, that standard conditioning is not an incontestable updating procedure in our context, simply because $\mathbb{P}_1(\cdot)$ is not a "true" measure over the class labels. Rather, it is only an estimated measure coming from a learning algorithm. Thus, it seems sensible to perform "conditioning" not on the measure itself, but rather on the learner that produced the measure. By this we mean retraining the learner on the original data without the $\lambda_\top$-examples, something that could be paraphrased as *empirical conditioning*. To emphasize that this type of conditioning depends on the data $\mathcal{D}$ and the model assumptions (hypothesis space) $\mathcal{H}$ and, moreover, that it concerns an *estimated* ("hat") probability, the conditional measure $\mathbb{P}_2(\cdot)$ could be written more explicitly as

$$\mathbb{P}_2(\cdot) = \widehat{\mathbb{P}}(\cdot \mid \lambda_x \neq \lambda_\top, \mathcal{D}, \mathcal{M}).$$

To motivate the idea of empirical conditioning, suppose that the estimated probabilities come from a classification tree. Of course, the original tree trained with the complete data will be highly influenced by $\lambda_\top$-examples, and the probabilities assigned by that tree to the alternatives $\lambda \neq \lambda_\top$ might be inaccurate. Retraining a classification tree on a reduced set of data might then lead to more accurate probabilities for the remaining labels, especially since the multi-class problem to be solved has now become simpler (as it involves fewer classes).

A problem of the above "ranking through iterated choice" procedure, that is, the successive selection of alternatives by estimating top-labels from (conditional) probability measures $\mathbb{P}_1(\cdot), \mathbb{P}_2(\cdot) \ldots \mathbb{P}_m(\cdot)$, concerns its computational complexity. In fact, realizing empirical conditioning by retraining a standard multi-class classifier comes down to training such a classifier for (potentially) each subset of the label set $\mathcal{L}$. As will be shown in the following, empirical conditioning can be implemented much more efficiently by our pairwise approach.

6.1 Implementing "ranking through iterated choice" by RPC

What kind of aggregation procedure is suitable for deriving an estimated probability distribution from pairwise classifications resp. valued preferences $\mathcal{R}(\lambda_i, \lambda_j)$? Let E_i denote the event that $\lambda_i = \lambda_x$, i.e., that λ_i is the target label, and let $E_{ij} = E_i \vee E_j$ (either λ_i or λ_j is the target). Then,

$$(m-1)\,\mathbb{P}(E_i) = \sum_{j \neq i} \mathbb{P}(E_i) = \sum_{j \neq i} \mathbb{P}(E_i \mid E_{ij})\mathbb{P}(E_{ij}), \qquad (9)$$

where m is the number of labels. Considering the (pairwise) estimates $\mathcal{R}(\lambda_i, \lambda_j)$ as conditional probabilities $\mathbb{P}(E_i \mid E_{ij})$, we obtain a system of linear equations for the (unconditional) probabilities $\mathbb{P}(E_i)$:

$$\mathbb{P}(E_i) = \frac{1}{m-1} \sum_{j \neq i} \mathcal{R}(\lambda_i, \lambda_j) \mathbb{P}(E_{ij})$$

$$= \frac{1}{m-1} \sum_{j \neq i} \mathcal{R}(\lambda_i, \lambda_j)(\mathbb{P}(E_i) + \mathbb{P}(E_j)) \tag{10}$$

In conjunction with the constraint $\sum_{i=1}^{m} \mathbb{P}(E_i) = 1$, this system has a unique solution provided that $\mathcal{R}(\lambda_i, \lambda_j) > 0$ for all $1 \leq i, j \leq m$ Wu et al. (2004).

Based on this result, the "ranking through iterated choice" procedure suggested above can be realized as follows: First, the system of linear equations (10) is solved and the label λ_i with maximal probability $\mathbb{P}(E_i)$ is chosen as the top-label λ_T. This label is then removed, i.e., the corresponding row and column of the relation $\mathcal{R}$ is deleted. To find the second best label, the same procedure is then applied to the reduced relation, i.e., by solving a system of $m-1$ linear equations. This process is iterated until a full ranking has been constructed.

Lemma 6.1. *In each iteration of the above "ranking through iterated choice" procedure, the correct conditional probabilities are derived.*

Proof. Without loss of generality, assume that λ_m has obtained the highest rank in the first iteration. The information that this label is incorrect, $\lambda_m \neq \lambda_x$, is equivalent to $\mathbb{P}(E_m) = 0$, $\mathbb{P}(E_m \mid E_{jm}) = 0$, and $\mathbb{P}(E_j \mid E_{jm}) = 1$ for all $j \neq m$. Incorporating these probabilities in (10) yields, for all $i < m$,

$$(m-1)\mathbb{P}(E_i) = \sum_{j=1...m, j \neq i} \mathbb{P}(E_i \mid E_{ij})\mathbb{P}(E_{ij})$$

$$= \sum_{j=1..m-1, j \neq i} \mathbb{P}(E_i \mid E_{ij})\mathbb{P}(E_{ij}) + 1\mathbb{P}(E_{im})$$

and as $\mathbb{P}(E_{im}) = \mathbb{P}(E_i) + \mathbb{P}(E_m) = \mathbb{P}(E_i)$,

$$(m-2)\mathbb{P}(E_i) = \sum_{j=1..m-1, j \neq i} \mathbb{P}(E_i \mid E_{ij})\mathbb{P}(E_{ij}).$$

Obviously, the last equation is equivalent to (10) for a system with $m-1$ labels, namely the system obtained by removing the m-th row and column of $\mathcal{R}$. □ □

As can be seen, the pairwise approach is particularly well-suited for the "ranking through iterated choice" procedure, as it allows for an easy incorporation of the information coming from futile trials. One just has to solve the system of linear equations (10) once more, with some of the pairwise probabilities set to 0 resp. 1 (or, equivalently, solve a smaller system of equations). No retraining of any classifier is required!

Theorem 6.2. *By ranking the alternative labels according to their (conditional) probabilities of being the top-label, RPC becomes a risk minimizer with respect to the position error (8) as a loss function. That is, the expected loss*

$$E(\tau) = \frac{1}{m-1} \sum_{i=1}^{m} (i-1) \cdot \mathbb{P}\left(\lambda_{\tau(i)} = \lambda_x\right)$$

becomes minimal for the ranking predicted by RPC.

Proof. This result follows almost by definition. In fact, note that we have

$$E(\tau) \propto \sum_{i=1}^{m} \mathbb{P}\left(\lambda_x \notin \{\lambda_{\tau(1)} \ldots \lambda_{\tau(i)}\}\right),$$

and that, for each position i, the probability to excess this position when searching for the target λ_x is obviously minimized when ordering the labels according to their (conditional) probabilities. □   □

7   Empirical Results

Regarding the ranking error, our RPC approach has already been investigated empirically in Fürnkranz and Hüllermeier (2003); Hüllermeier and Fürnkranz (2004). In this section, we shall therefore focus on the second type of loss function discussed in the paper, the position error, and present first results for the idea of empirical conditioning and the related "ranking through iterated choice" procedure.

Suppose any multi-class classifier, capable of producing probability estimates for the classes under consideration, to be given as a base learner. Depending on whether or not the multi-class problem is decomposed into a number of pairwise problems (to which the same base learner is of course also applicable), and whether or not the learning procedure is iterated, the following four learning strategies are conceivable.

- **Pairwise, iterated (PI):** This is the "ranking through iterated choice" procedure as outlined in Section 6.1.

Table 2. Win/Loss statistics for each pair of methods, using C4.5 (top) and Ripper (bottom) as base learners.

	PnI	PI	MnI	MI
PnI	—	9/6	13/3	9/8
PI		—	13/4	8/7
MnI			—	3/13
MI				—
PnI	—	9/4	13/3	12/3
PI		—	12/3	13/2
MnI			—	3/13
MI				—

- **Pairwise, non-iterated (PnI):** The original problem is decomposed into a number of pairwise problems, but the learning procedure is not iterated, i.e., the probabilities (10) are not recomputed. Instead, these probabilities are only computed *once* and the class labels are ranked according these probabilities.

- **Multi-class, iterated (MI):** The "ranking through iterated choice" procedure is implemented using the base learner in its original (multi-class) version.

- **Multi-class, non-iterated (MnI):** A ranking is produced by applying the base learner to the complete data set and ordering the class labels according to their probabilities.

As an aside, let us note that, in connection with selecting the top-label or ordering the labels according to their probability, ties are always broken through coin flipping.

As mentioned before, the strategy MI is tremendously inefficient from a computational point of view, since $m - 1$ multi-class classifiers have to be trained (and applied to the query case) in order to produce a single ranking of m labels: The first classifier is trained on the complete data, the second on the reduced data which does not include the examples of the first top-label, and so forth. Although this approach is hardly practical for real applications, we include it in our experiments as our main interest is to compare iterated with non-iterated learning. Our main goal is to find out whether the idea of iterating the learning procedure is beneficial or not.

Table 3 show the results that we obtained for a number of well-known

Table 3. Position error for conventional pairwise classification (PnI), iterated pairwise classification (PI), conventional multi-class classificiation (MnI) and iterated multi-class classification (MI) using C4.5 (left) and Ripper (right) as the base learner (better performance indicated in bold).

C4.5					
data	m	PnI	PI	MnI	MI
abalone	28	**3,492**	3,552	4,650	**4,004**
anneal	6	**1,023**	1,024	**1,023**	1,028
audiology	24	**2,668**	3,190	2,310	**2,186**
autos	7	**1,498**	1,502	**1,273**	1,293
balance-scale	3	1,357	**1,294**	1,397	**1,326**
glass	7	1,481	**1,449**	1,547	**1,486**
heart-c	5	1,224	1,224	1,231	1,231
heart-h	5	1,197	1,197	1,197	1,197
hypothyroid	4	**1,006**	1,008	**1,005**	1,007
iris	3	1,073	**1,053**	1,073	**1,053**
lymph	4	1,236	1,236	1,270	**1,250**
primary-tumor	22	**3,516**	3,531	4,254	**3,764**
segment	7	1,045	**1,042**	1,135	**1,042**
soybean	19	**1,183**	1,085	1,205	**1,113**
vehicle	4	1,327	**1,313**	1,411	**1,309**
vowel	11	**1,285**	1,309	2,314	**1,274**
zoo	7	1,178	**1,149**	1,238	**1,099**
letter	26	**1,170**	1,202	2,407	**1,279**

Ripper					
data	m	PnI	PI	MnI	MI
abalone	28	**3,466**	3,500	4,667	**4,358**
anneal	6	1,020	**1,017**	1,031	**1,028**
audiology	24	**2,863**	3,270	**2,394**	3,274
autos	7	**1,434**	1,449	1,449	**1,376**
balance-scale	3	1,256	1,256	1,406	**1,325**
glass	7	**1,444**	1,463	1,612	**1,486**
heart-c	5	1,218	1,218	1,218	1,218
heart-h	5	1,187	1,187	1,187	1,187
hypothyroid	4	1,007	1,007	1,012	**1,011**
iris	3	1,073	1,073	**1,067**	1,073
lymph	4	**1,291**	1,297	1,284	**1,277**
primary-tumor	22	3,499	**3,472**	4,478	**4,316**
segment	7	**1,059**	1,060	1,131	**1,075**
soybean	19	1,124	**1,073**	1,220	**1,123**
vehicle	4	**1,329**	1,343	1,489	**1,449**
vowel	11	**1,387**	1,423	2,501	**1,516**
zoo	7	1,228	**1,188**	**1,307**	1,327
letter	26	**1,176**	1,188	2,168	**1,375**

benchmark data sets from the UCI repository and the StatLib archive[4], using C4.5 and Ripper as base learners, respectively. For each data set and each method we estimate the mean (absolute) position error using leave-one-out cross validation, except for the data set "letter", for which we used the predefined separation into training and test data. Table 2 shows the numbers of wins and losses for each pair of methods.

In contrast to our expectations, the results suggest that iterating (empirical conditioning) does not pay off in the pairwise learning approach. More often than not, the average position error for the non-iterated variant is smaller than the one for the iterated version. On the other hand, empirical conditioning significantly outperforms conventional conditioning in the case of multi-class classification (the results are significant at a level of 2% according to a simple sign test which tests the hypothesis that the approaches have equal expected performance on all data sets).

Even though the results do not comply with our first expectations, they can be explained in an intuitively plausible way. In fact, one has to realize that the idea of empirical conditioning produces two antagonistic effects:

- Information loss: In each iteration, the size of the data set to learn from becomes smaller. This reduction of data comes along with a loss of information.
- Simplification: Due to the reduced number of classes, the learning problems become simpler in each iteration.

The first effect will have a negative influence on generalization performance, whereas the second one will have a positive influence. In RPC, the first effect manifests itself by a reduction of the number of "voters": In the k-th iteration of iterated choice, only $m - k + 1$ labels and, hence, only $(m - k + 1)(m - k)/2$ binary classifiers participate. Since the score of each label is thus derived from the votes of only $m - k$ instead of $m - 1$ such classifiers, the impact of each individual binary classifier on the final ranking increases. An erroneous prediction of a single binary classifier will have a larger effect if fewer classifiers are used to derive the ranking. Thus, the ranking scores become less reliable with a decreasing number of labels.

For conventional iterated choice, this is countered by the fact that the classifiers become increasingly simple, because it can be expected that the decision boundary for separating m classes is more complex than the decision boundary for separating $m' < m$ classes of the same problem. The crucial point is that this effect is disabled in the pairwise approach: Since the original learning problem is decomposed into pairwise problems right from the start, the simplification due to a reduction of class labels is already bailed out at the beginning. In later iterations, some pairwise prob-

---

[4]http://www.ics.uci.edu/ mlearn, http://stat.cmu.edu/

lems become irrelevant, but the remaining problems do not become simpler. Consequently, only the first (negative) effect remains, which in turn explains the deterioration for the pairwise approach. In contrast, the second (positive) effect often seems to dominate the first effect in the case of multi-class classification.

Despite the fact that the idea of empirical conditioning (iterative learning) does apparently not pay off in the case of pairwise learning, one should note that, according to Table 2, the best pairwise method, namely the non-iterated version, is nevertheless better than the best multi-class method, namely the iterated one.

8 Concluding Remarks

In this paper, we have first given an overview of recent research activities in a subfield of machine learning that we have called *preference learning*. Roughly speaking, preference learning is concerned with learning preference models from observed data. More specifically, we have focused on an especially simple class of preference models, namely *rankings*. In particular, we have studied the problem of *label ranking* in more detail.

To approach the label ranking problem, we have proposed an extension of pairwise classification, called ranking by pairwise comparison (RPC). By showing that RPC is a risk minimizer with respect to quadratic loss functions for rankings, this paper provides a sound theoretical foundation for ranking by pairwise comparison. The interesting point is that RPC can easily be customized to different performance tasks, simply by changing the ranking procedure employed in the second step of the method. By modifying this procedure, the goal of RPC can be changed from minimizing the expected distance between the predicted and the true ranking to minimizing the expected number of futile trials in searching a target label. This can be done without retraining the classifier ensemble.

The second type of loss function, the position error, is minimized by ordering the class labels according their (conditional) probability of being the target label. To improve the estimations of these probabilities, we proposed the idea of "empirical conditioning" and the related "ranking through iterated choice" procedure. In an experimental study, this procedure was compared with the standard ("non-iterated") variant where the probabilities are not recomputed, i.e., where the class labels are ranked according to the originally estimated probabilities. Our results suggest that empirical conditioning does indeed reduce the expected loss in the case of standard multi-class classification (where the "choice" of the top-label is realized by a multi-class classifier in each iteration), whereas it does not pay off in the case of pairwise learning. As an explanation, we offered the observation that the simplification effect (classifying becomes simpler if fewer classes are involved) does not grab in the pairwise approach or, stated differently, this effect is already fully exploited from the outset. And indeed, the non-iterated version of the pairwise approach is still superior to iterated multi-class classification, while being computationally much more efficient.

Regarding future work, there are many avenues and open problems. For example, instead of looking at particular types of loss functions as we have done in this paper, it would be interesting to find a more complete characterization of the type of loss functions for rankings that can can be minimized by the pairwise learning approach and those that cannot. Another open issue is an extension of label ranking to the learning of more general preference relations on the label set $\mathcal{L}$. In fact, in many practical applications it might be reasonable to relax the assumption of strictness, i.e., to allow for indifference between labels, or even to represent preferences in terms of partial instead of total orders.

Acknowledgments: This research was supported by the German Research Foundation (Deutsche Forschungsgemeinschaft, DFG).

Bibliography

C. Alonso, JJ. Rodríguez, and B. Pulido. Enhancing consistency based diagnosis with machine learning techniques. In *Proc. 10th Conference of the Spanish Association for Artificial Intelligence*, pages 312–321. Springer, 2004.

William W. Cohen, Robert E. Schapire, and Yoram Singer. Learning to order things. In Michael I. Jordan, Michael J. Kearns, and Sara A. Solla, editors, *Advances in Neural Information Processing Systems*. The MIT Press, 1998.

Jon Doyle. Prospects for preferences. In *Computational Intelligence*, volume 20, pages 111–136, 2004.

J. Fodor and M. Roubens. *Fuzzy Preference Modelling and Multicriteria Decision Support*. Kluwer Academic Publishers, Dordrecht, The Netherlands, 1994.

J. Fürnkranz. Round robin classification. *Journal of Machine Learning Research*, 2:721–747, 2002.

J. Fürnkranz and E. Hüllermeier. Pairwise preference learning and ranking. In *Proc. ECML-2003, 13th European Conference on Machine Learning*, Cavtat-Dubrovnik, Croatia, September 2003.

P. Haddawy, V. Ha, A. Restificar, B. Geisler, and J. Miyamoto. Preference elicitation via theory refinement. *Journal of Machine Learning Research*, 4:317–337, 2003.

S. Har-Peled, D. Roth, and D. Zimak. Constraint classification: a new approach to multiclass classification. In *Proceedings 13th Int. Conf. on Algorithmic Learning Theory*, pages 365–379, Lübeck, Germany, 2002. Springer.

Sariel Har-Peled, Dan Roth, and Dav Zimak. Constraint classification for multiclass classification and ranking. In Suzanna Becker, Sebastian Thrun, and Klaus Obermayer, editors, *Advances in Neural Information Processing Systems 15 (NIPS-02)*, pages 785–792, 2003.

R. Herbrich, T. Graepel, P. Bollmann-Sdorra, and K. Obermayer. Supervised learning of preference relations. In *Proceedings FGML-98, German National Workshop on Machine Learning*, pages 43–47, 1998.

E. Hüllermeier and J. Fürnkranz. Comparison of ranking procedures in pairwise preference learning. In Proc. IPMU–04, Perugia, Italy, 2004.

Eyke Hüllermeier and Johannes Fürnkranz. Learning label preferences: Ranking error versus position error. In *Advances in Intelligent Data Analysis VI*, Madrid, 2005. Springer.

T. Joachims. Optimizing search engines using clickthrough data. In *Proceedings of the 8th ACM SIGKDD International Conference on Knowledge Discovery and Data Mining (KDD-02)*, pages 133–142. ACM Press, 2002.

T. Joachims, L. Granka, B. Pan, H. Hembrooke, and G. Gay. Accurately interpreting clickthrough data as implicit feedback. In *Proceedings of the 28th Annual International ACM Conference on Research and Development in Information Retrieval (SIGIR-05)*, 2005.

Dorian Pyle. *Data Preparation for Data Mining*. Morgan Kaufmann, San Francisco, CA, 1999.

F. Radlinski and T. Joachims. Learning to rank from implicit feedback. In *Proceedings of the ACM Conference on Knowledge Discovery and Data Mining (KDD-05)*, 2005.

Gerald Tesauro. Connectionist learning of expert preferences by comparison training. In D. Touretzky, editor, *Advances in Neural Information Processing Systems 1 (NIPS-88)*, pages 99–106. Morgan Kaufmann, 1989.

J. Wang. Artificial neural networks versus natural neural networks: a connectionist paradigm for preference assessment. *Decision Support Systems*, 11:415–429, 1994.

TF. Wu, CJ. Lin, and RC. Weng. Probability estimates for multi-class classification by pairwise coupling. *Journal of Machine Learning Research*, 5:975–1005, 2004.

Constraints and Preferences: Modelling Frameworks and Multi-agent Settings

Francesca Rossi*

Department of Pure and Applied Mathematics, University of Padova, Padova, Italy

Abstract Preferences are ubiquitous in real-life. Moreover, preferences can be of many kinds: qualitative, quantitative, conditional, positive or negative, to name a few. Our ultimate goal is to define and study formalisms that can model problems with both constraints and many kind of preferences, possibly defined by several agents, and to develop tools to solve such problems efficiently. In this paper we briefly report on our recent work towards this goal.

1   Motivation and main goal

Constraints (Dechter, 2003; Rossi et al., 2006a) are requirements that we may state over the possible scenarios, and they must be met, otherwise we are not satisfied. Many scenarios can meet the given constraints, and they are all equally good, since they all satisfy the constraints. On the other hand, if a scenario does not satisfy some of the constraints, it is not acceptable. For example, when choosing a camera, we may be interested only in those that have a certain lens, and don't care about the other features. If a shop does not have cameras with that lens, then we would not buy a camera there. On the other hand, preferences are a way to model the fact that some scenarios are more desirable than others.

Preferences are ubiquitous in real life. In fact, as in the above example, most problems are over-constrained and would not be solvable if we insist that all their requirements are strictly met. Moreover, solvable problems have solutions with different desirability. Finally, many problems are more naturally described via preferences rather than hard statements. For example, when choosing a menu at the restaurant, we may prefer red wine

---

*This paper describes joint work done with the following collegues: K. Apt, S. Bistarelli, C. Domshlak, L. Khatib, J. Lang, P. Morris, R. Morris, M. S. Pini, S. Prestwich, A. Sperduti, K. B. Venable, T. Walsh, and N. Yorke-Smith.

to beer when eating meat, but pizza and beer may be more desirable than pizza and wine.

In some cases it could be more natural to express preferences in quantitative terms, as in "I like this at level 10 and that at level 20", while in other situations it could be better to use qualitative statements, as in "I like this more than that". Moreover, preferences can be unconditional, as in "I like a red car more than a blue car", or conditional, as in "If the car is convertible, I like it red more than blue". Furthermore, in many real life problems, constraints and preferences of various kinds may coexist. For example, in a product configuration problem, the producer may impose some constraints (for example, that no red cars are available at the moment) and may also add some marketing preferences, (for example, that it would be better to sell the white cars first), while the user may have preferences of various kind (for example, that he prefers red to the other colors if it is a sport car, and that he prefers a convertible to a sedan).

Because of the ubiquitous presence of constraints and preferences in real life, representing and reasoning about preferences is an area of increasing interest in theoretical and applied AI. Unfortunately, there is no single formalism which allows all the different kinds of preferences to be specified efficiently and reasoned with effectively. For example, soft constraints (Bistarelli et al., 1997) are most suited for reasoning about constraints and quantitative preferences, while CP-nets (Boutilier et al., 2004a) are most suited for representing qualitative and possibly conditional preferences. Our ultimate goal is to define and study formalisms that can model problems with both constraints and many kind of preferences, and to develop tools to solve such problems efficiently. Moreover, we also want to be able to deal with scenarios where preferences are expressed by several agents, and preference aggregation is therefore needed to find the optimal outcomes.

To move towards this goal, we have first compared the expressive power of two preference formalisms, soft constraints and CP-nets, and we have studied solvers for problems modeled by CP-nets and constraints together. Then, we have studied bipolar preferences, which allow for preference compensation. Finally, we have considered multi-agent scenarios, where the goal is to aggregate preferences, of possibly different kinds, specified by different agents, and to do that efficiently and satisfying certain properties. We have shown that existing multi-agent theoretical results and techniques can be used and adapted to the preference formalisms we use to improve the handling of preferences in the context of several agents. In particular, social choice theory and game theory seem to provide many tools to help us improve preference reasoning.

Parts of this paper appeared already in (Rossi, 2005).

2 Preference modeling frameworks: soft constraints and CP-nets

2.1 Soft constraints

Soft constraints (Bistarelli et al., 1997; Meseguer et al., 2006) model quantitative preferences by generalizing the traditional formalism of hard constraints. In a soft constraint, each assignment to the variables of a constraint is annotated with a level of its desirability, and the desirability of a complete assignment is computed by a combination operator applied to the local preference values. By choosing a specific combination operator and an ordered set of levels of desirability, we can select a specific class of soft constraints.

For example, in fuzzy constraints (Dubois et al., 1993, 1994, 1996a) preferences are between 0 and 1 (with 1 better than 0), and min is the combination operator. Weighted CSPs instead have preferences over the integers, with higher integers denoting a lower preference, and with sum as the combination operator. Classical constraints are soft constraints where there are only two levels of preference (true and false), where true is better than false, and where the combination operator is *logical and*.

Given a set of soft constraints, an ordering is induced over the assignments of the variables of the problem, which can be partial or total, and can also have ties. Given two solutions, checking whether one is preferable to the other one is easy: we compute the desirability values of the two solutions and compare them in the preference order. However, finding an optimal solution for a soft constraint problem is a combinatorially difficult problem.

Many search techniques have been developed to solve specific classes of soft constraints, like fuzzy or weighted. However, all have an exponential worst case complexity. Systematic approaches, like backtracking search and constraint propagation, can be adapted to soft constraints. For example, backtracking search becomes branch and bound where the bounds are given by the preference levels in the constraints. Constraint propagation, which is very successful in pruning parts of the search tree in constraint solving, can also be generalized to certain classes of soft constraints. Soft constraints are also not good at representing conditional and/or qualitative preference statements.

2.2 CP-nets

CP-nets (Boutilier et al., 2004a) (Conditional Preference networks) are a graphical model for compactly representing conditional and qualitative preference relations. They exploit conditional preferential independence by structuring a user's possibly complex preference ordering with the ceteris paribus assumption. CP-nets are sets of conditional ceteris paribus preference statements (cp-statements). For instance, the statement "I prefer red wine to white wine if meat is served" asserts that, given two meals that differ only in the kind of wine served and both containing meat, the meal with a red wine is preferable to the meal with a white wine.

CP-nets bear some similarity to Bayesian networks, as both utilize directed acyclic graphs where each node stands for a domain variable, and assume a set of features with finite, discrete domains (these play the same role as variables in soft constraints).

Given a CP-net, an ordering is induced over the set of assignments of its features. In general, such an ordering is a preorder (that is, reflexive and transitive).

Given an acyclic CP-net, finding an optimal assignment to its features can be done in linear time. However, for cyclic CP-nets, it becomes NP-hard. Comparing two outcomes is NP-hard as well, even when the CP-net is acyclic.

Summarizing, CP-nets and soft constraints have complementary advantages and drawbacks. CP-nets allow one to represent conditional and qualitative preferences, but dominance testing is expensive. On the other hand, soft constraints allow to represent both hard constraints and quantitative preferences, and have a cheap dominance testing.

2.3 Comparing their expressive power

It would be very useful to have a single formalism for representing preferences that have the good features of both soft constraints and CP-nets. To achieve this goal, we may start by comparing their expressive power.

We could say that a formalism B is at least as expressive as a formalism A if from a problem expressed using A it is possible to build in polynomial time a problem expressed using B such that the optimal solutions are the same.

If we apply this definition to soft constraints, we see, for example, that fuzzy CSPs and weighted CSPs are at least as expressive as classical constraints. If instead we we use this definition to compare CP-nets and soft constraints, we see that hard constraints are at least as expressive as CP-nets. In fact, it is possible to show that, given any CP-net, we can obtain in polynomial time a set of hard constraints whose solutions are the optimal outcomes of the CP-net. Thus, if we are only interested in the best solutions, CP-nets are not more expressive than hard constraints. This is useful to know, since it means that we can use the classical constraint-based machinery to find the optimal solutions of a CP-net.

It also means that soft constraints, which are more expressive than hard ones, are more expressive than CP-nets. Even hard constraints are more expressive than CP-nets. In fact, there are some hard constraint problems for which it is not possible to find in polynomial time a CP-net with the same set of optimals. This derives from the fact that not all solution orderings can be expressed via a CP-net. In fact, solutions which differ for just the value of one variable must be ordered, while in a constraint problem they could be equally valued (that is, both acceptable or both unacceptable).

However, we could be more fine-grained in the comparison, and say that a formalism B is at least as expressive than a formalism A iff from a problem expressed using A it is possible to build in polynomial time a problem expressed using B such that the orderings over solutions are the same. If we compare soft constraints and CP-nets by using this definition, then it is possible to see that CP-nets and soft (or hard) constraints are incomparable.

2.4 Ordering approximations

However, it is possible to approximate a CP-net ordering via soft constraints, achieving tractability of dominance testing while sacrificing precision to some degree (Domshlak et al., 2003, 2006; Kaci and Prade, 2007). Different approximations can be characterized by how much of the original ordering they preserve, the time complexity of generating the approximation, and the time complexity of comparing outcomes in the approximation.

It is vital that such approximations are information preserving; that is, what is ordered in the given ordering is also ordered in the same way in the approximation. Another desirable property of approximations is that they preserve the ceteris paribus property.

In (Domshlak et al., 2003) we have approximated CP-nets via soft constraints where the optimization criteria is the minimization of the sum of the preferences, and also via soft constraints where a lexicographic ordering is adopted. In both cases, the approximation is information preserving and satisfies the ceteris paribus property.

2.5 Constraints and preferences together

What about CP-nets and hard constraints together? Many problems have both constraints and qualitative and/or quantitative preferences. Unfortunately, reasoning with them both is difficult as often the most preferred outcome is not feasible, and not all feasible outcomes are equally preferred.

For example, consider a constrained CP-net, which is a CP-net plus a set of hard constraints. This structure allows to model both qualitative conditional preferences and hard constraints. Its optimal outcomes (called "feasible Pareto optimals" in (Boutilier et al., 2004b)) are all the outcomes which are feasible and not dominated in the CP-net by any other feasible outcome. It is possible to obtain all such optimal outcomes by just solving a set of hard constraints (Prestwich et al., 2005). In well defined cases, this avoids expensive dominance testing. If we want to avoid dominance testing completely, we can do that at the price of obtaining a superset of the feasible Pareto optimals by hard constraint solving. A similar constraint-based procedure can be used also when we add soft constraints to a CP-net.

3   Bipolar preferences

Whether they are conditional, qualitative, or quantitative, preferences often are of one of two kinds: positive or negative. A positive preference expresses a degree of desire, and a negative one expresses a level of unsatisfaction for a feature of an object. Preferences expressing both degrees of desire and levels of unsatisfaction are often called *bipolar*.

Bipolarity is an important topic in several domains, such as psychology, multi-criteria decision making, and more recently in AI (argumentation (Amgound et al. , 2005) and qualitative reasoning (Benferhat et al., 2002; Benferarth et al., 2006; Dubois and Fargier, 2005; Dubois and fargier, 2006)) and in decision theory (Labreuche and Grabish, 2006). In many real-life or artificial situations agents express what they like and what they dislike, thus often preferences are bipolar.

Positive and negative preferences could be thought as two symmetric concepts, and thus one could think that they can be dealt with via the same operators. However, it is easy to see that this would not model what one usually expects in real scenarios.

For example, when we have a scenario with two objects A and B, if we like both A and B, then the overall scenario should be more preferred than having just A or B alone. On the other hand, if we don't like A nor B, then we expect that the preference of the scenario should be smaller than the preferences of A or B alone. In fact, usually combination of positive preferences should produce a higher (positive) preference, while combination of negative preferences should give us a lower (negative) preference.

When dealing with both kinds of preferences, it is natural to express also indifference, which means that we express neither a positive nor a negative preference over an object. For example, we may say that we like peaches, we don't like bananas, and we are indifferent to apples. Then, a desired behavior of indifference is that, when combined with any preference (either positive or negative), it should not influence the overall preference. For example, if we like peaches and we are indifferent to apples, a dish with peaches and apples should have overall a positive preference.

Besides combining preferences of the same type, one may want also to be able to combine positive with negative preferences. We strongly believe that the most natural and intuitive way to do so is to allow for compensation. Comparing positive against negative aspects and compensating them w.r.t. their strength is one of the core features of decision-making processes, and it is, undoubtedly, a tactic universally applied to solve many real life problems.

For example, if we have a meal with meat (which we like very much) and wine (which we don't like), then what should be the preference of the meal? To know that, we should be able to compensate the positive preference given to meat with the negative preference given to wine. The expected result is a preference which is between the two, and which should be positive if the positive preference is "stronger" than the negative one.

Positive and negative preferences might seem as just two different criteria to reason with, and thus techniques such as those usually adopted by multi-criteria optimization could appear suitable for dealing with them. However, this interpretation would hide the fundamental nature of bipolar preferences, that is, positive preferences are naturally opposite of negative preferences. Moreover, in multi-criteria optimization it is often reasonable to use a Pareto-like approach, thus associating tuples of values to each solution, and comparing solutions according to tuple dominance. Instead, in bipolar problems, it would be very unnatural to force such an approach in all contexts, or to associate to a solution a preference which is neither a positive nor a negative one (and not even the indifference element).

Soft constraints and CP-nets are useful formalisms to model problems with quantitative preferences. However, they can only model one kind of preferences. Technically, soft constraints can model just negative preferences, since in this framework preference combination returns lower preferences, which, as mentioned above, is natural when using negative preferences.

This means that the soft constraint formalism based on semirings can be used to model negative preferences. A different algebraic structure is then needed to model positive preferences.

To model bipolar problems, we can link these two structures and we set the highest negative preference to coincide with the lowest positive preference to model indifference. A compensation operator between positive and negative preferences is then needed to model preference compensation.

A desirable property of compensation, that unfortunately often does not hold, is associativity. Non-associativity of preference compensation occurs in many contexts, thus we think it is too restrictive to focus just on associative environments. For example, non-associativity of compensation arises when either positive or negative preferences are aggregated with an idempotent operator (such as min or max), while compensation is instead non-idempotent (such as sum). Also compensative idempotent operators between min and max (such as the arithmetic mean) are almost never associative (Dubois and Prade, 1985).

We developed a framework for modeling and solving bipolar preference problems, which allows for (but does not force) non-associativity of preference compensation, since we want to give complete freedom to choose the positive and negative algebraic structures (Pini et al., 2006a). However, we also describe a technique that, given a negative preference structure, builds a corresponding positive preference structure and an associative compensation operator. Bipolar preference problems can be solved by suitable adapting both constraint propagation and branch and bound techniques.

4 Multi-agent preference aggregation

In many situations, we need to represent and reason about the simultaneous preferences of several agents over the same objects. To aggregate the agents' preferences, which in general express a partial order over the possible outcomes, we can query each agent in turn and collect together the results. We can see this as each agent "voting" whether an outcome dominates another. We can thus obtain different semantics by collecting these votes together in different ways.

In (Rossi et al., 2004a) we considered this scenario assuming that each agent uses a (partial) CP-net to express its preferences. For example, to obtain a Pareto-like semantics, we can say that an outcome A is better than another one, B, iff every agent says that A is better than B or that they are indifferent. An alternative criterion, that we may call majority, is that A is better than B iff a majority of the agents who are not indifferent vote in favor. A weaker criterion, that we may call Max, is that more agents vote in favor than against or for incomparability. Sometimes it is reasonable to assume that the agents are ordered in importance. If the first agent orders two outcomes then this is reflected in the final outcome. However, if they are indifferent between two outcomes, we consult the second agent, and so on. We say that A is lexicographically better than B iff there exists some distinguished agent such that all agents higher in the order are indifferent between A and B, and the distinguished agent votes for A.

4.1 Fairness

Having cast our preference aggregation semantics in terms of voting, it is appropriate to ask if classical results about voting theory apply. For example, what about Arrow's theorem (Kelly, 1978), which states the impossibility of a fair voting system? Can we fairly combine together the preferences of the individual agents?

In short, Arrow's theorem states that no voting system with two or more agents and which totally orders three or more candidates can be fair. More precisely, no voting system can be free, transitive, independent to irrelevant alternatives, monotonic and non-dictatorial.

Observe that in our context each agent can express both ordering and incomparability between two alternatives. The same would hold also if the agents used soft constraints rather than CP-nets. By comparison, the votes in an election express a total order without incomparability. As a result, Arrow's theorem does not immediately apply.

Before adapting Arrow's theorem to our scenario, let us consider the issue of fairness in more general terms, by assuming a scenario where each agent models its preferences via a partial order, and the ordering resulting from preference aggregation can be partial as well. Despite social welfare theory seldom considers partially ordered preferences, the possibility of using partial orders, both in the agents' orders and in the resulting order, can be easily justified. In fact, incomparability is a useful mechanism to resolve conflict when aggregating such preferences. If half of the agents prefer A to B and the other half prefer B to A, then it may be best to say that A and B are incomparable. In addition, an agent's preferences are not necessarily total. For example, while it is easy and reasonable to compare two white wines, it may be difficult to compare a red wine and a white wine. We may wish simply to declare them incomparable. Moreover, an agent may have several possibly conflicting preference criteria she wants to follow, and their combination can naturally lead to a partial order. It is thus reasonable to assume that both the preferences of an agent and the result of preference aggregation can be a partial order.

The definition of fairness considered by Arrow consists of the following desirable properties:

- Unanimity: if all agents agree that A is preferable to B, then the resulting order must agree as well.
- Independence to irrelevant alternatives: the ordering between A and B in the result depends only on the relation between A and B given by the agents.
- Monotonicity: whenever an agent moves up the position of one outcome in her ordering, then (all else being equal) such an outcome

cannot move down in the result.

- Absence of a dictator: a dictator is an agent such that, no matter what the others say, will always dictate the resulting ordering among the outcomes.

We have shown that, under certain conditions, it is impossible for a preference aggregation system over partially ordered preferences to be fair (Rossi et al., 2005; Pini et al., 2008). By moving from total orders to partial orders, we expect to enrich greatly our ability to combine preferences fairly. In fact, we can use incomparability to resolve conflict and thereby not contradict agents. Nevertheless, under the conditions identified, we still do not escape the reach of Arrow's theorem. Even if we are only interested in the most preferred outcomes of the aggregated preferences, it is still impossible to be fair.

4.2 Non-manipulability

Of course fairness is just one of the desirable properties for preference aggregations. Other interesting properties are related to the non-manipulability (also called strategy-proofness) of a preference aggregation system: it should not be possible for agents to manipulate the election by voting strategically. Strategic voting is when agents express preferences which are different from their real ones, to get the result they want. If this is possible, then the preference aggregation rule is said to be manipulable.

For social choice rules on totally ordered preferences, the Gibbard Satterthwaite theorem (Gibbard, 1973) proves that it is not possible to be at same time non-manipulable and have no dictators. Either there is a dictator (that is, an agent who gets what he wants by voting sincerely) or a manipulator (that is, an agent who gets what he wants by lying). In either case, there is an agent who gets what he wants no matter what the other agents say. This is clearly undesirable.

We extended this result to partially ordered preferences (Pini et al., 2006b, 2008). Even in this more general case, we prove that it is impossible for a social choice function to have no dictator and be non-manipulable at the same time. As with total orders, we conjecture that there will be ways around this negative result. For example, it may be that certain social choice functions on partial orders are computationally hard to manipulate. As another example, it may be that certain restrictions on the way agents vote (like single-peaked preferences for total orders) guarantee strategy-proofness.

4.3 Incompleteness

In a multi-agent context, some agents may decide to not reveal some of their preferences, because of privacy reasons. A pair of outcomes can thus be ordered, incomparable, in a tie, or the relationship between them may not be specified.

Notice that incomparability and incompleteness represent very different concepts. Outcomes may be incomparable because the agent does not wish very dissimilar outcomes to be compared. For example, we might not want to compare a biography with a novel as the criteria along which we judge them are just too different. Outcomes can also be incomparable because the agent has multiple criteria to optimize. For example, we might not wish to compare a faster but more expensive laptop with a slower and cheaper one. Incompleteness, on the other hand, represents simply an absence of knowledge about the relationship between certain pairs of outcomes. Incompleteness arises naturally when we have not fully elicited an agent's preferences or when agents have privacy concerns which prevent them revealing their complete preference ordering.

How do we modify preference aggregation functions to deal with incompleteness? One possibility is to consider all possible ways in which the incomplete preference orders can be consistently completed.In each possible completion, preference aggregation may give different optimal elements (or winners). This leads to the idea of the *possible winners* (those outcomes which are winners in at least one possible completion) and the *necessary winners* (those outcomes which are winners in all possible completions) (Konczak and Lang, 2005).

Possible and necessary winners have been shown to be useful in many scenarios, including preference elicitation. In fact, elicitation is over when the set of possible winners coincides with that of the necessary winners (Conitzer and Sandholm, 2002). In addition, preference elicitation can focus just on the incompleteness concerning those outcomes which are possible and necessary winners. We can ignore completely all other outcomes.

Computing the set of possible and necessary winners is in general a difficult problem. However, we identify sufficient conditions that assure tractability (Pini et al., 2007). Such conditions concern properties of the preference aggregation function, such as monotonicity and independence to irrelevant alternatives (Arrow et al., 2002), which are desirable and natural properties to require. We also studied this problem in the context of a specific voting rule (sequential majority voting), proving that for this rule it is easy to compute such winners, unless we put a restriction on the sequence of knock-out competitions performed by the rule (Lang et al., 2007).

5   Further issues in preference reasoning

Besides the issues discussed above, we have also followed several other lines of research, related to preferences. In the rest of this section we will briefly outline the main results we have obtained in such lines, or what we intend to pursue in the near future.

Learning preferences.   It is usually hard for a user to describe the correct preferences for his real-life problem. This is especially true for soft constraints, which do not have an intuitive graphical representation. We have shown that the use of learning techniques can greatly help in this respect, allowing users to state preferences both on entire solutions and subsets of the variables (Rossi and Sperduti, 2004).

Preferences and uncertainty.   Preferences can be seen as a way to describe some kind of uncertainty. When we are not sure about what should be allowed and what should be forbidden, we can pass from hard constraints to soft constraints, and use several levels of satisfiability. However, there is also uncertainty which comes from lack of data, or from events which are under Nature's control. Fortunately, in the presence of both preferences and uncertainty in the context of temporal constraints, we can reason with the same complexity as if we just had preferences (Rossi et al., 2004b; Khatib et al., 2007; Rossi et al., 2006b).

Many approaches to deal with uncertainty are based on possibility theory (Dubois and Prade, 1988a,b; Dubois et al., 2006b; Dubois and Prade, 1999; Dubois et al., 2001). While probabilities are useful when we have data, but they are variable, possibilities are useful when we reason under incomplete information. Technically, possibilities (and necessity) provide upper (and lower) bounds to probabilities.

The handling of the coexistence of preferences and uncertainty via possibility theory allows for a natural merging of the two notions and leads to several promising semantics for ordering the solutions according to both their preference and their robustness to uncertainty (Pini et al., 2005).

Preference formalisms and strategic games.   The notion of optimality naturally arises in many areas of applied mathematics and computer science concerned with decision making. When dealing with preferences, it is natural to ask for the optimal solutions according to the preferences. There are many areas in which preferences are considered. For example, strategic games are one of them. Strategic games are used to capture the idea that agents interact with each other while pursuing their own interests.

It is interesting to relate the notions of optimality in soft constraints, CP nets, and strategic games (Apt et al., 2008b). To relate the notion of optimality of CP nets to that in strategic games, in (Apt et al., 2006) we introduce a qualitative modification of the notion of a strategic game. We show then that the optimal outcomes of a CP-net are exactly the Nash equilibria of an appropriately defined strategic game in the above sense. This allows us to use the techniques of game theory to search for optimal outcomes of CP-nets and vice-versa, to use techniques developed for CP-nets to search for Nash equilibria of the considered games.

We also compare the notion of optimality used in soft constraints to that used in strategic games (Apt et al., 2008a), by means of two mappings. We show, for a natural mapping from soft constraints to strategic games, that in general no relation exists between the notions of an optimal solution and Nash equilibrium. However, for a class of soft constraints that includes weighted constraints, every optimal solution is a Nash equilibrium. In turn, for a natural mapping from strategic games to soft constraints, the notion that coincides with optimality for soft constraints is that of Pareto efficient joint strategy.

6 Conclusions

Much work has been done in the last years to model and solve problems with preferences. However, much remains to be done in order to achieve the ultimate goal of a single environment where most kind of preferences, single-agent or multi-agent, can be modeled and then efficiently dealt with. We think that our results constitute an interesting contribution to this research area, and we hope that, starting from them, many other significant results can be obtained.

Bibliography

L. Amgoud, J. F. Bonnenfon, H. Prade. An argumentation-based approach to multiple criteria decision. Proc. ECSQARU'05, 2005, pages 10-17.

K.R. Apt, F. Rossi, and K. B. Venable. CP-nets and Nash equilibria. In *Proc. of the Third International Conference on Computational Intelligence, Robotics and Autonomous Systems (CIRAS '05)*, pages 1–6.

K.R. Apt, F. Rossi, and K. B. Venable. A comparison of the notions of optimality in soft constraints and graphical games. to appear in "Recent advances in Constraints", selected papers from the 2007 ERCIM CSCLP workshop (Paris, June 2007), Springer LNAI, 2008.

K.R. Apt, F. Rossi, and K. B. Venable. Comparing the notions of optimality in CP-nets, strategic games, and soft constraints. To appear in Annals of Mathematics and Artificial Intelligence, 2008.

K. J. Arrow, A. K. Sen, and K. Suzumara. Handbook of Social Choice and Welfare. North-Holland, Elsevier, 2002.

S. Benferhat, D. Dubois, S. Kaci, and H. Prade. Bipolar representation and fusion of preferences in the possibilistic logic framework. In *KR 2002*. Morgan Kaufmann, 2002.

S. Benferhat, D. Dubois, S. Kaci, and H. Prade. Bipolar possibility theory in preference modeling: representation, fusion and optimal solutions. *Information Fusion*, 7(1):135–50, 2006.

S. Bistarelli, U. Montanari, and F. Rossi. Semiring-based Constraint Solving and Optimization. Journal of the ACM, vol. 44, n. 2, pp. 201-236, 1997.

C. Boutilier, R. I. Brafman, C. Domshlak, H. H. Hoos, and D. Poole. CP-nets: A tool for representing and reasoning with conditional ceteris paribus preference statements. Journal of Artificial Intelligence Research, 21:135–191, 2004.

C. Boutilier, R. I. Brafman, C. Domshlak, H. H. Hoos, and D. Poole. Preference-based constraint optimization with CP-nets. Computational Intelligence, vol. 20, pp.137-157, 2004.

V. Conitzer and T. Sandholm. Vote Elicitation: Complexity and Strategy-Proofness. Proc. AAAI/IAAI 2002, pp. 392-397, 2002.

R. Dechter. Constraint processing. Morgan Kaufmann, 2003.

C. Domshlak, S. Prestwich, F. Rossi, K. B. Venable, T. Walsh. Hard and soft constraints for reasoning about qualitative conditional preferences. Journal of Heuristics, special issue on preferences, vol. 4-5, September 2006.

C. Domshlak, F. Rossi, K. B. Venable, and T. Walsh. Reasoning about soft constraints and conditional preferences: complexity results and approximation techniques. Proc. IJCAI-03, 215–220. Morgan Kaufmann, 2003.

D. Dubois and H. Fargier. On the qualitative comparison of sets of positive and negative affects. In *ECSQARU'05*, pages 305–316, 2005.

D. Dubois and H. Fargier. Qualitative decision making with bipolar information. In *KR'06*, pages 175–186, 2006.

D. Dubois, H. Fargier, H. Prade. The calculus of fuzzy restrictions as a basis for flexible constraint satisfaction. Proc. of the 2nd IEEE Inter. Conf. on Fuzzy Systems, San Francisco, CA, March 28-April 1st, 1993, Vol. II: 1131-1136.

D. Dubois, H. Fargier, H. Prade. Propagation and satisfaction of flexible constraints. In: Fuzzy Sets, Neural Networks and Soft Computing (R.R. Yager, L.A. Zadeh, eds.), Kluwer Academic Publ., 1994.

D. Dubois, H. Fargier, H. Prade. Possibility theory in constraint satisfaction problems: Handling priority, preference and uncertainty. Applied Intelligence, 6, 1996, 287-309.

D. Dubois, H. Fargier, H. Prade. Possibility theory in constraint satisfaction problems: handling priority, preference and uncertainty. Applied Intelligence, 6, 287-309, 1996.

D. Dubois, H. Prade. A review of fuzzy set aggregation connectives. Information Sciences, 36 (1-2), 85-121, 1985.

D. Dubois, H. Prade. Possibility theory. Plenum Press, New York, 1988.

D. Dubois, H. Prade. Possibility theory: qualitative and quantitative aspects. In : P. Smets, Ed., Handbook on Defeasible Reasoning and Uncertainty Management Systems. Volume 1: Quantified Representation of Uncertainty and Imprecision. Kluwer, 169-226, 1998.

D. Dubois, H. Prade. Qualitative possibility theory and its applications to constraint satisfaction and decision under uncertainty. International Journal of Intelligent Systems, 14, 45-61, 1999.

D. Dubois, H. Prade. R. Sabbadin. Decision theoretic foundations of qualitative possibility theory. European Journal of Operational Research, 128, 459-478, 2001.

A. Gibbard. Manipulation of Voting Schemes: A General Result. Econometrica, 1973, vol. 41, pp. 587-601.

Souhila Kaci, Henri Prade. Relaxing Ceteris Paribus Preferences with Partially Ordered Priorities. proc. ECSQARU 2007: 660-671.

J. S. Kelly. Arrow Impossibility Theorems. Academic Press, 1978.

L. Khatib, P. Morris, R. Morris, F. Rossi, A. Sperduti, K. Brent Venable. Solving and learning a tractable class of soft temporal problems: theoretical and experimental results. AI Communications, special issue on Constraint Programming for Planning and Scheduling, vol. 20, n.3, 2007.

K. Konczak and J. Lang. Voting procedures with incomplete preferences. Proc. IJCAI-05 Multidisciplinary Workshop on Advances in Preference Handling, 2005.

Ch. Labreuche, M. Grabish. Generalized Choquet-like aggregation functions for handling bipolar scales. European Journal of Operational Research, 172(3), 931-955, 2006.

J. Lang, M.S. Pini, F. Rossi, K. Venable, T. Walsh. Winner determination in sequential majority voting. Proc. IJCAI 2007, Hyderabad, India, January 2007.

P. Meseguer F. Rossi and T. Schiex. Soft constraints. In T. Walsh F. Rossi, P. Van Beek, editor, Handbook of Constraint programming, pages 281-328. Elsevier, 2006.

M. S. Pini, F. Rossi, K. B. Venable. Possibility theory for reasoning about uncertain soft constraints. Proc. ECSQARU 2005, Barcelona, July 2005, Springer-Verlag LNAI 3571.

Maria Silvia Pini, Francesca Rossi, Kristen Brent Venable, Stefano Bistarelli. Bipolar preference problems. Proc. ECAI 2006 (poster paper), Riva del Garda, August 28-September 1, 2006.

M. S. Pini, F. Rossi, K. B. Venable, T. Walsh. Strategic voting when aggregating partially ordered preferences. Proc. AAMAS 2006 (5th international joint conference on autonomous agents and multiagent systems), Hakodate, Japan, May 8-12, 2006.

M.S. Pini, F. Rossi, K. Venable, T.Walsh. Incompleteness and incomparability in preference aggregation. Proc. IJCAI 2007, Hyderabad, India, January 2007.

M.S. Pini, F. Rossi, K. Venable, T.Walsh. Aggregating partially ordered preferences. To appear in Journal of Logic and Computation, Oxford University Press, special Issue on belief revision, belief merging and social choice, D. Gabbay, G. Pigozzi, O. Rodrigues eds., 2008.

S. Prestwich, F. Rossi, K. B. Venable, T. Walsh. Constraint-based Preferential Optimization. Proc. AAAI 2005, Morgan Kaufmann, 2005.

F. Rossi. Preference Reasoning. Proc. CP 2005 (invited paper), Sitges, Spain, October 2005.

F. Rossi and A. Sperduti. Acquiring both constraint and solution preferences in interactive constraint systems. Constraints, vol.9, n. 4, 2004, Kluwer.

F. Rossi, T. Walsh, P. Van Beek, editors. Handbook of Constraint programming, Elsevier, 2006.

F. Rossi, K. B. Venable, and T. Walsh. mCP Nets: Representing and Reasoning with Preferences of Multiple Agents. Proc. AAAI 2004, AAAI Press, 2004.

F. Rossi, M. S. Pini, K. B. Venable, and T. Walsh. Aggregating preferences cannot be fair. Proc. TARK X, Singapore, June 2005, ACM Digital Library.

F. Rossi, K. B. Venable, N. Yorke-Smith. Controllability of Soft Temporal Constraint Problems. Proc. CP 2004, Toronto, Springer LNCS 3258, 2004.

F. Rossi, K. B. Venable and N. Yorke-Smith. Uncertainty in soft temporal constraint problems: a general framework and controllability algorithms for the fuzzy case, Journal of AI Research, volume 27, pages 617-674, 2006.